Heidegger in Question

Philosophy and Literary Theory
Series Editor: Hugh J. Silverman

Robert Bernasconi, *Heidegger in Question*

Ulrike Oudée Dünkelsbühler, *Reframing the Frame of Reason: "Trans-lation" in and beyond Kant and Derrida*

Véronique M. Fóti, *Heidegger and the Poets*

Sabine Gölz, *The Split Scene of Reading*

Richard Kearney, *Poetics of Modernity: Toward a Hermeneutic Imagination*

Jean-François Lyotard, *Toward the Postmodern*

Jean-François Lyotard and Eberhard Gruber, *The Hyphen: Between Judaism and Christianity*

Louis Marin, *Cross-Readings*

Roy Martinez, *Kierkegaard and the Art of Irony*

Michael Naas, *Turning: From Persuasion to Philosophy—A Reading of Homer's* Iliad

Jean-Luc Nancy, *The Gravity of Thought*

Mario Perniola, *Ritual Thinking: Sexuality, Death, World*

Giuseppe Stellardi, *Heidegger and Derrida on Philosophy and Metaphor*

Wilhelm S. Wurzer, *Filming and Judgment: Between Heidegger and Adorno*

Heidegger in Question

The Art of Existing

Robert Bernasconi

ROWMAN & LITTLEFIELD
Lanham • Boulder • New York • London

Published by Rowman & Littlefield
An imprint of The Rowman & Littlefield Publishing Group, Inc.
4501 Forbes Boulevard, Suite 200, Lanham, Maryland 20706
www.rowman.com

86-90 Paul Street, London EC2A 4NE, United Kingdom

Copyright © 1993 by Robert Bernasconi

All rights reserved. No part of this book may be reproduced in any form or by any electronic or mechanical means, including information storage and retrieval systems, without written permission from the publisher, except by a reviewer who may quote passages in a review.

British Library Cataloguing in Publication Information Available

Library of Congress Cataloging-in-Publication Data

The Free Press edition of this book was previously catalogued by the Library of Congress as follows:

Bernasconi, Robert.
    Heidegger in question : the art of existing / by Robert Bernasconi.
       p. cm. — (Philosophy and literary theory)
    Includes bibliographical references and index.
    Originally published 1993 in hardcover by Humanities Press International, Inc., Atlantic Highlands, NJ. Reprinted in paperback 1996 by Humanities Press International, Inc.
    ISBN 978-1-5381-5034-4 (pbk)
    1. Heidegger, Martin, 1889–1976. I. Title. II. Series.

B3279.H49B453 1993
193—dc20
                                      92-23831
                                            CIP

Contents

Preface — vii

Acknowledgments — xi

Abbreviations of Works by Heidegger — xiii

Introduction — xvii

PART ONE: ETHICS AND POLITICS

1. The Fate of the Distinction between *Praxis* and *Poiesis* — 2

2. "The Double Concept of Philosophy" and the Place of Ethics in *Being and Time* — 25

3. Justice and the Twilight Zone of Morality — 40

4. Habermas, Arendt, and Levinas on the Philosopher's "Error": Tracking the Diabolical in Heidegger — 56

PART TWO: ART AND LITERATURE

5. Literary Attestation in Philosophy: Heidegger's Footnote on Tolstoy's "The Death of Ivan Ilyich" — 76

6. The Greatness of the Work of Art — 99

7. *Ne sutor ultra crepidam*: Erasmus and Dürer at the Hands of Panofsky and Heidegger — 117

8. "Poet of Poets. Poet of the Germans." Hölderlin and the Dialogue between Poets and Thinkers   135

PART THREE: HISTORY AND HISTORIOLOGY

9. Descartes in the History of Being: Another Bad Novel?   150

10. Bridging the Abyss: Heidegger and Gadamer   170

11. The Transformation of Language at Another Beginning   190

12. Deconstruction and the Possibility of Ethics: Reiterating the "Letter on Humanism"   211

Notes   225

Index   261

Preface

Research on Heidegger has proliferated over recent years.[1] Fortunately, most of the contributors have not simply been academics in search of something to write about. The study of Heidegger over the last 25 years, and especially over the last five, has established itself as one of the most exciting, demanding, challenging, and sometimes—as with Heidegger's political involvements—depressing arenas of scholarly endeavor. Nothing indicates this better than the attention Heidegger has attracted within fields other than philosophy. Theologians, literary critics, political theorists, sociologists, law professors, and historians have joined with poets, architects, and psychiatrists, not to mention journalists, in the apparently never-ending process of rereading Heidegger, not only because of the intrinsic interest of Heidegger's thought, but also because it has, particularly recently, inspired further insight, questioning, and innovation across all these disciplines and endeavors.

Corresponding to this massive activity, it is not surprising that many of the early studies on Heidegger suddenly seem remarkably dated, although in their time they were indispensable. Where once the tone was largely deferential, over the last 10 or 15 years commentators have become more questioning. Where once the task was to provide an exposition of texts that seemed virtually impenetrable, some of those texts now seem so familiar that scholars search for novel interpretations to breathe new life into them. To say that Heidegger research has now become more questioning is not to deny that Heidegger always had severe critics, but they tended to do their work by offering readings of his texts that were so diminished that they lacked credibility. As a result they were easily dismissed. The caricature that they offered provided some observers with an excuse to ignore Heidegger, but they left very little mark on how Heidegger was read.

The major reassessment of Heidegger's work that is now in progress, and to which it is hoped this volume will contribute, has been dominated by at least three events. The first is the ongoing publication of the *Gesamtausgabe*. The edition has not been without its critics, and every scholar that has made use of it must at one time or another have been frustrated by the uncertainties that surround it as a result of the decision, for which Heidegger himself was largely responsible, not to produce a critical edition in which editorial changes were clearly marked. Nevertheless, the individual volumes themselves have proved anything but a disappointment. Their cumulative effect confirms the legend of Heidegger's quite unparalleled achievement as a university lecturer. It is no surprise to find that the one book that has maintained its preeminence for almost 30 years is Otto Pöggeler's *Der Denkweg Martin Heideggers*.[2] Pöggeler had access to many of Heidegger's unpublished manuscripts, including the *Beiträge zur Philosophie*, a book that until its publication in 1989 was known to many only through Pöggeler's report of it. The process of reassessment will go on for some time. Almost all of the essays selected for the present volume rely heavily on the *Gesamtausgabe*. As further volumes appear, no doubt further revisions and refinements in our view of Heidegger will be called for. For example, the eventual publication of Heidegger's Marburg lectures on *Plato's Sophist* and *The Beginning of Modern Philosophy* will no doubt have an impact on the conclusions drawn in the first and ninth essays of the present volume respectively.[3] And who knows what the 1949 lectures *Einblick in das was ist* will show, when the scandalous remark juxtaposing "the production of corpses in the gas chambers" with agriculture as "a motorized food industry" is restored to its context?[4]

The second event that has dominated research on Heidegger over the last few years has been the recurrence of the controversy over Heidegger's politics. The central charge, that Heidegger lent his support to the Nazi regime in the notorious Rectoral Address of 1933 and never expressed remorse, remains unchanged. What fuelled the controversy in the late 1980s was the discovery of certain documents that showed that Heidegger, in constructing his defense after the war, had distorted the historical record concerning both his appointment and his conduct as Rector of the University of Freiburg. In the late 1940s and the mid-1960s, when the controversy also made headlines, there were already those who doubted Heidegger's version of events. The difference now is that there is no option but to accept what the documents show, however admiring one might be of Heidegger's philosophical accomplishments. The ground of the debate has shifted. Furthermore, lectures newly published in the *Gesamtausgabe*, especially those on Hölderlin's poetry, show just how the relation between Heidegger's thought and his politics is more complex than was previously believed.

The third event that has transformed the course of Heidegger scholarship has been the advent of deconstruction. The very word "déconstruction" was, according to Derrida, borrowed from *Littré* to translate Heidegger's word *Destruktion*.[5] Derrida's readings may not have been universally welcomed, which surely neither surprises nor disappoints him. Nevertheless, they are not the arbitrary inventions that Derrida's critics have complained of. Derrida reads with an attention to detail, a scrupulousness, and above all a certain remorseless determination not to be satisfied with surface impressions, that should put his overhasty critics to shame. The debt that Heidegger studies owes to Derrida extends far beyond Derrida's own essays on Heidegger, which are always notable for the way he draws attention to aspects of Heidegger's thought that have previously been neglected. Throughout all his writings Derrida has shown the vitality of a thinking that draws on the later Heidegger. Derrida's relation to Heidegger is addressed directly only in the last two essays of the volume, but its impact can be traced in all of them.

Derrida has been particularly important for shifting attention to Heidegger's history of Being and showing how that history produces a transformation of our relation to language.[6] This is because Derrida does more than study the history of Being. Deconstruction, as Derrida conceives it, is inconceivable without reference to the history of Being, notwithstanding the penetrating questions he poses to it. Most notably, Derrida's questions concern the way Heidegger tends to refer that history to the unity of metaphysics.[7] But Heidegger's presentation of metaphysics in its unity is always at the same time complicated by his reference to "another beginning," which is never a departure or rejection of metaphysics, but a rethinking of it, and in particular of its beginning. The history of metaphysics is therefore always in Heidegger the telling of a story and a disruption of that story, as one investigates the hidden resources of that history in the form of the words of Being.

The present volume is to be understood as a sequel to my *The Question of Language in Heidegger's History of Being*, published in 1985. Unlike the earlier book no single theme unifies *Heidegger in Question*. Given everything I have just mentioned—the explosion of secondary literature on Heidegger, the succession of volumes from the *Gesamtausgabe* throwing new light on old issues, and the proliferation of deconstructive readings that show how previously marginalized aspects of Heidegger's thought are anything but unimportant—this does not strike me as the time to attempt to write a definitive book on Heidegger. Instead, I have made select incisions into the Heideggerian *corpus* in an attempt both to extend and to revise my earlier book. The chief focus remains the history or destiny of Being (*Geschick des Seins*), in particular its distinction from, and yet its apparent dependence on, history (*Historie*) in the sense of a story or narrative. I continue to regard it as Heidegger's decisive, but still not always well understood, innovation. I have, however, also given extensive consideration in the essays collected here to ethics and politics. Certainly Heidegger is most vulnerable within this sphere of questioning, but there are more resources in his thought for understanding ethics, and even politics, than is usually recognized.

I have reserved for the Introduction a brief survey of the contents of *Heidegger in Question: The Art of Existing*, together with an explanation of both parts of the title. I have, of course, as yet only a vague sense of where this research is leading. Or, to put it differently, I cannot say now what a similar collection of essays written over the next five years or so would focus on, but I have my suspicions.[8] I believe that it would remain focused on the question of the history of philosophy, but would revolve around the question of the identity that Heidegger gives to philosophy. Heidegger repeatedly asserted that philosophy is essentially Greek (WP 31). Like Hegel before him, he entertained the idea of the centrality of Greek philosophy not least because of his belief in an inner relation between the Greeks, the Germans, and their respective languages. To say that philosophy is in its essence Greek meant to Heidegger, at the very least, that philosophy was Western or European. As I show in chapter 8, Heidegger also tended to argue his case in the rather narrower terms of the unique relation of the German language to the Greek language. In either case, our suspicions should be aroused. However, Heidegger did at least acknowledge the value of traditions that he might not have regarded as belonging to philosophy in the operative sense. The most famous instance is the case where Heidegger advised his Japanese visitors not to concentrate on Western philosophy but to study their own tradition (US 87; WL 3). How many other such invitations to other peoples should Heidegger not have issued? And does not Heidegger's own interest in at least some forms of Asian thought also indicate that this was not merely a question of each maintaining him- or her-self (impossibly) within his or her own tradition?[9] Philosophy, once it recognizes its finitude, encourages the proliferation of thought. This will surely prove all the more true once the prejudice that determines philosophy as essentially Greek loses its persuasiveness, as is already proving the case under the dual thrust of a questioning of the modern construction of the story of the exclusively Greek origins of Greek philosophy and a reevaluation of the determination of the non-Greek as essentially non-philosophical. On this basis, research on Heidegger and research inspired by Heidegger will certainly continue to proliferate, because there is every indication that his thought is more open to such developments than is the case for those philosophies that failed to reflect on their own historicity.

Acknowledgments

───◆───

Almost all of the essays in this volume have already appeared elsewhere. Although the essays are substantially unchanged, they have all undergone some revision, particularly where there is a need to alert readers to the publication of new primary or secondary sources.

I am grateful to the editors and publishers of the following journals and collections for permission to reprint and revise work which first saw the light of the day under their auspices:

Parvis Emad and Ken Maly for chapter 1, which first appeared in *Heidegger Studies* 2 (1986).

John Sallis and Humanities Press for chapters 2, 9, 10, and 11, which first appeared in *Research in Phenomenology* 18 (1988), 17 (1987), 16 (1986), and 13 (1983) respectively.

John Sallis and Indiana University Press for chapter 3, which first appeared in *Reading Heidegger: Commemorations* (Bloomington: Indiana University Press, 1992).

John Sallis and University of Chicago Press for chapter 12, which first appeared in *Deconstruction and Philosophy* (Chicago: University of Chicago Press, 1987).

Marcus Brainard for chapter 4, which first appeared in the *Graduate Faculty Philosophy Journal* 14, 2/15, 1 (1991).

David Wood and Routledge for chapter 5, which first appeared in *Philosophers' Poets* (London: Routledge, 1990).

James Risser and the State University of New York Press for chapter 6, which first appeared in *Heidegger: Toward the Turn* (Albany: SUNY Press, 1993).

Elaine Escoubas and La Part de l'oeil for chapter 7, which first appeared in a shortened version as "Ne sutor ultra crepidam: Erasme et Dürer aux mains de Panofsky et Heidegger," in *Dossier: Art et phénoménologie* 7 (1991).

This collection of essays is the latest product of over 20 years spent reading and rereading Heidegger's texts. Those years were not spent in isolation. The list of friends, colleagues, and students (including students who have become friends and colleagues) whose inspiration, guidance, and help is clearly marked on the following pages is too long to include here, as I found when I began to prepare the list. I can only hope that they know how much I am aware of my debt to them. This book is not only for them. It is theirs.

Special thanks go to Amit Sen, who made many helpful suggestions during the revision of the manuscript, to John Drabinski, who took on the burdensome task of preparing the index, and to Chris Harris, who prepared the manuscript for publication with skill and good humor and who corrected the proofs, and who always insisted that it be done to the sound of good music.

Abbreviations of Works By Heidegger

BP	*The Basic Problems of Phenomenology.* Translated by A. Hofstadter. Bloomington: Indiana University Press, 1984.
BR	"Brief an Richardson," *Heidegger. Through Phenomenology to Thought,* by W. J. Richardson. The Hague: Martinus Nijhoff, 1963.
BT	*Being and Time.* Translated by J. Macquarrie and E. Robinson. Oxford: Basil Blackwell, 1962.
BW	*Basic Writings.* Edited by D. F. Krell. New York: Harper & Row, 1977.
EB	*Existence and Being.* Translated by R. Hull and A. Crick. London: Vision, 1949.
EGT	*Early Greek Thinking.* Translated by D. F. Krell and F. A. Capuzzi. New York: Harper & Row, 1975.
EHD	*Erläuterungen zu Hölderlins Dichtung.* Frankfurt: Klostermann. Pages 1–143, zweite Auflage, 1951. Pages 152–193, vierte Auflage, 1971. The page numbers of the second edition, given in the margin of the fourth edition, will be cited.
EM	*Einführung in die Metaphysik.* Tübingen: Niemeyer, 1966.
EP	*The End of Philosophy.* Translated by J. Stambaugh. New York: Harper & Row, 1973, and London: Souvenir, 1975.
FD	*Die Frage nach dem Ding.* Tübingen: Niemeyer, 1962.
GA 13	*Aus der Erfahrung des Denkens.* Gesamtausgabe Band 13. Frankfurt: Klostermann, 1983.

ABBREVIATIONS OF WORKS BY HEIDEGGER

GA 20 — *Prolegomena zur Geschichte des Zeitbegriffs.* Gesamtausgabe Band 20. Frankfurt: Klostermann, 1979.

GA 21 — *Logik. Die Frage nach der Wahrheit.* Gesamtausgabe Band 21. Frankfurt: Klostermann, 1976.

GA 24 — *Die Grundprobleme der Phänomenologie.* Gesamtausgabe Band 24. Frankfurt: Klostermann, 1975.

GA 26 — *Metaphysische Anfangsgründe der Logik im Ausgang von Leibniz.* Gesamtausgabe Band 26. Frankfurt: Klostermann, 1978.

GA 29/30 — *Die Grundbegriffe der Metaphysik.* Gesamtausgabe Band 29/30. Frankfurt: Klostermann, 1983.

GA 32 — *Hegels Phänomenologie des Geistes.* Gesamtausgabe Band 32. Frankfurt: Klostermann, 1980.

GA 33 — *Aristoteles, Metaphysik IX, 1–3.* Gesamtausgabe Band 33. Frankfurt: Klostermann, 1981.

GA 39 — *Hölderlins Hymnen "Germanien" und "Der Rhein."* Gesamtausgabe Band 39. Frankfurt: Klostermann, 1980.

GA 43 — *Nietzsche: Der Wille zur Macht als Kunst.* Gesamtausgabe Band 43. Frankfurt: Klostermann, 1985.

GA 45 — *Grundfragen der Philosophie.* Gesamtausgabe Band 45. Frankfurt: Klostermann, 1984.

GA 47 — *Nietzsches Lehre von Willen zur Macht als Erkenntnis.* Gesamtausgabe Band 47. Frankfurt: Klostermann, 1989.

GA 50 — *1. Nietzsches Metaphysik. 2. Einleitung in die Philosophie.* Gesamtausgabe Band 50. Frankfurt: Klostermann, 1990.

GA 52 — *Hölderlins Hymne "Andenken."* Gesamtausgabe Band 52. Frankfurt: Klostermann, 1982.

GA 53 — *Der Ister.* Gesamtausgabe Band 53. Frankfurt: Klostermann, 1984.

GA 54 — *Parmenides.* Gesamtausgabe Band 54. Frankfurt: Klostermann, 1982.

GA 55 — *Heraklit.* Gesamtausgabe Band 55. Frankfurt: Klostermann, 1979.

GA 61 — *Phänomenologische Interpretationen zu Aristoteles.* Gesamtausgabe Band 61. Frankfurt: Klostermann, 1985.

GA 65 — *Beiträge zur Philosophie.* Gesamtausgabe Band 65. Frankfurt: Klostermann, 1989.

H — *Holzwege.* Frankfurt: Klostermann, 1972.

HB — "Die Herkunft der Kunst und die Bestimmung des Denkens," *Distanz und Nähe*. Edited by Petra Jaeger and Rudolf Lüthe. Würzburg: Königshausen und Neumann, 1983, pp. 11–22.

HCE *Hegel's Concept of Experience*. New York: Harper & Row, 1970.

HCT *History of the Concept of Time*. Translated by T. Kisiel. Bloomington: Indiana University Press, 1985.

HK *Heraklit*. Seminar WS 1966/67 with Eugen Fink. Frankfurt: Klostermann, 1970.

HNS *Martin Heidegger and National Socialism*. Edited by Gunther Neske and Emil Kettering. New York: Paragon House, 1990.

HPS *Hegel's Phenomenology of Spirit*. Translated by Parvis Emad and Kenneth Maly. Bloomington: Indiana University Press, 1988.

HS "Vom Ursprung des Kunstwerks. Erste Ausarbeitung," *Heidegger Studies* 5 (1989), pp. 5–22.

HT *Heraclitus Seminar 1966/67*. Translated by Charles H. Seibert. Alabama: University of Alabama Press, 1979.

I *Identität und Differenz*. Pfullingen: Neske, 1957.

ID *Identity and Difference*. Translated by J. Stambaugh. New York: Harper & Row, 1969.

IM *An Introduction to Metaphysics*. Translated by R. Manheim. New Haven: Yale University Press, 1973.

KM *Kant and the Problem of Metaphysics*. Translated by R. Taft. Bloomington: Indiana University Press, 1990.

KPM *Kant und das Problem der Metaphysik*. Frankfurt: Klostermann, dritte Auflage, 1965.

MFL *The Metaphysical Foundations of Logic*. Translated by M. Heim. Bloomington: Indiana University Press, 1984.

NG "Nur noch ein Gott kann uns retten," *Der Spiegel*, No. 23 (1976), pp. 193–219.

NI *Nietzsche*, Band 1. Pfullingen: Neske, 1961.

NII *Nietzsche*, Band 2. Pfullingen: Neske, 1961.

Ni *Nietzsche, Vol. 1. The Will to Power as Art*. Translated by D. F. Krell. New York: Harper & Row, 1979.

Nii *Nietzsche, Vol. 2. The Eternal Recurrence of the Same*. Translated by D. F. Krell. New York: Harper & Row, 1984.

Niii *Nietzsche, Vol. 3. The Will to Power as Knowledge and as*

	Metaphysics. Translated by J. Stambaugh, D. F. Krell, and F. Capuzzi. New York: Harper & Row, 1987.
Niv	*Nietzsche, Vol. 4. Nihilism.* Translated by F. A. Capuzzi. New York: Harper & Row, 1982.
OA	*De l'origine de l'oeuvre d'art. Premiére version (1935).* Edited by E. Martineau. Paris: Authentica, 1987.
P	"Plato's Doctrine of Truth." Translated by J. Barlow. In *Philosophy in the Twentieth Century,* edited by W. Barrett and H. D. Aiken, Vol. 3. New York: Harper & Row, 1971, pp. 173–192.
PLT	*Poetry, Language, Thought.* Translated by A. Hofstadter. New York: Harper & Row, 1971.
QT	*The Question concerning Technology and Other Essays.* Translated by W. Lovitt. New York: Harper & Row, 1977.
SD	*Zur Sache des Denkens.* Tübingen: Niemeyer, 1969.
SU	*Die Selbstbehauptung der deutschen Universität.* Frankfurt: Klostermann, 1983.
SZ	*Sein und Zeit.* Tübingen: Niemeyer, 1967.
TB	*On Time and Being.* Translated by J. Stambaugh. New York: Harper & Row, 1977.
TK	*Die Technik und die Kehre.* Pfullingen: Neske, 1962.
UK	*Der Ursprung des Kunstwerkes.* Stuttgart: Reclam, 1960.
US	*Unterwegs zur Sprache.* Pfullingen: Neske, 1959.
VA	*Vorträge und Aufsätze.* Pfullingen: Neske, 1954.
VS	*Vier Seminare.* Frankfurt: Klostermann, 1977.
W	*Wegmarken.* Frankfurt: Klostermann, 1967.
WB	"The Way Back into the Ground of Metaphysics." Translated by W. Kaufmann. In *Existentialism from Dostoevsky to Sartre.* New York: Meridian, 1956.
WCT	*What Is Called Thinking?* Translated by F. D. Wieck and J. Glenn Gray. New York: Harper & Row, 1968.
WD	*Was heisst Denken?* Tübingen: Niemeyer, 1954.
WDP	*Was ist das—die Philosophie?* Pfullingen: Neske, 1965.
WL	*On the Way to Language.* Translated by P. Hertz and J. Stambaugh. New York: Harper & Row, 1971.
WP	*What Is Philosophy?* Translated by William Kluback and Jean T. Wilde. German/English text. London: Vision Press, 1956.
WT	*What Is a Thing?* Chicago: Henry Regnery, 1970.

Introduction

❖

The phrase *Heidegger in Question* that forms the first part of the book's title needs little or no explanation, particularly in the current context; the phrase that follows it, *The Art of Existing*, is, however, more problematic and needs to be accompanied by an explanation. Does it not suggest a return to the long discredited existentialist reading of Heidegger? Today "Heidegger" is a body of arguments to be examined and, where found promising, submitted to revision and improvement in the alien context of philosophy of mind or philosophy of language. Or, "Heidegger" is a text whose strategies are to be scrutinized in terms of certain necessities imposed by the logic or *logos* of Western metaphysics, a logic that Heidegger himself helped to uncover and that has been investigated further by Derrida—even as this logic is found in Heidegger's texts themselves. Or again, "Heidegger" names an archive from which—to the extent that access to the archive is granted[1]—an intellectual biography can be constructed, but also on which judgment must be passed, because the archive does not allow the boundaries of the life of the mind and political life to remain distinct. I hope that the essays that follow reflect some of what is best in all these approaches. However, it is no secret, and it will in any case soon be clear to the reader of this book, that the deconstructive approach has had the most impact on this particular reader of Heidegger, not least because deconstruction has accomplished a certain renewal of the Heideggerian corpus that provides a context in which the other approaches have their place. Why, then, use a phrase like *The Art of Existing* in the book's title when, even if it escapes sounding like a manual or guide to the philosophical life for the uninitiated, it inevitably evokes a philosophical innocence that deconstruction above all has freed us from (or deprived us of)?

The phrase "*The Art of Existing*," or more precisely the word *Existierkunst*, is drawn from the Heideggerian corpus. It is a quotation from the so-called Appendix to section 10 of *The Metaphysical Foundations of Logic*.[2] Heidegger there distinguishes "the pedantry of a schematic system" from "the rigor of questioning" (GA 26, 200; MFL 157–58). The pedantry that is dismissed includes the belief that fundamental ontology could provide a firm foundation that would allow further supplementary disciplines to solve the problems of philosophy. Such a belief could be sustained only by ignoring the very finitude that Heidegger's analyses reveal at every turn. And yet, Heidegger says in a remarkable statement, "Not only do we need the analytic in general, we must produce the illusion ... that the given task at hand is the one and only necessary task" (GA 26, 201; MFL 158).[3] The analytic in question is twofold: the analytic of *Dasein* and the analytic of the temporality of Being (*Temporalität des Seins*). It embraces, therefore, not just the published portions of *Sein und Zeit*, but also the never-published third division of the first part, *Zeit und Sein*. The task of the analytic includes making explicit and thereby placing at our disposal what is implicit in human existence.

It is not often that one is asked to maintain an illusion, and it is tempting, although I suspect ultimately naive, to suggest that one cannot maintain an illusion *as such*. Heidegger seemingly attempts to bypass the epistemological problem by claiming that an illusion of this kind conforms with the art of existing. He claims that one must grasp at the same time the singularity of the specific course of action one is engaged in and its finitude. This makes the art of existing nothing else than "the clarity of action itself" hunting for genuine possibilities (GA 26, 201; MFL 158). In other words, the art of existing is a way of coming to terms with the finitude of existence, of not being overwhelmed by it, nor seeking an escape from action in self-reflection. This would be true of all action, but for the philosopher who gives preeminence to his or her own activity, it would amount to an acknowledgment that the action of philosophy cannot be freed from its relation to concrete existence, except as an illusion, an untenable working hypothesis, such as that Heidegger himself employs in the course of developing the program of fundamental ontology.

In "'The Double Concept of Philosophy' and the Place of Ethics in *Being and Time*," the second essay in this volume, I take up these themes in more detail. I show how the initial idea of fundamental ontology was compromised by the fact that Heidegger could not accomplish the analysis of existence without construing *Dasein* in terms of some concrete possible idea of existence: he had initially excluded this possibility on formal grounds (SZ 43; BT 69), but subsequently, as the analysis proceeded, conceded its inevitability (SZ 313; BT 361). I also suggest that the specific idea of existence operative in *Being and Time* is that of the philosopher. The question of the ontic fundament of fundamental ontology thus becomes a question of the *existentiell* understanding without which any existential analysis would be groundless. Behind any existential interpretation lies "an ontical way of taking existence which may be possible but need not be binding for everyone" (SZ 312; BT 360). On this reading Heidegger does not impose the model of philosophical existence on humanity, as some philosophers have done, but he nevertheless has it serve as the idea of existence governing the analysis of *Dasein*. The ideal of the philosopher is the route to, but not the result of, the analysis of *Dasein*. The difference might seem slight, but Heidegger explains it in *The Metaphysical Foundations of Logic*. On the one hand, he insists that the metaphysical isolation of *Dasein* is not to be confused with the factical *existentiell* sense of placing the one philosophizing at the center of the world (GA 26, 172; MFL 136). On the other hand, he makes clear that attaining the metaphysical isolation of *Dasein* is possible only on the basis of the extreme *existentiell* involvement of the philosopher (GA 26, 176; MFL 139–40). There is therefore a difference of levels that must be maintained. However, Heidegger does more than simply recognize the distinction. The initial reliance on the philosopher recoils on the subsequent analysis and establishes its limitations: "Since philosophizing is essentially an affair of finitude, every concretion of factical philosophy must in its turn fall victim to this facticity" (GA 26, 198; MFL 156). This takes place as metontology, as explained in the second chapter below.

In *The Metaphysical Foundations of Logic* Heidegger issues an extraordinary challenge. He suggests that a philosophy is to be judged according to the individual philosopher's success in the "art of existing." "The proofstone of philosophical truth consists solely in the loyalty the philosophizing individual has to himself" (GA 26, 22; MFL 17. Cf. SZ 391; BT 443). The philosopher and subsequently the thinker were important figures for Heidegger. Heidegger refused to separate the thinker from the thought.[4] But after the "error" of the 1930s, his defenders were increasingly forced to draw a distinction between them. Heidegger's own thought of "the art of existing" puts Heidegger, the thinker, in question. This is the focus of chapter 4 below, but a number of other essays in this volume address it too, especially those that discuss the relation of his writings on art and poetry to his politics.

In chapter 4 I situate Heidegger's political involvement with Nazism and his postwar silence on the Holocaust in relation to the tradition of the good philosopher as "a good man." The figure of the philosopher as "a good man" has proved an illusion, but, if one accepts authenticity to be doing service in Heidegger for goodness, which is admittedly not a simple matter, it is one to which Heidegger remained attached. The distinction between the philosopher's life and the philosopher's thought cannot be sustained as a way of resolving the issue where the thought is so explicit, as it is in Heidegger, that this thought itself is to be assessed with some reference to the life. But if the thinker's success in "the art of existing" is at least one of the standards to be appealed to, then "a personal failure" is no small matter.

Some people may gain comfort from such considerations, because it might seem that, while Heidegger might be dismissed on this basis, the tradition of the good philosopher as "a good man" survives. In "Habermas and Arendt on the Philosopher's 'Error'" I suggest, however, that, whereas Habermas betrayed himself by displaying such hopes while he passed judgment on Heidegger, Arendt and Levinas, even more so, both recognized that the lessons to be learned are nothing if not unsettling for the dominant tradition within Western philosophy and the way it approaches evil. It is not just Heidegger who is in question when the philosopher fails to exhibit any skills in the art of existing.

I have already mentioned that "the art of existing" was referred by Heidegger to "the clarity of action." Action—or rather *praxis*—is not a frequent topic in Heidegger, but its strategic place is crucial, especially in its relation to *poiesis*. Heidegger gives enormous importance to the notion of *poiesis* in his account of Western philosophy. It is in terms of *poiesis* that Heidegger not only explains the inner relationship between the Western philosophical tradition and technology, but also looks to poetry as a way of addressing the crisis or "danger" to which that tradition has been brought. During the tradition, and perhaps even in the way Aristotle himself conceived the relation between *praxis* and *poiesis*, *praxis* seems to become increasingly neglected or forgotten. In the first essay of the present volume, "The Fate of the Distinction between *Praxis* and *Poiesis*," I chart Heidegger's appeals to the distinction between *praxis* and *poiesis* and particularly the way his discussion of it is determined by the distinction's history. Heidegger seems both to be telling a story about the history of Western metaphysics and at the same time recalling that which is forgotten in that history and appears only by interrupting it. The essay plays a crucial role in the volume as a whole because it shows the dominance of *poiesis* in the Western tradition to be the dominance of storytelling or narrative in determining meaning, including the meaning of any action and indeed the meaning of existing as such: one's life makes sense to the extent that a story can be constructed round it. This is the Greek heritage.

Also for the Greeks, the question of *praxis* was a question of ethics or, rather, of *ethos*. *Praxis* does not answer the question "What should I do?" and by the same token Heidegger's phrase, "the art of existing," has little to do with "rules for existence." But there are other ways of framing ethical questions than by asking for directives, just as ethics need not be a matter of rules.[5] Although in both *Being and Time* and "Letter on Humanism" Heidegger apparently renounced ethical language, careful study of both texts shows that they still give a place to ethics. Just as in "'The Double Concept of Philosophy,'" which draws heavily on *The Metaphysical Foundations of Logic*, I explore the place that Heidegger gives to ethics in the period of *Being and Time*, in the final essay of this volume, "Deconstruction and the Possibility of Ethics," I explore the same question with reference to the "Letter on Humanism," extending it farther to include Levinas and Derrida. "Justice and the Twilight Zone of Morality," the third essay in the volume, suggests that, scattered through Heidegger's lectures and essays from 1935 for 10 years or so, are hints of another version of the history of Being from the one usually given. This other version begins with Anaximander's *dike* and ends with Nietzsche's *Gerechtigkeit*. It is concerned with the question of the history of the essence of justice, but as Heidegger relates this history it becomes more of a story, like Heidegger's account of the history of essence of truth, than *Seinsgeschichte*. It is as if Heidegger was opening up the way to another kind of history of ethics from that which is usually presented. Implicit in this history is an account of the relation of the transformations in the conception of morality to the history of Western metaphysics that has hitherto gone unrecognized and calls for further study.

The papers on art in the second section of this volume suggest that the question of art and poetry in Heidegger should not be approached independently from consideration of other aspects of his thought. This, of course, is entirely what one would expect from a thinker engaged in "the overcoming of aesthetics." The fifth essay, "Literary Attestation in Philosophy," is at one level a study of the use of literary examples in philosophy with specific reference to Heidegger's footnote in *Being and Time* to Tolstoy's "The Death of Ivan Ilyich." Within the context of the present book, it is perhaps more important that the essay helps clarify the largely ignored question of the structure of the first three chapters of the second division of *Being and Time*. Heidegger's discussion of Being-toward-death in the first chapter of the second division has received extensive attention in the secondary literature, but it has been read in isolation from the overall argument. Here restored to its context, it provides an appropriate setting for clarifying the relation between the existential and the *existentiell* on which a number of the essays in *Heidegger in Question* depend.

Two of the other essays on art and poetry—essays 6 and 8 in this volume—stress the overtly political character of Heidegger's discussions in this realm. For Heidegger after 1953, it is not only action, but also, and perhaps primarily, art that determines existence. This was, however, not a retreat on Heidegger's part from politics, as is clear from his expressed goal of turning the Germans from a public into a people. This notion of a people is in marked contrast with the individualistic bias of modern aesthetics, but it should not be dismissed simply because of the political connotations that it would have evoked among Heidegger's audience. Chapter 6, "The Greatness of the Work of Art," engages these questions with specific reference to the three versions of Heidegger's lectures on "The Origin of the Work of

Art," whereas chapter 8, "'Poet of Poets. Poet of the Germans.' Hölderlin and the Dialogue between Poets and Thinkers," takes them up with reference to Heidegger's various lectures and essays on Hölderlin. Both essays also help clarify the role Heidegger assigned to the thinker in this period: the thinker, in combination with the poet, is directed to the task of forming a people. It is perhaps here that the appearance of Heidegger's previously unpublished lectures has been most decisive in challenging the dominant interpretation. Retrospectively it is clear that Heidegger's readers—and I certainly include myself here—should have been more aware of the extent to which his writings on art and poetry, at least for the 10 years from 1933 and probably beyond, were dominated by political considerations. But there is a danger today that in an effort to show oneself sensitive to these issues, one simply leaves traditional aesthetics intact. Heidegger cannot be "saved" or "salvaged" by finding a residue of his thought on art, or anything else, that is free of art. Heidegger's contribution here is a very disconcerting version of what his contribution has so often been: to show how difficult it is to sustain the traditional boundaries of the various branches within philosophy as well the divisions between philosophy and other disciplines. Politics and political thought, or at least what used to go by those names, provide the most graphic examples, but by no means the only ones.

The seventh essay in the collection juxtaposes Heidegger's discussion of Dürer with that of the art historian Panofsky. It is an attempt to bring Heidegger's discussion of great art into the orbit of his discussion of the history of Being by focusing on a concrete example. It was perhaps no accident that the example Heidegger himself chose to offer in *The Will to Power as Art* was a German artist, Dürer, but the focus of this essay is on the attempt to reconstruct how Heidegger might have elaborated the few sentences to be found there, had he been asked to do so. One cannot broach this question without reflecting on the division between philosophy and art history as it appears in the academy. For this reason Heidegger's approach is compared with that of Panofsky, an art historian, who could also be described as a philosopher. The relation between philosophy and art history is so complex in this context because the place Heidegger gives to art is far from simple: art is certainly not subordinated to philosophy in the way that it is in Hegel. It quickly emerges that what differentiates Heidegger's approach from that of the art historians is that he regards the history of art from the standpoint of the history of Western metaphysics. "*Ne sutor ultra crepidam*: Erasmus and Dürer at the Hands of Panofsky and Heidegger" shows how differently such terms as "beauty" and "verisimilitude" appear, when examined from this standpoint. Although this essay is less directly concerned with the question of *Existierkunst* than most of the others, I have included it here because it shows the impact of Heidegger's account of the history of Being as it relates to the history of metaphysics in an arena where the historical issues are usually neglected, despite the extensive attention Heidegger's writings on art have received.

The thought of the history of Being is the later Heidegger's most characteristic thought, and the remaining essays in *Heidegger in Question* are also devoted to it. As I have already indicated, a number of the earlier essays in the volume have shown how Heidegger's discussions of the history of Western philosophy tend to collapse into the creation of narratives: narratives about technology, justice, and art, according to a principle explicated in the first essay in the volume. The focus of the remaining essays, specifically the ninth, tenth, and eleventh chapters, is the role of narrative in writing the history of philosophy. The ninth chapter examines how, in the late 1930s, under the impact of his recognition of the history of Being, Heidegger transformed the reading of Descartes he had given in the 1920s. In *Being and Time* and other works of the Marburg period, Heidegger challenged Descartes's claims to novelty. Subsequently, Heidegger seems to have become more prepared to give Descartes his traditional place as the founder of modern philosophy, albeit on a non-traditional basis. But the idea of a founder of modern philosophy is already part of a story, Descartes's own. The question then posed by Heidegger's reading of Descartes, as with all readings in the history of Being, is the relation of the narrative account to an interruptive reading. That Heidegger's history of Being was not always fully understood is apparent from a consideration of Gadamer's reading of Heidegger, which is the concern of the tenth chapter. I have attempted in the closing paragraphs of this essay to do justice to the uniqueness of Gadamer's own philosophical position, but for the most part the concern is with Gadamer's interpretation of Heidegger and his attempt to unite Heidegger's approach to the history of philosophy with that of Hegel, as if the two could be reconciled and were not essentially different, above all in their treatment of narrative.[6]

Finally, the eleventh chapter, "The Transformation of Language at Another Beginning," considers the relation between Heidegger and Derrida, and so brings to the surface considerations implicit in a number of the essays in this volume. This chapter is the oldest of all the essays included here, but I continue to stand by its reading of Heidegger's late essays on language, even if I now must acknowledge a failure to engage the "political" dimension of the question of language. Perhaps the most important aspect of the essay, in the context of the volume as a whole, is the explication of the notion of "another beginning," because it recurs in many of the other essays. The notion of "another beginning" that is nevertheless not a "new beginning" but a relation to the "first beginning" indicates what is most inviting, most challenging, and yet most disturbing in Heidegger's thought. It is inviting because it helps resolve a problem of strategy that is most acutely observed as a consequence of Derrida's warning that the idea of a new beginning that stood outside of the first beginning would remain bound to the traditional logic of oppositions and so resituate the new within the old. It is challenging because of the difficulty of walking this tightrope, as this and the other essays in the volume show. But it is above all disturbing, and it disturbs because Heidegger, as I note in chapter 8, thought "another beginning" specifically as the special relation between the Greek language and the German language. Once this special relationship is challenged, as I indicate in the book's Preface, Heidegger's own presentation of the *existentiell* foundations of the existential invites recognition of a multiplicity of philosophies, corresponding to the plurality of peoples and languages.

The title *Heidegger in Question: The Art of Existing* must be taken as a whole. The focus Heidegger places on existence establishes the finitude of thought, including his own. In other words, Heidegger's thought of *Existierkunst* itself places that thought in question. The essays in this volume attempt to continue that process. They not only pose questions about Heidegger, who was preeminently the thinker of the question, the one who wrote "Questioning Is the Piety of Thinking" (VA 44; QT 35). They also put questions to Heidegger. Sometimes the questions come from outside, but most often the thinking at work here operates by what might be called Heideggerian questions, which recognize that, in Heidegger's words, "Every posing of every question takes place within the very grant of what is put in question" (US 175; WL 71). There is also a process of self-questioning or of suspicion at work here, so that the questioning recoils on the essays themselves in a way which invites further questions, questions about the questions raised here, questions which would above all question the apparent innocence of questioning.[7] This, among other reasons no doubt, is what makes the essays in this volume at best only provisional, and happily so, in the face of a thinking that continues to challenge, even when it seems most questionable.

Part One

◆

ETHICS AND POLITICS

1

The Fate of the Distinction between *Praxis* and *Poiesis*

The distinction between *praxis* and *poiesis*—understood as a distinction between action and production, doing and making—is often thought of as Aristotle's own, because we must look to him, and specifically to Book Six of his *Nicomachean Ethics*, for its classic exposition. In fact, Aristotle explicitly tells us that he is taking up the distinction from "exoteric discourses" which were presumably well known to him and his contemporaries but are unfortunately unknown to us.[1] The familiarity of the distinction was such that he does not seem to have felt obliged to offer a sustained account of it, either in Book Six of the *Ethics* or elsewhere. Nor is there any clear agreement among scholars as to how the distinction is understood by him, in part because of attempts to interpret Aristotle's discussion in the light of contemporary debates within the field of ethics, and in part because of the difficulties scholars themselves have introduced by insisting that his language conform to our own contemporary standards of what constitutes an exact and consistent terminology.[2] Aristotle initially understands *poiesis* to be an activity that aims at an end distinct from the activity, whereas *praxis* is an activity whose end is nothing other than the activity itself. And he quickly assimilates this distinction to his own central distinction between the different kinds of being which belong to activities, a distinction he expresses in a number of different ways but is today most commonly referred to as the difference between *kinesis* and *energeia*.

Aristotle may be the fundamental source for our understanding of this distinction, but we should be aware that he has transformed it in the course of adopting it.[3] In its transformed sense, it governs his account of the ethical excellences or virtues, as well as his characterization of two of the five intellectual excellences, *phronesis* and *techne*, which correspond to *praxis* and *poiesis* respectively. I am more concerned here with posing certain questions for the reading of Heidegger which arise out of this distinction than with clarifying Aristotle's transformation of the distinction. But I am aware that the present essay suffers from the lack of a detailed account of what I understand by the "fate" of the distinction between *praxis* and *poiesis*, not just in Aristotle but in metaphysics generally. In the absence of such an account everything said here has only a preparatory status.

Heidegger's preoccupation with Aristotle during the Marburg period is well known and has been the subject of a number of studies.[4] Only recently, however, has Heidegger's reading of Aristotle's *Ethics* taken center stage.[5] The results of these studies are somewhat tentative and will remain so until the key source, the 1924/25 lecture course on Plato's *Sophist*, with its long opening discussion of Book Six of the *Nicomachean Ethics*, is published.[6] Meanwhile, since 1989 scholars have had at their disposal Heidegger's 1922 introduction to his never completed book on Aristotle.[7] On its basis it has at last been possible to begin to account for the impact Heidegger's course had on the students who attended it, an impact which eventually came to fruition in two particularly significant works of philosophy. The first of these is Hannah Arendt's *The Human Condition*, which, even if it does not mention Heidegger by name, is governed by the distinction between *praxis* and *poiesis*, first learned in his seminars on Aristotle.[8] The second is Gadamer's *Truth and Method*, where the distinction between *phronesis* and *techne* is appealed to in order to establish the kind of knowledge which characterizes the human sciences.[9] Both Arendt and Gadamer agree that it is not simply the failure to make the distinction which has distorted our understanding of the nature of politics and of the human sciences, but the predominance of *poiesis* and *techne*. Meanwhile *phronesis* and *praxis* have fallen into oblivion, although the manner in which they have done so is not sufficiently clearly articulated by either Arendt or Gadamer.

So far as possible I want to avoid speculating in this chapter on the details of Heidegger's reading of Book Six of Aristotle's *Ethics*, which still remain unclear. Nor do I intend to contrast Heidegger and Aristotle. Such comparisons between thinkers can be multiplied indefinitely, but the philosophical assumptions underlying enterprises of that kind have been challenged by Heidegger, in my view definitively. My question here is, in one sense at least, neither artificial nor extrinsic, but Heidegger's own. With reference to *Being and Time* and the Marburg lectures, it is the question of the destruction of the history of ontology. And, without wishing to restrict Heidegger to a single reformulation of his relation to previous thinking, that question subsequently came to be understood by him as the transformation of language at another beginning.[10] Within the terms of that question or questions, I shall pose the further question of the place of *praxis* with regard to the dominance metaphysics grants to *poiesis*. How far and in what way that is a question which properly belongs to Heidegger, or even can be profitably pursued with reference to Heidegger, cannot and should not be decided in advance.

To begin with *Being and Time*, it has frequently been said that with his analysis of the worldhood of the world, Heidegger attempted to transfer to readiness to hand (*Zuhandenheit*) the priority traditionally accorded to presence at hand (*Vorhandenheit*). This impression has no doubt been encouraged by the fact that Heidegger claims quite explicitly to have deprived *Vorhandenheit* and pure intuition of their priority (SZ 147; BT 187), a priority which, he also says, served as the foundation of Western philosophy since Parmenides (SZ 171 and 358; BT 215 and 410). But in referring *Vorhandenheit* to *Zuhandenheit* Heidegger does not attempt to offer an alternative foundation for ontology. It is not the task of so-called fundamental ontology to offer a rival thesis to that which has been maintained by the tradition. This is not simply a consequence of the fact that in *Being and Time* Heidegger explicitly puts in question the methodological tendency to derive everything and anything from a simple "primal ground" (SZ 131; BT 170). In *Kant and the Problem of Metaphysics* Heidegger explains, even more clearly than he does in *Being and Time* itself, that fundamental ontology does not attempt to issue a challenge to Greek philosophy: "Neither 'Being' nor 'time' needs to give up its previous meaning, but it is true that a more original interpretation of their justification and their limits must be established" (KPM 219; KM 165–66). This is also what is meant by the so-called repetition or retrieval of ancient philosophy.[11] The destruction of the traditional content of ancient ontology is directed not so much against that ontology as against its standard interpretation, which has come to provide an obstacle to its appreciation, blocking our access to the original experiences in which the first ways of determining the nature of being were achieved (SZ 22; BT 44). But Heidegger is clear that that may mean examining what philosophy has always overlooked, because of a certain naiveté on the part of ancient ontology (GA 20, 155; HCT 110; GA 24, 251; BP 186).

When we look to Heidegger's lectures and essays for an illustration of this process of referring traditional concepts to the experiences underlying them, we find that he frequently points to the importance of the experience of production for the development of the concepts of philosophy. In a lecture course delivered during 1927, the same year in which *Being and Time* appeared, Heidegger insisted that whereas the Kantian interpretation of existence is governed by perception, the interpretation of existence offered by ancient thought and Scholasticism was governed by productive behavior. This has important implications for the reading of *Being and Time*, as Heidegger himself indicates, when he restates the point in its own unmistakable terminology. The present at hand is "before the hand" and so in relation to *Dasein*. And it is so as something produced (GA 24, 143; BP 101).[12] This reference of presence at hand to production is something of a surprise after *Being and Time*, where it is primarily referred to theory and to knowledge. Even more puzzling might be the suggestion that for the Greeks "a *being* is synonymous with *a present at hand disposable*" (*vorhandenes Verfügbares*), for disposability had earlier on the same page been identified as the character of things of use, the ready to hand.[13] But this is no contradiction: present at hand and ready to hand are not opposed to each other as two separate realms, but rather belong together in what Heidegger, in an earlier lecture course, called "an exchange of presence" (GA 20, 264; HCT 194). It is not simply that, as Heidegger insists, the Greek word *ousia* bears the pre-philosophical meaning of "disposable possessions and goods" along with its philosophical meaning. This pre-philosophical meaning in some way also belongs to ancient ontology, which is not fully cut off from its pre-philosophical roots until the language of philosophy shifts from Greek to Latin. But ancient ontology, while harboring this meaning, nevertheless fails to articulate it, and this is what constitutes, according to Heidegger, its naiveté. Hence Heidegger can at this time conceive his task not as the overcoming of ancient ontology, but as the explicit elaboration of its basis (GA 24, 156–57; BP 111). The explicit recognition of the ready to hand in its relation to the present at hand and the acknowledgment of the determinative role of the experience of production belong to that elaboration.

If there are still any residual doubts about the crucial significance of the Greek interpretation of Being as production for the reading of the analysis of environmentality in *Being and Time*, these should be dispelled since the publication of Heidegger's 1931 lecture course on Book Nine of Aristotle's *Metaphysics* (GA 33). There, in the context of a discussion of Aristotle's account of the *episteme poietike* or *techne*, Heidegger refers to the interpretation of production (*Herstellen*) given by Plato and Aristotle and repeats that the basic concepts of philosophy have developed from this interpretation. He then explains that "it is necessary to clarify what it means that man has a relation to the works which he produces. It is for this reason that a certain book called *Being and Time* talks of dealings with equipment" (GA 33, 137). The remark still leaves unexplained the precise purpose of the discussion of equipment in *Being and Time*, but it leaves in no doubt that the importance of the discussion will be overlooked if we focus only on the supposed novelty of the descriptions to be found there, or its "phenomenological" credentials, and yet at the same time ignore its relation to previous thinking. As Heidegger says in *Kant and the Problem of Metaphysics*, "the existential analytic of everydayness does not want to describe how we use a knife and fork" (KPM 212; KM 160. See also GA 29/30, 262–63).

But what, then, is the significance of these references to Greek ontology for the reading of *Being and Time*? The account of equipmentality in *Being and Time* is not an account of production as such, but of our relation with things which have been produced. Nevertheless, these two are not so very different, given the way that our relation with what has been made exhibits the goals which already control production. A thing is made to be useful, and its making is already governed by the use to which it is to be put. Furthermore, the relations governing production and those governing use are not simply similar, but we understand them to be integrated. Just as the materials which are taken up and used when something is being made are already conceived from the standpoint of the product in the sense of the idea that the producer has in advance, so we understand that idea in its turn to have been conceived from the standpoint of the task for which the product is intended. Such a sequence of means and ends, whereby each end is the means for something else, leads to a notorious infinite regress, which a number of philosophers have entertained, including Aristotle. It is with reference to this dilemma that in Book One of the *Nicomachean Ethics* he introduces his examination of the idea of the Good. He subsequently returns to the problem in Book Six with his discussion of the *hou heneka*. It is a similar regress that provides the context for Kant's introduction of human being as an end in itself. When Heidegger appeals in *Being and Time* to the notion of the for-the-sake-of-which (*das Worumwillen*), he addresses the same problem to which these earlier thinkers were responding (SZ 113–17; BT 84–87).[14] This is confirmed by the way Heidegger introduced the for-the-sake-of-which in his lectures, not only with reference to Kant's account of the end itself, but also in order to elucidate the *hou heneka*, both as it occurs in Plato's discussion of the good in Book Six of the *Republic* and in Book Six of Aristotle's *Nicomachean Ethics* (GA 26, 137, 237, and 240; MFL 111, 184, and 186).

To emphasize these historical connections is not to diminish what Heidegger sought to accomplish in his thinking during this period. He characterized his thinking as a repetition, thereby removing it from the inside-outside opposition which tends to dominate contemporary discussions of how a philosopher relates to his forebears. Hence we should not be surprised to find a reference to *praxis* at the very point in *Being and Time* where Heidegger introduces the notion of equipment. He writes, "The Greeks had an appropriate name for 'things': *pragmata*—that is to say, that with which one has to do in one's concernful dealings (*praxis*)" (SZ 68; BT 96–97. Also GA 20, 250; HCT 185). And yet, in what would be another example of their so-called naiveté, they failed to think the ontological character of what they named, thereby setting Heidegger the task he takes up in these sections. "Ontologically, the specifically 'pragmatic' character of the *pragmata* is just what the Greeks left in obscurity; they thought of these 'proximally' as 'mere things.' We shall call those entities which we encounter in concern *equipment*." This reference to *praxis* is not to be understood in terms of Aristotle's distinction between *praxis* and *poiesis*. The sense meant is well explained in the 1935/36 lecture course published by Heidegger under the title *Die Frage nach dem Ding*. In a discussion of the meaning of *ta mathemata*, Heidegger distinguishes four other Greek senses of thing: *ta phusika*, things insofar as they originate and come forth from themselves; *ta poioumena*, things insofar as they are produced by the human hand and stand as such; *ta chremata*, things insofar as they are in use and stand at our constant disposal, whether *phusika* or *poioumena*; and finally, *ta pragmata*. *Ta pragmata* are explicated as "the things insofar as we have to do with them at all, whether we work on them, transform them, or we only look at and examine them—*pragmata* with regard to *praxis*: here *praxis* is taken in a truly wide sense, neither in the narrow meaning of practical use (*chresthai*), nor in the sense of *praxis* as moral action: *praxis* is all doing, pursuing and enduring, which also includes *poiesis*" (FD 53–54; WT 70).[15] It is this broad sense of *pragmata* that Heidegger evokes in *Being and Time*.

But even if in section 15 of *Being and Time* Heidegger evokes the broad meaning of *praxis*, and not its narrower sense where it is distinguished from *poiesis*, this does not resolve the fate of these terms with regard to *Being and Time*. I have already noted how in section 18 Heidegger passes from the sequence of serviceability and usability to the "for-the-sake-of-which," and how the last named is understood as echoing earlier discussions from the history of metaphysics. I shall here concentrate on the relation of Heidegger's discussion to Aristotle's *Nicomachean Ethics*, although that is not to deny the importance of the other echoes of metaphysics to be heard in this section.

The focus of Heidegger's preoccupation with the *Nicomachean Ethics* seems always to have been Book Six, where Aristotle turns from the ethical excellences to the intellectual excellences. Aristotle begins by recalling an earlier distinction between the so-called rational and irrational parts of the soul, one having the *logos* and the other being without it.[16] Aristotle then divides the former into the epistemic, which is invariable, and the deliberative, which is variable. Showing no concern to develop an unambiguous terminology, Aristotle then further divides the epistemic or theoretical into two parts, one of which is *sophia*, the other *episteme* itself. Similarly, he divides the deliberative or practical into *phronesis* and *techne*. Another name Aristotle gives to the deliberative is the "logistical," which is usually understood to mean the capacity for calculation.[17] Alongside the two epistemic excellences and the two practical excellences, there is a fifth excellence, *nous*, which is privileged above the others because it is concerned with first principles.[18] This framework is of particular importance because Aristotle maintains that within both the deliberative and epistemic parts of the soul there is an ordering, so that each has a *beltiste lexis*, a support faculty or disposition.

As regards the deliberative or practical, Aristotle attempts to show the superiority of *phronesis* over *techne* in various ways, but a particularly decisive passage is the following, where Aristotle subordinates *poiesis* to *praxis*:

> Thought alone moves nothing, but only thought for-the-sake-of-something [*hou heneka*] and concerned with action. This indeed governs *poiesis* also, since whoever makes something always has some further end in view: that which is made is not an end in itself, it is relative and for someone. Whereas that which is done [*to prakton*] is an end in itself, since doing well (*eupraxia*) is the end, and what desire aims at.[19]

But what does it mean for *praxis* to govern *poiesis*, or for the practical to be the principle of the productive? Aristotle conceives "principle" or *arche* with reference to his doctrine of the four causes. In the paraphrase attributed to Andronicus of Rhodes it is suggested that *arche* here means "efficient cause."[20] But this interpretation is not so much mistaken as misleading. The important point is rather that the practical is construed as the final cause of *poiesis*, as is indeed suggested by the reference to the *hou heneka* in the previous sentence. *Praxis* may bear its own end in itself, but how can it be the cause of *poiesis* without being conceived as an external goal? And if we grant to Heidegger that the doctrine of the four causes has its source in the experience of making, then Aristotle's reference of *praxis* to causality—be it the efficient or the final cause—places it within the referential teleology of *poiesis*.[21] In this way *praxis*—at the very time that it is privileged over *poiesis*—comes to be interpreted in the light of *poiesis*, and *phronesis* is referred to *techne* (GA 26, 146; MFL 118).[22] Even if I would hesitate before declaring this passage the decisive moment in the history of the traditional subordination of *praxis* to *poiesis*, it is striking that Aristotle appears to accomplish the reverse of what he intends. For when *praxis* is construed as the goal of *poiesis*, does it not cease to be *praxis*?

Aristotle's *Ethics* may be the fundamental philosophical source for an understanding of *praxis*, but the transformation *praxis* undergoes in being assimilated into the language of Aristotle's metaphysics, and the distortion it suffers when it is integrated into a structure which postpones it in favor of *poiesis*, better shows the problem of sustaining a recognition of *praxis* than it shows *praxis* itself. And this problem is inherent to *praxis*. There is a fundamental difficulty in providing pure examples of *praxis*, for it is not the object of a representation or of will, but is determined by the situation which calls for it. And yet, it is also true that the situation does not have its meaning in advance of the action, but is only shown to be the situation that it was retrospectively, in the light of the action. This retrospective determination of the situation and thus of the action itself arises, as Arendt has argued, in the construction of a story about it.²³ But such storytelling is itself a form of *poiesis*. It would seem that *praxis* shows itself only by submitting to the manner of revealing characteristic of *poiesis*, so that it does not show itself, except as a trace.

When, in section 18 of *Being and Time*, Heidegger refers the "toward which" of serviceability to the "for-the-sake-of-which," he repeats the Aristotelian integration of *poiesis* and *praxis* through the *hou heneka*, which, as we have seen, distorts the nature of *praxis*. But what is the significance of this echo, or repetition even, of an Aristotelian text at the heart of Heidegger's account of the worldhood of the world? Heidegger does not in fact confine the *Worumwillen*, or for-the-sake-of-which, to a form of teleological thinking. The for-the-sake-of-which is that wherein *Dasein* understands itself beforehand. It is that for which entities are freed, relating us to the horizon in which we are situated and in which entities may be encountered. Heidegger's introduction of the notion of horizon to elucidate the worldhood of the world and his subsequent reference to the *Lichtung*, or clearing, show instead that he is not so much underwriting as undercutting the tendency to understand the metaphysical tradition in terms of teleology. He does this not by turning his back on that tradition, but by repeating it in order to show its primordial sources.

The lecture courses from this period shed further light on this process. In various texts Heidegger understands *phronesis* (conventionally translated as prudence or practical reason) in terms of *Umsicht*, or circumspection, and *techne* as *Wissen*, or know-how, a knowledge which is governed by *Vorsicht*, foresight, as an advance look to the *eidos* (GA 24, 232; BP 163). In his 1927 lectures, *The Basic Problems of Phenomenology*, Heidegger explains that "the view in which the equipmental context stands at first, completely unobtrusive and unthought, is the view and sight of practical circumspection, of our practical everyday orientation."²⁴ This gives circumspection a broader signification than *phronesis* as the ability to recognize what action a situation calls for, but both are ways of seeing which are not directed to this or that, but which let a situation show itself. And it allows Heidegger to say that "all producing is, as we say, fore-sighted [*vor-sichtig*] and circumsighted [*um-sichtig*]" (GA 24, 154; BP 109). Circumspective seeing is thus placed within the context of the ontological constitution of production, as it was with Aristotle. Up to this point the discussion of circumspection in *The Basic Problems of Phenomenology* might seem to be straightforward phenomenological description, just as the account of the worldhood of the world in sections 15 to 18 in *Being and Time* is usually construed. But Heidegger here continues by pointing out that circumspection is prominent wherever ontology interprets what it is that is to be produced. He then suggests that even such preeminent expressions within Greek philosophy as *idea*, *eidos*, and *theorein* reflect the sight which pertains to production, a sight which "does not yet need to be a theoretical contemplation in the narrower sense but is first simply looking toward the produced in the sense of circumspective self-orientation." And then, having insisted on the role of production in Greek ontology, Heidegger repeats the claim of *Being and Time* that the access to the present at hand to be found in intuition, *noein* or even *theorein*, has dominated philosophy from Parmenides through Kant. In this way the 1927 lecture course confirms that the challenge to the priority of intuition is issued not from outside the tradition, but from the experience of production underlying it. *Theorein* is used by Greek philosophy to say "intuition," but a more penetrating hearing finds in it a reference to production.

But does the point of Heidegger's investigations into the role of the experience of making in the development of the concepts of Greek ontology lie in directing his readers to the opposition between production and pure theory? If that were his aim, it might be judged a serious matter that his account of production was in terms of practical circumspection. Would Heidegger not thereby have maintained the traditional indifference in which the distinction between *poiesis* and *praxis* has been held? And would he not thereby—to use the language of section 6 of *Being and Time*—remain the victim of the self-evidence which blocks our access to primordial sources as much as the traditional privileging of theory which he had sought to put in question? Certain passages from *The Metaphysical Foundations of Logic*, Heidegger's last lecture course at Marburg, may help us judge how appropriate such questions are.

The Metaphysical Foundations of Logic returns to the issue of transcendence, which in *Being and Time* was already the focus of the structure designated by the for-the-sake-of-which. But Heidegger makes clear that his approach toward such conceptions as intuition, *idea*, or *theoria* is governed by his conviction that they remain unsuitable for thinking transcendence because they lack a primordial rootedness in *Dasein*. And yet, in accordance with the explicit principle that insofar as transcendence was central to philosophy it must have come to light in all genuine philosophy—"be it only in a quite veiled way and not conceived as such" (GA 26, 234; MFL 182)—Heidegger suggests another possibility: "Dasein was also known to antiquity as authentic action, as *praxis*" (GA 26, 236; MFL 183). Not that Heidegger simply reverses the traditional privileging of theory over practice. To protect himself against this misinterpretation, he immediately warns that "if we now pose the problem of transcendence in connection with the problem of freedom, we must not take freedom in a narrow sense, so that it pertains to *praxis* in contradistinction to *theoria*." This would lead in the direction of Kantianism. "But the problem is the common root of both intuition, *theorein*, as well as action, *praxis*." And yet, if Heidegger thereby seems to withdraw the word *praxis* almost as soon as he offered it, a few lines later he returns to it as a name for the root of transcendence. "Though in Plato transcendence was not investigated down to the genuine roots, the inescapable pressure of the phenomenon nevertheless brought to light the connection between the transcendent intended by the *idea* and the root of transcendence, *praxis*" (GA 26, 237; MFL 184). Throughout this discussion Heidegger does not mention *poiesis*. Does that mean that *praxis* is here understood to include *poiesis*? The context is, after all, what Heidegger calls "a vague historical orientation to Plato's doctrine of ideas" (GA 26, 233; MFL 181). Or could it be that by "authentic action" Heidegger means *praxis* as opposed to *poiesis*? When, at the end of the discussion, Heidegger recalls that the *hou heneka*—"as that for-the-sake-of-which something is, is not or is otherwise" (GA 26, 237; MFL 184)—is particularly prominent in Aristotle, does he hear in the *hou heneka* a trace of *praxis* in the narrow sense, "be it only in a quite veiled way and not conceived as such," to use the phrase he introduced earlier in the discussion? To what extent does *praxis* survive its interpretation as the *hou heneka* of *poiesis*? Is it only the *poietic* that—to recall Heidegger's description of the linguistic work of art—determines what is holy and what is unholy, what great and what small, what brave and what cowardly, who master and who slave (UK 43; PLT 43. Cf. Heraclitus, Fragment 53)? Does not *praxis* also determine the situation which provokes it? And is this not what characterizes the truth or rather the *aletheia* of action to which Aristotle himself testifies in the *Ethics*?[25]

Leaving open for the moment the question of what Heidegger understands by *praxis* as the root of transcendence, this section of the last Marburg course helps with another question mentioned earlier, that of whether or not Heidegger in *Being and Time* should be understood as reversing the traditional privilege of the theoretical over the practical. The passages just quoted show that Heidegger's thinking is concerned with the question of transcendence rather than with the traditional distinction between theory and practice. Hence the difficulties which arise when one tries to construe Heidegger's scattered remarks on this theme in *Being and Time* as representing a single position of his own. There is some equivocation as to whether Heidegger asserts the primacy of the practical or whether he simply dissolves the distinction between theory and practice.[26] But this ambiguity is not accidental. It is a consequence of the ambiguity within metaphysics itself concerning the question of the relative priority of intuition or theory, on the one hand, and the experience of production, on the other. In finding support for the latter in the form of the priority of readiness to hand, Heidegger remains within the confines of a repetition of Greek ontology. Significantly, the ambiguity which surrounds the question of the relative priority of theory and practice in *Being and Time* reappears in later texts with reference to the dominance of the one or the other within the history of metaphysics. So one text asserts the supremacy of *theoria* for Greek life (VA 53; QT 164. Also GA 54, 220), while another from roughly the same time insists that "Plato experiences everything present as an object of making, indeed, decisively for the sequel" (VA 166; PLT 47). These references could be multiplied. I introduce them only to make all the more plausible my suggestion that the equivocation concerning the question of theory and practice in *Being and Time* arises from metaphysics itself and appears there in fulfillment of the task of the repetition and destruction of the history of ontology. Heidegger's discussion of theory and practice does not decide in favor of one or the other, nor is the distinction regarded as ultimate.

Both of the questions raised by a reading of these pages of *The Metaphysical Foundations of Logic*—the question of the nature of *praxis* and the question of the distinction between theory and practice—are taken up more explicitly in the "Letter on Humanism"; I shall take them up again in that context. Otherwise Heidegger focuses explicitly on *praxis* only rarely and his sights are clearly set on *poiesis*. Furthermore, this is not always the broad conception of *poiesis* which includes *praxis*, in the way that *praxis* may be understood to include *poiesis* both in *Being and Time* and the 1935/36 lectures referred to earlier. Rather, *poiesis* is in these last works often expressly referred to the experience of making. Heidegger repeats his early observation that a number of the most important Greek philosophical concepts were originally determined with reference to production. So, for example, in "The Origin of the Work of Art" Heidegger repeats the general conviction, already stated *Being and Time*, that "what seems natural to us is probably just something familiar in a long tradition that has forgotten the unfamiliar source from which it arose" (UK 17; PLT 24). He then proposes that the form-matter distinction in its universal application refers originally to the process of making and that the interrelation of form and matter is controlled beforehand by the purposes for which the thing is made (UK 20; PLT 26–27). Similarly, the first lecture course on Nietzsche declares that the distinction between form and matter arose in the sphere of equipment (NI 98; Ni 82). By the time of the 1962 "Seminar on the Lecture *Time and Being*," Heidegger shows the importance of the experience of making for Western metaphysics by sketching an account of metaphysics in terms of it: the presenting of what is present is interpreted by Aristotle as *poiesis*, from which it passes to subsequent metaphysics, where it comes to be understood as *creatio*, and later still as "positing" with reference to the transcendental consciousness of objects. "The fundamental characteristic of the letting-presence of metaphysics is production [*Hervorbringen*]" (SD 49; TB 45–46).

Only Plato's role in this history is left deliberately unclear, with his references to light more prominent than those to *poiesis*, particularly at first. It would require a more detailed survey than I could offer here in order to try and make sense of the different emphases of Heidegger's various accounts of the place of *poiesis*.

It is sufficient in the present context to show that in his reflections on *poiesis* Heidegger developed another relation to Greek thinking to that found in the Marburg period. This is most readily done with reference to the 1953 lecture "The Question concerning Technology."[27] This lecture contains Heidegger's most far-reaching thoughts on the role of *poiesis*, and the discussion is more carefully articulated than elsewhere. So, for example, he draws attention to the breadth of the Greek conception of *poiesis*, which should be understood to include *phusis* as well (VA 19; QT 10).[28] Furthermore, he emphasizes that the translation "making" is inadequate to the Greek understanding of *poiesis*, which means something more like "bringing forth."

And yet, nowhere in "The Question concerning Technology" does Heidegger mention *praxis*. The omission might not at first appear very serious, although it is at least surprising when one observes that Heidegger specifically refers to *Nicomachean Ethics* Book Six, chapters 3 and 4, where, in what he calls a "singular discussion," Aristotle distinguishes between *episteme* and *techne* (VA 21; QT 13). But, as everyone knows, Aristotle's discussion of the intellectual excellences also names *phronesis*, *nous* and *sophia*. Does it matter that Heidegger has given only a partial presentation of Aristotle's account? This misrepresentation of Aristotle might simplify Heidegger's attempt to show the centrality of *poiesis* within metaphysics, but it is no more than an easily recognized shortcut. In this passage Heidegger is more concerned with focusing on Aristotle's acknowledgment that *aletheia* in the sense of revealing belongs to the ancient words for knowing in the broadest sense, *techne* and *episteme*, than with their narrower delimitation in Aristotle. Can Aristotle's testimony be ignored in this way? Certainly *phronesis*, as the kind of knowing corresponding to *praxis*, is also a revealing.[29] But does this not challenge Heidegger's presentation more than it supports it?

In order to appreciate the role of "The Question concerning Technology" within the broader framework of Heidegger's thinking, it is important to recognize that in this essay he returns, even if only briefly and implicitly, to the structure already elucidated in *Being and Time* as the for-the-sake-of-which. Heidegger takes up Heisenberg's description of the technological age as one in which "it seems as though man everywhere and always encounters only himself" (VA 35; QT 27). Human beings are encouraged in their posture as "lords of the earth" by the illusion that everything they encounter is their own construct. Heidegger, however, does not limit himself to the familiar observation that wherever we go we encounter man-made creations: the tools of everyday life, machine-prepared food, and a countryside radically transformed by humanity. These were the phenomena to which Heisenberg referred in the lecture to which Heidegger directs us. Heidegger was concerned with the conception of truth in science and the recognition that science does not investigate nature as such, but only, for example, our *knowledge* of particles.[30] By contrast, Heidegger's observations extend to what he calls the blocking of *poiesis*, the annihilation of the thing and the refusal of the world. That is to say, in the technological age, the age of *Gestell*, the horizon of the for-the-sake-of-which has collapsed in on human beings.

Heidegger approaches the same theme elsewhere through his interpretation of Protagoras's saying that "Man is the measure of all use thing (*chremata*)." That "man always encounters only himself" can be understood as the modern counterpart of Protagoras's saying (H 94–98; QT 143–47. Also NII 127–73; Niv 85–122). This does not mean that the latter saying is to be understood with reference to modern technology, but rather the reverse: technology derives historically from *techne* as a mode of *aletheuein* (W 171; BW 220. Also GA 45, 178–79). And yet, what allows this history to be recognized is the sense in which it has completed itself. This is what lies behind Heidegger's statement in the essay on technology that it is an illusion—indeed "the final delusion"—to suppose that man encounters only himself. It is an illusion because in this situation human beings in fact fail to encounter themselves *in their essence*, that is to say, as addressed by being. But in "The Question concerning Technology," and also the essay "The Turning," Heidegger proceeds to show that the refusal of the world is that which allows revealing to be recognized as such. This is why it is described as the final delusion. The annihilation of the thing in the age of technology functions somewhat like the default of equipment in section 16 of *Being and Time*, and, as the latter revealed what was called the worldhood of the world, the former shows "the innermost indestructible belongingness of man within granting" (VA 40; QT 32). It is not a question of revitalizing our appreciation of ancient ontology by returning to its sources, but rather of another beginning, albeit that this too cannot take place without reference to the first.

This is why Heidegger must follow the lesson taught by Hölderlin in the poem *Patmos*:

> Wo aber Gefahr ist, wächst
> Das Rettende auch.

> Where danger is, that which rescues
> Burgeons too.

Having recognized the decisive role of *poiesis* within metaphysics, Heidegger does not turn his back on it, but attempts to come to terms with metaphysics through *poiesis*. That is also what lay behind his attempt to reinterpret the traditional doctrine of the four causes mentioned earlier. Here the multiplicity of meanings of *poiesis* which play off each other throughout the essay are made to culminate in a series of questions that lead to *poiesis*, in the sense of poetry, and the fine arts, in the sense of *techne*, an association already prepared for in "The Origin of the Work of Art" (UK 65–66; PLT 59). Heidegger asks if *poiesis* in the sense of poetry could not found anew "our vision of that which grants and our trust in it" (VA 43; QT 35).[31] His official answer is that "no one can tell," but the import of the question—and that is what Heidegger would have us attend to—is more positive. It is not simply an idle hope. It is a pious hope, expressed in the piety of questioning and based on the account of the history of metaphysics in terms of *poiesis*.

Poetry here does not mean everything that usually goes under the name of poetry. Other essays of the same period suggest that the sense of poetry here is related to that of "poetic dwelling." So, for example, in the essay " . . . *dichterisch wohnet der Mensch*. . ." poetry is explicitly associated not only with *poiesis*, which is mentioned only in passing, but also with building. "Poetry is, as a letting dwell, a kind of building" (VA 189; PLT 215). Two further kinds of building are also identified: first, the cultivation of what produces growth out of itself and, secondly, the construction of buildings and other works made by hand. Heidegger identifies these as, respectively, *colere* and *cultura*, on the one hand, and *aedificare*, on the other (VA 191; PLT 217). But could they not also be referred to *phusis* and *poiesis*? *Poiesis* in its narrow sense could be associated with *aedificare*, and by the same token building, as Heidegger understands it here, suggests *poiesis* in its broader sense. And yet, poetry is not simply one more kind of building among others, but another kind of building, the incipient (*anfänglich*) form of building. It lets dwell because it is the authentic gauging or measure of the dimension of dwelling (VA 202; PLT 227). In this notion of measuring which is developed at some length in the essay, one can hear an answer to Protagoras. But how are we to understand "dwelling"? In the lectures and essays in the 1940s, Heidegger offers it as his translation of the Greek *ethos* and thereby refers it to ethics (W 185; BW 233. Also GA 55, 205–6, and 214). The relation between *ethos* and ethics was indeed specifically acknowledged by Aristotle in the *Nicomachean Ethics*.[32] Furthermore, Aristotle takes it for granted that, as the intellectual excellence which corresponds with the ethical excellences, *phronesis* arises out of *ethos*.

To attempt to establish a relation between dwelling in Heidegger and Aristotle's *phronesis* would seem an artificial enterprise were it not for the

1951 lecture "Building, Dwelling, Thinking." I propose that its title should be understood as a form of remembrance of Aristotle's threefold division between the poetic or productive, the practical, and the theoretical.[33] Heidegger observes that we are accustomed to think of "dwelling and building as related as end and means" (VA 146; PLT 146). This is indeed how *phronesis* and *techne* present themselves in Aristotle as a consequence of the integration of *poiesis* and *praxis* within a single system of framework. And later in the essay, Heidegger is more explicit about the deficiencies of the Greek understanding in this realm. Heidegger suggests that the Greek conception of *techne* is not adequate to building in its narrow sense as construction. He writes, "The erecting of buildings would not be suitably defined *even* if we were to think of it in the sense of the original Greek *techne* as *solely* a letting appear, which brings something made, as something present, among the things that are already present" (VA 160; PLT 159). As in "... *dichterisch wohnet der Mensch* ...," Heidegger refers the twin senses of building, as cultivating and as constructing, to a third sense, building as dwelling. So it is not only production as understood in terms of outcome or results which is deemed insufficient. Even the broader conception of *techne* leaves unthought the relation of building to dwelling and so overlooks the essence of building as letting dwell: "To build is in itself already to dwell" (VA 146; PLT 146). Heidegger is saying that the inadequacy of the Greek concept of *techne* lies in its failure to think the nature of dwelling, a failure which is no doubt enhanced at the hands of Aristotle by its distinction from *phronesis*, with its trace of dwelling. Heidegger is concerned to combat the idea that building and dwelling are two separate activities. One should not be fooled by the fact that Heidegger calls the distinction "correct" (VA 146; PLT 146); this is one of Heidegger's favorite ways of dismissing an idea which he regards as insufficiently fundamental.

It is only with explicit reference to metaphysics that Heidegger can think in a way which is other than that of metaphysics. That is why, in my reading of such essays as "Building, Dwelling, Thinking," I emphasize the references to metaphysics to be found there. This is not to reduce what Heidegger says to what might already be found in metaphysics. Nor is it to establish a comparison external to the essential movement of the text, as the reference to *techne* in the essay shows. "Building" should not be reduced to *poiesis*, nor "dwelling" to *phronesis*, nor "thinking" to *theoria*. And yet, building, dwelling, and thinking can be thought only with reference to *poiesis*, *phronesis*, and *theoria* respectively. The remembrance of metaphysics is the only way in which the otherness of another beginning can be maintained. The fashionable, swift dismissal of metaphysics is as self-defeating as a half-hearted rejection of metaphysics is pointless. The thinking of another beginning does not oppose itself to metaphysics, because nothing would be more metaphysical than that. Heidegger attempts to think what the Greeks left unthought in the only way that is possible—with reference to what the Greeks did think. Heidegger makes exactly this point at the end of the 1957 lecture; "The Principle of Identity": "Only when we turn thoughtfully toward what has already been thought, will we be available for what must still be thought" (I 34; ID 41).

This can be illustrated with reference to the central thought of the essay "Building, Dwelling, Thinking." In the first instance it is expressed only negatively. Heidegger says there that "dwelling is never completely thought of as the basic character of human being" (VA 148: PLT 148). But, although it has neither been thought nor experienced, when Heidegger comes to say it in his 1944 lecture course on Heraclitus, he chose to say it in Greek and indeed in an echo of the traditional metaphysical definition of human being: *anthropos zoon ethos echon* (GA 55, 217, and 223). This is not the preferred way of saying it. At the end of "Building, Dwelling, Thinking" Heidegger offers the formula: "Dwelling is *the basic character* of Being in keeping with which mortals exist" (VA 161; PLT 160). But if it seems significant that in "Building, Dwelling, Thinking" Heidegger shows himself prepared to leave Greek behind and draw instead on Old English and High German to say and to establish the character of dwelling, then it should not be forgotten that in section 12 of *Being and Time* he had, with Grimm's assistance, already turned to ancient German and for the same purpose. Ancient German is not an alternative source to ancient Greek, to be preferred because it might be somehow outside metaphysics. What differentiates the early attempts to retrieve (*wiederholen*) metaphysics from later attempts to take the step back (*Schritt zurück*) into the essence of metaphysics is Heidegger's deeper appreciation of the situation from which thinking today must make its start. The difference has already been outlined with reference to his understanding of the essence of technology and of the final delusion to which we seem to succumb at the time of technology.

There is a tendency to want to understand dwelling as Heidegger's name for the condition to which he would like to lead us, a condition which would follow the technological world or rather its refusal of world. But this is to withhold from dwelling the place Heidegger gives it, a place which is at once both more provisional and more fundamental. In "The Turning" he writes that "unless man first establishes himself beforehand in the space proper to his essence and there takes up his dwelling, he will not be capable of anything essential within the destining now holding sway" (TK 39; QT 132–33). This helps to explain the outrageous statement with which Heidegger ends "Building, Dwelling, Thinking." It runs: "As soon as man *gives thought* to his homelessness, it is a misery no longer" (VA 162; PLT 161). It shows just how far remembrance of *ethos* might be from what would today pass for ethics. Can the statement be conceived as anything other than a mark of Heidegger's failure to come to terms with the split between theory and practice? It is surely not enough simply to say that Heidegger would not want to deny the need for new houses, but sees homelessness as a deeper problem than that of their construction. Ultimately, Heidegger is saying that were we able to think, we would already be dwelling. This is the import of my quotation from "The Turning," as also perhaps of the refrain from *What Is Called Thinking?*, that we are still not yet thinking. Heidegger is not simply trying to shock us, though no doubt that is part of it. And he is being deadly serious. The point is that homelessness is the danger and, like the blocking of *poiesis*, it might serve as that which rescues. The possibility we must entertain is that the statement about homelessness is already such a thinking, the thinking of a turning. If it is such, then this thinking is itself a form of *praxis*.

What that might mean was already the subject of the 1947 "Letter on Humanism," which predates the essays whose focus on *poiesis* I have just been considering. It is the only text by Heidegger that announces itself as concerned with action. The opening sentence runs: "We are still far from pondering the essence of action decisively enough" (W 145; BW 193).[34] The question is whether Heidegger succeeds in the essay to tell us anything more than about the essence of action. He explains that the failure arises because we think of action as causing an effect, which is in turn prized for its utility. One might suppose this means that the failure arises because we think of action in terms of production. But Heidegger himself immediately explicates the essence of action as "accomplishment" (*Vollbringen*), which he understands as "unfolding something into the fullness of its essence," or, in Latin, *producere*. This would seem to suggest that Heidegger was content to assimilate action to production, *praxis* to *poiesis*.

Heidegger seems to confirm this impression when he announces his task as freeing us from "the technical interpretation of thinking." The phrase is significant. The technical interpretation of thinking was already operative in Plato and Aristotle, who, according to Heidegger, took "thinking itself to be a *techne*, a process of reflection in service to doing and making. But here reflection is already seen from the perspective of *praxis* and *poiesis*" (W 146; BW 194). This means that they understood thinking "reactively." In an attempt to preserve the autonomy of thinking, it is set in opposition to acting and making, and thereby lets itself be determined by them. The reason why Heidegger quite properly finds the phrase "technical interpretation of thinking" more exact than, for example, "the practical interpretation of thinking" is that thinking is content to justify itself in terms of the service it performs. Thinking, one might say, no longer unfolds according to its essence but, removed from the element of being, comes to serve as an instrument of education: "Philosophy gradually becomes a technique for explaining from highest causes" (W 149; BW 197). Thinking opposes itself to the technical and the practical, but in the very process of denying the practical (in the broad sense) it becomes technical. Were it not that the "Letter on Humanism" was purportedly on action, one might suppose that the reference to *praxis* in the lines quoted above was entirely redundant.

At the end of the "Letter on Humanism" Heidegger rejoins the themes with which he opened the essay, and he does so with reference to the claim that thinking acts. We are told that, by its "inconsequential accomplishment" of bringing the unspoken word of being to language, the thinking of being exceeds all *theoria* and *praxis* (W 191–92; BW 239). What benefit it is to thinking to call it a deed is not made clear. It seems rather that the designation is more effective as a diminution of action. A little later he writes: "We measure deeds by the impressive and successful achievements of *praxis*. But the deed of thinking is neither theoretical nor practical, nor is it the conjuncture of these two forms of behavior" (W 192; BW 240). This would suggest that the issue had been decided against *praxis* and that Heidegger had introduced the question of action only to serve as a foil for his discussion of thinking.

And yet, the situation is perhaps not so simple. There are indications that Heidegger does address the essence of action in the "Letter on Humanism" and in the only way open to him—not directly, but discreetly. First of all, it could be suggested that *praxis* enters the essay in Heidegger's retelling of Aristotle's account of Heraclitus's encounter with some strangers. It is a story about the difference between the blindness of mere curiosity and the capacity to see a situation as an opportunity for word and action—what Aristotle calls *phronesis*. Although this is not why Aristotle introduces the story, it shows what he would have called *theoria*, *phronesis*, and *techne* in combination.[35] Heraclitus the thinker tells the strangers about dwelling. He says, *einai gar kai entautha theous*, which Heidegger translates as "for there are gods present even here." In "Logos," a subsequent essay on Heraclitus, Heidegger writes that "thinking changes the world" (VA 229; EGT 78). This is illustrated, albeit in a particular way, in the story about Heraclitus, for Heraclitus's words transform the situation. They are in this sense an action, and we know this action through a making, the story handed down for generations, until the present day (W 185–87; BW 233–35).[36] But only with Heidegger's retelling of the story does it point beyond the unity of the metaphysical terms, unknown as such to Heraclitus, to their remembrance in building, dwelling, and thinking.

In a second discreet reference to the difference between *praxis* and *poiesis* in the "Letter on Humanism," Heidegger makes what seems only a passing remark on the difference between speech and writing. He writes to Beaufret that his questions would have been better answered in direct conversation. Writing lacks the flexibility of conversation, whereas speaking remains purely "in the element of Being" (W 147; BW 195),[37] an element which has been deserted by the technical interpretation of thinking. On the other hand, the compensation of writing lies in its "wholesome pressure toward deliberate linguistic formulation." This Heidegger refers to in a later passage as "the now rare handicraft (*Handwerk*) of writing" and also as carefulness in saying, the cultivation of the letter (W 174 and 194; BW 223 and 241–42). A possible example of this rare handicraft might be found in his use of typography at the end of the "Letter on Humanism" and, indeed, in the two passages referred to earlier, where Heidegger sought to place thinking beyond the distinction between theory and practice. In both cases Heidegger refers to "praxis" and not to *praxis* in the Greek alphabet, which is his practice elsewhere in the essay.[38] This is perhaps Heidegger's way of indicating that in juxtaposing thinking with praxis, he is addressing not "authentic *praxis*" but praxis in its metaphysical determination, which we could call the "technical interpretation of *praxis*." In both passages Heidegger refers to the achievements (*Leistungen*) of praxis, and not its accomplishment (*Vollbringen*). But it was this latter word which at the beginning of the essay defines the essence of action. At the end of the essay it is used only of the thinking of being and the humbleness of its inconsequential accomplishment. "Inconsequential" means here that it is not judged in terms of its effects, not prized according to its utility. In other words, *praxis* does not display the essence of action.

At the same time and in the same way, Heidegger writes that the thinking of being exceeds theoria; as with the similar remarks about praxis, he avoids the use of the Greek alphabet. The explanation is no different in this case, but it is perhaps clearer to see. It should be recalled that at the beginning of the essay Heidegger had outlined his task of freeing us from the technical interpretation of thinking. "The characterization of thinking as *theoria* and the determination of knowing as 'theoretical' behavior occur already within the 'technical' interpretation of thinking" (W 146; BW 194). That is to say, the technical interpretation of thinking is as much a reduction of *theoria* as it is of thinking. It is theoria, not *theoria*, which is so easily surpassed. Underlying Heidegger's discussion of *theoria* and *praxis* in the "Letter on Humanism," and unknown to the first readers of this essay, is the 1942/43 lecture course on Parmenides, where both words receive an originary meaning. Indeed, the account of *praxis* there recalls the discussion 25 years earlier in *The Metaphysical Foundations of Logic*. Heidegger no longer writes of transcendence, but of *pragma* as "the one original inseparable whole of the relation between things and men" (GA 54, 124. See also GA 54, 118, and 219). We should allow the possibility that the word is given a fundamental status on both occasions and that as such it also underlies the "Letter on Humanism."

When Heidegger said that thinking acts, he was not diminishing the notion of action, however much it might sound like it from a contemporary perspective. But neither should one claim too much for this particular formulation. As Heidegger has reminded us, prior to the opposition of the theoretical and the practical the Greeks thought of *theoria* as the highest form of doing (VA 52; QT 164. See also GA 55, 203, and VS 91). They too could have made sense of his sentence, although not as Heidegger himself understood it. The full meaning of the saying that thinking is the most decisive form of action is, as the so-called Athens lecture of 1967 tells us, that through thinking the world-relation of human beings can begin to change. In other words, thinking acts through its role in the epochal destiny of the history of being. But above all, thinking is called to act at the time of the final delusion and the refusal of the world. And yet, Heidegger makes clear that if thinking is to act it must escape the inadequate distinction between theory and praxis by taking the step back to what was unthought in the beginning of Western thinking, to what was already named there and so dictated to our thinking—the inner connection between *phusis* and *techne* (HB 20–21).

Heidegger, in the "Letter on Humanism," may separate thinking from theory and praxis, but that does not mean that it is a narrow conception of thinking. "Thinking" as understood there already points in the direction of building and dwelling, and not as a conjunction of terms but through their inner connection. This is already suggested by the references to dwelling in the essay and the reference to poetry Heidegger feels obliged to add at its end, albeit somewhat artificially (W 193; BW 240). Whether or not my comments on the story about Heraclitus and on Heidegger's use of typography seem persuasive, it is important to see that Heidegger is not indifferent to the distinction between *praxis* and *poiesis*, like so many thinkers within metaphysics. He has not succumbed to a technical interpretation of *praxis*, which would understand it reactively with reference to *poiesis*. Heidegger's treatment is impressive for its reserve. It would have been very easy for him to adopt the attitude, now common, whereby it is imagined that one can attain a displaced or de-con-structed concept of action simply by edict.[39] There are those who would have us believe it is enough to *record* that a word is to be understood without reference to its metaphysical connotations from Aristotle or elsewhere to accomplish this. The present essay has tried to indicate the difficulties of such attempts.

So long as *praxis* is understood with reference to its distinction from *poiesis*, it amounts to "a technical interpretation of *praxis*," just as Heidegger wrote in the "Letter on Humanism" of the technical interpretation of thinking. In its technical interpretation *praxis* is only understood reactively and is thereby returned to *poiesis*. But how can *praxis* be understood other than reactively, given the dominance of *poiesis* in metaphysics? Does not the distinction between *poiesis* and *praxis* impose itself on our every attempt to circumvent it, even if it is a distinction which is impossible to maintain any longer in its metaphysical form?

Simply to ignore the distinction between *praxis* and *poiesis* is to succumb to the metaphysical dominance of *poiesis*. But to insist on *praxis* in contradistinction to *poiesis* is still to remain in the orbit of metaphysics. Heidegger seeks in the early Greek language an understanding of *praxis*—as also of *poiesis*—which might be said to be prior to their difference and so indifferent to it. These attempts correspond to what he was trying to say with the word "thinking" in the "Letter on Humanism." The extent to which *praxis* might originally have been undecided with regard to the standard alternative is quite other from its broad metaphysical sense, which includes both *poiesis* and *praxis* in the narrow sense of the words. But can we today think the early sense without reducing it to the broad sense or allowing it to be governed by the metaphysical distinction? When, in the lecture course on Heraclitus mentioned earlier, Heidegger attempts to return to an original sense of *praxis* and turns to *pragma* as "the one original inseparable whole of the relation between things and men," he comes to focus on the hands. The reference to hands is supported by the German word for action (*Handeln*), as also the words *vorhanden* and *zuhanden*. But is this not to return action to making? Has not the hand always been the fundamental instrument of making in its distinction from action and labor?[40] Such considerations haunt all attempts to pose the question of *praxis* without reference to its distinction from *poiesis*.

To claim to have at one's disposal a so-called deconstructed notion of action is simply to find a new way of repeating the metaphysical gesture. If the naiveté of Greek ontology lay in its failure to recognize its roots, the naiveté of today's attempts to overcome that ontology is found in the belief that we can take up what they left unthought as if we could make it our own. Heidegger confronted this difficulty by accompanying his attempts to think the early, the oldest of the old, with a remembrance of that which followed. He accepted the necessity whereby it is only in explicit relation to the history of metaphysics that the early sense of *praxis* can address the situation in which the thinking of *praxis* finds itself today. But to what extent could that history be conceived on the classical model? How far could it retain a similarity to the stories of the poets, with beginning, middle, and end? Heidegger's answer to these questions is found in his account of the essentially discontinuous destining of being. It is not a question simply of placing the oblivion of *praxis* within the context of the history of the dominance of *poiesis*. What does that mean?

The distinction between *praxis* and *poiesis* may quite correctly be recognized as metaphysical, and among philosophers it could even be said to be "exoteric" in the sense of "familiar." But it is "exoteric" also in another sense, that of being external to the history of metaphysics. It is metaphysical insofar as it leads to the subordination of *praxis* to *poiesis* and its consequent concealment. And it is anything but a metaphysical distinction insofar as *praxis* cannot be reduced to such a role and necessarily exceeds every attempt to contain it. The undoing of this subordination is a prime task of the thinking of another beginning and can only be accomplished insofar as it thinks in remembrance of the distinction. The concealment of *praxis* is not accidental, but a necessary consequence of the dominance of the poietical form of presencing. Yet *praxis*—as a mark of the exoteric and not simply as one concept among others—has left its trace, and not just in Aristotle. For example, Heidegger quotes a sentence from Eckhart which can illustrate the interrupting of metaphysics by *praxis*. This has nothing to do with the prevalence of Aristotelianism within metaphysics. Equally, the fact that the passage lacks political significance in any sense that would be recognizable to Aristotle (which is something which can, of course, be referred to the different conditions prevailing at the time when it was written) is not denied. But I have here left to one side the political dimension of *praxis* and its place with reference to the metaphysical determination of the theoretical, practical, and productive, albeit that to do so is a traditional prejudice of metaphysics. *Praxis* in the sense of that which interrupts is to be neither measured by nor limited to a specific idea of *praxis* which we might hold in advance.

In "The Turning" Heidegger asks the ethical question in its traditional form: *Was sollen wir tun?*—"What should we do?" (TK 40; QT 40). It might seem that Heidegger simply evades the question by postponing it. We must, he says, first ask, *Wie müssen wir denken?*—"How must we think?" But this too could be called an ethical question. I do not mean that it asks about the way moral considerations can be legitimately allowed to determine thinking. It is ethical in remembrance of the Greek sense of *ethos*. By contrast, the ethical question in its familiar form—"What should I do?"— already conceives ethics in terms of *poiesis*. Heidegger's deflection of the conventional question of ethics to thinking is not the straightforward evasion of ethics which it might seem.[41] What we should do cannot be said in abstraction, because what is essential is to recognize the specific situation for what it is. The capacity to do so corresponds to what Aristotle called *phronesis*, and it arises from dwelling. That is why Heidegger only posed these questions after he had insisted on the importance of dwelling in the sentence earlier. Between them Heidegger quotes a short sentence from Eckhart.

The sentence reads: "Those who are not of a great essence, whatever work they perform, nothing comes of it." It is drawn from *Die Rede der Unterscheidung*, which means "The Counsels on Discernment" but also "Discourse on Difference." The section in which it is found is called "On the Advantage of Self-Abandonment Which One Should Practice Inwardly and Outwardly." Eckhart contrasts acting and being. "If you are just, then your works too are just. We ought not to think of building holiness upon action; we ought to build it upon a way of being, for it is not what we do that makes us holy, but we ought to make holy what we do. However holy the works may be, they do not, as works, make us at all holy; but as we are holy and have being, to that extent we make all our works holy, be it eating, sleeping, keeping vigil or whatever it may be." Then comes the sentence quoted by Heidegger, and after it Eckhart's explanation. "Take good heed: We ought to do everything we can to be good; it does not matter so much what we may do, or what kinds of works ours may be. What matters is the ground on which the works are."[42] Within the context of Heidegger's discussion it is the notion of the ground which strikes us first. Heidegger says there that "modern man must first and above all find his way back into the full breadth of the space proper to his essence" (TK 39; QT 39). Essence is thought differently by Eckhart and Heidegger. In Heidegger this essence is understood with reference to dwelling, and specifically to dwelling in the truth of being. For Eckhart the great essence of man arises when man belongs to God. "A man's essence and ground—from which his works derive their goodness—is good when his mind [*Gemüt*] is wholly directed to God."

There is nothing arbitrary about Heidegger's reference to this passage. There are doubtless people who imagine that before any saying of Eckhart can properly take up a place in a text of Heidegger's it would need to be purified of its context in a thinker who the barest knowledge of historical chronology tells us belongs clearly within the time of metaphysics. But it can in fact be seen that restoring the sentence to its context in Eckhart's works allows it to contribute much more to Heidegger's own enterprise, notwithstanding that Eckhart thinks from a thoroughly different basis from Heidegger's. Eckhart advises against becoming attached to one's works or allowing goals and plans to govern one's life. In their place he counsels being free of one's works as soon as one performs them. This idea comes to fruition in his words *Gelassenheit* and *Abgeschiedenheit*. Heidegger's adoption of the first of these is well known. Many of his readers would prefer to free the word completely from its heritage, regarding that as only something accidental and without fundamental significance. But remembrance does not always simply draw thinking back into metaphysics. "Whatever and however we may try to think, we think within the sphere of tradition. Tradition prevails when it frees us from thinking back [*Nachdenken*] to a thinking forward [*Vordenken*], which is no longer a planning" (I 34; ID 41).

2

"The Double Concept of Philosophy" and the Place of Ethics in *Being and Time*

The familiar accusation against Heidegger that the existential analytic of *Dasein* in *Being and Time* amounts to an egoism is almost as old as *Being and Time* itself. This is clear from the 1928 lecture course now known under the title *The Metaphysical Foundations of Logic*. Heidegger there dismissed this and other related objections on the grounds that they arose from a primitive misunderstanding of his enterprise (GA 26, 240; MFL 186). A footnote to *Kant and the Problem of Metaphysics* shows that in 1929 Heidegger was still sufficiently incensed by the criticism to promise a special publication to confront these confused objections (KPM 211n; KM 160n). The promise was never fulfilled. Nevertheless, there is sufficient material in *The Metaphysical Foundations of Logic* to reconstruct Heidegger's response to the criticisms and indeed to reopen the vexed question of the place accorded to ethics by *Being and Time*.

The objection of egoism—and it has grown in currency rather than declined—took its starting point in Heidegger's claim that it belongs to the essence of *Dasein* to be concerned about its own Being (GA 26, 240; MFL 186). Heidegger could have pointed out that in the analysis of *Mitsein* in *Being and Time* he had also said that "*Dasein* is essentially for the sake of others" (SZ 123; BT 160). But this would have been to meet the criticism on its own level. Or rather, it would have left the question of levels unclarified. Heidegger preferred to try to answer the objection by focusing on the character of ontological statements. To say on the *ontological* level that *Dasein* is concerned about its own Being would not exclude the possibility that *in fact* it might be concerned with others. In other words, the charge of ethical egoism arose only because certain crucial distinctions had been overlooked. The objection confused the elucidation of *existential* structures for the assertion of an *existentiell* egoism (GA 26, 240; MFL 187). The corrective, as he advised in *The Metaphysical Foundations of Logic*, was to address *Dasein* in its "metaphysical neutrality" (GA 26, 246; MFL 191).

Throughout *Being and Time* Heidegger had warned against compromising the purity of the ontological analysis by failing to exclude certain ontical connotations from its language. So, for example, the ontological term "care" (*Sorge*) was not to be associated with words like "worry" (*Besorgnis*) or "carefreeness" (*Sorglosigkeit*) (SZ 192; BT 237). Similarly, he advised that his descriptions of fallenness did not amount to a "moralizing critique of everyday Dasein" (SZ 167 and 175; BT 211 and 220). Linking the charge of egoism with that of solipsism, Heidegger in 1928 complained against his unnamed critics that he had pointed out "many times, even *ad nauseam* that this Being qua Dasein is always already with others and always already with beings not of Dasein's kind" (GA 26, 245; MFL 190). It was his critics who, in their attempt to understand what was meant by *Dasein*, had inappropriately imported the standard idea of a solipsistic subject. Heidegger insisted therefore that it was not he who had been blind to the phenomena, but rather his opponents who had ignored his attempt to distinguish ontological questioning from subsequent levels of inquiry such as anthropology or ethics (GA 26, 171; MFL 136). Ontological questioning was "prior to every psychology, anthropology and characterology, but also prior to ethics and sociology" (GA 26, 21; MFL 17). The failure to make this distinction between two orders of discourse could only result in confusion (KPM 213; KM 161). To understand the word "care" in an ethical sense, rather than as the Being of *Dasein* in its structural unity, would render impossible from the outset any understanding of the existential analytic of *Dasein*. "No worldview-oriented position, i.e., one which is always ontically popular, and especially no theological position—or reject—whether it is approving or disapproving—comes as such in any way into the dimension of the problem of a metaphysics of *Dasein*" (KPM 214; KM 162). The metaphysics of *Dasein* was in this way set apart from all worldviews. Or rather, it sought to attain the realm in which ontical interpretations of *Dasein*, and hence worldviews, must move (SZ 200; BT 244).

Evidence of Heidegger's concern with the problem posed to philosophy by the proliferation of worldviews has long been available. It is known that Heidegger was preoccupied with this issue during his first period of teaching at Freiburg.[1] The publication of some of the Marburg lectures has shown for the first time just how complex Heidegger's response to that problem was in the late 1920s. Heidegger did not simply set fundamental ontology as the science of Being against the conception of philosophy as a worldview. To do so would have been to retain the same approach as the neo-Kantians, whose contrast between scientific philosophy and worldviews was, in Heidegger's view, neither the solution nor the statement of the problem but the problem itself. That is why Heidegger's first response was to look to the tradition for a different way of construing the question. So, for example, he appealed to the seventeenth-century distinction between *metaphysica generalis* and *metaphysica specialis*, to Kant's distinction between the academic and cosmic concepts of philosophy, and to Aristotle's distinction between first philosophy and theology.[2] Heidegger did not suppose that these distinctions were equivalent to each other. Still less did he underwrite the precise form they took. Rather, he sought in them a means to reformulate the terms of the problem which had come to be known as the problem of *Weltanschauungen*.

This can perhaps best be illustrated by turning to the 1927 lecture course, *The Basic Problems of Phenomenology*. Heidegger there questioned the tendency by neo-Kantians to appeal to Kant's distinction between the academic or scholastic concept of philosophy and the cosmic or cosmopolitan concept of philosophy in order to legitimate their own use of the distinction between scientific philosophy and philosophy as a worldview. Heidegger's complaint was that Kant by no means accorded to cosmic philosophy the task of developing a worldview. Both academic and cosmic philosophy were intended by Kant to be scientific in the sense of "radical, universal and rigorous" (GA 24, 22; BP 17) and hence ontological (GA 24, 16; BP 12). But—and here Heidegger's discussion is unfortunately curtailed, suggesting that he may have been drawing on an earlier lecture course or seminar, as yet unpublished—previous philosophy had failed to attain the status of a rigorous science. Does that mean that all philosophy had done no more than form worldviews and give practical advice (GA 24, 5; BP 4)? Heidegger answered this question in the negative. He regarded the idea of a worldview philosophy as "simply inconceivable" (GA 24, 16; BP 12). This is not to deny that philosophy is "a distinctive primal form of worldview" or to deny that it must concern itself with the possibility and structure of worldviews (GA 24, 13; BP 10). But to grant philosophy the task of forming worldviews would, Heidegger suggested, be absurd. The problem with the contemporary distinction between scientific philosophy and philosophy as the formation of worldviews was that philosophy could no more form worldviews than it could attain the status of a science. And yet—to use a form of argument which is today very familiar—if one term in an opposition is excluded (as happens when worldview philosophy is deemed inconceivable), then it must be acknowledged that the other term—here scientific philosophy—has also been in some way and to some extent inappropriately conceived. Scientific philosophy in these circumstances comes to be recognized as a pleonasm (GA 24, 5; BP 4). In this way Heidegger came to withdraw his initial insistence on referring to *scientific* philosophy (GA 24, 4, and 17; BP 4 and 13).

A parallel—though somewhat abbreviated—version of this discussion may be found in section 11 of *The Metaphysical Foundations of Logic*. It appears alongside Heidegger's response to the various objections to *Being and Time* as ethical egoism. Heidegger there explains that a worldview is the taking up or inhabiting of a position in the sense of an *existentiell* stance. A worldview philosophy, he confirmed, is nonsensical, unless what is meant is an inquiry into "the essence, the intrinsic necessary and possible form, of worldviews (GA 26, 230; MFL 179-180). The designation "scientific philosophy" is again said to be nonsensical, though on this occasion for the reason that philosophy is prior to all science, insofar as it is the eminent form of what science is only in a derived sense.

Even though the explicit discussion of the question of philosophy and worldviews was relatively brief in the 1928 lecture course, its centrality can readily be established. This can be done by recalling the manner in which Heidegger begins the course by setting out Aristotle's twofold characterization of metaphysics as both first philosophy and *theologike*. First philosophy (which Heidegger equates with ontology) is concerned with Being, whereas *theologike* is concerned with *to theion* in the sense of the overwhelming. *Theologein* is to be understood, not in terms of today's conception of theology, but as a contemplating of the *cosmos* (GA 26, 13; MFL 11). Its subject matter is beings as a whole (*das Seiende im Ganzen*) (GA 26, 33; MFL 24). Once again Heidegger's characterization is so swift, the moves he makes so abrupt, that one can only assume that he is drawing on an earlier discussion.[3] Certainly he does not use this occasion to persuade his audience of his unusual interpretation of Aristotle. When in subsequent writings he returns to the question of the relation between first philosophy and theology in Aristotle, he remarks that it is obscure (KPM 199-200; 150-51) and strangely ambiguous (H 157; HCE 135). Here he seems somewhat more confident. He refers ontology to *Existenz* and theology to *Geworfenheit* or thrownness, so drawing Aristotle's distinction within the orbit of *Being and Time*. His explicit intention is to attain a vantage point "for answering the question of the relation between philosophy and worldview" (GA 26, 17; MFL 14).

Heidegger does not suggest that Aristotle had already resolved this question. The problem was unknown to the Greeks, and Heidegger acknowledges that he needs, as he puts it, to "make clear" what Aristotle left quite vague under the term *theologike* (GA 26, 17; MFL 14). According to Heidegger, when Aristotle claimed that first philosophy is at the same time *theologike*, he must be understood as saying "that the basic ontological question of philosophy has somehow to do with the whole of beings (*das*

Ganze des Seienden), as well as thereby with human existence, and in such a way that the existence of the one philosophizing is in each case decided" (GA 26, 21–22; MFL 17). Past concentration on the scientific character of philosophy had led the philosopher to neglect him- or her-self. Heidegger attempts to redress this: "The proofstone of philosophical truth consists solely in the loyalty the philosophizing individual has to himself." And a little later he says, "There is, in fact, a philosophical worldview, but it is not a result of philosophy and not affixed to it as a practical recipe for life. It resides rather in philosophizing itself" (GA 26, 22; MFL 18). The question is this: Given that Heidegger does not understand philosophy as a worldview, what is the relation of this worldview to philosophy? He says of the philosophical worldview that it is not "to be read off from what the philosopher may say expressly about ethical problems, but it becomes manifest in what the philosophical work is as a whole." A bare statement of this kind is not only in need of further explication. It is in danger of appearing virtually indistinguishable from the sentimentalizing edification from which Heidegger is at some pains to separate himself.

"The philosophical work as a whole," which enshrines the worldview of the philosopher, unites ontology and theology. They are, Heidegger says, "at the same time." This is his answer to the question of whether theology is merely an appendage to ontology, a finishing touch, a worldview, or a conclusion (GA 26, 17; MFL 14). But then, what are the implications for Heidegger's own enterprise and its self-presentation as "fundamental ontology"? The published text of *The Metaphysical Foundations of Logic* takes up those issues in the so-called Appendix to section 10, concerned with *Being and Time*. The Appendix carries the title "Designation of the Idea and Function of a Fundamental Ontology."[4] It is here in the Appendix—and with two minor exceptions only here—that Heidegger appeals to the idea of a metontology.[5] There is a certain irony in the fact that Heidegger should designate his discussion of metontology an appendix: he had, as we have seen, already denied that Aristotle's *theologike*, to which it in many respects corresponds, could be regarded as an appendage. The status of metontology is curious in still another way. Although Heidegger in these pages will appear to use metontology in order to call fundamental ontology into question, the latter term survived the remainder of the lecture course and passed into *Kant and the Problem of Metaphysics* relatively unscathed. By contrast, the designation metontology barely survives the Appendix.[6]

What is the relation of fundamental ontology to metontology as it is set out in the Appendix? Fundamental ontology does not exhaust metaphysics. The references to the "totality of beings" (GA 26, 199; MFL 157) and to nature, along with Heidegger's situating of metontology in the ontic realm, contribute to giving the impression that the issue is some form of regional science or perhaps even a systematic application and completion of a project the foundation for which had been laid by fundamental ontology. The references to finitude, facticity, and thrownness guard against such a reading and suggest instead that Heidegger returned here to the problems of scientific philosophy in its relation to *Weltanschauungen*. Heidegger's explicit reference at the end of the Appendix to philosophy as both *prote philosophia* and *theologike* (GA 26, 202; MFL 158) confirms that he is returning to this question, with which the lecture course began.

It seems that Aristotle's *theologike* is evoked at the beginning of the 1928 lecture course and again at the end of the Appendix, not in an attempt to equate metontology with *theologike*, but rather in order to find some precedent for what Heidegger calls the discordance (*Zwiespalt*) of philosophy (GA 21, 410n), or what in section 12 he calls "the double concept of philosophy" (GA 26, 229; MFL 178).[7] The same is true of his references to the distinction between *metaphysica generalis* (ontology) and *metaphysica specialis* (as comprised of *cosmologia, psychologica*, and *theologia*) (GA 26, 223; MFL 174), both in this lecture course and again in *Kant and the Problem of Metaphysics*. According to Heidegger, Kant shifts the center of gravity to *metaphysica specialis* (KPM 19; KM 6). Even if Kant still saw the latter as the "final purpose" of *metaphysica generalis*, he succeeded in making ontology itself a problem (KPM 21 and 25; KM 8 and 10). Indeed, *metaphysica generalis* was understood by Heidegger as only a "preparation" for *metaphysica specialis* (KPM 21; KM 8), just as in *The Basic Problems of Phenomenology* he acknowledged that fundamental ontology was only preparatory. And yet, fundamental ontology is preparatory only with reference to the foundation of a "radical ontology," a repeating of the meaning of Being and the horizon of ontology at a higher level (GA 24, 319; BP 224). Can metontology, which appears to be associated with the ontic, contribute to this radical ontology? What would the projected radicalization amount to? In the Appendix Heidegger not only rejects as superficial and pedantic the idea that a further ontology with a new title could be added to it as a supplement (*Ergänzung*). He insists that metontology is possible only on the basis of and in unity with radical ontology (GA 26, 200; MFL 157). Metontology is not to be construed as a "summary ontic in the sense of a universal science." It is by virtue of its relation to fundamental ontology that the suspicion is eased that metontology might still be a "world-picture" (*Weltbild*). It is the discordance of metontology and fundamental ontology which is supposed to keep metontology from being a reinscription of the opposition between worldview philosophy and scientific philosophy.

Heidegger's remarks on Scheler in *The Metaphysical Foundations of Logic* throw further light on the relation of fundamental ontology to metontology.

Scheler's death led Heidegger to interrupt his plan for the course and begin the next lecture instead with an appreciation of his close friend. Heidegger tried to relate Scheler's thinking to the themes of the lecture course. Scheler asked the question, "What is man?" within "the whole of philosophy, in the sense of Aristotle's theology" (GA 26, 63; MFL 51). Later in the course Heidegger contrasted Scheler's optimism, that the central question of general philosophy was decided, with his own sense, that "now when the local official philosophical situation is hopeless" is the time "to risk again the step into an authentic metaphysics" (GA 26, 165; MFL 132). In other words, Scheler had accepted many theses from the tradition unquestioningly because he had failed to engage the question of Being. He had attempted, as it were, to bypass fundamental ontology. Does that mean that Scheler had jumped straight to metontology? I would suggest that in spite of the link that Heidegger makes between Scheler's work and Aristotle's "theology," Scheler's neglect of fundamental ontology excluded him from metontology. For all his "sensitivity for all the new possibilities and forces opening up" (GA 26, 63; MFL 51), Scheler had failed to find a way to avoid the danger of falling back into a worldview philosophy.

I shall return to the task of characterizing the discordance between ontology and metontology in a moment, but first it would be helpful to indicate more precisely the range of problems metontology was supposed to address. Heidegger's Appendix seems to be a response to two different kinds of objection to the program of fundamental ontology. The first kind of criticism was related to the problem of omissions. It is still one of the most frequently heard criticisms. It is said that Heidegger lacks an account of nature, of spatiality, of alterity, of ethics, of politics, and no doubt of much else besides. But the objection tends to be phrased in such a way as to assume that Heidegger's task had been to provide an exhaustive inventory of the different kinds of beings in the classical manner. The objection seems to ignore the very nature of fundamental ontology.

So, for example, it might be argued that in the process of focusing on time Heidegger had appeared, by comparison, to ignore spatiality. In fact, in *The Metaphysical Foundations of Logic* Heidegger conceded this without admitting it as a fault. He acknowledged that he had postponed a developed consideration of spatiality with a view to returning to it after he had addressed the problem of temporality. The lack was to be made good in a "metontology of spatiality," which would treat the metaphysical problem of space (GA 26, 174; MFL 138). Heidegger therefore continued to justify the order of his inquiry, but he also made it clear that it was not only for the sake of completeness that a fuller treatment of spatiality would have to be offered. A more penetrating reason was that "all languages are shaped primarily by spatial meanings." Language testifies to an irreducible spatiality. Indeed, he set out a similar line of thought in the 1925 lecture course *Prolegomena to the History of the Concept of Time*:

> The continual resistance to spatiality which we are forced to adopt in the determination of in-being . . . in the account of the environing world, the constant necessity here to suspend a specific sense of spatiality, suggest that in all of these phenomena a certain sense of something like spatiality is still in play. (GA 20, 230; HCT 170)

To this extent, even though a full thematic treatment of spatiality could be postponed, it would nevertheless always be latently in play within the analysis which preceded that treatment.

Of course, it would still be possible to argue that Heidegger's projected order of inquiry was inappropriate, so that one could not legitimately postpone consideration of space in favor of an examination of time. But it should be clear that the objections have then to be addressed to fundamental ontology itself. The complaint that, for example, Heidegger neglects sociality, politics, or the Otherness of the Other remains superficial if what is meant is simply that there is relatively little discussion of these themes in his published works. For the objection to stand it would be necessary to show that, because of Heidegger's starting point in fundamental ontology, their discussion would necessarily be inadequate. One can, for example, imagine an argument claiming that unless the radically Other is introduced at the very beginning of the inquiry, the Otherness of the Other will always be compromised, reduced, relativized, or derived. Nevertheless, this objection, unlike the first criticism, would need to address itself directly to the project of fundamental ontology.

The first objection, the complaint about omissions, ignores, therefore, the distinction between the two levels of inquiry upon which, as we saw, Heidegger insisted against his critics. Its tendency to turn into the second objection can be illustrated by taking the example of ethics. The example is Heidegger's own. Indeed, only ethics and spatiality are singled out and named by Heidegger as topics to be considered by metontology (although the question of nature would appear to be another possible candidate). It is as if there was a special urgency in these cases. So, in the Appendix, no sooner has the word "metontology" been introduced than we read, "here the question of ethics may be raised for the first time" (GA 26, 199; MFL 157). The phrase could be read as an answer to an objection of the first type. Or, recalling a passing remark in the "Letter on Humanism," it could be construed as Heidegger's answer to the young friend who, soon after *Being and Time* appeared, asked him when he was going to write an ethics (W 183; BW 231). Heidegger's answer—here the question of ethics may be raised for

"The Double Concept of Philosophy" and the Place of Ethics / 33

the first time—could perhaps be understood as saying that once he had finished with fundamental ontology, he would move on to metontology and write an ethics. But such an answer would no doubt have struck the questioner as peculiar, and not only for the reason that Heidegger, in *Being and Time*, had already apparently ruled it out by exposing the presupposition on which it was based. "The object we have taken as our theme is *artificially and dogmatically curtailed*, if 'in the first instance' we restrict ourselves to a 'theoretical subject,' in order that we may then supplement [*ergänzen*] it on the practical side by tacking on an 'ethic'" (SZ 316; BT 363–64). This answer, to which Heidegger later returned in the "Letter on Humanism," shows how foreign it would be to Heidegger's conception to suppose that metontology could be understood as an appendage which made up for what the earlier analysis had omitted. What, then, would be the place for ethics, if not as a supplement to fundamental ontology? Perhaps a clue can be found in the irreducibility of the spatial character of all language. Could the same not also be true for ethics, in spite of Heidegger's attempt to reduce the ontical connotations from ontological language? If all languages were already shaped by ethical meanings, would Heidegger still be able to eradicate the ethical character of language by simple edict? Would this not mean that there was at least in some sense an ethics already in place in *Being and Time*, for example, in the discussion of authenticity? But having dismissed as disingenuous Heidegger's own explicit denial of the ethical character of his language, the way is open for the return of one of the most common objections against *Being and Time*, that of ethical egoism.

It emerges on reexamination, therefore, that Heidegger is not readily able to sustain the purity of the distinction between the ontic and the ontological by which he seems to want to guard against the objection, for example, of ethical egoism. In fact, and this provides his commentators with a problem they have usually neglected, Heidegger shows that he himself was well aware of the difficulty. In *Being and Time* he had acknowledged a certain ontical priority of the question of Being, as well as an ontological priority (SZ 11–15; BT 32–35). In *Basic Problems of Phenomenology* he referred, in the context of a discussion of Aristotle's distinction between first philosophy and theology, to the ontical foundation of ontology—a phrase which would seem to undercut the scientific pretensions of fundamental ontology (GA 24, 26; BP 19). Similarly, at the beginning of the *Prolegomena* he presented the indissolubility of *Geschichte* and *Historie*, in spite of having introduced the former as that which precedes the latter. The same recognition dominates the Appendix. Heidegger there observed that even though Being is "the prior, the earliest, the *proteron*, the *a priori*," fundamental ontology, which takes Being as its subject matter, is not prior. This is because the understanding of Being presupposes the factical existence of *Dasein* to which this understanding belongs. "Since philosophizing is essentially an affair of finitude, every concretization of factical philosophy must in turn fall victim to this facticity" (GA 26, 198; MFL 156). It emerges, therefore, that Heidegger cannot and does not consistently sustain the precedence of the ontological over the ontic on which, nevertheless, the very project of fundamental ontology seems to depend.

It is this situation which leads to the emergence of the double concept of philosophy. Fundamental ontology is not to be equated with ontology, although Heidegger is not in every case careful to distinguish them. Sometimes Heidegger will say that fundamental ontology lays the foundation for ontology in general. Nevertheless this presents fundamental ontology simply in terms of what it is said to ground. More important to Heidegger, however, is the movement of its radicalization. This movement is characterized in three stages, listed both at the beginning and end of the Appendix. Heidegger names, first, the analysis of *Dasein* (as the taking up of the question of Being with reference to *Dasein's Zeitlichkeit*; second, the explication of Being itself in terms of *Temporalität*; and finally, as a result of this second stage, the development of an understanding of the limits of the problematic in the way which "ontology expressly runs back into the metaphysical ontic in which it implicitly remains" (GA 26, 201; MFL 158). This is referred to as the turn around (*Umschlag*) or turning (*Kehre*) of fundamental ontology.[8] It is the acknowledgment that fundamental ontology not only presupposes the ontic but must also explicitly return to that from which it arose. That is to say, the ontological investigation and clarification of human finitude and mortality draws fundamental ontology back to its ontic fundament. Heidegger says this in the Appendix by referring to "the intrinsic necessity that ontology turns back [*zurückschlägt*] into that from which it emerged." This formulation echoes a sentence from the end of the Introduction to *Being and Time* that is repeated again at the end of that book in section 85: "Philosophy is universal phenomenological ontology, and takes its departure from the hermeneutic of Dasein, which, as an analytic of *existence*, has made fast the guiding-line for all philosophical inquiry at the point where it *arises* and to which it *turns back* [*zurückschlägt*]" (SZ 38 and 436; BT 62 and 487).[9] This is the *Umschlag*: not a transformation of Heidegger's thinking at the point where it discovers its own failure and passes into something else, but the transformation of philosophy's own highest aspirations when it rediscovers its roots in the ontic. This *Umschlag*— or in Greek *metabole*—gives to metontology its name.[10] Metontology is not an addition but the recoil to that which precedes. According to Heidegger, fundamental ontology and metontology in their unity constitute metaphysics (GA 26, 202; MFL 158). And metaphysics is not only a discipline but the

"The Double Concept of Philosophy" and the Place of Ethics / 35

essence of *Dasein* itself. *Dasein* is metaphysical (GA 26, 274; MFL 212).

Fundamental ontology is therefore not fundamental, at least not in the sense of being a foundational science. Heidegger reiterated this in a lecture course on Hegel's *Phenomenology of Spirit* that he delivered during the winter semester, 1930–31. There Heidegger explained that the model of rigorous science (Husserl's model) and the model by which philosophy was understood as laying the foundation for the sciences and for knowledge in general were obstacles to rediscovering the basic problems of philosophy, which he still identified as those of ontology. Heidegger, in this context, accepted the thesis that "philosophy is not a science" and explained that it was already expressed, albeit somewhat more positively, in the title *Being and Time* (GA 32, 18; HPS 12). This confirms Heidegger's statement in the "Protocol on Time and Being" from 1962 that "what is fundamental in fundamental ontology is incompatible with any building on it. Instead, after the meaning of Being had been clarified, the whole analytic of Dasein was to be more originally repeated in a completely different way" (SD 34; TB 32). Without the Marburg lectures this sentence might seem to have been just another of Heidegger's attempts to rewrite his own history.

Nevertheless, in spite of the radical character attributed to fundamental ontology, it should not be understood as a new endeavor (KPM 184; KM 138). It is, according to Heidegger, "in every philosophy an occupied place and it is in each case transformed" (GA 26, 200; MFL 157). If fundamental ontology is neither fundamental nor new, how could Heidegger continue to maintain that "Being is the proper and sole theme of philosophy" (GA 24, 15; BP 11)? How could philosophy be construed as the science of Being? When Heidegger writes of the failure of all the great philosophies since antiquity (GA 24, 16; BP 12), is there not a suggestion that he will introduce a philosophy that could not fail? A careful reading of such sentences—and there are more than a few—would only be possible by returning them to the movement of the lecture courses in which they are found. For example, throughout *The Basic Problems of Phenomenology* Heidegger maintains that philosophy is scientific (e.g., GA 24, 455; BP 300), but alongside this thesis he places the assertion that "there is no such thing as the one phenomenology" (GA 24, 467; BP 328). Elsewhere too Heidegger acknowledges that fundamental ontology cannot claim to be the only approach possible (GA 26, 200; MFL 157). It might seem that there is little hope of reconciling these apparently conflicting tendencies in Heidegger's thought at this time. Nevertheless a resolution, albeit one of a fairly drastic kind, appeared in the Appendix to the 1928 course. Heidegger wrote that "not only do we need the [existential] analytic [of *Dasein*], but we must produce the illusion, as it were, that the given task at hand is the only one necessary task" (GA 26,

201; MFL 158). Perhaps the need to maintain the illusion helps to explain why this extraordinary admission can be found only in this Appendix. It is an admission even more remarkable than Husserl's, in the *Crisis of the European Sciences*, that the dream of philosophy as a rigorous science was over.[11]

Why must Heidegger produce this illusion? And what are the consequences for philosophy that it is not based on a firm foundation but maintained by an illusion, a deception (*Tauschung*)? Fundamental ontology is not so much foundational as preparatory. At the beginning of section 10 of *The Metaphysical Foundations of Logic* Heidegger explains that, although the existential analytic of *Dasein* is carried out with a view to fundamental ontology, fundamental ontology is itself preparatory in relation to the metaphysics of *Dasein*. It is preparatory and provisional because it must fall victim to facticity. This theme could be pursued through Heidegger's discussion of dispersion (*Zerstreuung*) in section 10 of *The Metaphysical Foundations of Logic*. It can also be shown to dominate *Being and Time* itself, and not least the question of the bracketing of ethical considerations.

That philosophy falls victim to its facticity is acknowledged specifically by Heidegger in section 63 of *Being and Time*, where he concedes that the existential interpretation has been governed by—and receives its guidelines from—an idea of existence which has been presupposed (SZ 313; BT 361). In spite of many prior indications that the purity of the analysis relies on keeping the ontic and the ontological separate, it emerges that the interpretation needs them to be kept in close touch with each other (SZ 295; BT 341). There is a "positive necessity" according to which "a definite ontical way of taking authentic existence, a factical ideal of Dasein," underlies the ontological interpretation (SZ 310; BT 358). Not that it is enough simply to admit this. The ideal must be carefully unfolded in the form of an existential analysis.[12]

The 1928 lecture course enhances our understanding of this necessity. The metaphysical neutrality and isolation of *Dasein* is not opposed to "the extreme *existentiell* involvement [*Einsatz*] of the one who projects" (GA 26, 178; MFL 140). On the contrary, the former is only made possible by the latter. This is because the finitude of *Dasein* is to be understood at the *existentiell* level. Heidegger again acknowledges that there is a problem as to the extent to which "there is an existentiell guidance, an indirect guidance, in the metaphysical project and in the existentiell involvement of the person who philosophizes" (GA 26, 176; MFL 140), without being fully explicit about how he intends to negotiate this problem. It would seem, however, that he allows the ideal of the philosopher to serve as the ontical model of authentic existence on the grounds that it will inevitably be in play already. So, given that "one of the possibilities of existence must serve for the concrete exposition of ontological selfhood," in *Being and Time* "an extreme model" is allowed to serve (GA 26, 243; MFL 188–89), "the extreme existential ontological construction" of "authentic self-choice" (GA 26, 245; MFL 190) This is reflected in the discussion of authenticity in *Being and Time* in the clear if unstated bias toward what in another context might be called the "virtues of the philosopher." The same tendency emerges very clearly in *The Metaphysical Foundations of Logic* when Heidegger comes to characterize the philosopher in distinction from the sophist. He focuses on curiosity, idle talk, and bluffing, the first two of which are included among the characteristics of everyday *Dasein* (GA 26, 15; MFL 12). Not that Heidegger regards the sophist and the philosopher as extreme opposites, any more than he regards authenticity and inauthenticity in this way. In any given historical culture "both [sophists and philosophers] belong together" (GA 26, 274–75; MFL 212). The philosopher is also evoked when Heidegger warns that "the metaphysical isolation" of the human being is not to be confused with the isolation of the human being "in the factical existentiell sense, as if the one philosophizing were the center of the world" (GA 26, 172; MFL 137). One might ask in response whether the philosopher can philosophize without placing him- or her-self at the center of the world. The question is a serious one. It is reflected in Heidegger's own tendency to place philosophy at the center. In the Appendix to the 1928 lecture course he says that "philosophy is the central and total concretion of the metaphysical essence of existence" (GA 26, 202; MFL 158).

A parallel point, which returns the discussion explicitly to the question of worldviews, is made when Heidegger considers the charge of atheism. The accusation would seem to warrant a reply similar to that which he gave to the charge of ethical egoism, and Heidegger begins in that vein:

> The existentiell involvement of fundamental ontology brings with it the semblance of an extreme individualistic radical atheism—this is at least the interpretation groped for when fundamental ontology is taken to be a worldview. Yet that interpretation must be tested for its legitimacy, and if it is correct it must be examined for its metaphysical, fundamental-ontological sense. (GA 26, 177; MFL 140)

Of course, Heidegger's expectation is that such an interpretation would be found unwarranted at the formal level. Nevertheless, Heidegger concedes that "it is preferable to put up with the cheap accusation of atheism, which, if it is intended ontically, is in fact completely correct" (GA 26, 211; MFL 165n). The passage continues: "But might not the presumably ontic faith in God be at bottom godlessness? And might the genuine metaphysician be more religious than the usual faithful, than the members of a 'church' or even the 'theologians' of every confession?" The suggestion would seem to be that atheism at the individual ontic level is a better starting point for the philosopher who seeks to penetrate the dimension of religion ontologically than allegiance to a community of believers would be. By the same token, the factical ideal of the philosopher, which at the *existentiell* level is indeed that of isolation and self-cultivation, would better serve to secure a genuine understanding of *Mitdasein* than an immediate, headlong rush into a discussion of the I-Thou relation. That is to say, a certain *existentiell* egoism by the philosopher seems to be the precondition for a genuine ontology that would open up the dimension in which relations with other human beings arise. But such a goal would itself not be entirely free of ethical considerations, ethical considerations implicit in the "philosophical worldview," that is to say, in philosophizing itself (GA 26, 22; MFL 18). In *Being and Time* Heidegger illustrates the "extreme possibility" of authentic solitude by appealing to the case of helping the Other "to become transparent to himself in his care and to become free for it" (SZ 122; BT 159). It would seem that insofar as fundamental ontology is directed to the difficult (and perhaps impossible) task of making care transparent to others, then it would not only be pursued within a certain *existentiell* egoism. It would also exhibit authentic solitude. So long as we no longer understand by "ethics" rules or directives, then ethics is indeed not a supplement or appendage to *Being and Time* (SZ 316; BT 364). *Being and Time* would be, to employ a phrase from the "Letter on Humanism" out of context, "original ethics" as well as "fundamental ontology" (W 187; BW 235).[13]

In conclusion, the interpretation I have proposed suggests that the Marburg lecture courses, and *Being and Time* in particular, should be submitted to a double reading corresponding to the double concept or discordance of philosophy as ontology and theology.[14] I have tried to outline what such a reading might be like in my treatment of Heidegger's claims that "Being is the sole and necessary theme of philosophy" and that it belongs to the essence of *Dasein* that it be concerned about its own Being.[15] The task of such a reading would take the language of the ontico-ontological assertions and seek to maintain the ontical and the ontological in their distinctness, while at the same time acknowledging that the two depend on each other in such a way that their separation cannot be sustained. Taking its starting point in the fact that neither the ontic nor the ontological holds an absolute priority over the other, the double reading would seek to halt—for a moment at least—the apparent collapse of Heidegger's distinctions. It would allow Heidegger the space to maintain the language of the ontic, the ontological and the metontological, terms by which he sought to transform both the concept of philosophy *and* the concrete existence of the philosopher who is held by it. To say with Heidegger that he had "answered the question" of the relation between philosophy and worldview would no doubt be to say too much, but the opposition between scientific philosophy and worldview philosophy is displaced, and in such a way that a place is found for ethics whereby it is no longer simply subordinated to ontology and so reduced to some kind of supplement or appendage.

3

Justice and the Twilight Zone of Morality

In *Being and Time* Heidegger excused himself from the task of providing a history of the concept of truth on the grounds that it could only be written on the basis of a history of ontology (SZ 214; BT 257). If after 1930 he repeatedly ventured what at least on the surface look like sketches of the history of the concept of truth, it was not because he had in the meanwhile completed a history of ontology. It would be more accurate to say that Heidegger came to recognize that the history of truth could not be separated from that of ontology. For a decade at least, he sought to present the history of ontology in terms of a history of truth. The result was not the history of truth as a concept but the history of truth in its Being. It was thus a history of the essence of truth in that unique Heideggerian sense of the phrase, such that in due course and with appropriate caution it would have to be thought of as a history of the truth of essence. One of the reasons for that need for caution is the difficulty of understanding how a term such as "history" might be understood in conjunction with the phrase "truth of essence." Would such a history of truth be *Historie* or *Geschichte*? And if *Geschichte*, would it be *Geschichte* in the sense of *Geschick*?[1] In other words, is this history of essence a story that strives to present above all a coherent picture of a continuous history? Or is it to be thought of as governed by the discontinuities of the sending of Being? Furthermore, at what point must truth be thought in terms of *aletheia*? Many years later Heidegger would acknowledge that "*aletheia* thought *as aletheia* has nothing to do with 'truth'; rather, it means unconcealment." He continued, "What I then said in *Being and Time* about *aletheia* already goes in this direction. *Aletheia* as unconcealment had already occupied me, but in the meantime, 'truth' came in between" (HK 260; HT 161). It is possible that what Heidegger understood as having intervened was precisely his attempt to write the history of the essence of truth, notwithstanding the fact that there were a number of instances in the 1930s and 1940s, particularly in the lecture courses, in which Heidegger warned his students that when he said truth in the context of the history of the transformation of its essence, they should hear it in terms of *aletheia*.

I am not proposing to pursue these questions directly. The history of the essence of truth, if I may be allowed to call it that provisionally, is not really my topic here, although it will prove easier to expel it formally than it will be to keep it from returning uninvited. It will suffice to begin by rehearsing the outline of that history as it is found in "Plato's Doctrine of Truth" (W 109–44; P 173–92),[2] an essay that spans the period 1930 to 1943. Heidegger identifies four stages in Plato's allegory of the cave from the *Republic*. One's journey begins with being chained in the cave. Then one is released from one's chains so that one can look around, before being forced into the sunlight and finally returned to the cave. Each stage is correlated with its own kind of truth or, rather, its own kind of unconcealment. Heidegger's reading assumes that for Plato, as for his predecessors, the self-evident and fundamental experience of *aletheia* is unconcealment. Heidegger's argument is not that *aletheia* as unconcealment disappears in Plato. Even though it comes under the yoke or mastery of the idea (W 135–36; P 187), it maintains a position (*Rang*) (W 130; P 183). That is to say, after Plato, "the essence of truth does not unfold from its own essential fullness as the essence of unconcealment, but is displaced [*sich verlagern*] to the essence of the *idea*." None of this is explicit in Plato. The passage between them is left unsaid by Plato. Although *aletheia* is said, *orthotes* or correctness is meant. Truth is both unconcealment and correctness, the correctness of perceiving and asserting based on *homoiosis*, the agreement of knowledge with the thing itself. The recognition of this ambiguity is a crucial moment of Heidegger's reading, although it is readily overlooked in the effort to reduce Heidegger's approach to the level of a doctrine.

For most of "Plato's Doctrine of Truth," Heidegger confines himself to a reading of a few pages of the *Republic*, but at the end of the essay he briefly continues the story beyond Plato. The same ambiguity identified in Plato is also found in Aristotle, where *aletheia* is set in opposition to *pseudos*, in such a way that truth as the correctness of an assertion is opposed to its falsity. To characterize the main epochs of subsequent metaphysics, Heidegger provides only three quotations and a minimal commentary. In Aquinas, *homoiosis* becomes *adaequatio*. Aquinas's location of truth in the understanding, following Aristotle, is subsequently sharpened by Descartes. Finally, Nietzsche, of whom the most is said, defines truth as incorrectness of thinking. Truth is a kind of error insofar as thinking necessarily falsifies the real by stabilizing or fixing becoming through representation. Nietzsche's conception of truth does not overturn *aletheia*; rather it is said to be the most extreme consequence of the transformation of truth from the unconcealment of beings to the correctness of sight. It is therefore only a change in the determination of the Being of beings as idea (W 139; P 189). In that way Heidegger can be said to point to what is sometimes referred to as the unity of metaphysics.

The history of the transformation of the essence of truth was not the only story that Heidegger was telling at the time. There were the stories Heidegger told to the German people about their role in the future of their country. I shall return to this briefly later in the chapter and at more length in chapters 4, 6, and 8. For the moment I want to concentrate on another story that Heidegger was telling, one which intersects with the story about *aletheia* and also perhaps the story of the *Volk*. It is the story of *dike*. The story has to be collated from a number of Heidegger's essays and lectures from this period. It has never been told as a story, not even by Heidegger, it seems, and the first task will be to reconstruct its outline from Heidegger's scattered remarks. I will give most attention to the roles of Anaximander and Nietzsche in this story, even though it was the publication in the *Gesamtausgabe* of the 1942/43 lecture course on Parmenides (GA 54), with its discussion of some of the intervening stages, that gave the clue to the importance of the history of *dike* in Heidegger.

Dike was among the first words of philosophy. Or, more precisely, the only sentence that survives from what is often called the oldest philosophical text known to us includes this word. Heidegger's interpretation of Anaximander is best known from his essay "The Anaximander Fragment" (H 296–343; EGT 11–35). Although in a 1941 lecture course Heidegger also takes up the Anaximander fragment, the references to *dike* are curtailed (GA 51, 98–99, and 118–20).[3] I shall therefore focus on the 1946 essay, albeit only to give a very partial account of it.

The fragment is preserved by Simplicius, who cites it from Theophrastus. In Burnet's *Early Greek Philosophy*, one of the commentaries Heidegger consulted, the fragment as found in Simplicius via Theophrastus is translated as follows: "And into that from which things take their rise they pass away once more, 'as is meet; for they make reparation and satisfaction to one another for their injustice according to the ordering of time,' as he says in these somewhat poetical terms."[4] Theophrastus's phrase, "in these somewhat poetical terms," encourages scholars, including Burnet, to judge the phrase in single quotation marks to be Anaximander's actual words and not just a paraphrase.[5] Heidegger decides that the direct quotation is briefer still.

Heidegger restricts the fragment to the phrase *kata to chreon. Didonai gar auta diken kai tisin allelois tes adikias*.[6] After careful consideration, he renders it *entlang dem Brauch; gehören nämlich lassen sie Fug somit auch*

Ruch eines dem anderen [im Verwinden] des Un-Fugs (H 342). In the English translation of Heidegger's essay this is translated in turn as "along the lines of usage; for they let order and thereby also reck belong to one another [in the surmounting] of disorder" (EGT 57). Heidegger's translation of *dike* as *Fug* can be rendered in English as "order" or possibly "juncture," although both words suggest themselves more from desperation than conviction. Other commentators use the more conventional translation of "justice" or, like Burnet, "reparation." Heidegger's translation is governed by a specific interpretation. What is at stake in this interpretation of Anaximander's saying?

From the outset, Heidegger contests the standard interpretation of the fragment according to which nature is being described in terms that derive from the human sphere. He dismisses the accusation that Anaximander's "moral and judicial notions get mixed in with his view of nature" (H 304; EGT 20). The criticism is anachronistic. Ethical or judicial issues were not at that time interpreted in terms of disciplines (see also GA 51, 99). If there are no boundaries to be drawn between, for example, ethics and physics as disciplines, "then there is no possibility of trespass or of the unjustified transfer of notions from one area to another" (H 305; EGT 21). But does that mean that law and the ethical are not at issue here at all? Heidegger carefully guards against such a claim. "Denial of such boundaries between disciplines does not mean to imply that in early times law and ethicality were unknown" (H 305; EGT 21). This can be clarified with reference to the contemporaneous essay, "Letter on Humanism." Heidegger there tries to disengage his thinking from the disciplines of ontology and ethics in order to think the truth of Being. This thinking, which Heidegger remarks could be called "original ethics," and which he says had already been attempted in a preliminary way in *Being and Time* under the title of "fundamental ontology," moves in the realm from which law and ethicality derive or from which they are assigned. As Heidegger wrote of *nomos*, it is "not only law but more originally the assignment contained in the dispensation of Being" (W 191; BW 238–39). Similarly, in the Anaximander essay Heidegger attempts to hear in the key words a more "original" meaning than their subsequent moral or juridical meaning would allow.

Heidegger speculates that the words criticized by Theophrastus as poetical were *dike, tisis, adikia*, and *didonai diken* (H 304; EGT 20). What underlies Theophrastus's judgment is not just his understanding that these words have primarily a moral or juridical meaning, but also the assumption that by beings (*ta onta*) Anaximander means natural things in the narrow sense (*phusei onta*) (H 305; EGT 21). Together the two assumptions result in a reading of the sentence as some kind of metaphor. Heidegger's diagnosis is that this reading is a consequence of the divorce of thinking from poetizing that took place with metaphysics (H 303 and 343; EGT 19 and 57). Heidegger offers an interpretation of the fragment in which these same words speak through the language of subsequent Greek thought, specifically through *phusis* and *logos*, *heris* and *moira*, *aletheia* and *hen*. "In the language of these fundamental words, thought from the experience of presencing, these words from the Anaximander fragment resound: *dike, tisis, adikia*" (H 325; EGT 39). The words deemed by Theophrastus to be inappropriate for philosophical thinking at its highest level are found to permeate the very words from which philosophy originally drew its inspiration. The fundamental words of Parmenides and Heraclitus, and thus of Western thinking generally, are from the outset words which, according to an old tradition, are derivative and thus extraneous to fundamental thinking. Heidegger in his reading of the fragment wants to upset that tradition and in such a way as to counteract the tendency to diminish the contribution of the early Greek thinkers.

On Heidegger's interpretation, the Anaximander fragment is concerned with Being (GA 51, 123). *Ta eonta*, in the sense of "the present, whether present or absent" (*das gegenwärtig und ungegenwärtig Answesende*), is designated by him as the unspoken, the unsaid in what is said in the Anaximander fragment. This establishes a continuity between the fragment and the thinking that follows it in the West. Heidegger writes of *ta eonta* that "this word names that which from now on, whether or not it is uttered, lays a claim on all Western thinking" (H 324; EGT 38). For Heidegger the Greeks thought Being in terms of presencing, and the words *dike* and *adikia* are to be construed with reference to it. *Dike* is associated with the idea of presencing as a lingering or tarrying. Such a conception is distinct from a notion of presence as permanence or persistence, but the two are not in simple opposition to each other. The fragment appears to be concerned with the relation between the two modes of presencing. Lingering in the former sense is recognized as an arising which subsequently passes away, and thus it recalls in certain respects Heidegger's attempt to articulate *phusis* in its Greek sense. But persisting is also a kind of lingering, and Heidegger describes *adikia* as an insurrection (*Aufstand*) on behalf of sheer endurance (H 328; EGT 43). Heidegger thus reads the fragment as foreshadowing the idea of Being as permanence which appears to govern Western metaphysics, while at the same time he claims that this idea is thought by Anaximander as bound to an idea of presencing as arising and passing away, an idea that Western metaphysics neglected.

Heidegger does not arrive immediately at the translation of *dike* as order (*Fug*) and *adikia* as disorder (*Unfug*). His initial translation employs the terms juncture or jointure (*die Fuge*) and being out of order (*aus der Fuge sein*) (H 327; EGT 41). The translation changes when Heidegger moves from understanding the fragment as saying that *adikia* is the essence of what is present (H 328; EGT 42)[7] to understanding it as saying that the presencing of what is present is a surmounting or coming to terms with *adikia* (H 335; EGT 49).[8] Heidegger uses the word *Verwindung* rather than the more forceful *Überwindung* to convey that *adikia* is not put to one side, once and for all, but is the non-essence (*Unwesen*) that belongs to the essence of presencing (GA 51, 119). Just as Heidegger understands Anaximander's fragment as concerned with Being, so Heidegger's essay should be understood as an attempt to engage in thinking the truth of Being. That is why Heidegger's reading of Anaximander's fragment does not culminate in *dike*. Nor for that matter does it focus on *to apeiron*, which is most often the central focus of Anaximander's commentators. The word that Heidegger identifies as "dictated to thinking in the experience of Being's oblivion" is *to chreon*. Heidegger translates it as *der Brauch*, which in the absence of a noun formed from the verb "to brook" is usually translated "usage" (H 340; EGT 54). This is the word that is assigned to the thinker of the truth of Being. But it would be wrong to think of the different words, *dike*, *apeiron*, and *chreon*, as alternatives from which one must be selected. With the word *to chreon* Anaximander, according to Heidegger, thinks the dispensing of justice and injustice, or rather, because these terms might return us to distinctions and realms which have been displaced, juncture and disjuncture. "Usage distributes juncture and reck in such a manner that it reserves for itself what is meted out, gathers it to itself, and secures it as what is present in presencing" (H 339; EGT 54). For Heidegger, to think *dike* in its relation to *to chreon* is not only to bring it into relation with the beginnings of philosophy, such that it allows us to proceed to a reading of Parmenides and Heraclitus (H 341; EGT 55). It is also to understand *dike* in terms of what still remains to be thought in the assignment of the truth of Being.

Heidegger appears to make little attempt to follow the thought of *dike* into Parmenides or Heraclitus. So far as I am aware, it is only in the summer semester of 1935, in *An Introduction to Metaphysics*, that Heidegger joins the company of the many scholars who juxtapose these three early thinkers of *dike*. In this context he introduces his translation of *dike* as *Fug* or juncture. In the previous semester Heraclitus's fragment 80 had been understood to be saying that right is strife, so that *dike* was translated by *Recht* (GA 39, 126). A few months later fragment 80 was understood to say "It is necessary to keep in view both setting apart as essentially bringing together and juncture as diverging" (EM 127; IM 166). What stands between the two translations is Heidegger's reading of Sophocles's *Antigone*, and in particular the famous chorus on human being. Heidegger, at the outset of his reading of Sophocles, rejects the translation of *dike* as "justice" or "norm" on the grounds that it gives the word a juridical and moral meaning at the cost of its basic metaphysical content, which he understands as the originary collectedness of *phusis* (EM 123; IM 160). Furthermore, Heidegger understands Sophocles's word *to deinon* in terms of the relation between *techne* as the violence of human know-how and *dike* as the overpowering juncture. The human being is in a violent struggle with *dike* as the overpowering. There are victories and defeats as the human being is tossed between juncture and disjuncture, but no final victory (EM 123; IM 161). It is not hard to recognize an echo of Anaximander in this account, even if it is one that Heidegger himself does not acknowledge explicitly.

What Heidegger does acknowledge is a much less obvious proximity between Anaximander and Parmenides. The reciprocal relation between *techne* and *dike* that Heidegger found in the chorus from *Antigone* is understood to be the same as the belonging together of thinking and being in Parmenides (EM 126; IM 165). Heidegger finds support for this in Parmenides's reference to *Dike* as holding the keys to the gates of the paths of night and day. He interprets this as referring to the path of being that discloses, the path of appearance that distorts, and the path of nothingness that closes off. Beings open themselves only insofar as the juncture of Being is preserved and protected. "Being as *dike* is the key to beings in their conjunction [*Gefüge*]." Heidegger will never again make so pronounced a statement about *dike* as this one from *An Introduction to Metaphysics*, but from this point on the word begins to take on an importance within his retrieval of Western metaphysics.

The importance is already reflected during the following year, in the lecture course *The Will to Power as Art*, in which Heidegger marks a transformation in the essence of *dike* which parallels the more famous transformation in the essence of *aletheia*. Once again the transformation takes place in Plato's *Republic*, albeit on this occasion the political dimension of the *Republic* is recognized in a way that perhaps reflects some of Heidegger's own political aspirations and disappointments. According to Heidegger, Plato's *Republic* is an attempt to show "that the sustaining ground and determining essence of all political Being consists in nothing less than the 'theoretical,' that is, in essential knowledge of *dike* and *dikaiosune*" (NI 193; Ni 165). Knowledge of *dike* is philosophy itself, with the consequence that philosophers should rule the state (NI 194; Ni 166). This does not mean that philosophers should conduct the affairs of state. It does mean, however, "that the basic modes of behavior that sustain and define the community must be grounded in essential knowledge, assuming of course that the community, as an order of being, grounds itself on its own basis, and that it does not wish to adopt standards from any other order." The passage derserves more attention than it has received in the current debates concerning the intersection of Heidegger's philosophy with Nazism. It should not be forgotten that when Heidegger made this observation he had already experienced what he understood as a series of rebuffs to his offer to help guide the development of National Socialism. However, if Heidegger understood his own public support for Nazism and his attempt to shape its direction as themselves modeled on the role of the philosopher in Plato's *Republic*, and there is clear evidence that he did, his account of the history of the transformations of *aletheia* and of *dike* should have led him to be suspicious of this appeal to Plato. The use of such a model could be more readily accommodated within the thinking of *Being and Time* or indeed almost any philosophy prior to it (except perhaps Nietzsche's) than within his later thinking, in which the sense of history is more radical and the suspicion of old models more acute.

Heidegger introduces *dike* into his discussion of the *Republic* by denying, as he had already done in his discussion of Anaximander and Parmenides, that it is a moral or legal concept. Once again he conceives it as "the conjoined juncture of the order of Being" (NI 227; Ni 195). Heidegger writes, "*Dike* is a metaphysical concept, not originally one of morality. It names Being with reference to the essentially appropriate articulation of all beings" (NI 194; Ni 166). Heidegger stresses the importance of retaining the metaphysical sense of *dike* for a reading of Plato. But when Heidegger says that *dike* is a metaphysical concept, the context shows that this cannot be taken to mean that it belongs to Western metaphysics. Nor can the phrase be understood as meaning that it is an "ontological" concept as opposed to a moral or juridical one. It is metaphysical in the sense of the word elucidated at the end of "What Is Metaphysics?" Or rather, it corresponds to what in the "Letter on Humanism" comes to be called either "original ethics" or "fundamental ontology." When Heidegger indicates, albeit only in passing, that in Plato's *Republic* there is a transformation from the metaphysical sense of *dike* to its moral sense, this could perhaps also be understood as a passage from "original ethics" to morality, although he does not say so explicitly. Heidegger writes, "To be sure, *dike* slips into the twilight zone of morality precisely on account of the Platonic philosophy" (NI 194; Ni 166). If such a passage could be confirmed, and the attempt to do so goes beyond what I am attempting here, it would be a decisive moment in the history of Western metaphysics.[9] Quite how decisive becomes clear from the subsequent history of metaphysics.

This history, as it relates to the question of justice, is outlined in the 1942/43 lecture course on Parmenides. Initially, Heidegger shows little or no interest here in Parmenides's account of *dike*. Heidegger bypasses the opening lines of the poem where *dike* is introduced. Nor does Heidegger pause over his translation of *dike* as *Fug* in line 28 of the poem (GA 54, 13), although, in the context of a discussion of Plato's *Republic*, Heidegger does return to the translation of *dike* in Parmenides as *Fug* to suggest that the Greeks might have heard in *dike* echoes of *deiknumi*, as showing, and *dikein*, as projecting. On this occasion it is not so much *dike* as *iustitia* that attracts Heidegger's attention. Elsewhere Heidegger thematizes justice almost always to renounce it as a topic because it was not an adequate translation for *dike*. Here *iustitia* is introduced in its own right, and, as we shall see, *dike* is put to one side. Even so, Heidegger's discussion of justice might readily be overlooked. This is because the chief focus of that part of the course in which it appears is the history of the transformation of the essence of *aletheia*. Indeed, it is Heidegger's fullest statement of that history for the period after Plato. Much of the discussion is dominated by the question of translation, first of all from Greek into Latin, a process which almost always in Heidegger marks a loss without compensatory gain.

The Romanization not just of *aletheia* but of *pseudos* is understood as a "transformation of the essence of truth and of Being" and as a genuine event in history (GA 54, 62). The polemical aspect of Heidegger's discussion is most pronounced when the Latin word passes into German. So, for example, Heidegger dismisses *falsch* as *ein undeutsches Wort* (GA 54, 57). *Falsum* is inadequate as a translation of *pseudos*, because it does not capture the connotation of disguise, the sense of something appearing to be other than it is (GA 54, 64). Heidegger uses the word "pseudonym" to illustrate his point (GA 54, 44, and 52–53). Although a pseudonym does in certain respects conceal the real name of the person, Heidegger, using Kierkegaard as his example, suggests that it should at the same time reveal what the author of the specific text is in truth. The Latin *falsum*, like *veritas*, is divorced from the issue of concealment and unconcealment which underlies the Greek experience of "truth." *Falsum* is associated with deception, and Heidegger notes the German word *Trick* is also to be regarded as "un-German." This time the word has been borrowed from English, a fact that Heidegger, at the height of World War II regards as somehow peculiarly appropriate (GA 54, 60). Heidegger even debates whether *Wahrheit* is "un-German." He hesitates to agree with the Grimm brothers that it is, but he does so finally, not on etymological grounds, but because its meaning has been determined by the Christo-Roman term *verum* (GA 54, 69). Nevertheless, on this occasion Heidegger is not content merely to mark the loss which takes place in the translation.

In the Parmenides lecture course, Heidegger goes farther than elsewhere in determining the positive content of *verum*. *Verum* is the upright (*das Aufrechte*) that is directed from above (GA 54, 71). It is related to *rectum* from *regere*, to rule, and hence carries a judicial meaning that is brought to the surface in the word *rectitudo*. Relating *verum* to *iustum* in the sense of law or right, and observing that Roman law (*ius*) also belongs to the essential realm of the command, Heidegger finds that both true and false are determined by the *imperium*, the command, and thus move in the essential realm of justice (GA 54, 59, and 66). Heidegger comments, in his only direct reference to *dike* in this part of the discussion, "For that reason *iustitia* had a completely different essential ground from *dike*, which presences [*west*] in terms of *aletheia*" (GA 54, 59). At first sight the reference to *dike* appears to be merely negative. There is a gulf between *dike* and *iustitia*, a gulf which might seem to exclude a history of the essential transformations of *dike* of the kind I am trying to expose. And yet, the clarificatory phrase added by Heidegger, that *dike* presences in terms of *aletheia*, reverses that judgment because it directs attention back to the transformations of *aletheia* in its essence. *Dike* gives way to *iustitia* as *aletheia* gives way to *verum*. Just as the latter change does not mean that the essencing of truth in the history of Western metaphysics is governed simply by *idea* without reference to *aletheia* as unconcealment, so the essencing of *dike* in the history of metaphysics is not wholly supplanted by *dikaiosune* in its moral or juridical sense. Nevertheless, the articulation of this continuity threatens to transform *Seinsgeschichte* into *Historie*. The essential difficulty is underlined by another passage from the lecture course in which Heidegger writes, "Roman *veritas* has become the 'justice' of the will to power. The circle of the essential history of the metaphysical conception of truth has closed. However, *aletheia* remains outside of the circle" (GA 54, 78).

In "Metaphysics as History of Being," a text written in 1941 and first published in 1961, Heidegger hints at a connection between the transformation of the essence of truth and theology (NII 421–23; EP 20–22). He develops this suggestion in the Parmenides lecture course. The political *imperium* gives way to the religious *imperium* of the Roman Curia (GA 54, 67). Its commands take the form of ecclesiastical dogma that divides people into believers and heretics and gives rise to the Spanish Inquisition. Heidegger associates the determination of the true as what is certain with Luther, who poses the question of whether and how someone can be certain and assured of eternal salvation. It is a question of whether and how one can be a "true" Christian, a question already posed in the Middle Ages by Aquinas, as Heidegger shows. The question of *iustitia* becomes a question of *iustificatio* or *Rechtfertigung* (GA 54, 75). Heidegger's familiar association of the beginning of modern metaphysics with Descartes's *certitudo* is here extended to include discourses of rightness and justification. Descartes is identified as a thinker concerned with the right use of reason (*usus rectus rationis*) as the faculty of making judgments (GA 54, 76). The use of reason which is not right is false in the sense of error. In Kant the question of the right use of reason is characterized by Heidegger as a "will to secure certainty" (*Wille zur Sicherung der Sicherheit*).

Heidegger completes the discussion in the Parmenides lectures of 1943/44 with a reference to Nietzsche. Western metaphysics is said to have achieved its pinnacle in Nietzsche's grounding of the essence of truth in certainty (*Sicherheit*) and justice (*Gerechtigkeit*) (GA 54, 77, and 85). This brief reference, like that in "Plato's Doctrine of Truth," draws on the lecture course from the summer of 1939 entitled "Nietzsche: The Will to Power as Knowledge." The 1939 lecture course is in some ways the most important of Heidegger's discussions of justice, but it only reveals its significance for the question of the history of (the essence of) justice in the context of the other texts already discussed. Heidegger remarks that it can be shown that Heraclitus's thought of *dike* sparked off Nietzsche in his reflections and constantly ignited his thinking. Two points are important. First, Heidegger, evoking the distinction between *Historie* and *Geschichte*, insists that he is not interested in questions of influence. Such historiological (*historisch*) observations are secondary. What is at issue is "the historical determination that the last metaphysician of the West obeys" (NI 632; Niii 137).[10] Second, Heidegger remarks on the absence in Nietzsche of any attempt to articulate the relation of justice to the essence of truth (NI 632; Niii 137–38). Heidegger is quite explicit that his own aim here is to think the essence of truth to the extreme and to show it to be the point at which the thought of justice becomes inevitable (NI 633; Niii 138). Heidegger's claim is that its necessity can be shown by a "historical reflection" (*geschichtliche Besinnung*).

The schema that governs Heidegger's reading of Nietzsche in this lecture course is set out in the context of his account of the concept of chaos. Heidegger observes that Nietzsche does not adopt the primordial Greek sense of chaos as the measureless, the groundless yawning-open. He follows the modern sense of chaos as the jumbled or tangled (NI 562–63; Niii 77). In addition, however, there is a further sense of chaos "originating from the basic position of Nietzsche's thinking." According to that third sense, chaos names "a peculiar preliminary projection of the world as a whole and for the governance of that world" (NI 566; Niii 80). There is therefore a "double meaning" to chaos in Nietzsche.[11] Chaos is "the inexhaustible, urgent, and unmastered abundance of self-creation and self-destruction," either thought originally as that in which law and its negation are first formed and dissolved, or thought superficially as it is encountered in the impression of confusion (NI 569; Niii 82). This is the basis on which Heidegger shows that Nietzsche's thought of chaos is both metaphysical, insofar as it falls short of Hesiodic chaos, and yet is not entirely confined to metaphysics by virtue of an ambiguity that escapes the oppositions and inversions in which Nietzsche is otherwise held (NI 617–18; Niii 124–25). Heidegger explains this in terms of the ambiguity of Nietzsche's concept of truth. The true, as a fixing or securing of what is in the course of becoming, is a denial of chaos, the truly actual. Hence, Heidegger's gloss on Nietzsche's statement that "Truth is the kind of error without which a certain kind of living being could not live."[12] Heidegger explains, "With respect to chaos, 'the true' of such a truth is not appropriate to that chaos; hence, it is untrue, thus error" (NI 619; Niii 125).

It is not only because Heidegger's treatment of chaos best shows the schema with which Heidegger was operating at that time that I am making it the basis for my attempt to recover what he has to say about Nietzsche on justice. Nietzsche's thoughts on chaos and on justice, according to Heidegger, are essentially related. The association is made through the concept of truth. In 1942 in "Plato's Doctrine of Truth" Heidegger quotes the same passage from *The Will to Power* that I have just quoted. He identifies it as the beginning of the unconditional fulfillment of the history of metaphysics (W 139 and 142; P 267 and 269). But "Plato's Doctrine of Truth" fails to specify what the 1939 lecture course makes clear, that the culmination of Nietzsche's attempt to think the essence of truth must be found in what Nietzsche calls "justice": "Nietzsche thinks the essence of truth at the outermost point as something he calls 'justice'" (NI 632; Niii 136. See also NII 20; Niii 173). Heidegger insists on this, in spite of the fact that Nietzsche's most decisive thoughts on justice belong to the period of *Thus Spoke Zarathustra* and are relatively few in number. Furthermore, as Heidegger acknowledges, Nietzsche was, in his final years, completely silent about what he called justice (NI 632; Niii 137).

Nietzsche failed to make explicit the connection between the thought of justice and that of the essence of truth (NI 632; Niii 137–38). Heidegger set himself the task of doing, or at least beginning to do, what Nietzsche was unable to do. The task is to penetrate the historical roots of the metaphysical question of truth so that it becomes clear why the thought of "justice" becomes inevitable after the abolition of the distinction between a true and an apparent world (NI 633–34; Niii 138). Heidegger takes two routes to this outermost point of the essence of truth. The first route is in terms of Nietzsche's understanding of truth as a holding-to-be-true. According to Heidegger, and the importance of the point is more readily apparent in the context of the Parmenides lecture course, such holding-to-be-true is usually thought of in terms of command (*Befehl*). The law of contradiction is such a command, the positing of a measure in the form of an imperative (NI 607–09; Niii 116–17). Heidegger poses the question of whether one can dispense with a standard (*Mass-gabe*) without succumbing to arbitrariness (NI 635; Niii 139). Heidegger will observe that not only can one not offer any such guarantee; the question itself seems to be formulated in such a way as to retain a standard against which the dispensing of standards is to be judged (NI 648; Niii 150). For himself, Heidegger refuses the question because it seems to be formulated in such a way as to retain a standard against which the dispensing of standards is to be judged (NI 648; Niii 150). He attributes to Nietzsche another answer: "Holding-to-be-true takes its law and rule from justice" (NI 643; Niii 145). The answer is metaphysical in that "justice" is here being taken metaphysically as the fundamental character of a thinking that is constructive (*Bauen*) or commanding, exclusive, and nihilative (NI 639-41; Niii 142-45).

The other route that Heidegger takes returns to the issue of the fixing or securing of chaos. Heidegger identifies the securing of permanence (*Bestand*) as assimilating and giving human direction to chaos. This assimilation (*Aneignung*) not only recalls the struggle between *techne* and *dike*; it corresponds to the Greek *homoiosis*. At the culmination of metaphysics, the essence of truth as *homoiosis* does not collapse but attains an exclusiveness it lacked when it operated within the orbit of the distinction between the true and the apparent world (NI 635-36; Niii 140). Nietzsche gives the essence of truth "the *metaphysical* name" justice (NI 637; Niii 141), although he may not have understood the historical reasons that led him to do so. According to Heidegger, after the publication of *Thus Spoke Zarathustra* Nietzsche thinks the essence of truth "always and everywhere... in terms of its ground of possibility, in terms of justice" (NI 637-38; Niii 141). Heidegger says "always and everywhere," even though he had earlier acknowledged that the word "justice" is rare in Nietzsche. If Heidegger's account is somewhat strained at this point, it is because, as with the other discussion, everything here is subordinated to establishing that Nietzsche's text remains governed by metaphysics.

What does Nietzsche understand by "justice"? Heidegger again issues the warning that the term cannot be given a juristic or moral meaning (NI 636; Niii 141). To approach Nietzschean *Gerechtigkeit* one must put aside Christian, humanistic, Enlightenment, bourgeois, and socialist moralities (NII 197; Niv 144 and NII 325; Niii 243-44). Ordinances of this kind are familiar in Heidegger and can never completely succeed. The difficulty of translating *Gerechtigkeit*—because all the likely candidates, justice, righteousness, justification, and so on, have what Heidegger at another time might have called different ontic commitments—is not entirely negative. The history of justice shows that the languages of the *imperium* and the Curia are also under scrutiny in this discussion. Meanwhile, Heidegger defines justice for Nietzsche as the unitary connection (*Zusammenhang*) of what is right, in the sense of the precise, the fitting, what gives direction (NI 637; Niii 141). Justice determines right and wrong from the standpoint of its own power and does not use an independent measure to help decide what is right and what is wrong (NII 198; Niv 144). It is the ground of the possibility of every kind of harmony of human beings with chaos, be it through art or knowledge (NI 638 and 647-48; Niii 141 and 149). "Justice is the preconstructive allotment (*Zuteilung*) of conditions that firmly secure a preservation, that is, an attaining and maintaining" (NII 327; Niii 245). Such an allotment "precedes all thinking and acting."

In employing these phrases Heidegger seems to point forward to the "Letter on Humanism" with its attempt to move into a realm prior to thinking and acting, as well as its attempt to pass beyond the distinction between ontology and ethics by reference to the prior realm of "fundamental ontology" or "original ethics." But the suspicion persists that the ontological sense remains privileged, and not just here in respect to Nietzschean *Gerechtigkeit*, but also in those places where Heidegger attempts to purify *dike* of its moral meaning.[13] Insofar as *Gerechtigkeit* is understood as occupying a place in the history of the essence of truth, then it is being determined not just metaphysically (in terms of the history of Western metaphysics) but also ontologically in a narrow sense. Only insofar as Nietzschean *Gerechtigkeit* is heard as recalling *dike* does it exceed the limitations of such a history.[14]

In the lecture "The Will to Power as Knowledge" Heidegger does not appear to find an ambiguity in Nietzsche's word "justice." He thus appears to close off the possibility of finding a Nietzsche who is not simply metaphysical, a possibility that had opened up with the ambiguity of Nietzsche's understanding of chaos. That he closes off this possibility conforms with the general tendency of Heidegger's reading of Nietzsche at this time, reflected in the lecture course by the statement that the "will to power in its *most profound* essence is nothing other than giving Becoming the permanence [*Beständigung*] of presence" (NI 656; Niii 156). And yet, in other texts from the same period, even those whose focus remains directed to the permanence of presence, this is understood to give rise to other possibilities, which Heidegger sometimes refers to as "the transition to another beginning" (NII 29; Niii 182). So, for example, in *The Eternal Recurrence of the Same and the Will to Power* Heidegger appears to go farther. The two lectures that go under this title were intended as a conclusion to all three courses on Nietzsche, although they were never delivered. The thrust of these remarks is the claim that Nietzsche "overcomes metaphysics" only in the limited sense of transforming it into its final possible configuration (NII 16; Niii 170). In this context, in clear anticipation of the account given 10 years later in "The Question concerning Technology," Heidegger provides an analysis of the age of consummate meaninglessness, where meaninglessness is understood as the "lack of the truth (clearing) of Being" (NII 20; Niii 174). Truth as "justice" is understood as the supreme will to power, the anthropomorphism of the unconditioned rule of human beings over the earth (NII 20; Niii 173).[15] This, the extreme position of Western metaphysics, marks the dominance of *techne*. In terms of *An Introduction to Metaphysics*, it is the apparent, *but impossible*, victory of *techne* over *dike*. Justice arises as the word of the last metaphysician precisely at the time when the loss of *dike* is most extreme. Nietzsche's word *Gerechtigkeit* is at once the extreme oblivion of *dike* and yet, for that very reason, according to a familiar Heideggerian law, provides the possibility for recalling *dike*. This is the way Heidegger fulfills the task of experiencing the necessity of another beginning at the culmination of metaphysics (NI 657; Niii 157).

Gerechtigkeit is not the fundamental word of Nietzsche's metaphysics, but it becomes so in Heidegger's reading of it. When Heidegger ultimately denies that justice can "be raised to the rank of the main heading in Nietzsche's metaphysics,"[16] the reason given is that "in Nietzsche's thought it remains veiled as to whether and how 'justice' is the essential trait of truth" (NII 331; Niii 249). Nietzsche says enough to enable Heidegger to attribute the thought to him, but not enough for the inevitability of that thought to emerge from a reading of Nietzsche. Nietzsche *should have* thought truth as justice. He needs to have done so. It is the thought that has its ground in "the historical determination that the last metaphysician of the West obeys" (NI 632; Niii 137). Nietzsche cannot attain this thought but he poeticizes (*gedichtet*) the ideal of the thinking of the last metaphysician in the figure of Zarathustra. Here there is another hint of the relation between "justice" and poetic thinking, albeit understood very differently from the way Theophrastus construed it.

Why is it inevitable that justice should have been the last word of metaphysics, its culmination (GA 47, 320)? Is it not possible to address this question with the resources of metaphysics alone, that is to say, with the resources of truth? The last word of metaphysics should have been justice because the first word of that thinking from which metaphysics divorced itself is and is not justice. More specifically, it is *dike*. Only engagement with the thinkers before metaphysics—Anaximander, Parmenides, Heraclitus—lets metaphysics appear in its unity and completeness. Conversely, it is metaphysics that lets *dike*, *aletheia*, and *logos* be tied together in a story. Heidegger can exhibit the inevitability of Nietzsche's obligation to think justice only by including in his narrative what at the same time he acknowledges does not belong to the story. Heidegger seems to admit as much: "Are we not forced into historical classification, which comes from without and looks only backward, or even into the historiological miscalculation [*Verrechnung*] of history, which is always captious and usually carping?" (NII 329; Niii 247). The story draws the pre-metaphysical into metaphysics, establishing a false continuity. Heidegger tries to resist this consequence by rejecting the translation of *dike* as justice. He must equally deny the translation from *dike* to *iustitia*. And that is perhaps why he left the history of the essence of justice scattered throughout his work, waiting to be discovered by the scavengers who came together a full century after Heidegger's birth and a full century after Nietzsche inevitably should have thought, and perhaps almost thought, truth as justice.

4

Habermas, Arendt, and Levinas on the Philosopher's "Error": Tracking the Diabolical in Heidegger

The scandal arising from Heidegger's political involvement with Nazism and from his postwar silence on the Holocaust refuses to go away, but the evident glee of Heidegger's philosophical opponents in the consequent damage to his reputation is misjudged. It is not only Heidegger, both the man and his thought, who is diminished by the whole affair, but also, and perhaps primarily, philosophy itself. What is disturbing is not just that, 45 years after the end of the war, philosophers still largely conduct the debate in clichés. What is under threat following Heidegger's "error" is one of philosophy's most exalted claims about itself.

The fundamental conviction at issue in the light of our growing knowledge of Heidegger's statements, his loyalties, his actions, and his silences concerns the nobility of the philosophical life. Philosophy tends to present itself not just as one historically conditioned form of life among others, but as a life in some sense and to some degree demanded of everyone, because it is the best life for human beings. It is the life against which all other lifestyles are to be judged. Not to be capable of pursuing it, whether because of lack of opportunity or lack of talent, is to be condemned to something less. Even Aristotle, who had an appreciation and understanding of the practical life that was unusual among philosophers, judged that "we ought either to pursue philosophy or bid farewell to life and depart from this world, because all other things seem to be utter nonsense and folly."[1] What must now be put under scrutiny is not any single claim about the merits of philosophy for human beings, but a whole tradition in which philosophy has been privileged as a way of life and not just a form of questioning or an area of study. Only a detailed historical investigation could show the full diversity of the forms the ideal has taken, but it is sufficient to recall the way that the philosophers of classical Greece sought to persuade their audiences of an essential tie between excellence in thought and in morals. To believe anything else than that to know what is good is to do what is good would be a disgrace for the philosopher, who is committed to the view that wisdom and knowledge are the highest of all things.[2] Hence, both Plato and Aristotle were haunted by the figure of the one who committed evil, knowing it to be such. They designated this the problem of *akrasia* and addressed it by supposing that the relevant knowledge cannot really have been operative at the appropriate time. Christianity may have displaced the site of wrongdoing, so that it was no longer referred to ignorance but to an evil will, but Christians remained sufficiently persuaded of the association between great thoughts and great lives to raise their most gifted theologians and philosophers to the rank of sainthood.

Even the recent domination of philosophy by a class of professional philosophers has not totally eradicated the ideal of the philosophical life. In fact, it has played a major, if largely unremarked, role in the discussion of Heidegger's moral and political "errors." It underlies the argument that Heidegger's moral and political failure is proof that he was not a great thinker. One major reason why there is so much interest in Heidegger's politics is because it is supposed that it will contribute to the reevaluation of his thought, even if nobody has yet succeeded in establishing on what precise basis this might be done.[3] In the continuing absence of any convincing arguments showing that Heidegger's political loyalties are at the root of his philosophy, and perhaps his moral failings reflected there also, a simple argument suffices:

> All great philosophers are moral.
> Heidegger was not moral.
> Therefore, Heidegger was not a great
>   philosopher.

If anyone doubts that it is possible to think like that, consider the anecdote told about Gilbert Ryle, who allegedly said early in 1960: "Heidegger. Can't be a good philosopher. Wasn't a good man."[4] Nevertheless, it should not be forgotten that the same major premise has been used by many commentators to avoid Ryle's conclusion, simply by focusing on the fact of Heidegger's importance as a philosopher, rather than the facts of his moral and political failings. That is why Lyotard's recent warning is worth bearing in mind:

"One should not seek to neutralize the intrinsic inequality of this affair by regulating it through its alternative: if a great thinker, then not a Nazi; if a Nazi, then not a great thinker—the implication being: either negligible Nazism or negligible thought."[5]

It is striking to find the ideal of the philosopher to be operative even where philosophy has, as in the case of Ryle, apparently abandoned all claim to be a way of life. One can compare Michael Dummett's more measured response to the discovery that Frege was antisemitic: "When I first read that diary, many years ago, I was deeply shocked, because I had revered Frege as an absolutely rational man, if, perhaps, not a very likeable one. I regret that the editors of Frege's *Nachlass* chose to suppress that particular item. From it I learned something about human beings which I should be sorry not to know; perhaps something about Europe, also."[6] That rational people are free from antisemitism and that good philosophers are good human beings are such deeply held convictions that knowledge of Heidegger's—and Frege's—failings presents a problem. In this essay, after a brief review of the forms the philosophical ideal took in Heidegger's writings, I examine the different ways in which four commentators—Rorty, Habermas, Arendt, and Levinas—have addressed the relation of those writings to his life.

Heidegger's failure was a moral failure—his behavior to his colleagues and friends, his apparent lack of remorse—as well as a failure of political judgment, a lack of *phronesis* in the sense of the capacity to recognize the situation, in this case Germany in the 1930s, for what it was. The failure was, furthermore, a failure of thought, at very least insofar as he did not succeed in incorporating what was so thought-provoking about the events he lived through into his thinking.[7] What makes Heidegger's failure all the more devastating is the knowledge that Heidegger's reputation as a thinker, especially in the early years, was greatly enhanced by his ability to convey the sense that his was a thinking which arose from life and would affect life. So the existential interpretation given in *Being and Time*, and in particular its account of authenticity, is guided by an idea of existence, an *existentiell* ideal, which would appear to be that of the philosopher (SZ 310–13; BT 358–61).[8] This focus on the philosophizing of the philosopher, over and above what the philosopher says, is explicit in *The Metaphysical Foundations of Logic* and in particular in the discussion of the art of existing (*Existierkunst*) (GA 26, 22, and 101; MFL 18 and 158), a phrase which appears to echo Cicero's reference to philosophy as the art of living (*ars vitae*).[9] Like Cicero, Heidegger privileges philosophy, as when he calls it "the central and total concretion of the metaphysical essence of existence" (GA 26, 202; MFL 158).

However, the figure of the philosopher or thinker, always prominent in Heidegger's thought, took on a special importance in the mid-1930s, when the thinker was given the task, either independently or in conjunction with the poet, of directing the people. The esteem in which the philosophical life was held, helps justify the directive function accorded to philosophy in a tradition which dates back to Plato. In the 1936/37 lecture course *Nietzsche: The Will to Power as Art* Heidegger finds "the decisive insight" of the entire *Republic* to be the statement that "it is essentially necessary that philosophers be the rulers" (NI 194; Ni 166).[10] Heidegger's explanation is also a commentary on his own intentions in the 1930s: "The statement does not mean that philosophy professors should conduct the affairs of state. It means that the basic modes of behavior that sustain and define the community must be grounded in essential knowledge . . ." Who would doubt that the knowing evoked here or at the end of "The Origin of the Work of Art" was not associated in Heidegger's mind with the *Wissensdienst* of the Rectoral Address or the Address on "National Socialist Education"?[11]

Subsequently Heidegger tried to understand his involvement as a mistake about the directive function of the thinker. In "The Rectorate 1933/34—Facts and Thoughts," dating from 1945, the admission was somewhat limited. He identified his assumption of the position of Rector as a renunciation of "the thinker's most proper vocation," but he still defined that vocation in such a way as to lead him to regret the fact that, in his teaching after 1934, his thinking "did not shape itself into a developing structure of a definite conduct [*ein werdendes Gefüge eines bestimmten Verhaltens*], which in turn might give rise to something primordial" (SU 38–39; HNS 29). The *Der Spiegel* interview of 1966, which in other respects is so disappointing, is strikingly direct in its denial of the philosopher's capacity for leadership: "Philosophy will not be able to bring about a direct change of the present state of the world" (NG 209; HNS 56–57). When the interviewer pressed Heidegger, the latter responded by saying, "The questions are so difficult that it would be contrary to the meaning of the task of thinking to make public appearances, to preach, and distribute moral grades" (NG 212; HNS 60). Even so, Heidegger continued to privilege the thinker in what constituted, at very least, the third version of the conception of the thinker to be found in his works. Heidegger initially held an existential version of the ideal of the philosopher, to the point where he could say that "The proofstone of philosophical truth consists solely in the loyalty the philosophizing individual has to himself" (GA 26, 22; MFL 17). By the 1930s, the philosopher had accumulated additional, political, loyalties so that the thinker was supposed not only to address the people with the question of who they are, but in so doing to help the poet form the public into a *Volk*.[12] Subsequently Heidegger shifted his focus away from the relation of the philosopher to the people and instead dwelled on the meditative thinker as the isolated spokesperson for Being. In spite of having renounced both the existential and political versions of the philosophical life, this third conception remains firmly in touch with the traditional account, not least by virtue of the way it seems to diminish all other forms of life.[13]

If it is true that the so-called Heidegger affair calls into question philosophy's self-conception—and to a certain extent its self-justification—many contributions to the debate fall short, precisely insofar as they leave the presupposition of the nobility of the philosophical life unexamined. When Christian Jambet presented Farias's *Heidegger et le nazisme* to the public for the first time, this was his starting point, although it is an issue that was soon overshadowed in the subsequent controversy.[14] One commentator who did not neglect the question was Richard Rorty in an essay in *The New Republic* called "Taking Philosophy Seriously." Rorty, targeting a view somewhat similar to that attributed to Ryle, denied that "learning about a philosopher's moral character helps one evaluate his philosophy."[15] This is perhaps the simplest version of the major premise of the argument against Heidegger. Rorty contests it by appealing to some familiar distinctions. The "philosopher" as the name of an ideal human being is not to be confused with the professors who have usurped the label of philosopher. The authors of great books may be great authors, but they are not necessarily great human beings. Rorty concludes that the authors of books worth reading are as "mixed-up as the rest of us" and that all we have to do in reading them is "to pull out from the tangle we find on the pages, some lines of thought that might turn out to be useful for our own purposes."[16] It is striking that in the course of diminishing the importance of the moral virtue of authors he also diminished their books, by his tone if not necessarily intentionally. Even though he is almost certainly right that there is no way to correlate moral virtue with philosophical importance, Rorty is problematic in his adoption of a kind of "pluralistic tolerance" to replace what he characterizes as the "fundamentalism" of those who take too seriously the rejection of a doctrine or an interpretation. The suspicion is that if Heidegger took philosophy too seriously, Rorty reduces both philosophy and the philosopher to the point where it is no longer clear why one bothers to any great extent with either. Rorty here operates with a simple pair of alternatives which forces a choice between either tolerance or insistence on authentic interpretation, at the same time that he appeals to a hermeneutics where one's reading is dominated in advance by "one's own purposes." To Rorty much of the excitement engendered by the debate about Heidegger is misdirected but easily corrected. It arises simply from the failure to distinguish between the moral condition of the author and the stature of the work. Here perhaps Rorty, in spite of himself, is the one guilty of exaggerating the efficacy of philosophy insofar as he imagines that one can dispel the confusion at the conceptual level without engaging in what might be called a destruction of the philosophical ideal. This task, which goes beyond what I might claim to be attempting here in this essay, would involve an analysis of, first, how the association between person and work arose and then attained the force of virtual self-evidence; secondly, what governed the historical variations in the way this association was both conceived and experienced; and finally, the manner in which it now finds itself under pressure in, among other places, the Heidegger affair. The last would have to include recognizing the way the association tends to remain in force, even when directly challenged.

Thus, when Habermas, in his foreword to the German edition of Farias's book, challenged Rorty's attempt to see the Heidegger affair as centered around the relation between person and work, he himself accepted another variation of the ideal philosophical life.[17] Habermas attempted to bracket the issue of Heidegger as a person without losing the critical leverage Heidegger's Nazism provided. Habermas joined with Rorty in rejecting the view, associated with Jaspers, that "whatever truth a philosophical doctrine contains must be mirrored in the mentality and lifestyle of the philosopher."[18] Such an insistence on the unity of work and person was "inadequate to the autonomy of thought and, indeed, to the general history of the reception and influence of philosophical thought."[19] Habermas hoped that this argument would be sufficient also to put a halt to comparisons between Heidegger's engagement with Hitler, on the one hand, and Bloch's and Lukacs's option for Stalin, on the other. But it is written under the rubric that "we" contemporary Germans would "do well to refrain from moral judgements on actions and omissions from the Nazi era."[20] Whether he is right or wrong about this, it is not what Habermas does. Habermas feels free to pass judgment on "Heidegger's apologetic conduct after the war, his retouchings and manipulations, his refusal publicly to detach himself from the regime to which he publicly adhered."[21] But how could one's sense of what it is appropriate to demand of Heidegger by way of apology in the 1950s and 1960s not be based on an assessment of what he had done in the 1930s? Habermas at this point is supposed to be treating Heidegger, his repressions and his falsifications, as symptomatic of a mentality still pervasive in the Federal Republic at least until the 1960s.[22] But Habermas does not simply correct the historical record; he establishes Heidegger's responsibility for distorting his relation to National Socialism. Furthermore, Habermas's treatment of ideological context in the foreword does not extend much farther than Heidegger's character. Perhaps he is attempting to expose the mystique of the thinker by suggesting that even retrospectively Heidegger exhibited no special power of insight into Germany's period of National Socialism. He "acted no differently from others."[23] In his attitude he was simply "one of many." But one has to suspect Habermas of disingenuousness when one recalls that in writing this foreword Habermas lends his name to a book he describes, remarkably generously considering its reputation, as "a detached evaluation of Heidegger's character."²⁴ Certainly Habermas attempts to distinguish the philosopher's task from that of the historian and so offers his remarks as a "supplement" to Farias's investigation. But if Habermas was serious about redirecting the debate about Heidegger, he would have seen that Farias's book not only distracts attention from the philosophical task at hand. It also fails to contribute to the historical work of presenting the context in which the ideological content of Heidegger's thought might be appreciated.²⁵

Habermas's expressed aim is to shift the focus from the relation between the person and the work, which is where Rorty located the issue, to the amalgamation of work and *Weltanschauung*. In so doing he returns to the familiar task of trying to establish an "*internal* connection between Heidegger's philosophy and his political perception of the world-historical situation." Here Habermas draws on his account of ideology as *Weltanschauung*, elaborated for example in *The Theory of Communicative Action*, to ask "whether issues of substance have been confused with those of ideology."²⁶ But what one finds, as Habermas charts the various stages of Heidegger's development, is not just an account of how, over the course of a few years, Heidegger obscured the original political context of ideas first introduced in the early 1930s, thereby detaching it "from all relation to surface historical reality."²⁷ Although Habermas may have little appreciation for what Heidegger understood by the history of Being—or for how Heidegger arrived at the idea—he is surely correct in his description of Heidegger's writings from the 1930s as a remarkable intertwining of genuine philosophical insight and distasteful political rhetoric.²⁸ In addition Habermas finds that a study of Heidegger's development leads to a focus on his changing conception of his role as a philosopher.²⁹ Habermas describes three different conceptions of the philosopher to which Heidegger conforms, corresponding to the three stages I identified earlier. The major difference in interpretation concerns the first stage, where Habermas is at some pains to show that the person of Heidegger is operative in *Being and Time*, but not in a way which "impeaches" the work.³⁰ Hence, Habermas's portrayal of Heidegger as a "German professor" who in 1929 "carried out a conscious break with academic philosophy, in order henceforth to philosophize in another, nonprofessional way."³¹ This is so that he can suggest, for reasons I shall explain in a moment, that the philosophy of *Being and Time* was subsequently swamped or distorted by the introduction of a worldview from outside, albeit this was possible only because of a loophole of *Being and Time* itself in the unhistorical framework in which historicity was addressed.³² But Habermas's interpretation can only be sustained by privileging the alleged neutrality of the academic philosopher and by failing to do justice to the radical break Heidegger had already made with the dominant conception of academic philosophy. It is a break testified to by the reminiscences of Heidegger's students and now confirmed by the publication of the lecture courses from this period in the *Gesamtausgabe*.[33]

By focusing on Heidegger's conception of the philosopher, it seems that ultimately, and in spite of what he set out to show, Habermas, in his objection against Heidegger, comes to rest on the relation of the person to the work. Habermas says it explicitly: "After 1929, Heidegger veered farther and farther away from the circle of academic philosophy; after the way he actually strayed into the regions of a thinking *beyond* philosophy, *beyond* argumentation itself . . . It was the consciousness of a mission cut to the form of one's own person . . ."[34] It would seem, therefore, that the conclusion that should follow from Habermas's sketch is that Heidegger's character and his philosophy were indeed intertwined. Habermas had no apparent hesitation in claiming that, had Heidegger been equipped with another character, he would have had another philosophy: "A self-critical attitude, an open and scrupulous comportment to his own past, would have demanded from Heidegger something that would surely have been difficult for him: the revision of his self-understanding as a thinker with a privileged access to truth."[35] So, in spite of Habermas's attention to *Weltanschauungen* in his own writings, in this essay on Heidegger he employs a distinction between arguments and their "ideological context" that is strikingly parallel to the neo-Kantian distinction between scientific philosophy and *Weltanschauung* philosophy that Heidegger addressed repeatedly from the oldest surviving lecture course (1919) onward.[36] The problematic character of that distinction determines the direction taken by *Being and Time*, and yet Habermas, in seeking to withdraw the ideological context from Heidegger's *"arguments,"* insists that the self-understanding, postures, and claims connected with Heidegger's *"role"* be set aside to arrive at the substance of his thought.[37] The amalgamation (*Verquickung*) of work and worldview is to be undone. Habermas would rewrite Heidegger's works as if they had been written by the ideal philosopher. The rewriting begins with Heidegger's very conception of the philosopher as if it was itself not philosophical, not part of the argument, but only the reflection of his character or perhaps a part of his *Weltanschauung*. This is why it is convenient for Habermas to present Heidegger as originally an academic philosopher and not one who from the outset was questioning the university in terms of the problem of *Weltanschauungen*. Could it not be, as Heidegger himself had already indicated in *The Metaphysical Foundations of Logic*, that philosophy, *Weltanschauungen*, and the *Existierkunst* of the philosopher are interwoven to the point where their interdependence is apparent?[38] Habermas's assumptions about philosophy may be questionable, as is his interpretation of Heidegger, but, more importantly in this context, his attempt to bracket the person of the philosopher achieves plausibility, such as it has, only insofar as the ideal figure of the philosopher as someone who is self-critical and who upholds the open society is already assumed to be in place.

A treatment of the relation between philosophy and morality much richer than that of either Rorty or Habermas is to be found in the works of Hannah Arendt, but it is no less problematic. Her intellectual life was dominated by the attempt to understand not only how Nazism happened, but also how a philosopher of such standing as Heidegger could become party to it. Arendt, who refused the title of philosopher for herself,[39] showed in her writings the extraordinary hold that the ideal of the philosophical life still had over her, in spite of her ambiguous relation to Heidegger. The tensions which show in reconciling her discussions of Heidegger with her more general assessment of the role of thinking are testimony to the way his failure to live up to the traditional ideal of the philosophical life issues a challenge to inherited categories.

One can say of Arendt what Levinas says of Plato, namely, that her philosophy is "obsessed by the possibility of tyranny."[40] Her first great book after the war, *The Burden of Our Time*, subsequently revised under the title *The Origins of Totalitarianism*, reflects this concentration.[41] In addition, she was both fascinated and appalled by "the attraction to the tyrannical," which, in her analysis, characterized so many of the great thinkers, with Kant the great exception.[42] However, her coverage of Adolf Eichmann's trial in Jerusalem in 1961, for *The New Yorker*, led her to what proved at the time to be a highly controversial conclusion. She came to associate some of the most dramatic and horrifying political events of the century with an observation which initially arose in the context of the everyday life of society, that "thoughtlessness—the heedless recklessness or hopeless confusion or complacent repetition of 'truths' which have become trivial and empty—seems to me among the outstanding characteristics of our time."[43] Arendt noticed that Eichmann spoke in clichés and sometimes, for example at his execution, in singularly inappropriate clichés. She thereby discovered "the fearsome, word-and-thought-defying *banality of evil*."[44] This was an analysis that provoked massive controversy, both at the time and subsequently. Arendt's claim about the banality of evil is particularly shocking within a moral framework, such as that which has tended to dominate since Abelard, where not the act so much as the intention to do evil is decisive. But Eichmann, on Arendt's analysis, was not equipped with an evil will. Nor was he stupid. He simply "never realized what he was doing."[45] "It was sheer thoughtlessness—something by no means identical with stupidity—that predisposed him to become one of the greatest criminals of that period."[46] It was not base motives, but the lack of any motives at all, other than those associated with his own advancement, which led him to do what he did.

This analysis of Eichmann served as the starting point of "Thinking and Moral Considerations."[47] Arendt posed the question of whether "the habit of examining and reflecting upon whatever happens to come to pass" did not condition human beings against evil-doing. She supported the hypothesis by associating thinking as the "dialogue between me and myself,"[48] with the knowing with and by myself of con-science.[49] If Arendt's proposal is to be associated with the preeminence tradition gives to philosophy, then it must be seen as a radical variation of it. Hence, Arendt draws on Kant's distinction between reason as the urge to think and the intellect, which is directed to verifiable knowledge. For it is not knowledge of good and evil with which Arendt is concerned, at least not in the form of moral propositions or commandments that would provide a final code of conduct.[50] Rather, thinking, which she insists with Kant must be a faculty ascribed to everyone, "dissolves accepted rules of conduct."[51] It becomes morally and politically significant, Arendt suggests, only in those rare moments of history, such as occurred with the rise of National Socialism, when everybody is "swept away unthinkingly by what everybody else does and believes in."[52] As Arendt had already described it in *Eichmann in Jerusalem*, "Those few who were still able to tell right from wrong went really only by their own judgments; and they did so freely; there were no rules to be abided by, under which the particular cases with which they were confronted could be subsumed."[53] It is no doubt true that the situation in Germany in the 1930s and early 1940s was unprecedented. But would it not also be possible to show that, in a world where inequality, injustice, and discrimination so often seem to have strong institutional support, those moments where the whole of respectable society seems to have succumbed to evil are not as rare as Arendt seems to indicate?[54]

Nowhere in "Thinking and Moral Considerations" is there any hint of the obvious problem that the Heidegger affair posed to this new variant of the attempt to connect thinking and the ability to tell right from wrong. How could Arendt, after some 30 years of deep reflection on the catastrophe which was such an intimate part of her own life, look to thought as a safeguard against evil, when she had the model of Heidegger before her? Her displacement of the moral force of philosophy to that of thinking only exacerbated the problem. Whereas history gives numerous examples of philosophers, Arendt was always cautious to provide the names of people who might serve as examples of thinkers. In fact, only two names recur with any regularity: Socrates, who is the example employed in "Thinking and Moral Considerations" and *The Life of the Mind*, and Heidegger. In other words, Arendt, blinded by her loyalty to her former teacher's devotion to thinking and captivated by the tradition of giving a moral and not just an intellectual status to the philosopher/thinker, ignores the fact that the case of Heidegger would appear to stand as a knock-down refutation of her thesis. Perhaps nothing could better show the continuing vitality of the association of the philosophical activity of thinking with resistance to evil than Arendt's insistence on casting a new version of it, in spite of the fact that it is in direct conflict with her knowledge of Heidegger's political involvements and his subsequent lack of remorse.

In "Martin Heidegger at Eighty," an essay which first appeared in 1969 only a few months before "Thinking and Moral Considerations" was delivered as a lecture, Arendt identified Heidegger with thinking. Recalling the early 1920s, she wrote, "The rumor about Heidegger put it quite simply: Thinking has come to life again . . . There exists a teacher; one can perhaps learn to think."[55] One cannot dismiss this judgment as the legacy of an earlier period of her thought that had not yet caught up with her new focus on the moral value of thinking, for the essay is with some justice generally regarded as one of the highpoints of Arendt's reassessment of Heidegger. One might contrast it, for example, with a 1946 essay which is remarkable for Arendt's attempt to close the book on Heidegger. Jaspers's philosophy is judged more modern than that of Heidegger: "Either Heidegger has said his last word on the condition of contemporary philosophy or he will have to break with his own philosophy. While Jaspers belongs without any such break to contemporary philosophy, and will develop and decisively intervene in its discussion."[56] This conclusion is striking, not so much because she proved so misguided in her relative assessment of Jaspers and Heidegger, but because, under the impact of the war and the Holocaust, she clearly deluded herself about her own relation to Heidegger's thinking. Arendt's subsequent writings offer powerful testimony to the "clues" it provided for contemporary philosophy. Indeed, Arendt's analysis of thoughtlessness is indebted to Heidegger insofar as it appears to take its starting point in Heidegger's claim that "most thought-provoking in our thought-provoking time is that we are still not thinking" (WD 3; WCT 6).

Although Arendt waited before acknowledging her debts to Heidegger in print, an unpublished address to the American Political Science Association in 1954 explained the role of the concept of historicity developed in *Being and Time*. Remarkably, Arendt specifies the importance of this concept in leading to the abandonment of the philosophical ideal of the wise man. His eternal standards separate him from "the perishable affairs of the city," even if "the old hostility of the philosopher toward the *polis* is only too apparent" in the "categorical opposition of . . . *das Man* against the self."[57] Although Arendt could never on her own account share the hostility toward the *polis* she attributed to Heidegger, she was ambiguous in her response to it. In a letter written to Jaspers soon after the war, she poured scorn on Heidegger's having withdrawn into the Todtnauberg hut as if it was a mousehole.[58] Twenty years later she would see things differently and would support the view that Heidegger went astray when he got involved in the world of human affairs, but that he had still been "young enough to learn from the shock of the collision" and so able "to settle in his thinking what he had experienced."[59] It is a story which has little support today, not least because the general view is that Heidegger failed lamentably to come to terms with his—and Germany's—past. Heidegger's "error," a term Arendt uses in this context always in quotation marks, was a going astray, a move from the thinker's residence to the political realm where he did not belong. His subsequent seclusion was an appropriate response, because it was an implicit acknowledgment by him of his proper place. The thinker is simply not at home in the world of human affairs. One recalls Aristotle's observation, "People say that men like Anaxagoras and Thales 'may be wise but are not prudent.'"[60] It seems that rejection of the classic dualism between theory and practice, as Heidegger himself attempts it in the Rectoral Address when he writes of the Greeks that "theory was to be understood as itself the highest realization of genuine practice" (SU 12; HNS 7), does not guarantee the success of the theorist in the practical realm.

But even if one were to accept Arendt's analysis—which in certain respects is very much in keeping with Heidegger's own defense of himself—and treat Heidegger as guilty of no more than a "misunderstanding of what it was all about," an "escape from reality," how could Arendt still give thinking a moral significance?[61] That she does so is clear from both "Thinking and Moral Considerations" and *The Life of the Mind*: "It looks as though Socrates had nothing more to say about the connection between evil and lack of thought than that people who are not in love with beauty, justice, and wisdom are incapable of thought, just as, conversely, those who are in love with examining and thus 'do philosophy' would be incapable of doing evil."[62] Furthermore, in both texts Arendt stresses the connection between thinking and conscience, where the latter is conventionally thought of, at least in principle, as available to everyone, just as thinking is usually thought of as the reserve of a few. Both thinking as the "dialogue between me and myself" and con-science as a knowing with and by myself are threatened by *self*-contradiction, contradiction within the self. In both cases the threat becomes operative only when I withdraw and face myself in solitude: "What makes a man fear this conscience is the anticipation of the presence of a witness who awaits him only *if* and when he goes home."[63] The problem remains that were there any basis for claiming "this moral side effect" of thinking, it would surely have displayed itself in Heidegger, once he too returned to solitude.[64]

Without relating the problem specifically to Heidegger, George Kateb sensed the tension in *The Life of the Mind*. Kateb reads *The Life of the Mind* as "a *qualified* accusation of *philosophical* thinking" and proposes that the political theory of the first volume of *The Life of the Mind* be identified as consisting in the thesis that "thoughtlessness and philosophy form a strange alliance."[65] To establish this interpretation, Kateb insists on finding in Arendt a distinction between "philosophical thinking" and what he calls "ordinary thinking." If this were indeed Arendt's point, Kateb could resolve what I have identified as her apparent inability to explain Heidegger's "error," by identifying Heidegger's thinking as philosophical thinking. But this is precisely not how Arendt sees it. Nor is Kateb's characterization of the thinking with a "moral side effect" as "ordinary" wholly appropriate, even if it acknowledges the importance for Arendt that, "as distinguished from the thirst for knowledge," it is not regarded as the privilege of the few, but as an ever-present faculty in everybody.[66] Arendt's own phrase is "thinking in its non-cognitive, non-specialized sense,"[67] and her characterization of it, like her question "What makes us think?", owes much to Heidegger, even if she does not share his elitism. Furthermore, part of Heidegger's importance for Arendt is that his focus on such thinking in his overcoming of metaphysics opened the way to her own dismantling of it.[68] Heidegger's thinking was not a form of thoughtlessness, but precisely the kind of thinking which, in conformity with the description given in "Thinking and Moral Considerations," "acts in a peculiarly destructive or critical way toward its own results."[69] Arendt could have approached the question of judgment without broaching that of thinking, just as she could have discussed thinking in this context solely in terms of what Eichmann lacked. There are numerous ways in which the role of the spectator seems to be divorced from the role of the thinker, and the more one stresses the Kantian context in which she develops her understanding of the former, the more true this becomes. The task here, however, is not to try and draw the distinction differently in ways which might make it easier to establish. The task is to understand better why she drew the distinction as she did.

Ultimately, Arendt was concerned not with thinking but with judging. The difference is that thinking deals with invisibles, which are absent, whereas judging "always concerns particulars and things close at hand."[70] However, Arendt's views on judging were never fully developed. In "Thinking and Moral Considerations" judging is introduced only in the closing paragraphs. *The Life of the Mind* remained unfinished, with the section on "Judging" the major casualty. The precise relation between thinking and judging as Arendt conceived it therefore remains unclear. Arendt's convictions about their proximity is somewhat puzzling, except insofar as one draws on traditional claims such as Plato's, whereby the philosopher preeminently possesses the ability to judge. But, whatever Plato says, great thinkers are not equipped with a greater capacity to tell right from wrong, beautiful from ugly. They are at least equally prone to judge a man's character by the beauty of his hands. Perhaps more so.

There is enough on judgment in Arendt, particularly associated with the idea of the spectator, to have some sense of why she turns to it in the face of the weakening, even the apparent reversal, of the basic moral commandments of Western morality in Nazi Germany and Stalinist Russia.[71] These situations called not for reliance on general rules under which to subsume particulars, but the ability to move from particulars to universals. That is why she did not have recourse to the traditional notions of *phronesis*, or practical reason, but instead adapted Kant's account of reflective judgment. What is not altogether clear is why Arendt insists on associating it with thinking. In any event, on Arendt's analysis Heidegger was in his political involvement guilty of a failure of judgment and not of thinking. Thinking may play its part in keeping judging from collapsing into the application of rules, but thinking is not judging. That is why Heidegger's political errors, and perhaps even his lack of remorse, do not on this account directly establish a failure of thinking. This is not to deny that there was such a failure in Heidegger. It lies most obviously in the absence of any evidence of sustained suspicion of the possible complicity of his thinking with "the works being peddled about nowadays as the philosophy of National Socialism," when Heidegger simply asserts their separation (EM 152; IM 199). But Arendt did not criticize Heidegger for failing to engage the political issues which concerned her. To her mind the problems arose precisely when he did attempt to take up these issues.

It has been necessary to introduce some of the intricacies of Arendt's account to help explain why her tendency to judge Heidegger's thought independently from his life was a consequence of her acceptance of the ideal of the solitary thinker and not the application of a clear distinction between person and works as found in Rorty. This becomes clear as soon as one compares her treatment of Heidegger with that of Jaspers. In her relation to Jaspers, Arendt seems to have accepted as axiomatic the unity of the person and the thought. Jaspers was everything Heidegger was not. On the occasion of her address when Jaspers was awarded the German Book Trade's Peace Prize, Arendt took full advantage of the fact that it was given "not only for 'excellent literary work,' but also for 'having proved oneself in life.'"[72] Arendt knew that to praise someone in these terms reflected badly on Heidegger. She hesitated to accept the invitation to give the *laudatio* for Jaspers because she knew that Heidegger would feel slighted.[73] But although Arendt did not dismiss the ideal of the philosophical life that Heidegger failed to live up to, she did not dismiss Heidegger for not being Jaspers. She recognized Heidegger's achievement in its own sphere. Indeed, Arendt's acknowledgment of the thinker's need for solitude is remarkable, given her earlier suspicion of it. The contrast between Heidegger's focus on "the absolute egoism" of the Self, "its radical separation from all its fellows," and the account of *Existenz* in terms of "the togetherness of men in the common given world," as developed by Jaspers, had been one of the fundamental points which had led Arendt to champion Jaspers.[74]

Arendt was generous in her judgment of Heidegger's "error" on the grounds that, as a thinker, his residence was elsewhere. She knew that she was making an exception. In the public realm the distinction between a person's life and a person's works had less force. This was the case with Jaspers, whom Arendt described as a citizen of the world. Arendt considered separation of the "objective work" from the person who produced it to be the misguided application of a distinction drawn from science and, in the final analysis, a consequence of the modern distrust of the public realm.[75] In conceding Heidegger his space, Arendt was not, as one might have anticipated, responding to the disappearance of the public realm, so much as acknowledging the underlying experience of Platonism in the face of her earlier celebration of Jaspers's affirmation of the public realm, an affirmation which she had once regarded as "unique because it comes from a philosopher and because it springs from the fundamental conviction . . . that both philosophy and politics concern everyone."[76] Arendt's later generous assessment of Heidegger should not be considered a personal matter. Rather, it would seem to be a version of the indulgence sometimes shown to the great whereby they are exempted from the ordinary moral code. Arendt even gives an explanation of why great thinkers might be expected to exasperate their admirers whenever they turn to human affairs.[77] Of course, the rhetoric of greatness is very much in question in this whole discussion, because it was an intimate part of Heidegger's own declarations in support of "the inner truth and greatness of the movement" (EM 152; IM 199).

Ultimately, Arendt appears to address the presumption about the association of philosophy and virtue in her discussion of the association of thinking, which is concerned with meaning rather than knowledge, and judging, which is most important in challenging dominant conceptions of morality or in unprecedented situations. Unfortunately, her attempt to articulate this relation was cut short, but it would seem that she takes the unusual step of insisting on the moral efficacy of thinking while excusing the great thinker. Arendt remains captivated by the ideal of the philosophical life in its various forms, even though it is only thinking, and not the life of the thinker, which ultimately holds importance for her. A world without thinking is liable to fall prey to every kind of excess, but the person who has withdrawn from the public realm in order to dedicate his or her life to thinking is, as the allegory of the cave already explained, liable to be disoriented when he or she returns to the common world.

No doubt Arendt's thesis about the banality of evil made it all the easier for her not to locate evil in Heidegger's thought, a thought which was marked in her eyes by an almost unique profundity. In *The Origins of Totalitarianism* Arendt had employed Kant's phrase, "radical evil," but in her own sense. The crimes of totalitarian regimes were neither punishable nor forgivable, at least according to the usual conceptions. In part this was because they were not conceivable in terms of evil motives or a perverted will: "It is inherent in our entire philosophical tradition that we cannot conceive of a 'radical evil.'"[78] At the time of the Eichmann book, in a letter to Gershom Scholem, Arendt expressly sets her thesis about the banality of evil against the idea of radical evil: "It is indeed my opinion now that evil is never 'radical,' that it is only extreme, and that it possesses neither depth nor any demonic dimension . . . Only the good has depth and can be radical."[79] However, these were just two attempts to address the same bewildering phenomenon of an absolute evil which at the same time did not always reveal itself as evil to the perpetrators, because whole moral systems had been perverted.[80]

It is on this question of evil that one can learn most from Emmanuel Levinas, who, like Hannah Arendt, was both a Jew and a former student of Heidegger from the 1920s. Levinas may not have much new to contribute directly to the issue of the ideal of the philosophical life, even though he makes it the starting point of a recent essay, "As If Consenting to Horror." Levinas there describes his "stupor and disappointment" when he heard of Heidegger's sympathy toward National Socialism. He recalls that he had hoped that it might have been only a "temporary lapse of a great speculative mind into practical banality," but his firm confidence in "an unbridgeable distance" between *Mein Kampf*, the criminal voice of evil, and *Being and Time*, which raised Heidegger to the highest ranks among European philosophers, was now in question, even though "nothing in this new phenomenology . . . portends any political or violent ulterior motive."[81] In what might be called a phenomenology of the Heidegger affair, Levinas describes the discomfort of wanting to believe that Heidegger's stature as a thinker must mean that his thought was separate from his political commitments, but at the same time being unable to sustain this conviction in spite of the lack of any evidence of a direct link, at least for the masterpiece, *Being and Time*.

There is, on the one hand, a work of philosophy whose "intellectual vigor and extreme analytical virtuosity he finds it impossible not to admire."[82] There is, on the other hand, and—as with Lacoue-Labarthe and Habermas— Levinas finds this decisive, Heidegger's distressing silence about the

Holocaust, which extends even to the *Der Spiegel* interview in which Heidegger tried to settle accounts:

> All the rest could, if necessary, still be attributed to the inevitable immorality of politics—haven't all states been responsible for wars? . . . But doesn't this silence, in time of peace, on the gas chambers and death camps lie beyond the realm of feeble excuses and reveal a soul completely cut off from any sensitivity, in which can be perceived a kind of consent to the horror?[83]

In this context Levinas employs with heavy irony the phrase a "human failure."[84] These were the words with which Heidegger had described his silence during Husserl's illness (NG 201; NHS 50). How could Heidegger have asked Husserl's wife forgiveness for that silence and yet apparently remained so oblivious of the effect of his other silence, his silence about the Holocaust?

Nothing so far in Levinas's essay prepares one for its closing questions, which appear to break the confines of the debate as decisively as his initial discussion seems destined to repeat it. Condemnation of the man, admiration for the work: this recipe might lead one to expect Levinas to repeat Rorty's solution, as a way of avoiding having to sacrifice Heidegger's works to his Nazism or deny his Nazism to save the works—except for the fact that Levinas's brief essay, unlike Rorty's, bristles with the anxiety created by this tension. Levinas's final questions arise from the recognition of this anxiety. Having reasserted his admiration for *Being and Time*, Levinas asks: "Can we be assured, however, that there was never any echo of Evil in it? The diabolical is not limited to the wickedness popular wisdom ascribes to it and whose malice, based on guile, is familiar and predictable in an adult culture. The diabolical is endowed with intelligence and enters where it will. To reject it, it is first necessary to refute it. Intellectual effort is needed to recognize it. Who can boast of having done so? Say what you will, the diabolical gives food for thought."[85] It is not only Heidegger that Levinas puts under suspicion under this rubric, but the whole ontological tradition. That is to say, Levinas's suspicions are directed not just at Heidegger, but at a certain style of thinking which is characteristic of Western philosophy. It is true that the person of Heidegger serves as a warning that our confidence in the moral efficacy of philosophy is probably misplaced. Levinas has never forgotten Heidegger's failings. But nor does he dwell on them either. The need to leave the climate of Heidegger's thought is the starting point of Levinas's own original thinking,[86] not the need to leave behind a teacher who had disappointed him. Hence, there is nothing disingenuous in Levinas's remark in "As If Consenting to Horror," that "I have not kept track of nor even remembered all the details" of Heidegger's involvement with

National Socialism.[87] They are not what needs to be thought. Nor is thoughtlessness as such the topic, if that would imply that the solution lay in a thinking which was itself to be left free from scrutiny. What is thought provoking is not thoughtlessness, but the diabolical. And because evil does not necessarily announce its presence unambiguously, it might be anywhere. It cannot be confined to the hearts or minds of agents, or to the projects and institutions they devise.

Arendt and Levinas share the recognition that evil extends farther than the intentions of the wicked. But whereas Arendt understands evil as lacking in depth or any demonic dimension, Levinas recognizes the diabolical element of thought, although tracking it is not easy. Indeed, Levinas had already in 1961 anticipated Arendt's observation about the banality of evil, only to challenge it: "It would be pointless to insist on the banality of murder, which reveals the quasi-null resistance of the obstacle. This most banal incident of human history corresponds to an exceptional possibility—since it claims the total negation of a being."[88] Violence is not the only response to violence. Already in advance of violence the face of the Other resists it ethically. Levinas appeals to the Other, and not to thinking, as Arendt does, to challenge the tyranny of norms of conduct.[89]

One could say that Heidegger, the man and the thinker, serves as philosophy's Other in the sense of challenging its norms, although not in a way that one could imagine Levinas being ready to accept. It might be better simply to say, therefore, that in Heidegger philosophy sees what it has long hidden from itself. The point is not simply that a thinker of Heidegger's stature was misled, so that we must draw some distinctions to protect our most cherished illusions about philosophy. It is no longer enough to separate person and work, or *Weltanschauung* and work, or the realm of the thinker from the public realm. Heidegger's failings, which extend beyond the political and the moral to thinking itself, reflect not just on him, or on a school of philosophy, but on the very ideal of the Western philosophical tradition as a way of life. This ideal constitutes a conviction about philosophy so deeply held that only a philosopher's apparent blindness to events as cataclysmic as those witnessed in Europe in the middle of the century could destroy it. Here is an end of philosophy, of philosophy's self-conception. It was not the same end of philosophy that Heidegger had envisaged in his works. Nor was it brought about in his works alone. He enacted it in his life and works by showing what for too long had gone unsuspected, that great thoughts, under the mask of nobility, can lead us astray. The task of thinking this end, the task of ploughing through the wreckage, not just to track down the diabolical, but to see what can be scavenged, has barely begun.

Part Two

♦

ART AND LITERATURE

5

Literary Attestation in Philosophy: Heidegger's Footnote on Tolstoy's "The Death of Ivan Ilyich"

Tolstoy's name appears only once in Heidegger's published writings. He is named in a footnote to the discussion of Being-toward-death to be found in the first chapter of the second division of *Being and Time*. The footnote reads, "L. N. Tolstoi hat in seiner Erzählung 'Der Tod des Iwan Iljitsch' das Phänomen der Erschütterung und des Zusammenbruchs dieses 'man stirbt' dargestellt." Macquarrie and Robinson provide the following translation: "In his story 'The Death of Ivan Ilyitch' Leo Tolstoi has presented the phenomenon of the disruption and breakdown of having 'someone die'" (SZ 254; BT 495 n12). The footnote seems straightforward enough. It would appear to invite a reading of Tolstoy's story which would serve to illustrate Heidegger's account of the phenomenon of everyday Being-toward-death.

The context of the footnote helps to confirm this meaning. The footnote is in section 51 of *Being and Time*, entitled "Being-toward-death and the Everydayness of Dasein." The previous section had provided a preliminary sketch of the existential-ontological structure of death in an effort to show how *Dasein*'s existence, facticity, and falling reveal themselves in the phenomenon of death. But in the same place Heidegger acknowledged that a *formal* sketch of this kind was insufficient on its own.

Being-toward-death must be exhibited in everydayness; the connection between Being-toward-death and care must be given phenomenal confirmation. Hence, section 50, which provided a *formal* sketch of the ontological structure of death guided by the account of care arrived at in the final chapter of the first division of *Being and Time*, was followed by section 51, which provided a *concrete* analysis of everyday Being-toward-death with the aim of confirming the formal sketch. However, insofar as the analysis was limited to the everyday, it remained essentially incomplete. For that reason, in section 52, the exposition went into reverse (*Umkehr*) and the interpretation of everyday Being-toward-death was interrogated in preparation for the introduction of authentic Being-toward-death. The latter was supposed to complete or supplement the former with a view to forming the "full existential concept of death."

This program is not unproblematic. How are formal structures to be provided with concrete confirmation? In the Introduction to *Being and Time* Heidegger had employed a distinction between the existential and the *existentiell* in order to address the problem of our access to these structures, and he returned to it whenever their basis was in question. The distinction operated in the following way. "The question of existence is an ontical 'affair' of Dasein" (SZ 12; BT 33). That is to say, it is a question which can only be "cleared up" or "brought to order" through existing. Heidegger gave the name *existentiell* to the kind of understanding which arises in this way. It was specifically divorced by him from the theoretical transparency of the ontological analysis of existence, which he described as *existential*. Heidegger returned to the question of theoretical research, its praxis and its source in authentic existence, in the second part of section 69, but only to postpone a full discussion of these questions to a part of *Being and Time* which was never written. Nevertheless, he said enough there to indicate that this cluster of problems had widespread implications, even for the conception of phenomenology set out in the Introduction. I will not pursue these questions here. I shall on this occasion set artificial limits around the question of the ontic foundation of ontology—the question of so-called metontology raised in chapter 2—so as to focus on some preliminary issues suggested by the chapter on Being-toward-death.

In spite of the attention the chapter on Being-toward-death has received, commentators have tended to ignore the fact that, far from being a self-contained unit, it leaves authentic Being-toward-death without ontic attestation. This can be shown simply by observing the structure of the chapter. Section 53 provided only the existential projection of an authentic Being-toward-death. It explored the existential conditions of the *existentiell* possibility of authentic Being-toward-death, but without offering a sketch of the *existentiell* possibility itself. That is to say, it was directed to the formal structures of existence insofar as they condition this ontical potentiality-for-Being. But the chapter ended without the addition of a concrete analysis which would confirm these structures in the way that section 51 had supported the formal sketch found in section 50. The omission governs the next two chapters of *Being and Time*. The *existentiell* possibility of authentic Being-toward-death had been elucidated in its existential conditions in the first chapter of the second division. Ontic attestation of this *existentiell* possibility remained to be established.

I have suggested that Heidegger employed the distinction between the existential and *existentiell* in order to describe how the ontological analysis of *Dasein* was supported at the ontic level. But *existentiell* descriptions, which are supposed to help confirm the existential analysis, can also serve to compromise it. At the end of section 49 Heidegger observed that, from an ontic perspective, ontological characterization is liable to appear formalistic to the point of emptiness (SZ 248; BT 292). The concrete analyses of everyday Being-toward-death were supposed to compensate for this. All *existentiell* possibilities of Being-toward-death must be consistent with the ontological structures. Indeed, the latter would provide the basis for the former. But the reverse cannot be countenanced: the existential definition of concepts must remain unaccompanied by any *existentiell* commitments (SZ 248; BT 293). This requirement had already been stated in section 9 and had necessitated the adoption of *Dasein*'s average everydayness as the starting point of the inquiry. This was to avoid construing *Dasein* "in terms of some concrete possible idea of existence" (SZ 43; BT 69).

In the context of section 49 this meant that the existential analysis of death had to be kept rigorously separated from other interpretations. So, for example, all "ontic other-worldly speculation" about an afterlife must be rigorously excluded. The ontological interpretation of death is characterized as "this-worldly." Not, as Heidegger made clear in one of his lecture courses, that this prejudges the traditional questions of immortality and resurrection (GA 20, 434; HCT 314). It is rather the precondition for posing such questions in a legitimate manner. But can *existentiell* commitments and ideals ever be excluded? Heidegger is unambiguous in the answer that he gives at the end of the chapter. The ontological investigation has, he says, taken place "without holding up to Dasein an ideal of existence with any special 'content,' or forcing any such ideal upon it 'from outside'" (SZ 266; BT 311). One can legitimately ask whether this answer would have been quite so persuasive had the elucidation of the *existentiell* possibility of authentic Being-toward-death not been postponed to a later chapter. Of course, its omission from this chapter does nothing of itself to secure the purity of the analysis. The absence of an explicit account of authentic Being-toward-death at the ontic level is no guarantee of the lack of an ideal of existence operating implicitly within the analysis. But this consideration turns out to be unimportant anyway. Heidegger was to undercut this line of questioning later in the book when he conceded that, after all, there had indeed been "a definite ontical way of taking authentic existence, a factical ideal of Dasein, underlying our ontological interpretation of Dasein's existence" (SZ 310; BT 358). I shall return to this point later. I mention it now only as some indication of how serious the question of the relation between the existential and the *existentiell* will prove for the analysis. It is not too much to say that what is at stake is the very possibility of fundamental ontology as usually conceived. The purpose of this chapter is to suggest that Heidegger's brief reference to Tolstoy's story plays a more intimate role in this drama than might at first be imagined. But first the footnote itself must be submitted to a more careful examination.

The footnote, as I have already said, is in section 51. The section takes up the phrase "one dies" (*man stirbt*). This "one" is the "they" (*das Man*) of everydayness, the nobody (*das Niemand*), and the phrase gives rise to an analysis of three kinds of fleeing in the face of death. The three—temptation, tranquilizing, and alienation—are drawn from the four phenomena used in section 38 to characterize falling. The fourth, entanglement or *Verfängnis*, in the sense of exaggerated self-dissection, is omitted from section 51, although later "the fetters of a weary 'inactive thinking about death'" (SZ 258; BT 302) and "brooding over death" (SZ 261; BT 305) gain Heidegger's attention. Here the temptation is said to be that people try to persuade the "dying person" that he or she is not dying; tranquilization takes the form that even when someone dies the tranquility and carefreeness of the public is not to be disturbed; and finally the alienation of *Dasein* from its ownmost nonrelational potentiality-for-Being occurs when anxiety in the face of death comes to be regarded as fear and passed off as weakness. The reference to Tolstoy is appended to the discussion of the second of these, tranquilization or *Beruhigung*. Specifically, it is attached to the sentence, "Indeed the dying of Others is seen often enough as social inconvenience, if not even a downright tactlessness, against which the public is to be guarded" (SZ 254; BT 298).

No reader of Tolstoy's story would have any difficulty in recognizing how it illustrates the phenomenon in question. From the first chapter, which opens with the announcement of the death of Ivan Ilyich, Tolstoy is concerned with "the exceedingly tiresome demands of propriety."[1] These are exhibited in the context of both the requiem service and the issuing of condolences to the widow. Both interrupt "the recognized order of things"—namely, a regular game of cards such as Ivan himself used to play.[2] The expression on the face of the dead man serves as "a reminder to the living," but one they prefer to ignore as having nothing to do with them.[3] Similarly, it is remarked later in the story that Ivan's daughter was "impatient with illness, suffering and death because they interfered with her happiness."[4] So Tolstoy's story illustrates what Heidegger calls the social inconvenience of death. It also provides examples of the other kinds of fleeing in the face of death. The temptation to talk "the 'dying person' into the belief that he will escape death" (SZ 253; BT 297) is exhibited by a belief both in wonder-working icons[5] and in the curative powers of medicine: "Stimulate the sluggish organ, check the activity of another—secretion ensues, and everything would come right."[6] Other people—with the exception of the young peasant Gerassim—come to mean falsity: "Gerassim alone told no lies."[7] And finally, Ivan Ilyich exhibits his alienation—which is the third form of fleeing in the face of death—not only by his fear of death, but also by the way he goes along with the attempts of people around him to persuade him that he is getting better. It would even be possible to illustrate the fourth phenomenon of falling by pointing to the entanglement in the frenzied self-dissection which Ivan engages in as part of his revolt against death and his attempt to find a moral explanation of why he must die.

Details such as these, as well as the placing of the footnote within section 51 of *Being and Time*, no doubt encouraged Macquarrie and Robinson to offer the translation of it which they did: "In his story 'The Death of Ivan Ilyitch' Leo Tolstoi has presented the phenomenon of the disruption and breakdown of having 'someone die.'" The disruption and breakdown is the social inconvenience (*gesellschaftliche Unannehmlichkeit*) which the illness and death of someone causes for those in the immediate vicinity. That this is the interpretation underlying the translation receives partial confirmation in Macquarrie's book on *Existentialism*, where he draws on Tolstoy's story to "illustrate" Heidegger's account. "For everyone except Ivan (and even for him up till the moment when he becomes aware that he is mortally ill) death is a most inconvenient and disagreeable subject, not to be thought about or talked about. For Ivan, it becomes a theme of engrossing importance, coloring everything else."[8] Macquarrie, doubtless recalling the description of the phenomenon of entanglement, denies that Heidegger is recommending morbid brooding over death: "He explicitly rejects such brooding." But Macquarrie does not look to Tolstoy's story for a concretization of anything but the everyday attitude to death.

Nevertheless, Heidegger's footnote permits another reading, which corresponds more closely to the German. It would run: "L. N. Tolstoy, in his story 'The Death of Ivan Ilyitch,' has presented the phenomenon of the shattering and the collapse of this 'one dies.'" On this reading Heidegger's point would not be that Tolstoy's story exhibits the everyday attitude to death, or at least not that only. The story would also be called upon to show the shattering of the everyday attitude. Tolstoy, having presented the way we for the most part refer death away from ourselves to everyone else, shows how one individual, Ivan Ilyich, comes to confront his own death. But at what point in the story does this happen? How might the everyday attitude be brought to a point of collapse? And would that mean that

Tolstoy's story was cited in preparation for the analysis of authentic Being-toward-death?

The shattering and breakdown of the "one dies" takes place in the first instance as the recognition that I myself am going to die. This is something certain. Not in the everyday manner of being certain, which is a question of the kind of certainty we can have about beings as we encounter them. The certainty which belongs to anticipation—or rather "running ahead" (*Vorlaufen*)—is somewhat different (SZ 265; BT 309). In the story we read that Ivan comes to realize that the textbook syllogism "Caius is a man, men are mortal, Caius is mortal" does apply to him after all. "If I had to die like Caius I should have known it was so, some inner voice would have told me. But there was nothing of the sort in me, and I and all my friends, we knew that it was quite different in our case. And now here it is!"[9] Tolstoy comments, "Strangely enough all that used to cover up, obscure and obliterate the feeling of death no longer had the same effect."[10] This is registered in the sixth of the 12 chapters. And in the seventh chapter, the pretense, the lie, the temptation to believe that he would get better is less a comfort than a torment to Ivan.[11] At these moments everyday evasion of death is no longer effective. But does it amount to a "shattering and collapse of the 'one dies'"?

From chapter 6 through chapter 11, Ivan Ilyich's attitude to death fluctuates. Even at the beginning of the last chapter, we can still read that Ivan's doubts remain unresolved.[12] Ivan had already begun to entertain the suspicion that his life had in some way been misspent, but as the final chapter opens, he still maintains that he led a proper life. Because he appears to believe that the nature of his death should be in some way related to the quality of his life, he continues his revolt against death. "That very justification of his life held him fast and prevented him from advancing, and caused him more agony than anything else."[13] Ivan Ilyich is still caught up with himself, as is illustrated by the way he wants to be pitied. Has the inauthentic evasion of death been shattered so long as Ivan Ilyich is still in this frame of mind?

Authenticity is not be understood as a simple alternative to inauthenticity. It is true that at the beginning of the existential analysis, and when he is rehearsing that beginning as in section 45, Heidegger gives the impression that authenticity, inauthenticity, and indifference are formally equivalent modes. But Heidegger makes few attempts to maintain this impression. The inauthentic and the indifference of averageness frequently merge in everydayness and the fallenness of the "they." As soon as Heidegger posed the question of the who of *Dasein* in its everydayness, another tendency emerged. It came to be recognized that "*Authentic Being-one's-Self* does not rest upon an exceptional condition of the subject, a condition that has been detached from the 'they'; *it is rather an existentiell modification of the "they"—of the 'they' as an essential existentiale"* (SZ 130; BT 168). That is why Heidegger can ask whether *Dasein* can maintain itself in an authentic Being-toward-its end: "How is the ontological possibility of an *authentic* Being-towards-death to be characterized 'Objectively,' if, in the end, Dasein never comports itself authentically towards its end . . . ?" (SZ 260; BT 304. Cf. also SZ 169; BT 213). His answer—which is that *Dasein* cannot be said to *be* authentic in the same manner in which *Dasein is* inauthentic—returns us to the question of attestation: "The question of Dasein's authentic Being-a-whole and of its existential constitution . . . can be put on a phenomenal basis which will stand the test only if it can maintain a possible authenticity of its Being which is attested by Dasein itself" (SZ 267; BT 311). The sentence should be read with the emphasis on possibility. It is the possibility of authenticity which is crucial, and indeed it is this focus on possibility which enables Heidegger to reverse the alleged priority of the "they" to say that the they-self is an *existentiell* modification of the authentic self (SZ 317–18; BT 365–66). Or, as was already said in section 52, "inauthenticity is based on possible authenticity" (SZ 259; BT 303). So, if there was a shattering of the everyday in Ivan's case, this means not that he was held in authenticity as some kind of constant state, but in its possibility. It is hard to see, even on these terms, that there was such a shattering prior to the brief last chapter of "The Death of Ivan Ilyich." This is the center of gravity of most readings of Tolstoy's story anyway. Examining now two very different attempts to relate Tolstoy's story to Heidegger's account of death, it will be no surprise to find that they both also come to focus on this final chapter.

The most extravagant claims have been made by Walter Kaufmann, who provided the alternative, more literal, translation of Heidegger's footnote that I quoted above. He insisted that "Heidegger on death is for the most part an unacknowledged commentary on 'The Death of Ivan Ilyitch,'"[14] an uncritical repetition of "Christian commonplaces in secularized form."[15] Kaufmann maintained this thesis by emphasizing Ivan Ilyich's courage, specifically his having the courage at the end to defy propriety and shriek.[16] Kaufmann appears to have understood this moment as a passage from an evasive fear of death to anxiety or dread in the face of death. It was, in other words, an overcoming of the alienation of *Dasein* from its ownmost non-relational potentiality-for-Being. But Kaufmann did not explain the significance of the fact that in Tolstoy's story, Ivan Ilyich subsequently becomes quiet. Kaufmann emphasized Ivan Ilyich's anxiety before death as expressed in the scream, but he said nothing about the moment when it seems that there is neither fear nor the shock of anxiety, because, in Ivan Ilyich's own words, "death is over."[17] This suggests that one cannot identify Heidegger with Tolstoy, at least on the basis of the minimal and highly selective reading that Kaufmann offered.

William Spanos has written on the relation between Heidegger and Tolstoy's story in more detail and with much greater sensitivity than Kaufmann.[18] And yet, Spanos's reading is also in certain respects onesided. Whereas Kaufmann selected only those passages from the story which assist him in his attempt to reduce Heidegger to Tolstoy, Spanos was inclined to see only those aspects of Tolstoy's story which conform with his picture of Heidegger. So, for example, Spanos focused on the image of the black sack which Tolstoy introduces in chapter 9 to show Ivan resisting his death. Spanos understood this resistance as having its source in Ivan's dread (*Angst*). It is Ivan's dread or anxiety in the face of death which prevents him from "perceiving anything positive in the weak impulse to assist the process of dying." But that left Spanos in difficulty when it came to providing an interpretation of the passage in the last chapter where Tolstoy has Ivan entering the black sack, now described as a hole, and finding light within it.[19] Spanos confronted this problem by leaving behind the language of *Angst* from *Being and Time* and turning instead to the later Heidegger's notion of releasement (*Gelassenheit*). That Tolstoy wrote "Let the pain be"[20] might seem to provide some justification for this reference to *Gelassenheit*. But what is the relation between Ivan's *Angst* and his *Gelassenheit*? It is hardly surprising that Spanos avoided this question. It goes far beyond the question of the relation of the early and the late Heidegger. It might perhaps be conceded that *Angst* is not wholly lacking from the later Heidegger and that *Gelassenheit* is not altogether absent from *Being and Time*. But to establish a proximity between *Angst* and *Gelassenheit* would only serve to suggest that if Ivan exhibited *Gelassenheit* in his last moments when accepting death, then his earlier resistance of death should have been construed by Spanos, in terms of Heidegger's well-known distinction, as fear rather than dread. Spanos identified certain "Heideggerian" moments in "The Death of Ivan Ilyich" but it is at best unclear whether he succeeded in giving a coherent reading of Tolstoy's story in terms of Heidegger.

Spanos understood his treatment of the story as an attempt "to get below the exclusively socio-moral readings that interpret death as merely a judgement against the hollowness of his life." He believed that Tolstoy's ultimate point was not simply a moralistic or ontic one, "but rather, or at least primarily, an ontological one."[21] With his introduction of this distinction Spanos touched on the central problem of the relation between the existential and the *existentiell*, outlined above, even if he did not seem fully aware of its contours as a problem. Spanos joined with Kaufmann in identifying Tolstoy's moralizing as the major obstacle to securing some form of unity which would join Tolstoy and Heidegger. This is hardly surprising, given Heidegger's frequent renunciation of the moralizing tone which his language tends to evoke. But the fact that Heidegger's language evokes this tone in spite of his expressed intentions cannot be dismissed so quickly, as I shall try to show later.

The strength of Spanos's reading of Tolstoy's story lies in his treatment of its temporality. The ever-quickening tempo of the story corresponds with a transformation in Ivan's temporality. The weakness of Spanos's essay, on the other hand, is found in his failure to confront the difficulties of giving a reading of the end of the story consistent with a Heideggerian intention. As to the first, Ivan's encounter with death is for Spanos an encounter with temporality.[22] Spanos was right to observe that Ivan's confrontation with death was not something sudden, reserved until the end of his life: "the process is not abrupt." He situated in Book Six Ivan's "first positive intimation" of the imminence of death, "faint and brief though it is."[23] But this qualification is perhaps not readily reconcilable with a rather bolder claim made by Spanos also about Book Six. Referring to Ivan's crucial encounter with the "my-ownness of death," Spanos wrote that "he has been driven out of the refuge provided by the public spatial structure of *das Man* into authenticity."[24] The difference in emphasis between these two judgments is not a simple consequence of indecision on the part of Spanos. The tension in Spanos should be referred to the tension within Heidegger's own treatment of authenticity. Heidegger, I noted earlier, seems ultimately to focus on possible authenticity and not on the sense in which one might *be* authentic as one might *be* inauthentic. The question has further ramifications beyond those I have introduced here. I mention it now largely in order to be able to indicate the depth of Spanos's understanding of the last chapter. There, at the "instant of surrender," Ivan "dis-covers 'the right thing': that life is *relationship* and ... redemption is never lost to the past, but is *always* a possibility of the future."[25] In this way Spanos seems to opt for an understanding of authenticity as *possibility*.

Nevertheless, it is at this same point that the difficult passage from *Angst* to *Gelassenheit* is situated. Spanos presented Ivan's last words—"Death is finished"*—as meaning that death has undergone a paradoxical metamorphosis—"death, in the courageous act of confrontation, undergoes a paradoxical metamorphosis: *It* becomes a benign agent, a *Thou*." Spanos called this a "de-structed sense."[26] His references to Greek and Hebraic archetypes at this point are not, however, sufficient to clarify precisely what he meant. The *It* belongs to Book Six, where, Spanos told us, it occurs over a dozen times. But there is some difficulty explaining the source of the *Thou*, without having recourse to Buber's famous and, in this context, somewhat inappropriate dichotomy.

---

* In the translation Spanos uses, Ivan's last words are not "death is over" but these words instead.

Spanos's introduction of the *Thou* alerts us, if only unwittingly, to the fact that if the familiar characterization of Heideggerian Being-toward-death is followed, the last pages of Tolstoy's story seem to represent an almost unambiguous collapse into the inauthentic. Is Ivan's exclamation of joy not the denial of anxiety in the face of death? Are not his final words—"Death is over. It is no more"—inserted into the novel as "a way of escape, fabricated for the 'overcoming of death'" (SZ 310; BT 357)? Is not their echo of the final words of Jesus Christ suggestive of an unwarranted introduction of "ontical other-worldly speculation" (SZ 248; BT 292)? Is not Ivan's recourse to his wife and son in his final hours, after he had neglected them throughout his life, a pathetic failure to acknowledge that he must die alone? Does not the conclusion of Tolstoy's story slide into inauthenticity with its proposal of what amounts to "norms and rules for composing oneself towards death ... for 'edification'" (SZ 248; BT 292)? And is not the story simply propaganda for Tolstoy's own unsubstantiated idea that "the better a man's life the less dreadful death is to him and the easier it is for him to die"[27]—a view which represents a temptation for the dying person no less inauthentic than that of a hope in doctors or icons? It would appear that a Heideggerian reading of the story must stop short of the last moments of Ivan's life, for good reason. It runs completely counter to the *existentialist* picture of man dying alone which has been drawn from Heidegger's discussion of death by critics from Sartre onwards. That would help explain—without legitimating—Spanos's sudden shift of gear, whereby his references to *Being and Time* gave way to talk of *Gelassenheit*.

Both the existentialist approach to death and that represented by Tolstoy's moralizing would, insofar as they come into conflict, have to be characterized as *existentiell*. Spanos, by contrast, sought to give an ontological reading of the story. He explicitly opposed his reading both to Kaufmann's existentialist interpretation and to what he regarded as the more conventional literary interpretation, which treats the story as "essentially a *vehicle* for a moral (ontic) assertion."[28] Nevertheless, it may prove as hard to reduce the moralizing weight of Tolstoy's "The Death of Ivan Ilyich" as it has proved difficult for Heidegger to convince his readers that his own discussion was, as he claimed, "far removed from any moralizing critique of everyday Dasein" (SZ 167; BT 211).

At this point it is tempting to have recourse to another reading of Tolstoy's story, one less intent on diminishing the moral basis of the story but at the same time securing its philosophical significance. A reading inspired by the ethical philosophy of Emmanuel Levinas might well meet these requirements.[29] Certain parallels would quickly emerge between Tolstoy's story and Levinas's discussion of death, a discussion developed in specific contrast to Heidegger's account in *Being and Time*. So, for example, Levinas insists that death has the temporality of a perpetual postponement. Death is always "ever future," leaving time "to be for the Other."[30] Ivan's discovery that "It was still possible to put it right" evokes Levinas's insistence that "There is before death a last chance that heroes seize, which is not death."[31] Does that mean that, insofar as Heidegger uses Tolstoy's story as evidence for his own analysis, the evidence in fact goes against him? According to Heidegger, it is "they," not the hero or the authentic *Dasein*, who have more time (SZ 425; BT 477). Other details could be used to support a Levinasian reading. The important question—"What if in reality my whole life has been wrong?"—arises when Ivan Ilyich was looking at "Gerassim's sleepy, good-natured face,"[32] thereby recalling Levinas's claim that it is the face of the Other which puts me into question. And above all, do not the concluding pages of Tolstoy's story well suit Levinas's description, where "Death, source of all myths, is *present* only in the Other, and only in him does it summon me urgently to my final essence, to my responsibility"?[33] So, according to Levinas, the relation with death maintains the social conjuncture. He regards the doctor as an a priori principle of human mortality, so that death approaches accompanied by hope in someone.[34] And the crucial transformation in Ivan's relation to his own death comes when, in Levinas's phrase, he is "liberated from the egoist gravitation."[35] But decisions for and against rival philosophical interpretations of a story cannot be made on the basis of a few details. It would be necessary to attempt a sustained Levinasian reading of "The Death of Ivan Ilyich." But to what purpose? And what does it mean to call a reading of a story after the name of a philosopher? Valuable though it might be to explore such a reading on some other occasion, in the present context it would distract from the question of the character and legitimacy of philosophical readings of literature, or, more precisely, the question of the use of literature within philosophy.

What is the role of literary examples within philosophical texts? What is literary attestation? Could an attestation not only fail to attest, but in certain cases actually refute what it was introduced to support? Or must formal structures always govern the consideration of concrete possibilities? In this essay I can provide no more than a prolegomenon to a serious consideration of such questions. I undertake it in the conviction that, by appealing to Heidegger's language of the existential and the *existentiell*, I may put the question in a particularly forceful way. The difficulties that accumulate around Heidegger's distinction, such that it sometimes seems appropriate to talk of the collapse of the distinction and thus the breakdown of the very project of fundamental ontology, do not count against this. They are rather to be considered as evidence of the power of the terms themselves. Nobody has yet shown that subsequent philosophy, including that of the later Heidegger, is better able to answer these questions simply because it has turned away from the difficult—perhaps impossible—distinction between the existential and the *existentiell*.[36]

Heidegger introduced the footnote on Tolstoy in a section on the everyday attitude to death. This concrete treatment was introduced as a response to the "peculiar *formality* and emptiness of any ontological characterization" (SZ 248; BT 292). But the problem extended farther than that. So long as the account was formal, it was in danger of being arbitrary. It needed confirmation. Heidegger had already encountered a similar problem in his presentation of care as "a basic existential-ontological phenomenon" (SZ 196; BT 240). In order to defend himself against the charge of arbitrariness, Heidegger had felt obliged to show that there was a prior ontico-existentiell basis for this ontological interpretation. "In explicating Dasein's Being-as-care, we are not forcing it under an idea of our own contriving, but we are conceptualizing existentially what has already been disclosed in an ontico-existentiell manner" (SZ 196; BT 241). It is for this reason that in section 42 Heidegger cited one of the ancient fables of Hyginus on care. Heidegger described the document as "pre-ontological." It was, he said, a primordial expression of *Dasein*, "unaffected by any theoretical interpretation and without aiming to propose any" (SZ 197; BT 241). This claim was somewhat compromised when Heidegger conceded that the priority of care maintained by the fable arose in the context of the familiar interpretation of man as a compound of body and mind or spirit (*Geist*) (SZ 198; BT 243). Furthermore, in a lecture course Heidegger acknowledged that he was in the first instance drawn to the phenomenon of care not by the fable, which he noticed only subsequently, but in his reading of Augustine and Christian anthropology in general (GA 20, 418; HCT 302). But the primary question here is not whether we find Heidegger's justification of his selection of the phenomenon of care convincing. The question is why he should have recourse to a "pre-ontological" document to justify the existential-ontological interpretation. His answer reversed familiar categories: "The testimony which we are about to cite should make plain that our existential interpretation is not a fabrication [*Erfindung*], but that as an ontological 'construction' it has a basis which has been sketched out beforehand in an elemental way" (SZ 197; BT 242). In other words, the suspicion is less that the fable is a fabrication or a fiction, than that without its testimony the existential interpretation itself would have to be regarded as one.

The same issues are at stake in the chapter on Being-toward-death. The task is to provide phenomenal confirmation for the ontological status accorded to care understood as the totality of Being-a-whole (SZ 252; BT 296). The danger is that the attempt to provide an existential projection of an authentic Being-toward-death would result in no more than "a fanciful undertaking" (*ein phantastisches Unterfangen*) and "a merely fictitious arbitrary construction" (*eine nur dichtende, willkürliche Konstruktion*) (SZ 260; BT 304). At the end of the first chapter of the second division, Heidegger confirmed that authentic Being-toward-death, although now shown to be *existentially* possible, still had the status of a fanciful or fantastical exaction (*eine phantastische Zumutung*) at the *existentiell* level (SZ 266; BT 311). The implication is that fundamental ontology would lose its scientific credentials and be reduced to the status of mere literature, a work of fiction. For, as Heidegger had already warned, the character of an arbitrary fiction (*willkürliche Erdichtung*) is that it lacks the testimony of the thing at issue, which alone is the proper basis of conviction (SZ 256; BT 300). The problem is not resolved in the chapter on Being-toward-death. Heidegger chose to emphasize the problems of a characterization of authentic Being-toward-death. Was it because the presentation of everyday Being-toward-death in section 51 was relatively unproblematic, being a simple application of the structures already outlined in chapter 5 of the first division? Or was it not because, from the outset and *contrary to the order of presentation*, the possibility of authenticity had underpinned the analysis so that all doubts must ultimately come to be directed to it? This latter hypothesis is partially confirmed by the way in which the "obviousness" of the analyses in division one are put in question in the course of division two (SZ 332; BT 380). Division one of *Being and Time* does not provide a secure foundation for division two.

The hypothesis under examination, based on the revised translation of Heidegger's footnote, is that Heidegger's reference to "The Death of Ivan Ilyich" serves not only to confirm the account of everyday Being-toward-death, but also to mark a place where the factical idea of authentic existence intervenes. As Heidegger subsequently admitted, such ideas had inevitably determined the formal analysis from the outset. To put it another way, Heidegger would subsequently attempt an *existentiell* confirmation of the existential structures in an effort to save fundamental ontology from being reduced to the status of an arbitrary fiction. Meanwhile, this footnote reference to Tolstoy's story was a kind of holding operation, a temporary measure, although perhaps not without permanent consequences for the meaning of *Being and Time*.

The language to which Heidegger has recourse in the face of the difficulties threatening to overwhelm the quest for fundamental ontology gives a centrality to the question of the relation of philosophy and literature that readers of *Being and Time* seem not to have observed. The rhetoric implies that fiction is outside the truth. Were the ontological analysis to prove a fiction, it would no longer be philosophy. But Heidegger's own practice belies that rhetoric, even on the restricted reading of the footnote provided by Macquarrie and Robinson. The analysis of everyday Being-toward-death was supported, not by the evidence of direct observation, but by a work of fiction. This is not accidental. If we could readily face up to this evasion as a matter of course, if it was obvious to us, if we only needed to have it drawn to our attention for us to be able to acknowledge it, then Heidegger's account of everydayness would have to undergo radical revision. Rather than confirming *Dasein*'s fallenness, all claims about the predominance of fallenness would have been compromised. And yet, Heidegger began with everydayness on the grounds that it is ontically closest to us, notwithstanding that it is also ontologically the farthest from us. Under what circumstances does the inauthentic show itself as such? What is the point of access to *Dasein* in all its modes—authentic, inauthentic, and undifferentiated between the two? I shall not rehearse that controversy here.[37] There is some suggestion in section 9 that Heidegger looked to averageness as the everyday undifferentiated character of *Dasein* in order to circumvent the difficulty that *Dasein* might be construed in terms of some concrete possible idea of existence (SZ 43; BT 69). However, the difficulty of situating the everyday in relation to the inauthentic and the undifferentiated makes this interpretation far from easy to sustain. There is also some difficulty in correlating it with Heidegger's explicit references both to anxiety, as that which makes the authentic and inauthentic manifest to Dasein as possibilities (SZ 191; BT 235), and to conscience, as revealing *Dasein*'s lostness in the "they" (SZ 307; BT 354). These seem to point to authenticity as performing the role of providing this access. In that case, Tolstoy's story must itself in some way share in authenticity. For, even on the minimal reading of the footnote, "The Death of Ivan Ilyich" is required to reveal *Dasein* in its inauthenticity.

I shall not try to follow Heidegger through all the stages of the second chapter of the second division during his search for testimony of authentic existence as an *existentiell* possibility. Nor shall I repeat the analysis in chapter 3, where he attempted to secure an essential connection between this *existentiell* possibility and the ontological possibility already projected in the chapter on Being-toward-death. Nevertheless, I can briefly indicate that the subsequent analysis took the form it did precisely because Heidegger kept two questions separate. First, there was the question of *existentiell* attestation of *Dasein*'s authentic potentiality-for-Being. Second, there was the question of correlating this *existentiell* attestation with the existential structures already arrived at in the chapter on Being-toward-death, that is to say, with *Dasein*'s authentic potentiality-for-Being-a-whole. The first question pointed to resoluteness, through a discussion of what the everyday interpretation of *Dasein* calls "the voice of conscience" (SZ 268; BT 313). The second question was that of how resoluteness as an *existentiell* tendency could be brought—or even "welded" (SZ 305; BT 353)—together with "running ahead" (*vorlaufen*) as the existential structure of Being-toward-death (SZ 302; BT 349). The minute care with which Heidegger charted his course is some indication of the importance he attached to these questions.

It was thus not until chapter 3 that Heidegger attempted to address directly the question already raised in chapter 1 of the second division as to whether the existential conception of death is possible in an *existentiell* way or whether it is an arbitrary fiction (SZ 303; BT 350). And, on the basis of a repetition of section 53 now rethought in terms of resoluteness, the answer soon follows that this conception is not just a fictional possibility forced upon *Dasein*, but is a mode of an *existentiell* potentiality-for-Being attested by *Dasein* (SZ 309; BT 357).

This reconstruction of Heidegger's attempted resolution will have to suffice for the present purpose. Heidegger was well aware of how far his discussion fell short of fundamental ontology, if it were to be regarded, in Husserl's phrase, as a rigorous science. The lecture courses of the Marburg period show this most clearly, but it is apparent from *Being and Time* itself. For example, at the beginning of the third chapter Heidegger asked if the attempt to bring together resoluteness and running ahead did not amount to an "unphenomenological construction" (SZ 302; BT 349). Heidegger's rejection of this proposal rendered inevitable a revision of the concept of phenomenology of the kind he called for in the fourth chapter of *Being and Time*. He had by then already conceded that it would be mistaken to conceive *Dasein*'s authentic potentiality-for-Being-a-whole in terms of proof: "It would be a misunderstanding to shove this existentiell possibility aside as 'unproved' or to want to 'prove' it theoretically" (SZ 309–10; BT 357). Three times in as many pages, Heidegger insisted that the formal idea of existence which he had elucidated was not binding on his readers in an *existentiell* way (SZ 312–14; BT 360–62). He warned that the phenomenon needed to be "protected against the grossest perversions" (SZ 310; BT 357), but did not indicate how this might be done. If as a first step one might try to make the concrete ideal of existence as explicit as possible, it has to be said that Heidegger did not accomplish very much in this direction. There is a sentence which helps to explain why: "Philosophy will never seek to deny its 'presuppositions,' but neither may it simply admit (*zugeben*) them" (SZ 310; BT 358). Philosophy cannot admit its presuppositions in the sense of granting them or acceding to them. It must constantly fight against these ontic presuppositions, even if it can never be presuppositionless. But for that very reason, a philosophy will often give the illusion of being more rigorous or compelling, to the extent that it fails to acknowledge its presuppositions and simply keeps silent about them.

With this in mind I return now to Heidegger's footnote on "The Death of Ivan Ilyich." We were left with the choice between, on the one hand, the translation by Macquarrie and Robinson which restricted the significance of the reference to the everyday and, on the other hand, the alternative translation which left the problem of interpreting the final chapter of Tolstoy's story in an effort to find there the shattering of the "they," the shattering of the "one dies." Because the first alternative adopts a somewhat forced reading of Heidegger's footnote, it is important to pursue the second route.

Literary texts have a certain autonomy, but what happens to them when they are submitted to philosophically inspired readings? How does a literary example function within a philosophical text? Heidegger says that "the ontological 'truth' of the existential analysis is developed on the ground of the primordial existentiell truth. However, the latter does not necessarily need the former" (SZ 316; BT 364). We may not be able to decide for sure whether Tolstoy's story provides the *existentiell* basis for Heidegger's existential analysis, but Heidegger eventually admits that he cannot do without some such *existentiell* ideal. And novels are peculiarly effective at this level. Just as the Greeks recognized that only the poetic could preserve *praxis*, so we need literary texts to show resoluteness and Being-toward-death. Authentic Being remains hidden from others (SZ 260; BT 304). Tolstoy has his own way of telling us this by means of the story itself. The first chapter—first in order of presentation, but last according to the internal time story—shows very clearly that Ivan Ilyich's wife had not understood his deathbed experience. Nor can we read such an understanding into the bloodshot eyes and morose look of his son. Even Gerassim, who it will subsequently emerge is not to be condemned, appears in the first chapter to be part of the conspiracy: "'It's God's will. We shall all come to it some day,' said Gerassim, showing the even white teeth of a peasant—and like a man in the thick of urgent work he briskly opened the front door . . ."[38]

In the context of Book One, when Gerassim responds to one of the departing guests that "It's God's will. We shall all come to it some day,"[39] he could readily have been taken to exhibit a further form of the inauthentic attitude to death, one which refers it to an external power. Only retrospectively do we recognize that Gerassim understood more of death than the others, so that his words—"We shall all come to it some day"—are not another form of the "one dies" but an expression of Being-toward-death. Only subsequently does it emerge that he alone is capable of exhibiting the pity that acts, until in his last moments Ivan too learns it. In this way Tolstoy's reserved introduction of Gerassim serves to confirm the same point that Heidegger made when he suggested that "in accordance with its very meaning, this authentic Being must remain hidden from the Others" (SZ 260; BT 304). It is not only that Ivan's death remains unintelligible to the everyday, commonsense approach of Ivan's wife (cf. SZ 309; BT 357). Until informed by the narrator, the reader is no more able to understand Gerassim than the characters in the story. The novelist as narrator alone can penetrate the veil which conceals a person's attitude toward death. This power of the storyteller to reveal aspects of the fictional characters, which in real life nobody could ever know with certainty about even their most intimate friends, is just one of the ways literature threatens to mislead us in its very attempt to instruct. As we shall see, when it comes to the more extravagant example of what Ivan is thinking at the moment of his death, Tolstoy exhibits a certain reticence.

Close examination of the last chapter shows that Tolstoy offers alongside each other two accounts of Ivan Ilyich's death. In one version, death is the key and, in the second, the emphasis is placed on the Other. The different versions are not offered as alternatives, but that is not to say that they can immediately be dissolved into one. And yet, Tolstoy's doubling of his text at this point, so far as I am aware, has provoked no comment in the vast secondary literature on the story.[40]

The first version is given with reference to the image of a black sack. Tolstoy introduced it in chapter 9 at the point where Ivan had sent his wife away and gone to sleep with his legs resting on Gerassim's shoulders. It seemed to Ivan that he was being thrust into a narrow, deep, black sack. He had both cooperated with and resisted this agonizing process until, at the moment when he burst out of the sack, he regained consciousness. He awoke to find Gerassim still attending him, but he too was now sent away. Alone Ivan cursed God and questioned his life. In the face of his pain he declared, "Here's my sentence. But I am not guilty."[41] The sack has been variously interpreted.[42] It most likely represents death or, more precisely, the dying person's acceptance or refusal of death. So long as Ivan insists that his life has been good, he is unable to accept his death and, in terms of the image, is unable to enter the sack. In chapter 12, the final chapter, Ivan Ilyich is again found resisting being forced into the black sack or black hole: "That very justification of his life held him fast and prevented him from advancing."[43] But the obstacle disappears and death is no longer regarded as an enemy force. "Suddenly some force smote him in the chest and side, making it still harder to breathe; he sank through the hole and there at the bottom was a light."[44] Tolstoy is making the point that Ivan has at last recognized his guilt, which he had previously refused to do.

I have tried to show that Heidegger's account of Being-toward-death cannot be treated in isolation, as has been done all too often. The first chapter of the second division of *Being and Time* leads into a discussion of the connection between Being-guilty and Being-toward-death. This connection, which according to Heidegger must "be elucidated phenomenally" (SZ 305; BT 353), is well illustrated by Tolstoy's story. The shattering of Ivan's everyday attitude takes place in guilt. Not that the guilt arises from the failure to perform some long-recognized duty. Ivan Ilyich at this point ceases to look for past failures or omissions which would serve to explain why he had to suffer this pain. It is at least plausible that his guilt is detached from relationship to any law or "ought" (SZ 283; BT 328), leaving the possibility open that Ivan is guilty *authentically* (SZ 287; BT 333). In order to act, Ivan has to stop being preoccupied with the question of what he had specifically done to make him guilty, just as Heidegger in section 59 passed from this everyday conception of guilt to a formal conception of it (SZ 283; BT 328). "'No, it was all wrong,' he said to himself, 'but no matter.' He could, he could do the right thing. 'But what *is* the right thing?' he asked himself, and abruptly grew quiet."[45] This quiet cannot be understood as a quieting of the screaming which had continued for three long days, for Tolstoy records in the next paragraph that "the dying man was still shrieking desperately."[46] It is a quieting of the internal soliloquy brought on by uncertainty as to what might be the right thing to do. It is the silence of conscience.

However, at this point Tolstoy interrupts the narrative and subjects it to a form of repetition. The details of Ivan's self-questioning are repeated and the questioning is again apparently resolved in a quieting of his thoughts. The transition between the two accounts is marked by the phrase "It was at this very same moment . . ." Here is the text:

This was at the end of the third day, an hour [sic] before his death. At that very moment his schoolboy son had crept into the room and gone up to his father's bedside. The dying man was still shrieking desperately and waving his arms. His hand fell on the child's head. The boy seized it, pressed it to his lips and burst into tears.

It was at this very same moment that Ivan Ilyich had fallen through the hole and caught sight of the light, and it was revealed to him that his life had not been what it ought to have been but that it was still possible to put it right. He asked himself: "But what *is* the right thing?" and grew still, listening. Then he felt that someone was kissing his hand. He opened his eyes and looked at his son.[47]

The same recognition, "It was all wrong," followed by the same question, "But what *is* the right thing?" The same silence and then the discovery of his son. Up to this point there are no important differences between the two accounts, even if some of the details raise the question of whether Tolstoy might have added to the text at some later stage. For example, in the passage just quoted Tolstoy says that these events took place one hour before Ivan's death, but a little later we read that "for those present his agony lasted another two hours."[48] These two unreconcilable accounts of objective time make it tempting to attach the statement that it was one hour before his death to the passage that immediately precedes, it and the statement that it was two hours to the description of his final encounter with his son and his wife. Not that anything is resolved thereby. Both take place "at this very same moment."[49] But it is as if, by what was perhaps no more than a slip of Tolstoy's pen, we can more readily separate two different descriptions of Ivan's changing relation to his own death. One simply marks the transformation of his guilt, while the other seems to refer that transformation to an encounter with his son and his wife. That separation might have been used to mark the difference between what might be called a standard Heideggerian interpretation from a Levinasian one, had I not earlier renounced using Tolstoy's text to stage a confrontation between these two philosophers. Instead, I shall focus on further moments of indeterminacy in the story.

The difference between the two different versions of the events one or two hours before Ivan's death lies in the fact that, whereas the first version offers only an external account of Ivan's recognition of his son at his bedside, the second version goes further by telling the reader what Ivan felt and thought, albeit with a certain reticence on Tolstoy's part. In the second version, Ivan's quietness is only temporary. He finds an answer to the question "But what *is* the right thing?" and he appears to find it by looking at his son and looking at his wife and feeling sorry for them both. Ivan comes to the conclusion that "It will be better for them when I die." He wants to say this but does not have the strength. Instead, he sends his son away and apologizes. "'Take him away . . . sorry for him . . . sorry for you too . . .' He tried to add 'Forgive me' but said 'Forego' and, too weak to correct himself, waved his hand, knowing that whoever was concerned would understand."

Ivan had already come to the conclusion that action was at this point more important than words. "'Besides, why speak, I must act.'" Perhaps the suggestion is that, by apologizing and by asking his son to be taken away, he had in fact acted. Had Ivan simply told those around him what the reader is told about how he felt—that he knew he was a misery to them and that he knew it would be better for them were he to die—he would by contrast have relied only on words. Ivan does not try to explain himself. He tries to do something to make it less painful for them. He is not asking to be understood and in that sense he has chosen solitude.

This concern for action marks a change. Ivan has now learned the lesson that Gerassim seemed to know instinctively: for each person the recognition of mortality—Being-toward-death—should guide his or her actions. The young peasant had earlier given his own death as a reason for going to the assistance of his master: "We shall all of us die, so what's a little trouble?"[50] But Ivan's concern that his son should be spared seeing him in his pain and Ivan's words of apology to both his son and his wife did not satisfy his concern to act. The unease recurred: "He felt full of pity for them, he must do something to make it less painful."[51] The word for pity is *zhalet*. The same word was prominent at the end of chapter 7, when Ivan Ilyich wanted to be pitied as he was pitied when he was ill as a child. Now he feels pity not for himself, but for others.[52] The first thought of those around him at his death was for themselves.[53] Ivan's last thought was not of himself, but of them. He had at the last chosen to live for Others and this meant, in the situation in which he found himself, the acceptance of his own death.

Ivan no longer answered his own question, "What *is* the right thing?" by reference to a conception of his duties, as he had once done.[54] He now finds the answer in the situation which confronts him. He sees his son and wife and responds to them. In responding to their faces he finds his responsibility (cf. SZ 288; BT 334). This is the approach Heidegger also adopted in *Being and Time*, following Aristotle, from whom Heidegger's account of conscience, resoluteness, action, and situation in large part derives. The situation as Ivan now saw it, having looked at his wife and his son, was that he must do something for them: "release them and release himself from this suffering."[55] By focusing on them as well as on himself, his own pain does not disappear, but he is able to *let it be*. And at the same time his habitual fear of death also dis-appears. It is then that Ivan discovers light in place of death, a light which corresponds to that he found at the bottom of the hole in the first account of his recognition and acknowledgment that his life had been wrong.[56] In this way he passes through the hole.

This indeterminacy of the second account in spite of the greater detail Tolstoy provides is highlighted by the confusion which arises when Ivan means to say "*prosti*" (forgive), but only succeeds in uttering the word "*propusti*" (let [me] pass through). Ivan does not even try to correct himself, but he is said to be content in the knowledge that "whoever was concerned would understand."[57] If Ivan was asking for forgiveness from those around him, then he was deceived in thinking he was understood.[58] There is no indication that anyone was aware of Ivan's change of heart. Hence, it is more likely that the reader will think of God at this point, although to do so might simply be another example of what Heidegger called "ontical other-worldly speculation" (SZ 248; BT 292). If Tolstoy does not make the reference more explicit, it is for a reason. Literature too can be more persuasive to the degree that it does not admit its presuppositions.

Many of the problems of interpretation which arise in reading Tolstoy's story lie in the indeterminacy of the final lines of the story. Some of the difficulties already emerged in the examination of the obstacles to Spanos's attempt to establish a correlation between Heidegger's existential account of Being-toward-death and Tolstoy's story. For example, there is the difficulty that Ivan's fear gives way ultimately to joy, not anxiety. That difficulty can perhaps be addressed by observing that Heidegger does indeed give a place to joy: "Along with the sober anxiety which brings us face to face with our individualized potentiality-for-Being, there goes an unshakable joy in this possibility" (SZ 310; BT 358). Similarly, the fact that, in response to a bystander's comment that "it is all over," Ivan utters "in his soul" the words "Death is over. It is no more" need not prove a stumbling block.[59] What is striking is that although it lends itself to a religious reading—in which case it is taken as a reference to the last words of Christ, *consummatum est*[60]—no single interpretation is forced on the reader. Does it indicate an "overcoming of death" of the kind Heidegger condemns as a perversion (SZ 310; BT 357)? Or could it be Tolstoy's way of remarking the impossibility of experiencing death?

So long as our focus is on the story as a work of literature, it is not obvious that we must decide this question. Tolstoy raises the question, leads the reader toward an answer, but holds back from giving an unambiguous answer. The reader has shared in Ivan's preparation for death, but is excluded from his final moments. One of the more striking features of the traditional treatment of literary and philosophical texts is that ambiguity or undecidability is not only tolerated, but often admired in art. By contrast, it has not been acceptable in philosophy, at least for long periods. It might even be suggested that the religious reading of the phrase "Death is over" belongs to the second more concrete account of Ivan's last moments. Similar problems of interpretation arise in connection with the phrase "whoever was concerned would understand" as applied to Ivan's failed attempt to say "forgive" or even "goodbye." It presumably refers to either God or the son, but by virtue of its indeterminacy the way is open for it to be included in a more open reading of the final pages of the book. "The Death of Ivan Ilyich" was the first story Tolstoy published after his conversion.[61] As such, one might have expected it to be more specific in its Christian message, although in that case Heidegger would have had to renounce the story as an example of inauthentic otherworldly speculation.

But why does Tolstoy give what looks like two accounts of the same event? Tolstoy describes the scene and then repeats it in what can most readily be understood as a flashback.[62] If the second account, the flashback, offers a more concrete account this is because it encapsulates certain *existentiell* commitments, whereas the earlier, more reticent version is, by contrast, to be understood as an attempt to withdraw from those ideals of existence. More specifically, the flashback provides the sketch of an answer to the question of why Ivan grows quiet and is able to find light in place of dark. And it seems that such an answer can only be given at the concrete or *existentiell* level. There is thus a remarkable appropriateness to Heidegger's reference to "The Death of Ivan Ilyich," because the final pages of Tolstoy's story struggle in their own way with a similar problem of reticence that faced Heidegger.

Heidegger cannot simply underwrite Tolstoy's account: "The idea of existence which we have posited gives us an outline of the formal structure of the understanding of Dasein and does so in a way which is not binding from an existentiell point of view" (SZ 313; BT 361). Heidegger cannot avoid *existentiell* commitments, but nor is his formal analysis reducible to the one which is operative through his text. It is not a matter of indifference or irrelevance which *existentiell* ideals have influenced his thought and presentation of the existential. And yet, Heidegger's reticence about the ideals of existence governing his analysis serves to protect against the reduction of the formal existential analysis to the *existentiell* level. Nevertheless, this silence left the way open for another ideal—for convenience, I might call it the existentialist ideal—to serve in its place and dominate the reading of his text. Is it a failing by Heidegger's readers that they have inserted an *existentiell* to mask the existential? Or is it not the case that it is impossible to maintain the formalization of the existential without concretization? And, just as the distinction between existential and *existentiell* cannot ultimately be maintained, neither can the distinction between philosophy and literature. On a number of occasions Heidegger commented on how an existential analysis does violence to the everyday and its tranquilized obviousness (SZ 311; BT 359). Is there not here also a basis for an understanding of the violence literary examples perform within philosophy? Such examples—and all examples are in a sense literary—destroy the autonomy and integrity of the philosophical text.

BIBLIOGRAPHY OF SECONDARY LITERATURE CONSULTED ON TOLSTOY'S "THE DEATH OF IVAN ILYICH"

Bartell, James. "The Trauma of Birth in 'The Death of Ivan Ilych': A Therapeutic Reading," *Psychocultural Review* 2, 2(1978), pp. 97–117.

Donnelly, John. "Death and Ivan Ilych," in *Language, Methaphysics, and Death*, edited by John Donnelly. New York: Fordham University, 1978, pp. 116–30.

Jahn, Gary R. "The Role of the Ending in Leo Tolstoi's 'The Death of Ivan Il'ich,'" *Revue Canadienne des Slavistes* 24, 3 (1982), pp. 228–38.

Jankélevitch, Vladimir. "Tolstoi et la mort," in *Sources*. Paris: Seuil, 1984, pp. 23–31.

Kaufmann, Walter. "Existentialism and Death," in *Existentialism, Religion and Death*. New York: New American Library, 1976, pp. 192–218.

———. *Discovering the Mind. Volume 2.* New York: McGraw-Hill, 1980, pp. 209–16.

Kulenkampff, Jens. "'Der Tod des Iwan Iljitsch.' Sterblichkeit und Ethik bei Heidegger und Tolstoi," in *Sterblichkeitserfahrung und Ethikbegründung*, edited by Walter Brüstle and Ludwig Siep. Essen: Verlag Die Blaue Eule, pp. 164–79.

Matual, David. "The Confession as Subtext in 'The Death of Ivan Il'ich,'" *International Fiction Review* 8, 2 (1981), pp. 124–28.

Olney, James, "Experience, Metaphor, and Meaning: 'The Death of Ivan Ilych,'" *Journal of Aesthetics and Art Criticism* 31, 1 (1972), pp. 101–14.

Ovsyaniko-Kulikovsky, D. N. "On Ivan Ilich," in *Tolstoy: The Critical Heritage*, edited by A. V. Knowles. London: Routledge and Kegan Paul, 1978, pp. 419–24.

Pachmuss, Temira. "The Theme of Love and Death in Tolstoy's 'The Death of Ivan Ilyich,'" *American Slavic and East European Review* 20, 1 (1961), pp. 72–83.

Paskow, Alan. "What Do I Fear in Facing my Death?," *Man and World* 8 (1975), pp. 146–56.

Perrett, Roy W. "Tolstoy, Death and the Meaning of Life," *Philosophy* 60 (1985), pp. 231–45.

Rohde, Eric. "Death in Twentieth-Century Fiction," in *Man's Concern with Death*. London: Hodder and Stoughton, 1968, pp. 160–76.

Russell, Robert. "From Individual to Universal: Tolstoy's 'Smert' Ivana Il'icha," *Modern Language Review* 76 (1981), pp. 629–42.

Smyrniw, Walter. "Tolstoy's Depiction of Death in the Context of Recent Studies of the 'Experience of Dying,'" *Canadian Slavonic Papers* 21 (1979), pp. 367–79.

Spanos, William V. "Leo Tolstoy's 'The Death of Ivan Ilych': A Temporal Interpretation," in *De-Structing the Novel: Essays in Applied Postmodern Hermeneutics*, edited by Leo Orr. Troy, N.Y.: The Whitson Publishing Company, 1982, pp. 1–64.

Turner, C. J. G. "The Language of Fiction: Word-clusters in Tolstoy's 'The Death of Ivan Ilyich,'" *Modern Language Review* 65 (1970), pp. 116–21.

Van der Eng, Jan. "The Death of Ivan Il'ic," *Russian Literature* 7 (1979), pp. 159–92.

Wasiolek, Edward. "Tolstoy's 'The Death of Ivan Ilyich' and the Jamesian Fictional Imperatives," *Modern Fiction Studies* 6, 4 (1960–61), pp. 314–24.

———. *Tolstoy's Major Fiction.* Chicago: University of Chicago Press, 1978, pp. 165–79.

Wexelblatt, Robert. "The Higher Parody: Ivan Ilych's Metamorphosis and the Death of Gregor Samsa," *Massachusetts Review* 21 (1980), pp. 601–28.

Williams, Michael V. "Tolstoy's 'The Death of Ivan Ilych': After the Fall," *Studies in Short Fiction* 21 (1984), pp. 229–34.

Wiltshire, John. "The Argument of Ivan Ilyich's Death," *The Critical Review* 24 (1982), pp. 46–54.

6

The Greatness of the Work of Art

In the mid-1930s Heidegger indulged in a certain rhetoric of greatness. The most notorious instance of this rhetoric is the sentence from *An Introduction to Metaphysics* where Heidegger distinguishes "what is today being put about as the philosophy of National Socialism" from "the inner truth and greatness of this movement" (EM 152; IM 199).[1] More revealing—and more disturbing still—are the comments in the Rectoral Address of 1933, where Heidegger declares that there is a "will to greatness" and that the decision between it and the decline which occurs whenever things are just allowed to happen determines the fate of "the march that our people has begun into its future history" (SU 14; HNS 9). Other instances of the rhetoric of greatness could be multiplied,[2] but I will focus on a somewhat more discreet use of it in "The Origin of the Work of Art." The phrase in question is so familiar to everyone that it is readily overlooked. Only as one reads and rereads the text do the puzzles and enigmas to which "The Origin of the Work of Art" gives rise come to settle on the phrase "great art."

At the beginning of the second of the three lectures that constitute the essay, Heidegger observes that, compared with the work, the artist remains inconsequential in great art. Only in passing does he indicate that great art alone is what is under consideration here: "Gerade in der grossen Kunst, und von ihr allein is hier die Rede, bleibt der Künstler gegenüber dem Werk etwas Gleichgültiges, . . ." (H 29; PLT 40). The extent and significance of this restriction is far from clear. How far does this "here"extend? Does the restriction refer to the essay as a whole? Or is it confined to the immediate context of the phrase? From where does Heidegger borrow the concept of "great art" and to what extent does he underwrite it? On the surface, the concept of "great art" belongs to aesthetics, and yet "The Origin of the Work of Art" is allegedly engaged in overcoming the aesthetic tradition. The question of whether Heidegger succeeds in twisting the concept of art free of its metaphysical heritage will prove to be all the more acute when raised with reference to the concept of great art.

Throughout Heidegger's writings the self-evidence which accompanies inherited concepts, simply by virtue of their familiarity, is put in question. It was in those terms that Heidegger introduced the task of the destruction of the history of ontology in *Being and Time* (SZ 21; BT 43). That is why one must be cautious when Heidegger appeals to our familiarity with artworks in an attempt to resolve the problem which threatens to stop the inquiry from ever getting started. At the outset of "The Origin of the Work of Art" Heidegger observes that the question of the origin of the work of art cannot be answered with reference to the artist, because the artist is an artist only by virtue of the work. And yet the work needs the artist. Each needs the other. Furthermore, one cannot turn directly to art, as this in turn exists only in works. Heidegger suggests that we must start from actual works, because that is where art prevails, but he is well aware of the difficulty: "How are we to be certain that we are indeed basing such an examination on artworks, if we do not know beforehand what art is?" (H 8; PLT 18). Heidegger breaks the circle, or rather he is able to embrace it, because "works of art are familiar to everyone" (*Kunstwerke sind jedermann bekannt.*) (H 8; PLT 18). That is why, in order to discover what art is, he begins by posing the question of the work.

The question of the work sets the first part of the essay on a circuitous route. In outline, the question of the work becomes a question of the thingly aspect of the work. Hence, Heidegger attempts to distinguish the prevalent concepts of the thing. Because the thing is often confused with equipment, Heidegger is led to investigate what equipment is. It is only at that point, with Heidegger pursuing a trajectory which threatens to be always postponing the question of art, that, by what is presented somewhat disingenuously as sheer good fortune, something is discovered about the work: "unwittingly, in passing so to speak" (*unversehen, gleichsam beiher*) (H 24; PLT 35). This is because, contrary to the design of the inquiry, which was to proceed via the thingly aspect of the thing to the thingly aspect of the work, the apparent diversion into equipmentality proved to be a shortcut insofar as it was a work that instructed us about equipmentality. Everyone is familiar with equipment, such as a pair of shoes (*Jedermann kennt sie . . . Jedermann weiss, was zum Schuh gehört.*) (H 22; PLT 32–33). It was simply out of convenience that recourse was made to a painting of a pair of shoes. The reader is told that a pictorial representation would help with the description. Only subsequently does it emerge that the painting proved to be more than simply a convenience. The painting allows us to notice the shoe's reliability (*Verlässlichkeit*), something which the wearer of the shoes, the peasant woman in Heidegger's example, knows without being specifically aware of it. Certainly there was no mention of reliability in *Being and Time*. There the Being of equipment was understood to be usefulness, on the basis of an analysis which relied on the obtrusiveness which arises when, for example, the shoes are worn out (H 24–25; PLT 34–35. Cf. SZ 73; BT 103). The shoe's reliability or dependability would never have been discovered without the help of the painting (H 24; PLT 35). Such is the curious itinerary of the first of the three lectures, rendered all the more circuitous when in the third lecture it is discovered that the thingly aspect of the work was rather its earthy character, so that the premise on which the inquiry set out was false (H 57; PLT 69). One suspects that Heidegger's itinerary in the first part of "The Origin of the Work of Art" is governed in large measure by a need to redress the discussion of readiness to hand in *Being and Time*, in preparation for the revision of the concept of world, now that it is to be juxtaposed with that of the earth.

The elaborate trajectory I have just rehearsed was not part of the original outline of the essay. The discussion of Van Gogh's painting and of the different concepts of the thing in the first part of "The Origin of the Work of Art" were added to the text only when the original lecture was expanded into three lectures during 1936. The three lectures were delivered in Frankfurt in November and December 1936, and they form the basis of the edition published in 1950 in *Holzwege* with the addition of an epilogue.[3] Two earlier versions of the lecture have now been made available, and this makes it possible to reread the familiar version with fresh eyes. In 1987 an unauthorized edition of the original lecture was published in France (OA). This is the version Heidegger delivered in Freiburg on 13 November 1935, a full year before the Frankfurt version. Heidegger repeated it in Zurich in January 1936. The publication of this text as "the first version" seems to have provoked the editors of the Heidegger *Gesamtausgabe* into releasing an undated, but clearly earlier, version under the title "Vom Ursprung des Kunstwerks. Erste Ausarbeitung" (HS).

A comparison of the three versions—which I will refer to as the first draft, the Freiburg lecture, and the Frankfurt lectures respectively—helps to reveal the dynamic of Heidegger's questioning and allows certain neglected features of the text to be highlighted. Furthermore, the differences between the three versions show Heidegger negotiating—or perhaps rather evading—the political realities of his time. However, even if I succeed in showing that there is an unsavory political dimension to the essay, this does not mean that the essay can simply be dismissed. It is not difficult to show that a language is contaminated, especially when that serves to restrict a text to a monotonous or monological reading, one which deprives the text of any truth it might convey. However, before judging Heidegger's political stance on the basis of such an analysis, one would need to compare Heidegger's language not just with the Nazi discourses on art of the same period, but also with other discourses on art.

To take just one example, it is not enough to show that Heidegger shares the Nazis' enthusiasm for the word *Volk*, not least because it was already a common term in German discussions of art prior to the twentieth century. It is instructive in this context to recall Gadamer's observations in an essay written in 1966 on "The Universality of the Hermeneutical Problem." At one point in the essay Gadamer focuses on the experience of the alienation of aesthetic consciousness which arises when one judges works of art on the basis of their aesthetic quality. He observes that the problem had already been recognized in a particularly distorted form when National Socialist politics of art, "as a means to its own ends, tried to criticize formalism by arguing that art is bound to a people."[4] Gadamer did not mention Heidegger by name, nor is there any indication there or elsewhere that he would subsume Heidegger's essay under this label, but what he went on to say would apply perfectly well to "The Origin of the Work of Art." "Despite its misuse by the National Socialists, we cannot deny that the idea of art being bound to a people involves a real insight. A genuine artistic creation stands within a particular community, and such a community is always distinguishable from the cultured society that is informed and terrorized by art criticism." The notion of the *Volk* has tended to play only a minor role in the interpretation of "The Origin of the Work of Art." Gadamer fails to mention it in his introduction to the Reclam edition of Heidegger's essay.[5] It is possible that the word has been ignored, wittingly or not, out of a certain sensitivity, an attempt to safeguard Heidegger's text from being reduced to an address to the German people, which in certain respects is exactly what it was—even when delivered to the student body at Zurich University. Far from it being the case that Heidegger retreated into a discussion of art in consequence of his political disillusionment, as used to be said on occasion, the texts on art and poetry have a strong political component.[6] Indeed, to neglect the political dimension of Heidegger's text is to risk restricting "The Origin of the Work of Art" to the realm of aesthetic alienation, instead of recognizing it as a response to aesthetic alienation.

The recently published *Beiträge zur Philosophie* confirms that Heidegger's essay belongs to the overcoming of aesthetics. In a section entitled "'Metaphysics' and the Origin of the Work of Art" Heidegger writes that "The question [of the origin of the work of art] stands in innermost connection with the task of the overcoming of aesthetics and that means at the same time of a specific account of beings as objectively representable" (GA 65, 503). It is clear that Heidegger means "The Origin of the Work of Art" to put aesthetics radically into question, but this introduces a difficulty. Is it not possible that the concept of art is irretrievably marked by aesthetics? That Heidegger is engaged in a radical questioning of the concept of art is confirmed by *An Introduction to Metaphysics*. In the context of his statement that for us moderns the beautiful is what reposes and relaxes, such that art is a matter for pastry cooks, he says, "We must procure for the word 'art' and that which it names a new content on the basis of an original and recaptured basic position to Being" (EM 101; IM 132): "Wir müssen dem Wort 'Kunst' und dem, was es nennen will, aus einer ursprünglich wiedergewonnen Grundstellung zum Sein einen neuem Gehalt verschaffen." The question is how far "The Origin of the Work of Art" accomplishes this task. When Heidegger answers the question of the origin of the work of art by designating art to be an origin, has he given the concept of art a new content? Does reliance on the familiarity of art, and specifically of great art, not imply a certain reliance on aesthetics?

The relation between great art and aesthetics is specifically explored by Heidegger in his account of the "Six Basic Developments of the History of Aesthetics" in the first of the lecture courses on Nietzsche. Heidegger offers this history in preparation for a reading of Nietzsche, but it is an indispensable accompaniment to "The Origin of the Work of Art," especially as it belongs to the same period as the Frankfurt version of the lectures. The text explores the relation between the history of the essence of aesthetics and the history of the essence of art (NI 94; Ni 79). The correlation Heidegger establishes across the six stages is an extraordinary one. Prior to metaphysics, there is great art, but there is as yet no aesthetics. Only when great art comes to an end, at the time of Plato and Aristotle, does aesthetics begin. The third stage, which corresponds to modernity, is characterized by the formation of a dominant aesthetics in terms of *aesthesis*. It is accompanied by the decline of great art. In Hegel, the fourth stage, aesthetics achieves its greatest possible height. Meanwhile, great art comes to an end. Nevertheless, the history has two further stages to run. The fifth stage is referred to Wagner and the collective artwork, which marks the dissolution of sheer feeling and which, in its effects, is the opposite of great art. Aesthetics becomes psychology in the manner of the natural sciences, and at the same time art history develops. Finally, aesthetics is thought to an end by Nietzsche in the physiology of art. Heidegger himself does not here directly underwrite the idea, which he attributes to Nietzsche, of art as the countermovement of nihilism, although it could be argued that he does so in "The Question concerning Technology."

It might seem that in this history art takes an inordinate time to die and suffers many false deaths in the process, like the hero or heroine of a Victorian melodrama. In other respects, however, this story of decline is typically Heideggerian, even mirroring in its stages Heidegger's account of the history of the essence of truth (cf. H 68; PLT 81). But in this case Heidegger seems to have been more determined than ever to have history convey a moral. Art and aesthetics are not compatible. Aesthetics prospers as art declines. Aesthetics is great when it tells what great art used to be.

Heidegger constructs this history from a framework borrowed largely from Hegel, while using the inclusion of Nietzsche to subvert the Hegelian starting point.[7] Although Hegel is presented as the *Vollendung* or completion of aesthetics, Heidegger will later in the lecture course acknowledge that Nietzsche is its extreme form (NI 152; Ni 129). Great art is defined not on the basis of aesthetic judgments concerning the relative merits of different artistic styles but, in Hegel's phrase, as an "absolute need" (NI 100-01; Ni 84-85). Its task, in Heidegger's paraphrase of Hegel, is to be "the definite fashioner and preserver of the absolute" (NI 108; Ni 90). In Heidegger's own language, great art is "the definitive formulation and preservation of beings as a whole" (NI 106; Ni 89). But Hegel is clear that in these terms, the work performed by great art passed to religion and finally to philosophy. That is the meaning of the famous sentence, "Art is and remains for us, on the side of its highest vocation, something past."[8]

Heidegger's sketch of the history of art and aesthetics does nothing to ease the suspicion that surrounds the quest for a non-metaphysical concept of art. This is because Heidegger is hampered by the lack of a Greek concept of art. The Greek word *techne* is associated with the second stage of the history of art and aesthetics, not its first stage, which is where Heidegger locates great art. When in "The Origin of the Work of Art" Heidegger appeals to *techne*, it is in the context of his observation that it is difficult to distinguish the essential features which separate the creation of works from the making of equipment, an observation which looks as if it might threaten his attempt to separate the two. To compound the difficulty he recalls the fact that the Greeks not only used the same word for both art and craft, they did not distinguish between craftsmen and artists. Indeed, both translations of *techne*, "art" and "craft," are misleading: *techne* is a form of knowing. Heidegger's redetermination of *techne* as *Wissen*, a "knowing which supports and conducts every irruption into the midst of beings" (NI 97; Ni 81), is something on which he insists in a number of different contexts. But Heidegger fails to address the question of why the Greeks, who belonged to the time of great art and who allegedly "understood something about works of art" (H 47; PLT 59), did not leave in their language any mark of the distinction between the artwork and equipment.

Nevertheless, Heidegger does give an account of how within metaphysics the same conceptuality, the conceptuality of production—the notion of *eidos* in Plato, the notions of form and matter in Aristotle—are applied indiscriminately to works of art and to equipment. "All reflection on art and the artwork, all art theory and aesthetics since the Greeks stands until now under a remarkable fatality. With the Greeks (Plato and Aristotle) reflection on art employed the characterization of the artwork as a thing which was made, that is, a work of equipment [*Zeugwerk*]. Thereby the artwork is at first, and that means here in its actual Being, formed matter" (OA 52). Elsewhere Heidegger explains that the distinction between matter and form arose in the realm of manufacture and was subsequently transferred to that of art (NI 98; Ni 82). That metaphysics blocks our access to the work as work is an idea easily accommodated within a Heideggerian framework. What is hard to reconcile with it is the apparent lack of any recognition among the Greeks of the kind of distinction between work and equipment Heidegger seeks. In contrast to the broad conception of *techne* employed by the Greeks, he wants a highly restricted conception of great art. This does nothing to ease the suspicion that Heidegger's conception of art is trading off the very aesthetics which it is supposed to question. It seems that at various junctures Heidegger's discussion relies precisely on the kind of self-evidence which a thoroughgoing destruction is supposed to put in question (cf. H 12; PLT 22).

How else is one to understand the absence from "The Origin of the Work of Art" of any sentence which would say for art what Heidegger said for religion in his lectures on Heraclitus in the summer of 1943: "There is no Greek religion at all" (GA 55, 13)? This is of particular importance given Heidegger's tendency to equate what is Greek with what is fundamental and to relegate what the Greeks lacked to the realm of the derivative and deficient. For Heidegger, religion, both as word and thing, is Roman. Why does Heidegger not say "There is no Greek art at all"? This would not commit him to saying that there is no Greek tragedy, no Greek music, no Greek dance, and so on. It would simply acknowledge that the Greeks did not share the fairly recent sense that these activities have something in common which can be designated art. In fact, he seems to assume the collectivity of the fine arts, as when he refers to the way the Greeks accorded a primacy to poetry among the arts (NI 192–93; Ni 164–65).[9] The evidence is rather that they lacked that conception of the arts which would lead one to juxtapose poetry and, for example, architecture or music. In other words, Heidegger appears to take the modern system of *les belles artes* for granted and incorporates it into his conception of art.[10]

Although Heidegger can be faulted for the way he approaches the concept of art, he is more circumspect in his approach to the artwork itself. Because metaphysics serves to obstruct access to the work as work, the question of the accessibility of the work is central to Heidegger's attempt to overcome aesthetics. It is the problem with which Heidegger begins the draft version of "The Origin of the Work of Art," just as it introduces "The Work and Truth," which is the second of the three lectures constituting the Frankfurt version. Heidegger repeats in this context the observation that the usual or inherited concepts of the thing have blocked our access to the work-being of the work. He suggests that to gain access to the work it is necessary to remove it from all relations to everything else. This presumably means that the work should not be referred to anything other than itself. For example, the work is not to be referred to the artist. This proposal is made to sound the most natural way to proceed. Perhaps it would have been prior to the publication of *Being and Time*, where the analysis in sections 15 to 18 showed that only when things are approached in their interconnection can one discover the relational structure which exhibits the readiness to hand of equipment. This suggests that Heidegger is being disingenuous when he of all people poses the question of the self-subsistence (*Insichselbststehen*) of the work in precisely these terms. Nevertheless, it proves to be a highly convenient way of focusing on the context in which art appears, and, importantly, given Heidegger's remarkable neglect of this aspect elsewhere in the essay, quite explicitly with reference to equipment (H 21; PLT 32), it introduces an historico-cultural perspective. Artworks have been torn out of their own space to be exhibited in museums. Indeed, it often seems that the museum, as the place where art is exhibited, determines for the public what is and what is not art. A short essay on Raphael's *Sixtina*, written in 1955, develops the point at greater length: "Wherever this picture may yet be 'exhibited' in future, it has lost its place [*Ort*]. That it might unfold its own essence incipiently, that is to say, that it might itself determine its place, remains denied to it. Transformed in its essence as artwork, the picture wanders into the alien. Presentation in a museum levels everything into the indifference of 'exhibition.' In an exhibition there are only sites, but no places" (GA 13, 120). The exhibition, the museum, corresponds in respect of location to the time of aesthetics.

Even if a work remains in its original location, as usually happens with architectural works, once the world of the work has perished, nothing can be done to restore it. As a result of the withdrawal and decay of its world, the works are no longer works. They are past (H 30; PLT 41. Also OA 22). Although Heidegger does not say *vergangenes* but *Gewesenen*, the reference to Hegel's claim about the past character of art is clear. The self-subsistence of the work has fled. It is not simply that the art industry combines with the ordinary inherited concept of the thing to obstruct our access to the work as work, which might suggest that the work-being of the work remained concealed but intact. No amount of textual emendation, no extensive critical apparatus, can restore Sophocles' text to its own world and so let it be a work once more.

The work does not belong to the museum world, the world documented by historians, or the world of the art industry. It belongs to the world it opens up by itself. Heidegger illustrates the working of art with the following example: "The temple, in its standing there, first gives to things their look and to men their outlook on themselves." He immediately adds, "This view remains open as long as the work is a work, as long as the god has not fled from it." With the flight of the god from the temple, the self-subsistence of the work has fled with it (H 30; PLT 41). If Heidegger had indeed visited "the remains of a Greek temple," for example that at Paestum, he would have found not a place but a site, or in the words of *Being and Time* simply "a bit of the past . . . still in the present" (SZ 378; BT 430).

This raises the question of Heidegger's own access to the work. How did he arrive at his description of the temple? Can he account for his text at this point? He does at one point suggest that a recollection (*Erinnerung*) of the work can bring back what is past even to the point where such a recollection might offer the work a place from which to shape history. Nevertheless, this is to be distinguished from the case "where the work is preserved in the truth that happens by the work itself" (H 56; PLT 68). The draft version makes clear what is at issue in this distinction. Historical recollection may enable us to experience the temple at Paestum or the cathedral at Bamburg as an "expression" of their respective ages. They testify to the previous splendor and power of a people, but that does not mean that they are still works in Heidegger's sense. "Our 'glorious German cathedrals' can be an 'inspiration' to us. And yet—world decline and world withdrawal have broken their workbeing" (HS 7). In other words, because of world withdrawal, the Germans of the 1930s should not look to German cathedrals to *do* the work of art. Being in flight, being away (*Wegsein*) remains at hand (*vorhanden*) in the work in such a way that world decline could be said to belong to the work (HS 10). There are no immortal works of art (H 66; PLT 79). On this view great art is from its outset always dying.

The world of the temple, like the world of Raphael's *Sixtina*, has withdrawn. This shifts attention to Heidegger's other examples, most notably the poems of Hölderlin and Van Gogh's painting of the shoes. Heidegger at one point in "The Origin of the Work of Art" establishes a clear parallel between the temple and the Van Gogh painting. "Truth happens" in both. One cannot distinguish the two cases by suggesting that Van Gogh's painting works only within the limited sphere of disclosing the equipmentality of equipment, "what the equipment . . . is in truth" (H 25; PLT 36), whereas in the case of the temple "beings as a whole are brought into unconcealment" (H 44; PLT 56). Heidegger in the second Frankfurt lecture is quite explicit that the truth of the Van Gogh painting cannot be so restricted. Truth happens in Van Gogh's painting in such a way that "that which is as a whole—world and earth in their counterplay—attains to unconcealedness" (H 44; PLT 56): the earth to which the shoes as equipment belong and the world of the peasant woman which protects it (H 23; PLT 34). It would seem, therefore, that if the temple was great art in its time, the Van Gogh painting must also qualify as great art. Similarly, the role Heidegger gives to Hölderlin, particularly in the first two versions of "The Origin of the Work of Art" and in the 1934/35 lecture course, would seem to warrant a similar status for his poetry (GA 39). But how could this be reconciled with the sketch of the history of art and aesthetics given in the Nietzsche lectures, where Heidegger seems to accept Hegel's claim that "art is and remains for us, on the side of its highest vocation, something past"? And, above all, if Hölderlin's poems and Van Gogh's painting were so clearly great art, what sense could one make of the questioning in which "The Origin of the Work of Art" culminates, particularly its final version? One would have to suppose that these questions were simply rhetorical, even false.[11]

All three versions of the lecture pose the question of how far and why art still exists. Contrasting the different versions, it seems that Heidegger does not proceed toward an answer so much as he succeeds in placing his initial answer in question. When in the draft Heidegger asks if truth as "the openness of the there" must happen in the way that it arises in the origin as art, he gives a relatively unambiguous response. Because "truth is essentially earthy," then "the work, that is art, is necessary for the happening of truth" (HS 21). It hardly needs to be emphasized that this focus on the unique status of art contrasts with the recognition in both the Freiburg and Frankfurt versions that there are other ways in which truth might happen: the founding of the political state, the questions and sayings of the thinker, and so on (OA 44. H 50; PLT 61).[12] This establishes a clear difference between the draft and the subsequent versions that is not simply a matter of omissions.

Even so, it is tempting to refer this difference to an omission. What intervenes between the draft and the lectures Heidegger delivered at Freiburg and at Frankfurt is, at least on the surface, Hegel. The Freiburg version culminates in a discussion of Hegel's statements about the past character of art, and while the *Holzwege* text relegates the explicit discussion of Hegel to an epilogue, which presumably means that it was not included in the lectures as delivered, it can be shown that Hegel's discussion of art permeates the conclusion of the main body of the text. Nothing better marks the intervention of Hegel than the definition of great art to be found in the different versions. I have already noted how in *The Will to Power as Art* Heidegger explicitly adopts the Hegelian definition, which is then adopted in the Freiburg lecture as well as the Frankfurt lectures. This is not the case in the first version of "The Origin of the Work of Art," where great art is characterized very differently. According to the draft, art is made great not only by its power of unfolding, its being an origin, but also by its related power to destroy (*Zerstörung*). Specifically, great art destroys the *Publikum* (HS 8). This constitutes the political agenda of Heidegger's discussion of art, which in the *Holzwege* version is sufficiently discreet to have allowed most readers of this essay, including myself, to have downplayed it until recently. For Heidegger, art destroys the public to form a people. In Germany in the 1930s nothing could have been more politically charged.

The crucial discussion is found in the final paragraphs of each of the three different versions. Although they use the same terms and so look remarkably similar, they point in different directions. What they share is the distinction between, on the one hand, an art which is an origin (*Ursprung*) and as such a *Vorsprung*, and, on the other hand, an art which remains a mere supplement (*Nachtrag*), a routine cultural phenomenon. What has to be decided, according to Heidegger, is whether art is to remain something secondary, as happens when it is conceived in terms of expression and elucidated further in terms of such concepts as embellishment, entertainment, recreation, and edification; or whether art is to be an instigator of our history (*ein stiftender Vorsprung in unsere Geschichte*) (HS 22). This distinction serves as a reinscription of the distinction between great art and subsidiary forms of art, although it remains to be seen how radical a reinscription it is.

All three versions also use the language of decision, but in the draft the connection is much closer to the kind of decision to which Heidegger called the German people in the Rectoral Address, just as the idea of art as an instigator of our history echoes what he calls in the same place "the march that our people has begun into its future history." When Heidegger asks whether or not we are in the neighborhood of the essence of art as origin, it seems clear, even if he does not spell it out, that "we" means the German people. And when he says that clarity about who we are and who we are not already constitutes the decisive leap into the neighborhood of the origin, one can at least provisionally understand this as a question about whether the Germans are to be a *Publikum* or a *Volk*. The stridency of the draft means that Heidegger left relatively undeveloped any doubts he might have had about whether the German people would take the path he was laying out for them. Instead, there was a polemical tone about the draft, found also in the Hölderlin lectures from the same period, and in both cases it was directed against the expression theory of art that he associated with Erwin G. Kolbenheyer, Oswald Spengler, and the racist ideologue Alfred Rosenberg, and which was widely prevalent at the time (GA 39, 26–27; HS 17–18). Although nothing is spelled out, the implication is that by combatting the philosophy of art as expression, Heidegger is preparing for the time when the Germans would be ready to choose their destiny. So long as art was restricted to being a form of expression, the public might be inspired, for example, by a German cathedral, but a people would never come to be founded.

The brief discussion of Hölderlin in the draft exhibits the same degree of conviction that can be found in the 1934/35 lecture course on Hölderlin.

Hölderlin institutes German Being (*Seyn*) by projecting it into the most distant future (GA 39, 220). Heidegger is quite explicit about the political significance of this conviction. To side with Hölderlin is "politics" in the highest and most authentic sense, to the point that one no longer has any need to talk about the "political" (GA 39, 214). That Hölderlin is not yet a force in the history of the German people simply means that he must become one. Similarly, in the draft of "The Origin of the Work of Art" Hölderlin's poetry is introduced as "the untrodden center" of the world and earth of the German people, where their great decisions are held in reserve (HS 15). The poems may scarcely be attended to, but they are more actual in the language of the German people than all the theater, cinema, and verse in circulation. The draft ends with a brief quotation from Hölderlin's "Die Wanderung," which although its meaning is not explicated is said to provide the key to what precedes it.

> Schwer verlässt,
> Was nahe dem Ursprung wohnet, den Ort.
>
> Hard it is,
> For what dwells near the origin, to leave its place.

How Heidegger meant these lines to be understood is not easily decided. The context suggests that the focus falls on knowing whether or not we dwell near the origin and, if we do, the manner in which we stay in proximity to the work as the only place where truth happens (HS 21).

The Freiburg lecture puts in question what the draft had presupposed by asking whether there must always be art and a work for truth to happen (OA 44). Heidegger himself acknowledges this question to be a turning point in the essay. Whereas the draft insisted that there must be a work for there to be truth, the Freiburg version says only that if there is to be a happening of truth of the kind that one finds in art, there must be a work (OA 42). In other words, as already noted, art as a setting into work is now presented as only one of the ways in which truth happens. The result is that when in the Freiburg lecture Heidegger returns to the themes found at the end of the draft, the focus of the investigation has undergone a decisive shift. The question has now become whether there is great art any longer and, indeed, whether there could still be great art. That is to say, it is no longer a question of whether art is an origin, but whether it can be an origin again, and not just the accompaniment or supplement it has become. In this context Heidegger again emphasizes the transitory character of art. Great art is never timely. An art is great if it sets into a work *the* truth which is to become the standard for a period (OA 48). That is to say, an artwork is great for a specific time, but only for a time.

The question of whether art itself is destined to remain only a supplementary announcement is posed in terms of Hegel's pronouncements of the past character of art. Heidegger agrees with Hegel that we no longer have any absolute need to present a content in the form of art, but Heidegger during the course of the lecture disputed Hegel's conviction that art is presentation (OA 52). So Heidegger says that a final decision about Hegel's judgment is still awaited. This decision, however, is not to be confused with the judgments of a critic or an art historian who might inform us about the quality and originality of certain works.[13] It is a "spiritual decision" in which a people determines who they are. Or, rather, as Heidegger is addressing the Germans, the question is that of "who *we* are." As in the draft, the role of the thinker is not clearly elaborated, but Heidegger's growing clarity about the nature of the decision now makes it possible for him to specify that a people's knowledge of what the artwork could and must be in their historical existence contributes to that decision. Presumably the thinker contributes to the people's knowledge of what the work can do, through delivering lectures like "The Origin of the Work of Art."

The Frankfurt lectures can be read as taking a stage further the transformation in the questioning which occurred between the draft and the Freiburg lecture. At the end of the Frankfurt lectures Heidegger is quite explicit that the question of the essence of art, the question of the origin of the work of art, is to be displaced by a more genuine questioning (H 65; PLT 78). The rhetoric of these closing pages is striking. Heidegger's questions follow after a series of assertions lasting several pages. Never had Heidegger been more assertive in his discussions on art and never was he to be so questioning. The question of what art is, such that it could properly be called an origin (H 58; PLT 71), has changed to become the question of whether art is or is not an origin in our historical existence, the question of whether and under what conditions it can and must be an origin (H 65; PLT 78). That is to say, even though the references to Hegel were relegated to the Epilogue, the question of the past character of great art governs the inquiry.

The question of the past character of art or, one might say, the question of the coming poets, dominates the inquiry as it becomes more enigmatic for Heidegger. As Heidegger insists in the Epilogue, he does not claim to solve the riddle of art (H 66; PLT 79). And as he says in the Addendum, written in 1956 and first included in the Reclam edition of 1960, "What art may be is one of the questions to which no answers are given in the essay" (UK 99; PLT 86). Given the political agenda of the draft, in keeping with the explicitly acknowledged politics of the Hölderlin lectures, it is no surprise to find that this change in tone reflects a change in the relation between the thinker and the people. In the draft version the thinker is not named. What matters is clarity about "who we are and who we are not," because such clarity is "already the decisive leap into the neighborhood of the origin" (HS 22). The question "Who are we?" as a question addressed to the people had been developed in the first Hölderlin course (GA 39, 48–59). Heidegger acknowledges the time of this question as the time of the poet, the thinker, and the founder of the state insofar as they found the historical existence of a people (GA 39, 51). But the draft version of "The Origin of the Work of Art" focuses only on the relation of the poet to the decision of the people. When, in the Freiburg version, Heidegger emphasizes that this decision "can only be *prepared for by long work*," it is possible to recognize this preparation as the contribution of the thinker, even though the thinker is still not named in this context. What is made clear in this version is how meditation on art since Plato and Aristotle, particularly in its form as "art theory," has proved to be an obstacle to a proper posing of the question of who we are. But only in the Frankfurt lectures, where the question of who we are is not explicitly posed, does the "we" become problematic. It becomes problematic to the extent that Heidegger seems unable to control it.

Alongside the "we" of the German people is the "we" of the thinker, the one who meditates on art: "We ask about the essence of art. Why do we ask in this way? We ask in this way in order to be able to ask more genuinely whether art is or is not an origin in our historical existence, whether and under what conditions it must be an origin" (H 65; PLT 78). In the last of these sentences a transition is made from the "we" of Heidegger, the "we" of the thinker, to the "we" of "our historical existence" as a people. This transition to the "we" of the people is confirmed three sentences later when Heidegger asks, "Are we in our existence historically at the origin? Do we know, which means do we give heed to, the essence of the origin? Or, in our relation to art, do we still merely make appeal to a cultivated acquaintance with the past?" The identity of the people is made explicit when Heidegger, returning to the quotation from Hölderlin with which the draft version had also ended, acknowledges that the poet's work "still confronts the Germans as a test to be stood."

The lines from Hölderlin themselves no longer convey the same sense that they had in the draft. The context is no longer that of the question of why truth has to happen as art and the emphasis is no longer on dwelling near the origin. By the time that one reads in the Frankfurt version

> Schwer verlässt
> was nahe dem Ursprung wohnet, den Ort.

the emphasis has shifted to the oppressiveness of this departure from art as the place of origin. The earlier stridency with which Heidegger had challenged the theory that German art is an "expression" of the people (HS 18) has been replaced by a certain *Schwermut*, or melancholy, which matches the isolation that the thinker now experiences in his meditation on art. Is it a mistake to hear in this change of mood Heidegger's growing awareness of his political isolation? Does not a space open up between the thinker and the people precisely as Heidegger's recognizes that he was not to be given the role in determining the direction of the Nazi Party that he had projected for himself?

In all three versions importance had been attached to a knowing which was not theoretical but the site of the decision about art. Only in the third version was this knowing specifically associated with meditation on art and thus with the thinker. The thinker's role was specified again in 1943 when Heidegger wrote, "For now there must be thinkers in advance, so that the word of the poets may be taken up" (EHD 30). The thinker prepares a space for the work, a path for the creators, and quarters for the preservers (H 65; PLT 78). The coming preservers are an historical people (H 62; PLT 75), whose knowing lets the work be a work and maintains its self-subsistence (H 55; PLT 68). Although Heidegger fails to acknowledge it fully in his text, the "we" becomes as enigmatic as the work of art. Heidegger for the most part writes of the Germans as this thrown people, but the Germans in this sense are no more than a public who fail to recognize their poet. The German people that Hölderlin's poetry addresses are yet to be constituted. However marked the different versions of "The Origin of the Work of Art" might be with a certain political rhetoric, which betrays Heidegger's still shocking involvement with the Nazi Party, he himself experiences the untimeliness of this thinking, a non-synchronicity between his audience as he addressed them and as they heard him—as in the famous "Become who you are." Insofar as Heidegger forced the issue and assumed the existence of the audience only the artwork could open up, he in a sense became part of the art industry, perhaps even the Nazi machine. At other times he was more sensitive: "We do not want to make Hölderlin relevant to our time but, on the contrary, we want to bring ourselves and those who are coming under the measure of the poet" (GA 39, 4).

Perhaps the enigma of whether Van Gogh's painting of the shoes is great art or not shares in the uncertainty created by the political context. It would seem that the Van Gogh painting is supplementary art, rather than great art. That is to say, it is a work, but not an origin. It expresses a world rather than instituting one. In keeping with this one might note that, although there was a time when the people in Greece who lived in the shadow of the temple relied upon the temple, the peasant woman depends on her shoes, not the painting. However, simply to see the issue in these terms is to ignore the political component of Heidegger's discussion that the present reading of "The Origin of the Work of Art" has brought to the surface. For Heidegger, the political meaning of the Van Gogh painting can be seen in *An Introduction to Metaphysics*, where it is clear that he is doing more than evoking a world already in place or threatening to disappear. Heidegger described the painting in this pastoral passage: "As to what is in the picture, you are immediately alone with it as though you yourself were making your way wearily homeward with your hoe on an evening in late fall after the last potato fires have died down" (EM 27; IM 35). One is tempted to ask further about this way of "reading" paintings whereby one projects oneself into the world it represents, but more urgent is the question of whether the picture is not being evoked by Heidegger—according to the notorious phrase Heidegger apparently added to the lecture course later—as part of the encounter between global technology and modern man (EM 152; IM 199). It seems that Heidegger would have liked the painting to have been not just an expression of a culture which had had its time. He wanted it to be a still untimely work of great art, one whose preservers were awaited. In that case the question of whether the Van Gogh painting warranted the title great art, in the all-important sense of helping a people determine who they are, was still undecided in 1936, so far as Heidegger was concerned. It was undecidable by the thinker at the time because the answer would come only when and if the public made their decision to become a *Volk* in the requisite sense, a *Volk* living from the earth. It was, for Heidegger at that time, no doubt also a question about the future direction of National Socialism. Hence, the introduction has a melancholic mood. By the same token, it was not so much for Heidegger himself but for the people to decide. It is a question of whether or not art would again become "an essential and necessary way in which truth happens in a decisive way for our historical Dasein" (OA 54; H 67; PLT 80).

This third version is not the last version of the closing pages of "The Origin of the Work of Art," even if one takes into account the Epilogue and the Addendum. Once one recognizes the importance of the issue of the dominance of technology and "the spiritual decline of the earth" (EM 29; IM 37–38) operative in "The Origin of the Work of Art," it quickly becomes apparent that the last two pages of "The Question concerning Technology," a text known in a version dating from 1953 (VA 42–44; QT 48–49),[14] represent what was at least Heidegger's fourth attempt to write a conclusion to "The Origin of the Work of Art." Heidegger's discussion moves through at least five stages, which recapitulate, supplement, and revise the essay of almost 20 years before. The discussion starts with the ambiguity of the word *techne*. In "The Origin of the Work of Art" its breadth seemed to constitute an obstacle to Heidegger's attempt to mark the difference between the artwork and equipment. In "The Question concerning Technology" this very problem seems to provide the basis for addressing the challenge of technology. Hence, Heidegger's second step is to recall that when the arts were at their highest level, they not only bore the modest name *techne*, but were understood in terms of *poiesis* as revealing. Heidegger's third step is to understand the revealing of *poiesis* as poetical. Specific reference to *poiesis* was absent from "The Origin of the Work of Art," but the privilege given to poetry within the arts can be found in all three versions of the essay.[15] In "The Question concerning Technology" Heidegger relates art and *poiesis* by looking to the fine arts in their poetic revealing to awaken anew and found our vision of and trust in that which grants (VA 43; QT 35). Heidegger turns to art not because of its power to destroy, nor because of its radical difference from the technological order. It is the proximity between art and technology, between the work and equipment, which opens the possibility that art might offer an essential meditation upon and a decisive confrontation with technology. The lack among the Greeks of a concept of art clearly marked off from other forms of *poiesis* is now used to advantage, although it has to be said that the reference to "the fine arts" suggests that the concept of art has still not been submitted to an adequate historical destruction.

The question of the people, the question of who we are, is no longer the issue. In a fourth step, Heidegger passes directly to the question of whether there may or may not be some rescue from the entrenchment of technology. And the decisive thought guiding the question is again Hölderlin's.

> Wo aber Gefahr ist, wächst
> Das Rettende auch.
>
> Where the danger is, that which rescues
> burgeons too.

So far as the essay's response to technology is concerned, the impact of this quotation cannot be overemphasized, particularly when placed in the context of the history of metaphysics that Heidegger had developed earlier in the essay and elsewhere.[16] Strikingly, the context is that of the end of philosophy, thought not as Hegel thought the consummation of philosophy, but more as Hegel thought the past character of art. Heidegger looks not to philosophy as such, which has in a sense exhausted its possibilities, but to the dialogue of thinking with poetizing, as evidenced by the appeal to Hölderlin.

The future of art remains a question in "The Origin of the Work of Art," just as in "The Question concerning Technology" the future of technology is left open. But what of art in the later essay? In the closing pages of "The Question concerning Technology" Heidegger continued the task of withdrawing the politically charged vocabulary that had marked the draft of "The Origin of the Work of Art" and which he had already begun to sanitize in the Freiburg and Frankfurt versions.[17] He omitted all reference to the *Volk*, to decision, and to "great art" as such. Heidegger found a way of continuing his confrontation with technology away from the nightmare of National Socialist politics. But meanwhile the question that "The Origin of the Work of Art" left open, the question of whether there may yet be art (UK 99; PLT 86), appears no longer to be in question.[18] The fate of technology may not have been decided, but Hölderlin's authority as "the poet" is submitted neither to the people nor apparently to any other kind of future for decision. In other words, Heidegger came to terms with his disastrous political involvement only by allowing himself to turn his back not just on politics but "on the people," a phrase which was admittedly almost always dangerous on his lips, as it usually meant for him *the* people, the Germans. In consequence, the successive rewriting of "The Origin of the Work of Art" in 1935 and 1936—through even to 1953—leaves a question as to whether the mutual isolation of the poet and the thinker in the 1950s did not mark a return to a form of aestheticism. Perhaps Heidegger should have persisted with the question "Who are we?"—even, perhaps especially, in the *absence* of an answer—whereas he appears to have simply displaced the question of the German people into that of the German language. A discussion of art addressed to *the* people justifiably provokes suspicion. But to reject "The Origin of the Work of Art" for a philosophy of art that excludes reference to the communities that not only spawn art, but are established by art, would seem, as Gadamer already warned, to amount to a restoration rather than an overcoming of aesthetics.

7

Ne sutor ultra crepidam: Erasmus and Dürer at the Hands of Panofsky and Heidegger

In his *Natural History* Pliny told the story of how, when the painter Apelles exhibited his works, he would hide himself nearby so that he could overhear the comments of the passersby. According to Pliny, this was because Apelles trusted the judgment of the people over his own (*vulgum diligentiorem iudicem quam se praeferens*). Pliny gave as an example the case when, after a cobbler complained that one of the paintings showed a pair of sandals with an insufficient number of loops, Apelles took note of the criticism and corrected the mistake. But, the anecdote continued, the cobbler was so proud of having caused Apelles to make the change, that the next day he began to criticize the way Apelles had portrayed the subject's legs. This so incensed Apelles that he called out from his hiding place, in words that had already become a proverb by Pliny's day, *Ne sutor ultra crepidam*, "Let the shoemaker stick to his last."[1]

Pliny does not comment further on the anecdote, but it appears that if Apelles valued the criticism of the people, he also insisted on his critics confining their comments to their area of expertise. Such sentiments are frequently expressed by specialists jealously guarding their preserve, often out of frustration at the mistakes and errors to which trespassers are prone. This is very much the thrust of Shapiro's criticism of Heidegger's use of Van Gogh in *The Origin of the Work of Art*.[2] As Derrida presents it in *La verité en peinture*, "one of the two is a specialist. Painting, and even Van Gogh, is, so to speak, his thing, he wants to keep it, he wants it returned."[3] Shapiro makes a number of complaints against Heidegger, who fails to identify precisely which painting he is describing; who refers to the shoes as those of a peasant woman; who insists that the Being of the shoes is only uncovered in the painting and could not have been "imagined in looking at a real pair of peasants' shoes";[4] and who overlooks the artist's presence in the work. "Alas for him, the philosopher has indeed deceived himself." The implication is that the paintings are safe only so long as the art historians are their sole curators. Shapiro does not find Heidegger's claims about art as a disclosure of truth even worth examining, presumably because the account of the Van Gogh painting on which they are initially based is so flawed from the point of view of the art historian.

Perhaps in an effort to respect the disciplinary divisions that Heidegger fails to observe, Shapiro in his response neglects his role as a distinguished art theorist, and restricts himself to art history narrowly conceived. Shapiro does not touch on the philosophical content of Heidegger's essay and, indeed, he gives no indication of how small a proportion of the essay he is considering. Heidegger somewhat disingenuously offers his description of the shoes as being "without any philosophical theory" (H 21–22; PLT 32) and so provides Shapiro with the opening he needs. But philosophy cannot be so easily bracketed, either from ordinary description, particularly as Heidegger provides it, or from art history, even as Shapiro practices it here. That it is not quite so easy to keep art history free from philosophy is one of the things that emerges from Derrida's examination of Shapiro's essay in "Restitutions."[5] Derrida draws attention to some of the assumptions Heidegger and Shapiro share in their desire to attribute the shoes to someone or something. Both of them assign each of the shoes to a foot, insofar as they are agreed that the shoes form a pair. Both appropriate the shoes to their own realm, so that the peasant Heidegger assigns them to a peasant woman, whereas Shapiro, the city dweller, returns them to Van Gogh, who was "by that time a man of the town and city."[6] And, most important for Shapiro, the art historian, there is the attribution of the painting to a painter, something which, as Derrida could also have pointed out, is not without its economic significance in terms of the art market. Shapiro is so determined to confine his comments to the allegedly non-philosophical portion of *The Origin of the Work of Art* that he ignores the fact that Heidegger had already questioned the tendency to refer the work of art to the artist: "It is precisely in great art—and it alone is being addressed here—that the artist remains inconsequential as compared with the work, almost like a passageway that destroys itself in the creative process for the work to emerge" (H 29; PLT 40).

Heidegger has no such problems with the artist in the case of his other famous example, a Greek temple, but one can imagine a Shapiro asking questions about the relation between Heidegger's description and the building that he purports to describe. Foremost among them would be the question of which temple is under scrutiny. Heidegger did not visit Greece until 1962. Because Heidegger makes reference to the temple at Paestum (H 30; PLT 40), the focus would fall on Heidegger's visit to Rome in April 1936. Philosophers would be asking each other if Heidegger followed in Goethe's footsteps and made an excursion there. Then there would be the question of which of the temples at Paestum is meant, the temple of Poseidon or the temple of Ceres, although scholars regard the dedications as only conjectural. Or perhaps even the Italic temple, dedicated to the Capitoline triad, Zeus, Juno, and Minerva? A pair of Greek temples and an Italian one: Which to choose? Publication of the 1935 version of Heidegger's lecture resolved the question by showing that the reference to Paestum predated the trip to Rome (OA). Furthermore, Heidegger referred to "the temple of Zeus" (OA 24), which suggests to Martineau, the editor of the lecture, that Heidegger's temple never existed: "Alas, this time round, for Shapiro and the history of art generally, Heidegger's temple is unquestionably an ideal one" (OA 56 n3). And yet, is it not legitimate to insist that Heidegger should not only have visited a temple before describing one, but that he should specify which one? Only then would it be possible to confirm or deny the verisimilitude of his account. At one level it seems a reasonable demand to make of him. But is this Heidegger's level? Heidegger is not describing what happens when one visits the remains of a temple and finds, as he put it in *Being and Time*, "a bit of the past . . . still in the present" (SZ 378; BT 430). Heidegger's point at this stage of *The Origin of the Work of Art* is that even when we visit a temple today, we find that the world of the work has perished. So long as the temple is a work it opens up a world. Once the god has fled, the work is no longer a work (H 32; PLT 43). This means that even if one were able to identify the object of Heidegger's description and verify the factual components of his account, it would no longer be the great work it once was. And yet, Heidegger's description seems to aim at the truth of the work during the time when it was still great art, not unproblematically, as I tried to indicate in the previous chapter. Who can underwrite the description?

Brief though the reference to Dürer is in *The Will to Power as Art*, a lecture course held in the winter semester 1936/37, it seems to offer the possibility of evading at least this difficulty.[7] The reference to Dürer improves on the discussion of the temple, with its ambiguity about the source of the description, in that Heidegger takes as his basis a comment by one of Dürer's contemporaries, Erasmus. Erasmus wrote of Dürer that "from the position of one thing, he expresses more than the one aspect that offers itself to the beholder's eye" (*ex situ rei unius non unam speciem sese oculis intuentium offerentem [exprimit]*).[8] Erasmus's credentials are established through his association with Dürer. When Heidegger quotes from

Erasmus's eulogy to Dürer, he supports it with the observation, shared by many commentators, that "the statement expresses a thought that obviously grew out of a personal conversation" (GA 43, 230; NI 217; Ni 186). It is true that we know from Dürer's diary of his journey to the Netherlands that he met with Erasmus more than once, although what they discussed on these occasions is largely speculation.[9]

Erasmus was no art critic. Panofsky tells us that he left few descriptions of individual works of art that were not portraits of himself or his friends, and that his eulogy on Dürer is his only characterization of an individual artist.[10] This eulogy is included, somewhat gratuitously, in the dialogue *De recta Latini Graecique sermonis pronuntiatione* (*The Right Way of Speaking Latin and Greek*). At a certain point one of the participants in the dialogue recommends that young boys, while they are learning to write, should also learn drawing and painting, and to this end he recommends they read Dürer's *Underweysung der Messung mit dem Zirckel*. This is the excuse for Erasmus's panegyric for Dürer, most of the terms and expressions of which he drew from Pliny's account of Apelles in the *Natural History*. It was a book Erasmus knew well; he wrote notes for an edition published in 1516, and, in a letter which served as a preface to an edition which appeared in 1525, he went so far as to put Pliny's work above all the works of all the sculptors and painters that were referred to in it.[11] The comparison between Dürer and Apelles was not a new one. It was not unusual in Italy for painters to be compared with Apelles and it also became something of a set piece in respect of Dürer.[12] Erasmus in his letters to their mutual friend Willibald Pirckheimer had grown accustomed to referring to Dürer simply as Apelles as early as 1523, four years before the eulogy.[13] In *De recta pronuntiatione*, however, it was more than this. The art historian and Dürer scholar Erwin Panofsky has not only exhibited how carefully constructed the eulogy was, but he also judges that "all in all . . . Erasmus's synthetic portrait does not lack verisimilitude."[14]

Verisimilitude (*similitudo*) also happens to be what Apelles stood for in the history of art.[15] His skill in this respect was legendary: if one presented some horses with a series of paintings of horses, the horses would apparently neigh only at those by Apelles.[16] And a person who claimed that he could tell a person's age and could prophesy the date of their death from that person's face, found that he could work as well from Apelles' portraits as he could from "real life."[17] That Dürer was the new Apelles meant that Dürer was another master of verisimilitude. This is still Dürer's reputation. For example, Panofsky judges that even Dürer's phantasmagoric works are based in verisimilitude: "Every increase in verisimilitude and animation strengthens rather than weakens the visionary effect."[18]

It seems, therefore, that Dürer was not praised by Erasmus for doing something new in contrast with Apelles. Rather, Dürer proved his virtuosity by doing the same as Apelles, but with less at his disposal. Whereas Apelles accomplished his feats of verisimilitude by using color, Dürer established a remarkable likeness more economically, in monochrome. Nevertheless, there are a couple of phrases in Erasmus's eulogy which do not appear to be drawn from Pliny, as well as what is apparently a deliberate misquotation.[19] One of the passages not drawn from Pliny is the sentence cited by Heidegger. It is also the most puzzling phrase in the eulogy. In preparation for examining Heidegger's reading of it, I shall briefly turn to the interpretations offered by two of the most eminent Dürer scholars, Heinrich Wölfflin and Erwin Panofsky. But having already evoked the topic of Shapiro and Heidegger, I should say at once that I am not attempting to set up a rematch between Heidegger and the art historians.

Without saying so explicitly, both Wölfflin and Panofsky understood Erasmus's phrase as identifying the point at which Dürer goes beyond verisimilitude, although, of course, this begs the question about what verisimilitude in art consists in. Wölfflin does not just say that Dürer presents things not as they appear but according to their plastic content. He understands Erasmus to say that Dürer's art is directed at what is essential and decisive (*Wesentliche und Entscheidende*).[20] So, reading *species* as the *malerische Erscheinung* or "pictorial appearance," Wölfflin understands Erasmus to be drawing a contrast between the view of the object which is determined only by chance and that which gives an exhaustive image of the object so that it appears in complete clarity.[21] Writing in 1951, Panofsky judged that Wölfflin's interpretation "may be in harmony with Dürer's intentions but it does not . . . express the meaning of Erasmus."[22] The basis of this distinction between what Dürer wanted to say and what Erasmus said on his behalf seems to lie in the fact that whereas Wölfflin's interpretation is consistent with what Dürer seems to stand for in the history of art, there are certain difficulties in imposing precisely this meaning on Erasmus's words.

Panofsky doubts that *res* meant here a kind of Platonic idea or that the *species* was a particularized and merely phenomenal appearance. Not least, this would leave the phrase *ex situ* unexplained. So Panofsky suggests that it is the language of optics and not the language of philosophy that is operative here. "*Res* is the three dimensional object seen; *situs* its position in space; and *species* its visual image or 'aspect' which is, by definition, a flat projection of the object. In ordinary visual experience, Erasmus means to say, one object placed in a given position in relation to the eye will present only one aspect. Dürer, however, 'expresses more than this one aspect' . . . ; he manages to suggest that the object is a complete, three-dimensional entity extending, as it were, behind the one surface image which 'presents itself to the beholder's eye.'"[23] Erasmus would therefore be praising Dürer as a master of perspective who succeeded in producing the illusion of three-dimensionality, although Erasmus used language drawn from Pliny's praise of Parrhasius, who painted "the surface [of the object] . . . in such a manner that it promises something else behind itself and shows what it hides."[24] Nevertheless, perspective takes Dürer beyond verisimilitude, as Panofsky noted elsewhere. "The strange fascination which perspective had for the Renaissance mind cannot be accounted for exclusively by a craving for verisimilitude."[25] At its very simplest, the fact that we have two eyes and not one means that "exact perspective is not always 'natural.'" Perspective was not only "a guarantee of correctness but, even more, a guarantee of aesthetic perfection."[26]

What Heidegger understands by Erasmus's phrase is less clear. Heidegger does not offer a translation, but he does give a paraphrase: "By showing a particular thing from any given angle, he, Dürer the painter, brings to the fore not only one single isolated view which offers itself to the eye." This directly contradicts Plato's discussion of art in the *Republic*, at least as Heidegger interprets it: "The painter can bring the table into view only from one particular angle. What he pro-duces (*her-stellt*) is consequently but *one* aspect, *one* way in which the table appears. If he depicts the table from the front, he cannot paint the rear of it. He produces the table always in only one view or *phantasma*" (*Republic* 598b) (GA 43, 229; NI 216; Ni 186).[27] Heidegger says in the more strident tones of the *Gesamtausgabe* edition, "It is quite obvious that Erasmus here speaks expressly against the position Plato adopts in this dialogue; it is not by any means an arbitrary assumption to presuppose that the humanist Erasmus knew this dialogue of Plato and this passage on art" (GA 43, 230). Heidegger insists that Erasmus is responding not just to Platonism, but to Plato. Indeed, one wonders why Heidegger is so determined to establish Erasmus's sources, unless he fears another reading, like Panofsky's, which would take Erasmus away from a strictly philosophical discourse. It is striking to observe the ease with which Heidegger moves between a discussion of Erasmus's reading, on the basis of which the phrase is understood as a response to Plato, and Erasmus's conversation with Dürer, whereby the phrase is assigned equally to Dürer: "That Erasmus and Dürer could speak in such a fashion . . ." (GA 43, 230; NI 217; Ni 187). So far as Heidegger is concerned, Erasmus and Dürer speak with one voice.

Heidegger's interpretation seems to locate the meaning of Erasmus's phrase within the language of philosophy rather than, for example, of optics. There is no mention of perspective even though Dürer was a master of it, though not perhaps as great a master, either in theory or practice, as some of the Italians.[28] But although the reference to Dürer occurs only as an apparent aside in a discussion of the relation of art and truth, Heidegger does much more than simply suggest that Dürer reverses Plato. The decisive step is taken when he announces that he is going to complete or supplement Erasmus's statement. In doing so he transfers the discussion from the language of Platonic philosophy into the language of Being: "By showing any given individual thing as this particular thing, in its singularity, he [Dürer] makes Being itself visible: in a particular hare, the Being of the hare; in a particular animal, animality" (GA 43, 230; NI 217; Ni 187). Erasmus and Dürer speak with the voice of Being.

Dürer's "Hare" is a work of stunning realism, and one which has been described as "probably the first example of a self-contained, figurative nature study."[29] Its novelty gives it a certain ambiguity. The same commentator reminds us that Dürer's watercolor appeared at a turning point in history, where new forms of expression were being used for traditional meanings, so that this nature study might also have evoked a symbolic meaning, that of fertility or "sanguine sensuality."[30] However, Heidegger's introduction of the "Hare" in this context is unfortunate and tempts one to say that he should have "stuck to his last." Given that Erasmus's eulogy praised Dürer for what he could accomplish without using color, it is barely conceivable that Erasmus could have had a watercolor in mind at this point. Indeed, Erasmus remarks at one point of Dürer's engravings, that "were you to spread on colors, you would injure the work."[31] By introducing a watercolor, Heidegger has added color to his account, extraneous color of a kind that no specialist would dream of imposing. Of course, there are questions, questions in the spirit of Derrida, that one could ask about Heidegger's choice of example. One could ask if Heidegger had only seen a black and white reproduction of the "Hare" so that he thought it was an engraving. Or perhaps he saw an engraving based on the watercolor. Then there is the question of which of Dürer's paintings of hares is meant, because even though there is one obvious candidate, one could no doubt suggest that the Being of the hare emerges more clearly in some of the other hares found in Dürer. And, particularly in the case of some of Dürer's other hares, there is a question as to whether they are indeed hares and by Dürer. One recalls that hare, which in spite of the presence of Dürer's monogram is now attributed by art historians to Hans Hoffmann, who apparently, like a number of other artists, would draw his hares using rabbits for models.[32] With symbolic meanings, reproductions unfaithful to the original, forgeries, and false models, even the most realistic-looking works of art depart from truth in the sense of correspondence.

Dürer's "Hare" shows the Being of the hare, just as Van Gogh's painting shows what the peasant woman knows without reflecting, the Being of the shoes. If this parallel is appropriate Heidegger would want to say that the Being of the hare is disclosed only in the watercolor and could not be

Dürer, *Hare*. 1502. Watercolor with opaque white. Albertina, Vienna.

imagined by looking at a live hare. The parallel would mean that Erasmus, albeit only after his text has been "supplemented" by Heidegger, provides justification for the use to which Heidegger puts the Van Gogh painting in the contemporary essay on "The Origin of the Work of Art." And this, in turn, raises a number of questions. To what extent does this understanding of art, which one would normally think of as Heidegger's, belong already to modernity? And to what extent does this change, in an understanding of the relation of the work to Being, itself reflect a change in art as such? Heidegger indicates how he might approach such questions when at the end of the Epilogue to *The Origin of the Work of Art* he writes that "The history of the essence of Western art corresponds to the change in the essence of truth" (H 68; PLT 81).

Heidegger thereby refers the history of art to the history of Western metaphysics, just as Dürer is referred to a transformation in the understanding of Being. Indeed, in the *Gesamtausgabe* edition of the lectures the words "vgl. Nominalismus" are added in parenthesis after the reference to the understanding of Being. Another text from the previous semester helps clarify the character of this transformation, one which Heidegger conceives at this time as being essentially rooted in Germany. "Through German Protestantism in the Reformation not only Roman dogma was changed, but also the Roman-Oriental form of the Christian experience of Being was transformed. What was already being prepared in the Middle Ages with Master Eckhardt, Tauler and Seuse and in the 'German *Theologia*' is brought to bear in a new beginning and in a more comprehensive way by Nicolas of Cusa, by Luther, Sebastian Frank, Jacob Boehme—and in art by Albrecht Dürer" (SA 37-38; ST 30). Dürer belongs to the advent of modernity, which is construed in several ways: the meaning of Being is determined by the self-certainty of thinking; the truth of faith as established by church doctrine gives way to the demand of a search for a new foundation for knowledge; and, with "the liberation of man to himself," art becomes the decisive way in which human creativity is freely unfolded (SA 38; ST 31). This reference to art needs to be balanced by the account given in the "Six Basic Developments in the History of Aesthetics," which can be found in the same lecture course as the discussion of Dürer. Heidegger's history records how, as aesthetics develops, great art declines. The decline of great art takes place irrespective of the high quality of what is produced or the preeminence accorded to art in modernity, as reflected in the high value placed on creativity, taste, and genius. This is because great art is understood by Heidegger in another sense from that which refers it to the taste of its audience. Great art is conceived in Hegelian terms as "an absolute need" or, in Heidegger's paraphrase of Hegel, as "the definite fashioner and preserver of the absolute" (GA 43, 107; NI 108; Ni 90). In Heidegger's own terms, great art makes manifest "what beings as a whole are, preserving such manifestation in the work" (NI 100; Ni 84).[33] Whether Dürer's watercolor of the hare is great art in this sense is an open question, just as it is with Van Gogh's painting of the shoes.

Whether "great art" or not, Dürer's "Hare" is introduced by Heidegger not in terms of its place in the history of art, but in terms of the transformation in the understanding of Being that was in process at the time. That is to say, Heidegger refers Dürer's "Hare" to a change that, as he puts it in his sketch of the history of art and aesthetics, "does not arise immediately from art or from meditation on it" (GA 43, 96; NI 98; Ni 83). It is tempting to suppose that by referring the work to the history of Being Heidegger compromises the work as work, its self-subsistence. But it must be understood first of all, that Heidegger's account of the artwork, as an account of great art, is with reference to the way it fulfills the task of fashioning or, at very least, preserving, "the absolute in the realm of historical man" (GA 43, 98, and 107; NI 100 and 108; Ni 84 and 90). In other words, from the outset Heidegger conceives the work of art quite differently from the ways the work has conventionally been conceived by art history.

The juxtaposition of Heidegger with Panofsky raises the question of what it might mean to treat a work of art as a work of art. Panofsky's early theoretical writings attempt to construe works of art not in relation to something outside themselves (such as their historical circumstances, psychological prehistory, or stylistic analogies), but "exclusively in relation to their own being."[34] Even so, his studies of Renaissance art led him directly to Renaissance optics, symbolism, and religion. Furthermore, there is the question of the framework in which this study takes place. The tension between a rigorous art history based on documentary sources and, one trusts, a no less rigorous attempt to justify the conceptual schema Panofsky brought to these works, dominates his subsequent investigations. Indeed, the tension between Dürer's realism and his idealism, in the form of the twin categories of verisimilitude (*Richtigkeit*) and beauty, not only dominates his first major work, his 1915 dissertation *Dürers Kunsttheorie*, it also reflects his own basic dilemma. Panofsky's scholarship is impressive to the point where it obtrudes upon the work as work. The documents satisfy the obsessive demand for correctness. They have a corrective function (*berichtigende Funktion*), for example, when they prove that "a change of meaning in the formal components has altered the effect which a work of art has upon us today."[35] But the documents serve only as the presupposition for the perception of artistic volition (*Kunstwollen*), which lies beneath the surface of the phenomenon as its immanent meaning.

Panofsky's way of letting the work be a work is, of course, as different from Heidegger's as his neo-Kantian starting point is different from Heidegger's phenomenology. Panofsky was convinced that the *Kunstwollen* could be comprehended only in "fundamental concepts which are deduced *a priori*,"³⁶ but he failed to arrive at such an a priori system of concepts that he could impose on the historical facts, and was unwilling to restrict himself to questions of artistic development. Michael Podro has charted the way that Panofsky sought a solution by identifying his own neo-Kantian viewpoint with the Renaissance perspective construction.³⁷ Using the Renaissance perspective construction as both a historical and at the same time a transhistorical reference point means that Panofsky can locate his own viewpoint both within and beyond the history he is examining. However, Panofsky never succeeds in resolving the difficulty that arises from taking as absolute what he is determined to show lacks unique authority and represents only one way of organizing the depiction of spatial relations.³⁸ Panofsky claims that in antiquity objectively straight lines were seen as curved, whereas in the Renaissance under the impact of plane perspective they were seen as straight.³⁹ Irrespective of questions about how he might find evidence for this change, there are questions arising from the "objectivity" accorded to the Renaissance. As we have seen, Panofsky himself elsewhere granted that Renaissance perspective lacked "verisimilitude." It is perhaps no wonder that by 1931 Panofsky had recast the tension between historical facts and a priori concepts in terms of the violence of interpretation. To justify this change in his position Panofsky turned to Heidegger's *Kant and the Problem of Metaphysics*: "Every interpretation must necessarily use violence" (KPM 183; KM 138).⁴⁰ But there is no evidence that Panofsky's indebtedness to Heidegger extended farther than this book, which, of course, had been the subject two years previously of a notorious debate with Panofsky's former associate, Ernst Cassirer.

In *The Origin of the Work of Art* and in other writings on art from the 1930s, Heidegger does not attempt to identify a transhistorical reference point, as Panofsky had done. The destruction of the Platonic tradition of aesthetics takes place by reference to the work as work. This can be approached in terms of Heidegger's third reference to Dürer (H 58; PLT 70). Heidegger quotes a sentence from the third book of the *Vier Bücher von Menschlicher Proportion*. The sentence runs, "For in truth, art lies hidden within nature; he who can wrest it from her, has it."⁴¹ Heidegger's focus is on the word "wrest" (*herausreissen*), but in order to be clear as to what is at stake it is necessary to return the sentence to its context.

Panofsky appropriately describes the third of the *Four Books on Human Proportion* as "the final statement of what may be called Dürer's philosophy of art."⁴² It is here that Panofsky chooses to explain the "more" beyond verisimilitude, which Dürer calls beauty. Neither beauty nor verisimilitude can be attained without theoretical knowledge, "art" in the narrow sense.[43] Geometry alone would reveal the best proportions for the human figure.[44] This is not to say that Dürer thought that only an idealized form of beauty should be represented or that there was only one form of perfect beauty. Dürer's theory of human proportions is by no means free from prejudice, but he gives more place to difference (*Unterschied*) than almost any of his contemporaries.[45] Restored to its context the statement that Heidegger quotes from Dürer is concerned with the question of fidelity to nature. Dürer advises artists to observe nature carefully and to avoid assuming that by departing from it they will invent something better. To do so would be to assume that one could improve on what God accomplished when he created nature. Insofar as an experienced artist can produce a beautiful image from his imagination, this is only because he has been schooled by copying from nature. This is the sense in which art is embedded in nature.[46]

Panofsky understands this passage in a way which reflects the tensions within his own philosophy of art. He suggests that Dürer is trying to avoid seeking beauty either in geometry, in the sense of an a priori theory of proportions, or in a single human being that one adopts as one's model.[47] Dürer rejects the latter because nobody embodies all beauty. He rejects the former because he considers that God made men as they should be: "I maintain that true perfection of form and beauty is contained in the mass of all men; I would rather follow whoever can properly extract it [*der das recht herausziehen kann*] than the one who wants to introduce a newly fabricated proportion [*ein neu erdichtte Mass*] that human beings have had no part in."[48] Panofsky equates this *herausziehen* with the *herausreissen* cited earlier.[49] The process of extraction is a part of the creative process, which nevertheless still subordinates itself to nature. It is not a priori, it is not invention, but it is not simply copying. The "double demand" to imitate nature and yet at the same time improve upon it might appear to represent a contradiction, but a study of Renaissance art theory shows that the two demands were incompatible only subsequently.[50]

The relation of art to nature troubles Heidegger. He employs the sentence from Dürer for the first time in the Freiburg version of *The Origin of the Work of Art* in November 1935, at the moment when he introduces the word *Riss*, or rift, as if to provide some warrant for his use of the word, although an even earlier version employs *Riss* and *hereinreissen* without appeal to Dürer's authority (HS 12). Heidegger says that the self-enclosed is extracted into the open by a kind of "drawing out," which takes place in drawing and engraving (OA 50). In the 1936 version of the essay, the only one Heidegger himself published, he uses the Dürer quotation to explore certain difficulties that he had not addressed previously. Heidegger had already introduced *Riss* some pages earlier, and the sentence from Dürer forms part of a discussion of the relation between the work of art and nature, the things of the earth. Heidegger's task at this point is to establish the originality of the work. The problem he faces is that if the work is to bring thingness into the open, it would appear that it must already be in relation to nature. But would this not compromise the sense in which the work of art is an origin? Heidegger cites Dürer not in support of his position, but in developing a possible objection to his view. If art is already in nature, the work would be a copy of what is in nature, and it would simply be a matter of releasing what nature already contains. Hence, Heidegger's response to Dürer is that "this art hidden in nature becomes manifest only through the work, because it lies originally in the work" (H 58; PLT 70). That is to say, art is in the work, rather than in nature or the artist. Dürer is in this way assimilated by Heidegger to the Platonic conception, which he had already set himself against, most explicitly in the first draft of *The Origin of the Work of Art* (HS 14).

One should not overlook the fact that Dürer intended his sentence on extraction as a revision of his earlier Platonism. Dürer is tempering his passion for artistic creativity by emphasizing the need for observation and even measurement. It seems that he had read in Ficino about how the Saturnian melancholic was filled with divine influences and oracles from on high, so that he could always devise something new and unusual.[51] Associating this with the Platonic ideas, Dürer wrote:

> The great art of painting has been in great esteem with the powerful kings many hundred years ago, for they made the outstanding artists rich and honored them, considering such talent to be a creative thing like unto God. For a good painter is inwardly full of figures, and if it were possible that he live forever, he would have from the inner ideas, of which Plato writes, always something new to pour out in his works.[52]

The sentence Heidegger quotes in *The Origin of the Work of Art* can be read as part of Dürer's later correction of this enthusiasm for a kind of Platonism he had learned at the hands of the Italians.

Heidegger's quotations from Dürer and Erasmus are more closely connected, therefore, than might at first sight appear. Both are against Plato and both reflect the transformation in the understanding of Being, at the advent of modernity—in all its ambiguity. Dürer's commitment to verisimilitude could be said to reflect the transformation of truth to correctness. The negotiation between beauty and verisimilitude that dominates not only his practice (*Brauch*) but his *techne*, his *Kunst*, is submitted to geometry, the art of measurement. All of this could easily be accommodated to Heidegger's account of modernity, although Dürer, as was typical in the Renaissance, would have been more inclined to see it as a return to the art of the ancients.

Dürer understood his writings on the art of measurement to be in the tradition of the missing books of Apelles and Protogenes. Yet Dürer also understood art as subordinated to God's creativity, and his ultimate purpose in painting to be not verisimilitude but "the great honor and glory of God."[53] If he had been asked what constituted the difference between these ancient artists and himself, Dürer would have drawn on a conceptuality which Heidegger almost invariably minimizes in his account of modernity, preferring to confine it to the Middle Ages, and regarding its subsequent appearances mere throwbacks, residues, like the remains of the temple.

Dürer felt free to appropriate the art of the ancients for the glory of God. One could represent Christ, "the fairest of all the earth," in the proportions that had been used for Apollo, or show Mary in the same beautiful form that had been used for Venus. Panofsky juxtaposes this quotation with one from Erasmus which is "in diametrical opposition" to it.[54] In his *Ciceronian Dialogue* Erasmus writes, "Suppose now, if you like, that Apelles, who in his time surpassed all painters in the representation of gods and men, were by some miracle to reappear in our own century and were to paint the Germans as he had once painted the Greeks, or the monarchs [of our time] as he had once painted Alexander, although nobody like them exists nowadays: would he not be said to have painted them badly?—Badly, because not fittingly [*male quia non apte*]."[55] Erasmus concludes that if someone today painted as Apelles used to paint, they would not be painting like (*similem*) Apelles. This is because the sign, the appearance (*species*), would no longer be congruent with the thing. Certainly Panofsky is right that Erasmus and Dürer are not on this occasion talking as one, but they are not in direct contradiction either. Dürer is talking about ideals of beauty, which, it must always be remembered, are for him many, puzzlingly so in terms of the Platonic legacy. Erasmus is addressing the problem that verisimilitude is also not always the same. It is not only that the subject of a portrait changes with age, so that a likeness ceases to be lifelike as the subject grows older, something he was all too aware of, as we shall see. The very question of verisimilitude cannot be freed from what the thing signifies. This may be most obviously true of representations of the gods, but it was also true of human portraits. Erasmus however, seems to have had a problem with verisimilitude when it was he himself who was being depicted.

There are portraits of Erasmus by Massys, Holbein, and Dürer. Posterity has come to prefer Holbein's portrait, as perhaps Erasmus himself did. There is thus a temptation to judge the verisimilitude of Dürer's portraits of Erasmus on the basis of their resemblance to the more famous representations by Holbein. What does it mean for an artist to give a true picture of someone? Is a portrait to be judged on how closely it resembles the person? Or should it tell us something about that person, something that the sitter

Dürer, Erasmus of Rotterdam, 1526. Engraving. Museum Dahlem, Kupferstichkabinett, Berlin

might not even know or be capable of recognizing, so that he would not by any means be the best judge?[56] Although Erasmus was ready to praise Dürer for his skill as a portraitist, he nevertheless considered that he was the better judge of what would constitute a good likeness of him. On seeing Dürer's portrait of him, Erasmus wrote, "Dürer has portrayed me, but it is not at all like me [*sed nihil simile*]."[57] To another correspondent, who happened to be in close touch with Dürer, he was rather more tactful, suggesting that it was the passage of time which explained the failure of the engraving to match its original. Erasmus sat for Dürer twice, both times in 1520, at which point Erasmus already struck Dürer as "a little old man [*ein altes Maenniken*]."[58] The second drawing does not survive. The first, a charcoal sketch now in the Louvre, served as the basis for an engraving which Erasmus completed in 1526. To help Dürer's memory, Erasmus sent a medallion by Quinten Massys, but that dated from 1519. Writing in 1525 to Pirckheimer, while still trying to encourage Dürer to go ahead, Erasmus confided, "If he can contrive something from memory and with the aid of the medallion, then he may do with me what he did with you, whom he made rather too fat."[59] Dürer himself inscribed the portrait in Latin and Greek. The Latin inscription—*Imago Erasmi Roterodami ab Alberto Durero ad vivam efficiem de deliniata*—ignored the time delay and simply recorded that Dürer had drawn Erasmus from life. The Greek inscription—*Ten kreitto ta suggrammata deixei* ("The writings portray him better")—was copied from the medallion by Quinten Massys. Under other circumstances Erasmus might have appreciated the joke that Dürer copied the disclaimer from Massy's portrait but not the portrait itself. In any event, Massys and Dürer display a different attitude from Holbein, who inscribed the first version of a woodcut of Erasmus with the words: "If anyone has not seen Erasmus in his bodily shape, this cut, drawn from life, will give his counterfeit."[60]

When Erasmus heard from Pirckheimer that Dr. Edward Lee, Bishop of Colchester in England, had been criticizing Dürer's work, he responded, "I am delighted that our Dürer has met his cobbler" (*Gaudeo Durero nostro contigisse sutorem suum*).[61] The Bishop of Colchester had been in dispute with Erasmus for some time, and the joke seems to be that Dr. Lee was being a shoemaker to both Erasmus and Dürer, in the sense of being a critic who did not recognize his limitations. Perhaps the joke was on Erasmus, who subsequently became a critic of Dürer's own attempt at a "likeness" of him. Dürer himself had warned, "The art of painting can only be judged by those who are themselves good painters."[62] Erasmus and Lee, a pair of shoemakers? But only two? Heidegger also appears to have exceeded his bounds, for example, with his reference to a watercolor as if it was an engraving. And no doubt in this context a certain Heideggerian invective could be used to expose Panofsky's philosophical pretensions. But it would be out of place for either a Panofsky or a Heidegger to dismiss the other on the grounds that they have exceeded their proper limits. Both Heidegger and Panofsky, in trying to let the work be a work, found that what first comes under scrutiny are the boundaries which determine the realm of art. Panofsky found that his studies of Renaissance art referred him to Renaissance optics and Renaissance symbolism and Renaissance religion. Similarly, Heidegger in *The Origin of the Work of Art* did not subordinate art to philosophy. The thinking of Being, the founding of a state, and the production of an artwork are all ways in which truth establishes itself (H 50; PLT 62).

Dürer insists on the preeminence of the judgment of the artist. Pliny's story about Apelles can also be understood as championing the artist in the realm of the arts. And yet, when it comes to shoes, even Apelles is prepared to concede that the cobbler knows more. The story thus follows the hierarchy established by Plato in the tenth book of the *Republic*, where the painter is said to be an imitator, "the producer of a product three removes from nature," the producer of the appearances, not the producer of being in truth (*Rep.* 597e and 596e. GA 43, 218. Cf. NI 206–07; Ni 177–78). Van Gogh, in a passage which also serves as the epigraph to Derrida's "Restitutions," writes, "But truth is so dear to me, and so is the *seeking to make true*, that indeed I believe I would still rather be a cobbler than a musician with colors."[63] Still governed by an idea of verisimilitude, Van Gogh appears to think of the shoes that the cobbler made as being more true than the shoes the painter depicted. It is this that Heidegger challenges, on the basis of his reading of Van Gogh's painting and on the basis of Erasmus's testimony about Dürer. The painter reveals, and he does so in accord with truth not as verisimilitude but as unconcealment.

Within Platonism, and thus within Western aesthetics generally, according to Heidegger, art and equipmentality are submitted to the same conceptual schema and so are inadequately distinguished. Heidegger claims, particularly in the first version of *The Origin of the Work of Art*, that the Western conception of art remains modelled on what a craftsman, for example, a cobbler, does. The shoes the cobbler makes are not just modelled on the idea of a shoe, they are modelled so as to fit the last, the wooden model of the foot, which represents what a foot should be. So too the painter works to a series of models, the Platonic Ideas, on the one hand, and on the other, the mathematics of proportions, for example, human proportions, which would also say what size and shape a foot should be. In terms of this tradition, Apelles could be understood to say to the cobbler, you stick to your models, as I will to mine. It is here that Heidegger intervenes. Great art is not like production. In great art the artist abandons the model, breaks the mold. This is what Heidegger in the *Beiträge* calls "artlessness" (GA 65, 506). Art history, however, understands such breaks according to a stylistic analysis, whereas for the Heidegger it is in terms of the counterplay of world and earth. Is Dürer's "Hare" great art? Heidegger equates great art preeminently with the Greeks, before aesthetics. But insofar as one could succeed in associating Dürer with the transformation which takes place in thought and in religion at the advent of modernity, then it shares in a certain greatness, the greatness of a transformation in the history of Being. Heidegger celebrates this greatness because it does not just help mark the inauguration of modernity, but points beyond it to "The Origin of the Work of Art," where the work is found to reveal Being.

8

"Poet of Poets. Poet of the Germans." Hölderlin and the Dialogue between Poets and Thinkers

The phrase "The Dialogue between Poetry and Thinking" is unmistakable. It is readily decoded as referring to the dialogue between Hölderlin and Heidegger. One scarcely notices that, in its reinterpretation, poetry has been defined in terms of a poet and thinking in terms of a thinker, even though to do so runs counter to the tendency of *The Origin of the Work of Art*, where the artist as creator is referred to the work and not vice versa (H 29; PLT 40).[1] Not that the work, in the sense of the poem, is precisely what is at issue. Heidegger's preferred word was not *das Gedicht* or *die Dichtung*, but *das Dichten*, which suggests the act of composing a poem, versifying. I shall follow the usual convention and translate it, somewhat unhappily, as "poetizing," and thus I shall refer to the dialogue between poetizing and thinking. The dialogue between poetizing and thinking establishes a relation, perhaps even a community, between the poet and the thinker. What is the character of this community?

In the Postscript to "What Is Metaphysics?" Heidegger wrote that "we know nothing of the dialogue [*Zwiesprache*] of poet and thinker," and then added, in words borrowed out of context from Hölderlin's "Patmos," that they "dwell near on mountains farthest part" (W 107; EB 392. Cf. WP 94). The use of the image suggests that, in spite of his disclaimer, Heidegger did know something about the relation between poets and thinkers. Moreover, the image of the mountain seems to place both poet and thinker "above" men (cf. GA 39, 166). Heidegger's more rarefied essays on language, from the 1950s, and above all his cult of the thinker, might lead one to suspect that the thinker and the poet join with each other to the exclusion of everyone else. This picture of an isolated community of two would also fit with the image of Heidegger retreating into poetry in disillusionment, following his allegedly brief and certainly ill-fated excursion into politics in 1933.[2] But the recognition that Heidegger's political interest was longer lasting than many commentators had previously thought, or wanted to think, and the publication of some of the relevant volumes of the *Gesamtausgabe*, along with the early versions of *The Origin of the Work of Art*, suggest a very different picture.[3] Before reexamining the evidence it is useful to recall some of Heidegger's better-known statements characterizing the dialogue between poetizing and thinking.

The tendency to refer the dialogue between poetizing and thinking to a dialogue between the poet and the thinker is encouraged by the confidence that we can more readily identify a poet or a thinker than we can the acts of poetizing or thinking. But we identify the poet in the light of the tradition of aesthetics, in which poetry is reduced to what Heidegger called poesy (*Poesie*), just as the thinker is thought of as a figure in the philosophical tradition. This sets the poet and the thinker apart, in opposition to each other, because conventionally philosophy is generally opposed to poesy, just as art, which is referred to beauty, is usually distinguished from truth. The dialogue between thinking and poetizing is not a dialogue between philosophy and poesy (GA 52, 6). Furthermore, once art is subordinated to philosophy, as already happened in Plato (GA 53, 142), the path is set for art's function to be taken over by philosophy. This process reached its culmination in Hegel's statement about the so-called end of art (cf. H 66–67; PLT 79–80 and NI 100–01; Ni 84–85). Aesthetics is therefore an obstacle to the dialogue between thinking and poetizing, because it has already decided in advance in favor of thinking, specifically the unique historical form of thinking called philosophy. The precise relation between poetizing and thinking in the dialogue remains unclear, undergoing some variation across Heidegger's various accounts. Nevertheless, there is perhaps more differentiation within Heidegger's discussion of the dialogue between thinking and poetizing than is usually recognized, with Heidegger marking a difference between the dialogue of thinking *with* poetizing, in which the former is subordinated to the latter, and the dialogue of poetizing *with* thinking, in which the reverse is true.

When Heidegger referred to what he was doing in his essays on poetry as a dialogue of thinking *with* poetizing (e.g. US 38; WL 160–61), the formulation did more than reflect the one-sidedness of a dialogue being conducted by someone who identified himself preeminently as a thinker, whatever one may think of his efforts at writing poetry. By using the phrase "dialogue of thinking with poetry," Heidegger also acknowledged his subordination to the authority of the poet. The idiosyncracy of Heidegger's essays on Hölderlin, of which Hölderlin scholars have often complained, has its basis in this dual structure, whereby Heidegger acknowledged the poet but at the same time appropriated the poet to his own concerns. Heidegger was engaged in a work of transformation, as much as one of clarification or elucidation. The objections to Heidegger's dialogue with Hölderlin raised by scholars such as Max Kommerell[4] are not dissimilar to those that have been levelled against the equally notorious "dialogue between thinkers." Heidegger's defense of the latter was that the dialogue between thinkers is "bound by other laws, laws which are more easily violated," than those which govern the methods of historical philology (KPM 8: KM xviii). Whenever Heidegger rendered a text barely recognizable, the temptation is to suggest that he was engaged less in a dialogue than in a monologue (cf. US 265; WL 134). It might even be possible to establish some measure of agreement on the point that only one voice is heard. Critics complain that it is Heidegger's own. Heidegger himself says that it is the voice of Being. "The thinker says Being," is how he explained it in the Postscript to "What Is Metaphysics?" (W 107; EB 391). In the same place it was said that "the poet names the gods." Does that mark a difference between the poet and the thinker? Or is the naming of the gods to be assimilated to the saying of Being? If so, by whom if not the thinker? Heidegger did not address these questions directly, but he did insist in "Hölderlin and the Essence of Poetry" that "poetry is the founding of Being by means of the word" (EHD 38; EB 304). Nevertheless, in his 1953 essay on Trakl, Heidegger wrote that "the authentic dialogue with the poet's poem is the poetic dialogue" (US 38; WL 160). That seems to imply that the thinker's dialogue is somehow less than authentic. In other words, Heidegger not only acknowledged that his writings on poetry were a certain kind of distortion—a disaster, a misfortune (*ein Unglück*), as he conceded in response to Kommerell.[5] He also admitted that the discussion of a poem as it takes place within the thinking dialogue with poetizing interferes with that listening which allows the poem to sing (US 39; WL 161).

The thinking dialogue with poetry and the poetizing dialogue with thinking have different aims. Thinking and poetizing each define differently the region of their neighborhood (US 173; WL 70) and each are in the service of language in quite different and distinctive ways (WP 95). Nevertheless, in spite of the differences which hold them apart, poetizing and thinking are no longer to be thought of as separated in the sense of being cut off in a relational void (US 196; WL 90). Hence, it is no surprise to find Hölderlin described as "one of our greatest, that is, one of our coming thinkers, because he is our greatest poet" (GA 39, 6). Hölderlin is not a thinker by virtue of an interest in philosophy. It is as a poet that he is a thinker. Heidegger makes a similar comment with respect to Mörike. In his correspondence with Emil Staiger about Mörike's poem "On a Lamp," Heidegger insisted that "the poet does not need to concern himself with philosophy, for a poet, of course, grows ever so more poetical the more thoughtful he is" (GA 13, 101). The dialogue of poetizing with thinking is unconcerned with the question of identifying precisely which philosophical texts have influenced which poets. It is said to have a deeper, more intimate, source. For Heidegger, therefore, the dialogue between thinking and poetizing does not begin only when a thinker turns to poesy or when a poet draws on philosophy. Certainly, when a thinker like Heidegger takes up a poem, there is a thinking of the poem (e.g. GA 52, 11–12). But the dialogue *between* poetizing and thinking, as opposed to the dialogue of thinking *with* poetizing, does not await a thinker who is prepared to break the confines of his or her trade; poetizing and thinking are not joined together in dialogue as a result of the dialogue between poet and thinker (US 189; WL 84). In 1957, in "The Essence of Language," Heidegger wrote that "We must discard the view that the neighborhood of poetry and thinking is nothing more than a garrulous cloudy mixture of two kinds of saying in which each makes clumsy borrowings from the other" (US 196; WL 90). Thinking and poetizing do not need to be brought together. "All meditative thinking is poetic, and all poetry in turn is a kind of thinking" (US 67; WL 136). They already belong together. They already reside in an intimate, essential dialogue long before they are differentiated, and it is this proximity which makes possible the dialogue between thinker and the poet: "The neighborhood of poetry and thinking is not the result of a process by which poetry and thinking—no one knows from where—first draw near to each other and thus establish a neighborhood. The nearness that draws them near is itself the appropriation by which poetizing and thinking are directed into the ownness of their essence" (US 196; WL 90).

Heidegger's first step in the redetermination of thinking and poetizing was to reexamine their relation in the early Greek period, a task he began already in *An Introduction to Metaphysics*. He observed that the early Greeks had a strikingly different perspective on the distinction between poetizing and thinking: "The thinking of Parmenides and Heraclitus was still poetic which in this case means philosophical and not scientific" (EM 110; IM 144). It is no accident, therefore, that Heidegger's 1946 essay, "The Anaximander Fragment," was the occasion of some of his most extreme assertions of the close proximity of poetizing and thinking. As the first fragment of Greek thought, the Anaximander fragment was prior to the advent of conceptual language (H 314; EGT 29). Heidegger wrote in this context that "Thinking is primordial poetry, prior to all poesy, but also prior to the poetics of art, since art shapes its work within the realm of language. All poetizing, in this broader sense, and also in the narrower sense of the poetic, is in its ground a thinking" (H 303; EGT 19). And again, "Thinking is the poetizing of the truth of Being in the historic dialogue between thinkers" (H 343; EGT 57). In saying what the truth of Being dictates, the thinker poetizes the primordial saying of Being. Drawing on the etymology of the German word *dichten*, Heidegger related it to the Latin word for saying: thinking, that is to say, "the poetizing essence of thinking," is "the original *dictare*" (H 303; EGT 19). The thinker's recollection of the primordial saying of Being, for example, in the course of translation, is also a poetizing. Hence, *der Brauch*, which is the word Heidegger selected to translate *to chreon*, is said to be "dictated to thinking in the experience of Being's oblivion."

This last phrase confirms that the dialogue of thinking and poetizing is historical. If scholars in their study of Greece have often kept "the poetic thinking of Parmenides and Heraclitus" separate from "the thinking poetry" of tragedy (EM 110; IM 144-45), it is clear that the distinction results from what philosophy and art have subsequently become. Poetic thinking, where "thinking has priority," has come to be appropriated retrospectively by philosophers who have judged them according to their own standards. Confidence in the separation of poesy and philosophy is a product of the history of Western metaphysics, but it was by no means characteristic of the beginnings of that history. Heidegger was quite explicit, with regard to poetizing and thinking, about the extent to which "each needs the other" (*brauchen einander*). And yet, that need has been concealed by the prejudice sustained for centuries that thinking is to be understood as *ratio*, calculation in the broadest sense (US 173; WL 70). It is perhaps only at the end of philosophy, at the uttermost extremity of the oblivion of Being, that the dialogue between poetizing and thinking could take the form of a dialogue between poet and thinker. The alleged separation of poetry and thinking which denied their proximity would collapse, but not as a consequence of the dialogue between Hölderlin and Heidegger. Rather, the dialogue between Hölderlin and Heidegger will have been possible, on this scenario, only because the tradition of philosophy and of art which upheld this separation was at an end. Nevertheless, Heidegger's reading of Hölderlin helped him formulate his account of the history of philosophy as the history of Being. That the dialogue with Hölderlin would institute a history, the idea of which would have been entirely foreign to Hölderlin, instructs us in the complex nature of how thinking rediscovers itself in the thinking dialogue with poetizing.[6]

Heidegger wrote in the *Beiträge* that "the historical determination of philosophy reaches its summit in acknowledging the necessity of creating a hearing for Hölderlin's word" (GA 65, 422). Why Hölderlin in particular? What is his *seynsgeschichtliche Einzigkeit*? Until recently it was still possible to address this question independently of the political context in which Heidegger gave Hölderlin a privileged role. The texts initially available to scholars were relatively silent about this context. In the 1936 Rome lecture "Hölderlin and the Essence of Poetry" Heidegger maintained that the reason why he was focusing on Hölderlin, in his attempt to show the essence of poetry, was because Hölderlin was "the poet of poets" (EHD 32; EB 294). It was Hölderlin's vocation to poetize the essence of poetry that singled him out. In Heidegger's thoughtful dialogue with Hölderlin, the poet's ability to institute what remains gives rise to the claim that the essence of poetry is the founding of Being in language (EHD 39; EB 305). Poetry in this sense was said to be "doubly bound" (EHD 42; EB 310), bound to the gods and to the people. Yet the nature of this relation was far from clear in "Hölderlin and the Essence of Poetry." On the one hand, the speech of the poet apprehends the hints of the gods so as to pass them on to his own people. Poetizing as the original naming of the gods is thus possible only when the gods themselves bring us to language (EHD 42; EB 311). On the other hand, the poetic word is only the interpretation of the "voice of the people" (EHD 43; EB 311). The poet is thus identified as the one cast out into the realm between men and gods. What Heidegger left obscure in the Rome lecture was how the poet could give to the people the hints of the gods while at the same time serving as their voice, just as he left unclarified what he had in mind in describing Hölderlin's poetry as determining and defining a new time. However, much that Heidegger left unsaid in the Rome lecture he had already set out quite clearly over a year earlier, in the 1934/35 lecture course from which it was drawn. But *Hölderlin's Hymnen "Germanien" und "Der Rhein"* was not published until 1980, and it has taken some years for its significance to be generally appreciated.

The main difference between the two texts is that, whereas in the lecture Heidegger was clear that Hölderlin was "the poet of poets," it is only in the lecture course that he specified that Hölderlin was "the poet of poets" *as* "the poet of the Germans" (GA 39, 214). Heidegger here clarified his claim that the founding of Being in language could take place only as the founding of a people, so as to include acknowledgment of the fact that Hölderlin had not yet become a power in the history of the German people (GA 39, 214). As the early versions of *The Origin of the Work of Art* emphasized, the German public were, in Heidegger's view, not yet a people.[7] Hölderlin is "the poet of the Germans" in the sense that he awaits the German people; he stands before them (H 65; PLT 78. GA 39, 1). The crucial point is that it was as a thinker that Heidegger assigned himself the task of elevating Hölderlin to this role in German history (GA 39, 214). He knew that to do so was to engage in "politics," albeit politics "in its highest and most authentic sense," a politics that did not need to talk endlessly about the political. In other words, the dialogue between thinking and poetizing was, at least at the time it was introduced, political. It was political in the specific sense of being concerned with the founding of a people. The poet had the central role in the accomplishment of this task, to which the thinker made a preparatory contribution. It is true that in the lecture course Heidegger had only relatively little to say about the role of the thinker. Indeed, at one point Heidegger explicitly acknowledged that he was concentrating on the poet at the expense of what belongs to thought and its necessities (GA 39, 151). But it is clear, at least, that there was not supposed to be anything exclusive about the company that the thinker kept with the poet—even if "the voice of the people" speaks only in a few (GA 65, 319). The thinker's task in this context, like the poet's, was directed to the coming people. In other words, the questions of the identity and community of the poet and the thinker cannot be posed appropriately independently of the question of the constitution of the people.

The strange, paradoxical temporality which characterizes the foundation of "we, the people," according to classic social contract theory, such that the people must already be a people in order to constitute themselves as a people, undergoes some variation in the case of the poet's foundation of a people. Poetry institutes, founds, and would bring us to the site of the historical existence of a people, a site on which, Heidegger observed, we are not yet standing, although it awaits "us," would "we" but attend to what it says (GA 39, 113). And yet, poetry awaits the people, as the people awaits poetry. It is in respect of this relation that the 1934/35 lecture course was more specific than the subsequent lecture. Hölderlin is said to transmit the hints of the gods to the people only to the extent that he gives voice to the people, and so helps to bring them to existence. Hölderlin's "time" can be understood only with reference to the history of the still-awaited German people. Who Hölderlin is is not yet decided and will only be decided by the German people. And yet, in a sense it is in that decision that they become the German people. All talk of a dialogue between poetizing and thinking, at least with reference to the 1930s, must be understood as directed to, and in an important sense sustained in advance by, the future or coming people. It is in this respect, and for this reason, that with some consistency Heidegger continued to join thinking, poetizing, and the founding of the state or *polis*, following the Greek model (GA 39, 51. EHD 83).[8]

The description in "Hölderlin and the Essence of Poetry" of poetry as the original language (*Ursprache*) of an historical people, and as the saying which first makes language possible (EHD 40; EB 307), was offered by Heidegger without clarification. He did not explore how this reference to the past related to the time that Hölderlin's poetry anticipates (EHD 44; EB 313). Only in the lecture course did he specify that this original language was to accomplish an essential transformation of the experience of the essence of language in the historical existence of a people, a transformation of their existence to bring them back into the original realm of Being (GA 39, 64). This original language was not a "primitive language," as the English translation has it (EB 307). Heidegger contrasts it with idle talk (*Gerede*) and thereby seems to keep the discussion within the orbit of the fundamental ontology of *Being and Time* (GA 39, 64, and 217). But that impression is deceptive, because the question of "who we are" is here posed in terms of whether we enter into the original historicity of our historical language, a question of whether language itself comes to language in relation to the decision of the *Weltzeit* of our people (GA 39, 76–77). Heidegger's answer lay in introducing the language of the "Fatherland." The Fatherland, far from being the source of "unruly patriotism," was presented as "the historical Being [*Seyn*] of a people" (GA 39, 120).

The question which naturally arises at this point is whether this focus on the people governs Heidegger's understanding of poetizing and thinking only in the brief period following Hitler's rise to power and Heidegger's Rectoral Address, or whether it persisted longer. The answer can be found in the interpretation of Hölderlin's poem "Homecoming" that Heidegger offered in 1943.[9] At the end of the essay Heidegger took up the final lines of the poem:

> Sorgen, wie diese, muss, gern oder nicht, in der Seele
> Tragen ein Sänger und oft, aber die anderen nicht.
>
> Cares like these, whether he likes it or not, a singer
> Must bear in his soul and often, but the others not.

Heidegger identified these "others" as the poet's kin. Without rehearsing all the details of Heidegger's reading, it can be said that Heidegger interpreted the poem as itself a homecoming (EHD 24; EB 281), in the sense of a call to the "others" in the Fatherland to hear the poem so that they might for the first time come to know the essence of the homeland (EHD 28; EB 287). This homecoming is therefore "the future of the historical essence of the Germans" (EHD 29; EB 288). For this reason Heidegger strained the final lines of the poem until they displayed an ambiguity: the others as the carefree ones are said to be free only of the cares of poetic saying, but not from the cares of hearing the poetic word (EHD 28; EB 286). By contrast, the careful hearers are those others who, together with the poet, *think* "the mystery of the reserving proximity" and so, in turning toward the same thing that occupies the poet, become the poet's kin. The kin are in this way identified by their thinking, a thinking which prepares for what is to come: "For now there must be thinking in advance, so that the poetizing words may be heard" (EHD 29; EB 288). The German people are prepared for this not just by the poet, but by the dialogue between poetizing and thinking. That is why Heidegger described them as "the people of poetizing *and* of thinking" (EHD 29; EB 288). "The others" are not just those who do not share the cares of the poetic word. They are at the same time those who hear the poetic word and in thinking about it become the poet's kin. Heidegger ended the essay by emphasizing how the poet cannot easily hold to the word of the reserving proximity and so needs this help (EHD 30; EB 289–90). "The others" seem therefore to perform the task assigned to the preservers in The Origin of the Work of Art (H 56–58; PLT 68–71).[10]

Three or four years after offering this interpretation of Hölderlin's "Homecoming," Heidegger returned to it in a remarkable passage in "The Letter on Humanism." There was nothing surprising about Heidegger's insistence that "homeland" (*Heimat*) be thought "not patriotically or nationalistically." One does not need to refer to the fact that World War II had meanwhile ended. The stipulation recalls Heidegger's comment over 10 years earlier that "Fatherland" should not be thought in terms of unruly patriotism. However, there was one decisive change. Instead of referring the Fatherland to the historical Being of a people, the *Heimat* is now thought in terms of the history of Being (W 168; BW 217). The change in vocabulary is underlined when, in his attempt to support Hölderlin's effort to help his "countrymen" (*Landesleute*) find their essence, Heidegger rejected what he called "the egoism of a people," preferring to speak instead of "the destiny of the West" (W 169; BW 218). On the face of it this would appear to be an attempt to purge his previous account of its focus on the German people. The impression is reinforced when the notion of "the West" is itself made the subject of reinterpretation by being understood "regionally as the Occident in contrast to the Orient, [and] not merely as Europe, but rather world-historically out of nearness to the source." At this point Heidegger offered two brief observations, each referring the reader to poems he had discussed in lecture courses held in 1942. Heidegger's first comment was to suggest that we have still scarcely begun to think the mysterious relations to the East to be found in Hölderlin's poetry. A note directed the reader to "Der Ister" and to the third strophe of "Die Wanderung," where Hölderlin declared himself "bound for the Caucasus" and celebrated an earlier encounter by the Black Sea between the Germans and "the children of the sun." Yet Heidegger's own lectures on "Der Ister" did not reflect this interest. Their focus had fallen heavily on the relation between Greece and Germany at the expense of Hölderlin's references to the East (GA 53, 170).

It would seem, therefore, that in saying that the mysterious relations to the East had not been adequately thought, Heidegger was implicating himself in the general criticism. The temptation is to say the same about the second comment, which referred explicitly to the final pages of Heidegger's essay "Andenken," first published in 1943 and drawing on an earlier lecture course. Heidegger wrote, "'German' is not spoken to the world so that the world might be reformed through the German essence; it is spoken to the Germans so that from a fateful belongingness to the nations they might become world-historical along with them." But Heidegger's reference to the essay "Andenken" is of no help here. Just as, earlier in that essay, Heidegger seemed more interested in the German women of the poem "Gesang des Deutschen" than "the brown women" of "Andenken" (EHD 101–02), so also the discussion at the end of the essay about the need for the German people to learn to be at home is left unencumbered, either by references to other nations or to what he would elsewhere call "historical dwelling in the nearness of Being" (W 169; BW 218). Heidegger does nothing here, or elsewhere, to complicate the simple picture by which the Greeks and the Germans alone are singled out. Or, rather, they are paired, so that every claim about the originality of the Greeks, from *Introduction to Metaphysics* on, indirectly bolsters the Germans. Hence, Heidegger systematically excludes Egypt from his reading of Hölderlin.[11]

It would seem, therefore, that in these brief remarks in the "Letter on Humanism" Heidegger engaged in what was for him the all too familiar task of ontologizing ontic language. In this case, the seemingly nationalistic language of the Hölderlin essays was the issue, just as a few pages earlier he had sought to ontologize the seemingly anthropological language of *Being and Time* (W 156–58; BW 205–07). The attempt was by no means unambiguous, because almost always in such attempts Heidegger would not fail to underline the ontic sense at the very moment he was withdrawing it. This was no exception. Returning to the poem "Andenken" and the notion of homelessness, Heidegger commented that "When confronted with death, therefore, those young Germans who knew about Hölderlin lived and thought something other than what the public held to be the typical German attitude" (W 170; BW 219). A strange scene to evoke in a letter written to a French officer in 1946!

It seems that the 1959 lecture "Hölderlins Erde und Himmel" fulfilled Heidegger's attempt to reread Hölderlin as primarily a world-historical poet rather than as simply the "poet of the Germans." Heidegger's reading of "Das Griechenland" was governed by his understanding of Hölderlin's letter to Böhlendorff from the autumn of 1802, just as the reading of "Andenken" had been governed by his understanding of Hölderlin's 1801 letter to Böhlendorff about the indispensability of the Greeks and the difficulty of the Germans learning what is proper to them. By focusing on Greece the problematic of the Germans disappeared into the notion of the West, as Heidegger had proposed it should in "The Letter on Humanism." If Heidegger, contrary to the "Letter," then went on in this essay to refer the West to Europe, it was not in geographical terms. If the West has become Europe, it is in terms of a certain technological and industrial dominance. Heidegger posed the question here of whether the advent of another dawn of world history must not arise in Europe, given what he took to be the fact that the present condition of the world was in its essential origin European through and through (EHD 176–77).[12] But the German people had not disappeared from Heidegger's agenda, any more than their relative absence from "Hölderlin and the Essence of Poetry" was anything but an illusion. As "the poet of poets," Hölderlin remained "the poet of the Germans" for Heidegger. This was the premise underlying all of Heidegger's writings on Hölderlin.

The notorious *Der Spiegel* interview, conducted in 1966 but not published until Heidegger's death 10 years later, confirms this.[13] In an attempt to lead Heidegger "away from generalities to a specific destiny of the Germans" (NG 214; HNS 62), the interviewer confronted Heidegger with a passage from his 1936/37 lectures "The Will to Power as Art," in which Hölderlin and Nietzsche are said to have "placed a question mark after the task of the German people to find their essence historically" (NI 124; Ni 104). Heidegger's first answer was in the language of the essay "Hölderlins Erde und Himmel": "I could put what is said in the quotation in this way: I am convinced that a change can only be prepared from the same place in the world where the modern technological world originated." Only when the interviewer repeated the question, "Do you allocate a special task specifically to the Germans?" did Heidegger revert to his earlier language and concede, "Yes, in that sense, in dialogue with Hölderlin" (NG 217; HNS 63). Furthermore, Heidegger specified that what suited the Germans for this task was "the special inner relationship between the German language and the language and thinking of the Greeks."

It would seem, therefore, that Heidegger never entirely displaced the reference to the Germans as the third party which dominated—albeit for the most part without being explicitly mentioned—his account of the dialogue between poetizing and thinking. If in the 1950s Heidegger referred that dialogue less to the politically charged notion of the people and more to that of language, this does not succeed entirely in concealing the continuity in Heidegger's thought on this point.[14] Language, for Heidegger, was always the language of a people. It is no accident that the two quotations from Wilhelm von Humboldt which close the 1959 lecture on language both concern the transformation of the language of a people: "Through inner illumination and the favor of outer circumstances, a people might so utterly impart a different form to the language bequeathed to it, that this language would thereby become an entirely different and new one."[15] It is true that this is not how Heidegger would have presented the issue himself. He would have emphasized the sense in which a people first become a people in this transformation of language, whereas von Humboldt was describing how, long after the original creation of a language, an already available sound-form might be applied to the inner purposes of language. Heidegger's second quotation from von Humboldt is similarly heard differently, in the context of Heidegger's text, from the way it reads in its original context. Von Humboldt was concerned with the way there is some latitude in every language as regards sentence structure and the ordering of speech, such that a people's literature, particularly its poetry and philosophy, can produce new idioms and so bring to language what it does not yet possess. In the context of Heidegger's essay one understands that the transformation of our relation to language can be brought about through the belonging together of poetizing and thinking (US 267; WL 136). Time can introduce new meaning to old words and old laws of syntax can give rise to different ideas. "This is a continuing harvest from the *literature* of a people, though especially there from its *poetry* and *philosophy*."[16] More striking still is the fact that the questions dominating the essays on language, questions about undergoing an experience with language and about bringing language to language, were already raised in the first lecture course on Hölderlin with an explicitly "political" aim in mind (GA 39, 76). The indications are, therefore, that Heidegger did not purge the dialogue between poetizing and thinking of its "political" reference to the foundation of a people, so much as conceal it.

That he did so is disturbing, but of itself it probably cannot be regarded as sinister. It is not the reference to a people that compromises Heidegger's thought by tying it to the political context of Germany in the 1930s. It is the fact that he employs the idea of *the* people, which in context means, of course, the German people. It would be a mistake to suppose that Heidegger's insistence specifically on the German people was simply the product of the nationalism of his times. The story according to which the Germans were the privileged heirs of the Greeks and shared a unique relation with them was not original to the twentieth century, although—as Heidegger himself pointed out (GA 53, 98)—it took a particularly distorted form among the National Socialists. Even if Heidegger did misrepresent Hölderlin's account of the relation of the Greeks with the Germans by excluding reference to Egypt, he nevertheless relied heavily on that account to understand the task of thinking at the end of philosophy.

However, the dialogue between poetry and thinking went farther than confirming a traditional, if often neglected, truth that poetry is the poetry of a people, just as philosophy is the philosophy of a people. It went beyond privileging, according to a version of the history of Western philosophy that Heidegger accepted and rewrote, the Greek and German peoples (GA 65, 42). Heidegger neither ignored the idea of a people nor took it for granted. He posed the question of the way in which a people becomes a people. The poet and the thinker, as "the few" in which "the voice of the people speaks out rarely [*selten*]," was Heidegger's answer to this question (GA 65, 319): "The people first becomes a people when the most singular ones arrive and begin to presage [*ahnen*]" (GA 65, 43). The verb *ahnen* had special echoes for Heidegger. Hölderlin in *Wie wenn am Feiertage* had written of nature:

> Drum wenn zu schlafen sie scheint zu Zeiten des Jahrs
> Am Himmel oder unter den Pflanzen oder den Völkern,
> So trauert der Dichter Angesicht auch,
> Sie scheinen allein zu seyn, doch ahnen sie immer.

> Thus if she seems to sleep at times of the year
> In the heavens or among the plants or peoples,
> So the faces of the poets also mourn.
> They seem to be alone, but are always presaging.

The poets, like the thinkers, may appear to be alone, but in their presaging they, as the coming poets, are not alone. Presaging, the poet names the holy, a word which "still unheard, is preserved in the language of the Germans" (EHD 74), and which served to call the German people to themselves.

The dialogue between poetizing and thinking originally provoked suspicion because it appeared to establish the exclusive community of the poet and the thinker, "on mountains farthest part," neighbors to each other in their isolation from the rest of humanity. The publication of the lecture courses from the 1930s and early 1940s has given rise to a new suspicion directed at Heidegger's politics and his evocation of "the German people," at a time when such remarks were at best "unpropitious" and at worst damning. Nevertheless, in the urge of Heidegger's readers to distance themselves from this gesture, there is a danger that they miss the fact that his reference of poetry to a people serves as a decisive step in withdrawing art from its subordination to aesthetics. The community between poet and thinker arises as the community that founds community, the community of a people who are more than a public. Such a conception, Heidegger insists, breaks the arts, and poetry in particular, from their confinement within aesthetics, where they stand divorced from the broader realm of political concerns. Of course, art within aesthetics was never entirely free from politics. Within humanist aesthetics one might be regarded as somehow less of "a man," even less than human, to the extent that one was a barbarian or a philistine, unable to appreciate the nobility of the arts. Heidegger's conception is ripe for continuing the same tyranny of taste, where the capacity to discriminate within the arts reflects and justifies discrimination between peoples and within a people. Heidegger's rhetoric is not free from remarks of that tenor, but they arise to the extent that he forgets the paradoxical temporality of the constitution of the people. It is not the poet who, with the thinker, founds a people simply. It needs a people to prove the poet to be a poet in the operative sense and to prove the thinker a thinker. It is in the coming community of a people that the community of the poet and thinker will have been established.

Part Three

◆

HISTORY AND HISTORIOLOGY

9

Descartes in the History of Being: Another Bad Novel?

What is Descartes's place in the history of metaphysics? The usual answer is that Descartes stands at the beginning of modern philosophy, and Heidegger seemed most often to accept this.[1] However, Heidegger could also be found, for example, in his 1935/36 lecture course, contesting the customary portrait of Descartes on which he believed that this answer is based. According to this picture, Descartes was someone who, through the procedure of doubting, discovered the *ego sum* as an indubitable foundation and so liberated philosophy from its subordination to theology and its stultification in the mere analysis of concepts and the discussion of traditional opinions (FD 76–77; WT 98–99). My question here is not how adequate or just Heidegger's caricature of the standard portrait of Descartes was to the philosophers and scholars of his day.[2] Nor shall I ask whether the changes since undergone in the study of Descartes would complicate this representation. More serious still, because it exaggerates the provisional status of my treatment of these issues, I shall have to forgo a detailed discussion of Descartes's own texts. My question is limited to the judgment that places Descartes at the beginning of modern philosophy. Insofar as Heidegger accepted this view, what could he have meant by it? What happens when such a thesis from the history of philosophy is taken up into the so-called history of Being?

The terms in which Heidegger in 1935/36 rejected what he regarded as the standard account of Descartes will help to explain my title. The passage in the translation of W. B. Barton, Jr., and Vera Deutsch runs, "This story of Descartes, who came and doubted and so became a subjectivist, thus grounding epistemology, does give the usual picture; but at best it is only a bad novel and anything but a story in which the movement of being becomes visible" (FD 77; WT 99). It should be noted that the word twice translated as "story" is *Geschichte*, which is also a word for history. When Heidegger uses *Geschichte* to refer to the history of Being, he emphasizes its proximity to *Geschick*, with its connotations of sending, fittingness, and destiny. *Ge-schick* is a "gathering sending" (*versammelndes Schicken*) (VA 32; QT 24). Had the translators not been concerned to show that the same word is used twice, they would no doubt have found it more natural to translate it differently on each occasion. The passage would have read, "This story of Descartes, who came and doubted and so became a subjectivist, thus grounding epistemology, does give the usual picture; but at best it is only a bad novel [*ein schlechter Roman*] and anything but a history in which the movement of Being [*Sein*] becomes visible." If the remark is not to recoil on Heidegger, the implication must be that the history of Being is not a novel, at least not a bad one.³ There is, of course, another word for history in German, *Historie*, but it does not so readily bear the double sense that the word *Geschichte* enjoys, except perhaps archaically.

I should mention that in place of the standard interpretation Heidegger focuses on how "the further destiny [*Schicksal*] and form of modern philosophy" was determined on the basis of Descartes's reflection on the mathematical in the *Regulae ad directionem ingenii* (FD 79; WT 102). It is primarily because of a radicalization of the mathematical and the axiomatic, rather than as a consequence of doubting, that the I becomes defined as the special subject from which, through representation, all other things "mathematically" receive the thingly character of being an object. The word *subjectum*, which had previously covered all things at hand, is now reserved for the "I" of the I think. *Objectum*, a word which had previously been reserved for what one cast before oneself in mere fantasy, was now extended to designate things in their relation to the subject. This, Heidegger observes, marks a transformation in the language of philosophy that is no mere terminological change, but "a radical change of *Dasein*, that is, of the *Lichtung* of the Being of beings on the basis of the predominance of the *mathematical*." Heidegger continues, "*It is a stretch of the way of authentic [eigentlich] history necessarily hidden from the usual view*, a history which always concerns the openness of Being—or nothing at all" (FD 82; WT 106).

The question is how such a history, once brought to light, might avoid being simply another bad novel. What does the thesis that modern philosophy begins with Descartes mean if it is not the plot of a novel? It would be a novel of which Descartes wrote the first draft in the *Discourse on the Method of Rightly Conducting One's Reason and Seeking for Truth in the Sciences*. Descartes himself describes his treatise "simply as a history, or, if you prefer, a fable." Or, instead of "a history" one should perhaps translate *une histoire* as "a story," since there is a similar ambiguity governing the French word as has already been observed in the case of the German *Geschichte*.⁴ Subsequently Descartes warns his reader against fables and histories, and even though he does not show himself aware that this warning must apply equally to the history or fable which issues the warning, it is not impossible that he does. For, along with castigating both fables (for making one imagine events to be possible which are not really so) and histories (for their omissions), he warns against taking them as models for one's own conduct, since anybody who did would be liable to "conceive plans beyond their powers"; and this warning is one which Descartes explicitly issued to his readers with respect to his own project.[5]

If Descartes's own *Discourse on Method* was the first draft of this novel, there have been subsequent versions of the story. Heidegger was particularly fond of quoting Hegel's lyrical praise of Descartes in his lectures on the history of philosophy, where the philosophy of the modern world was said to have begun with Descartes: "Here, we may say, we are at home and, like the sailor after a long voyage, we can at last shout 'Land ho.' "[6] While Hegel was giving his lectures in Berlin, in Munich Schelling was similarly describing Descartes as the "initiator of modern philosophy." According to Schelling, Descartes "had begun to break off all connection with earlier philosophy, to wipe away, as if with a sponge, everything that had been accomplished in this science before him, and to rebuild philosophy again from the start, as though no one had philosophized before him."[7]

However, it would seem that it was neither Hegel nor Schelling whom Heidegger had in mind in rejecting the standard reading of Descartes as a bad novel, but rather the neo-Kantian interpretation. In *The Basic Problems of Phenomenology* Heidegger had observed that "The Neo-Kantianism of recent decades introduced the historical construction that with Descartes a completely new epoch of philosophy begins. Everything before him back to Plato, who was himself interpreted in terms of Kantian categories, was supposed to be mere darkness" (GA 24, 174; BP 124). Heidegger continues, "In opposition to this notion, it is rightly stressed today that modern philosophy since Descartes still continues to work with the ancient metaphysical problems and thus, along with everything new, still remains within the tradition. But this correction of the Neo-Kantian interpretation of the history of thought does not yet touch the decisive point for a philosophical understanding of modern philosophy." Heidegger rejects the claim of the scholars that the new metaphysical problems were posed on the foundation of the old, which would deny the claim of modern philosophy to be a turning point. "On the contrary, by this turnabout, by this allegedly critical new beginning ancient metaphysics became dogmatism, which it had not earlier been in this style; it had become a mode of thought that with the aid of traditional metaphysical concepts seeks to gain a positively ontical knowledge of God, the soul, and nature" (GA 24, 175; BP 124).

These remarks from *The Basic Problems of Phenomenology* serve as a decisive clue for understanding what Heidegger was attempting in his discussion of Descartes in *Being and Time*, and in particular the role it plays in the so-called destruction of the history of ontology. Heidegger's first lectures in Marburg, held in the winter semester, 1923/24, and devoted to Descartes, had for their title *Der Beginn der neuzeitlichen Philosophie*. At the time of my writing, the publication of these lectures is expected soon and the significance of the title can only then be examined in its context. Meanwhile, to reread *Being and Time* is to find that at that time Heidegger showed relatively little interest in the question of the beginning of modern philosophy. On the single occasion when he refers to this claim, he does so not in his own voice, but by saying that "one" credits Descartes's discovery of the *cogito sum* with being the departure point of modern philosophy (SZ 45–46; BT 71). The whole emphasis of the discussion of Descartes in the published sections of *Being and Time*, and particularly sections 19 to 21, is on Descartes's lack of radicality. And Heidegger gives his reader sufficient indications of the proposed but never published discussion of Descartes's *cogito* in Part Two, division two of *Being and Time*, for there to be no reason to doubt that this emphasis would have been maintained. So, "by working out the unexpressed ontological foundations of the *cogito sum*" (SZ 24; BT 46), that is, by a "phenomenological destruction of the *cogito sum*" (SZ 89; BT 123), Heidegger would have reversed the *cogito sum*, so that it would be shown that the *sum* in the sense of "I am in the world" precedes the *cogito* (SZ 211; BT 254). In so doing he would have reiterated a point he had already anticipated five years earlier in Freiburg (GA 61, 171–75).

It seems that in the 1920s Heidegger believed that Descartes stood at the beginning of modern philosophy, understood in terms of the dominance of the mathematical science of nature (GA 29/30, 83). But that was a relatively unimportant issue within the general framework of the destruction of the history of ontology. What was crucial to Heidegger was, first, to challenge the claim that Descartes established a new beginning for philosophy, a claim which would run counter to Heidegger's return to the Greeks to find "the original experiences in which we achieved our first and subsequently guiding determinations of Being" (SZ 22; BT 44). And secondly, alongside this, to show how Descartes, far from challenging these determinations of Being, merely accepted them in their essentials. Indeed, what is said to set Descartes apart from his predecessors and justify his claim to begin modern philosophy is his readiness to accept previous ontological decisions unquestioningly. Heidegger's approach to Descartes was in this way dominated by the task of the destruction of the history of ontology. The destruction was not an attack on Western philosophy in general or indeed on any of its "representatives," including Descartes. There is an unquestionably critical tone to Heidegger's discussion of Descartes in *Being and Time*, made all the more noticeable because of the high esteem in which Descartes is usually held.[8] This tone is present when, for example, Heidegger identifies one sentence in Descartes as an evasion (SZ 93; BT 126) or when he notes Descartes's general "lack of mastery of the basic problem of Being" (SZ 94; BT 127).[9] But when Heidegger calls his account of Descartes in *Being and Time* a "critical discussion" (SZ 98; BT 131), the word criticism is to be understood primarily in the same positive sense it has when Heidegger laments the fact that Descartes's own basic ontological orientation toward the tradition was "devoid of any positive criticism" (SZ 98; BT 131). Of course, it is not possible to bemoan the lack of positive criticism in a thinker without oneself making a negative criticism. But the positive criticism which Heidegger attempts to pursue and which he says is absent from Descartes consists in putting *Dasein* in question (GA 29/30, 30). In other words, it is the raising of the question of Being. Heidegger's negative criticism is directed less against those figures who might be called the representatives of the tradition than against "the inept guardians" of the tradition, for example, the neo-Kantians (GA 26, 197; MFL 155).

The destruction was concerned with staking out the positive possibilities of the tradition. There is even an indication in *Being and Time* of how the Cartesian analysis of the world in terms of *extensio* might still be "rescued" by referring it to Kant's discussion of spatiality (SZ 101; BT 134). The negative role of destruction was limited primarily to a criticism of the contemporary approach to the history of ontology. And that tended to mean neo-Kantianism, including its presentation of Descartes as the founder of modern philosophy. Descartes, standing at the beginning of modern philosophy, was for Heidegger a signpost on the way back to the Greek beginnings. The beginning which took place with Descartes was not new, although the temptation to mark the modern era as new is particularly strong if one writes in German, where the word for the modern period is *die Neuzeit*.

To take up briefly the first aspect of the destruction, Heidegger, as I have said, issued a challenge to the claim that Descartes established a new beginning for philosophy. That this was to have been, at least in part, the concern of the discussion of Descartes in Part Two is indicated by its projected title—"The ontological foundations of Descartes' *cogito sum*, and how medieval ontology has been taken over into the problematic of the *res cogitans*" (SZ 40; BT 64)—and more particularly by certain remarks in the second half of section 6 of *Being and Time*, which offers a brief preview of the unpublished sections. We read there that

> the seemingly new beginning which Descartes proposed for philosophizing has revealed itself as the implantation of a baleful prejudice, which has

kept later generations from making any thematic ontological analytic of the "mind" such as would take the question of Being as a clue and would at the same time come to grips critically with the traditional ancient ontology. (SZ 25; BT 46)

And in Part One of *Being and Time*, as well as in lecture courses from the Marburg period, Heidegger shows how Descartes had to a large extent adopted and maintained the scholastic vocabulary of Aquinas and particularly Suarez. It was an observation familiar to Descartes scholars of the 1920s.[10] But it lent credence to the view that Descartes operated under the "unbroken ascendancy of the traditional ontology" (SZ 96; BT 129). Indeed, in comparison with the scholastic notion of analogy—and here Heidegger refers explicitly to Cajetan—"Descartes is always far behind" (SZ 93; BT 126).

If the primary task was to show Descartes's dependence on previous thinking, the secondary task was to show the dependence of subsequent thinking on Descartes. The priority between the two enterprises was indicated at the beginning of the discussion of Descartes, in the first division of the first part of *Being and Time*. "The account we shall give of these matters will enable us to know upon what basically undiscussed ontological 'foundations' those interpretations of the world have come after Descartes—and still more those which preceded him have operated" (SZ 89; BT 122). The priority simply reflects the direction of the inquiry. It was not Descartes who diverted philosophy from the phenomenon of the world toward nature. This is a consequence of the interpretation of Being to be found in Plato and Aristotle. Similarly, only the "proximate roots" of the distinction between nature and spirit are found in Descartes (SZ 89; BT 123). There was indeed a shift in Descartes "from the development of traditional ontology to modern mathematical physics and its transcendental foundations" (SZ 96; BT 129).[11] But what was crucial for Heidegger at this time was the ontological dogmatism which accompanied this shift, in which all subsequent philosophy was implicated. It was a question, for example, of "how ontologically groundless are the problematics of the Self from Descartes' *res cogitans* right up to Hegel's concept of spirit" (SZ 320n; BT 497nxix). If Heidegger did not feel as at home with Descartes as Hegel did, this was for essential reasons. Nor did the sequence stop with Hegel. Heidegger associated Husserl and indeed all phenomenology with the Cartesian framework.[12] Nor, ultimately, was Kant an exception. "Notwithstanding all the essential respects in which he had gone beyond him" (SZ 24; BT 45), Kant adopted Descartes's position quite dogmatically and simply occupied a place, albeit a decisive one, between Descartes and Hegel (GA 24, 177; BP 125).

If Descartes's ontological definition of the world was in error (SZ 95:

BT 128), if he was accused of skipping over the phenomenon of the world, these were understood as characteristics not simply of modern philosophy but of the ontological tradition from its very beginning in Parmenides, as the missing third division of the first part of *Being and Time* was to have shown (SZ 100; BT 133). Descartes was simply "the most extreme tendency" of a certain ontology (SZ 66; BT 95), "the most extreme form in which it has been carried out" (SZ 89; BT 122), "the most extreme counterinstance of the determination of the Being of the entity as a world" (GA 20, 232; HCT 172). But Descartes's extremism was not of the kind which would leave him isolated on the sidelines. It was rather what assured him his centrality within the history of Western philosophy:

> In his analysis and determination of the Being of the world he stands at a characteristic place in the development of this question [of the structure of the Being of the world]. On the one hand, he assumes the determinations of the Being of the world as they were drawn by the Middle Ages and so by Greek philosophy. And yet, on the other hand, because of *the extreme way* in which he raises the question of the Being of the world, he prefigures all the problems which then emerge in Kant's *Critique of Pure Reason* and elsewhere. (GA 20, 232; HCT 172. My italics)

This seems to suggest that Descartes did raise the question of the Being of the world. What underlies this claim? Heidegger was clear that Descartes (like Plato and Aristotle) raised the question of Being only in the limited sense of the Being of nature. But Heidegger nevertheless gave particular prominence to Descartes's recognition that the Being of a being does not "affect" us, a recognition which Heidegger also identified as underlying Kant's claim that "Being is not a real predicate." Descartes wrote in the *Principles of Philosophy* that "Substance cannot be first discovered merely from the fact that it is an existing thing, since this alone does not of itself affect us."[13] In *Being and Time* Heidegger understood Descartes's admission that Being is "inaccessible" and so "incapable of clarification" in the light of his alleged evasion of the question of Being (SZ 94; BT 127). But in the 1925 lecture course Heidegger had seemed to suggest that—"without Descartes knowing it and also perhaps without Kant ultimately understanding it"— this "peculiar principle" that Being does not affect us was perhaps the most clear-cut formulation of the Being of "world." For it pointed to the fact that "we are not capable of apprehending the Being of beings primarily and in isolation, but always first apprehend *what* a being is" (GA 20, 236–37; HCT 175). This introduced the possibility of a more open or generous account of Descartes, a possibility which *Being and Time* did not take up.

On the present evidence there is no reason to doubt that in the Marburg period Heidegger placed Descartes at the beginning of modern philosophy.

But what began with Descartes was not regarded by Heidegger as essentially new except insofar as its ontological dogmatism could be said to be new. Heidegger expressed this view again very clearly at the beginning of the 1930s, when he said that the new orientation toward consciousness in modern philosophy since Descartes was not a radically new beginning which broke with Greek philosophy. But, whereas the Greeks interpreted Being as *logos*, the fact that this ancient starting point was now transferred to the subject indicated that the motives and goals determining the philosophy of antiquity were no longer understood (GA 32, 196). Underlying this interpretation was Heidegger's conception of the unity of philosophy. And this interpretation was to be complicated, though not essentially challenged, in the 1930s, then Heidegger construed the history of philosophy in terms of three epochs—the Greek, the Medieval, and the Modern.

This conventional division was not totally absent from the Marburg period, even if it was not at that time understood epochally. But how is the introduction of epochality to be understood? Is Heidegger's account of the three epochs any less a story than that told by the neo-Kantians? How does the notion of epochality function alongside the list of the words which say the transformation of Being? If the whole of modern metaphysics taken together, as Heidegger suggested, is contained within the interpretation of beings and of truth prepared by Descartes (H 80; QT 127), how is this whole marked by the chain or list of the transformations of Being? The division into three epochs is taken over from Hegel, but what is the significance of the fact that Heidegger elucidates the notion of epoch in terms of *Ansichhalten*, in the sense of a holding back? It would require a broader inquiry than is possible here to chart how the discourse of the growing oblivion of Being is interwoven with the language of the saying of Being. But it clearly signals a transformation of Heidegger's understanding of his task, which is no longer conceived in terms of the destruction of the history of ontology, at least as construed in *Being and Time*. In 1941—that is, after most of the texts I shall be considering—Heidegger was able to refer to the destruction as introduced in *Being and Time* and say that it had "not yet been thought in terms of the history of Being" (NII 415; EP 15).

The difference between the destruction of the history of ontology, on the one hand, and the history of Being, on the other, is perhaps best indicated by comparing the treatment of the subject-object distinction within each. Whereas in *Being and Time* Heidegger regarded the subject-object distinction, for all its "facticity," as ontologically inadequate, he would emphasize later its truth rather than its vacuity: "Man becomes subject" (H 81; QT 128).[14] It is, one might say, an ontological event. Similarly, Descartes's maintenance of Scholastic terminology, which in *Being and Time* was seen as evidence of his lack of radicality, was subsequently greeted as "the sign of a genuine transition." "It almost seems as if in the beginning of modern metaphysics the traditional essence of reality, *actualitas*, is maintained just as it is . . ." (N II 428; EP 25). I cannot now rehearse the details of this transformation in Heidegger's thinking. And it should be understood that if I sometimes use the label "the history of Being" in discussing this transformation, I am referring to more than simply the sketches of the early 1940s that bear this title. In this context what is most important is Heidegger's recognition of the end of philosophy in the sense of the exhaustion of its possibilities. That Descartes was the founder of modern philosophy meant, for Heidegger, not only that "the whole of modern metaphysics taken together, Nietzsche included, maintains itself within the interpretation of beings and of truth that was prepared by Descartes" (H 80; QT 127). More than that, Descartes "begins the completion and consummation of Western metaphysics" (H 91; QT 140). There is a unity to the modern epoch which is in turn enclosed within the larger unit of metaphysics itself, so that the three epochs of the history of metaphysics together constitute the single epoch of metaphysics.[15] Heidegger attempted in this way to retain the unity of metaphysics in spite of the discontinuity which marks the relation of the three epochs to each other. The difficulty this presents can be indicated by the tension found within the following sentence from "The Age of the World Picture": "The fundamental metaphysical position of Descartes is taken over historically from the Platonic-Aristotelian metaphysics and moves, despite its new beginning, within the same question: What is a being [*Was ist das Seiende*]?" (H 91; QT 139). Is the phrase "new beginning" used here ironically? Does Heidegger mean to say that the question persists "in spite of the *claim* that there is with Descartes a new beginning"? When Heidegger says that Descartes moves within the same question as previous metaphysics—the question of the being—is he repeating the so-called *Destruktion* of *Being and Time*, where Descartes's failure is the characteristic failure to criticize or put in question the ontological prejudices of the tradition he inherited? Or has Heidegger found a sense of "the new beginning" which reconciles it with Descartes's use of traditional language? The next sentence provides an answer: "That this question [the question of beings], formulated in this way, does not come to the fore in Descartes' *Meditations* only proves how essentially the modified answer to it already determines the fundamental position." This is Heidegger's own reply to his treatment of Descartes in *Being and Time*. The transformation which takes place with Descartes, and which Heidegger is prepared—at least provisionally—to call a new beginning, does not depend on the introduction of a new terminology or even, it seems, a fundamental questioning of the character of Being.

The 1940 lecture series on European Nihilism helps to clarify the apparent enigmas of the 1938 lecture on "The Age of the World Picture." Heidegger again observed the way Descartes's language was that of medieval scholasticism. In particular Heidegger drew attention to Descartes's designation of God, the *substantia infinita*, as *summum ens* and *creator*, and to the understanding of *substantia finita* as *ens creatum*. Heidegger wrote, "Thus all being is seen from the point of view of *creator* and *creatum*, and the new delineation of man through the *cogito sum* is, as it were, simply sketched into the old framework. Here we have the most palpable example of earlier metaphysics impeding a new beginning for metaphysical thought. A historiological report on the meaning and nature of Descartes' doctrine is forced to establish such results" (NII 163; Niv 115). This was, of course, the conclusion drawn in *Being and Time*, and Heidegger focuses on it as if he wanted to emphasize the contrast. For, in the 1940 lecture course, Heidegger immediately proceeded to contrast Descartes's intentions with Descartes's language. "A historical meditation on the inquiry proper, however, must strive to think Descartes' principles and concepts in the sense he himself wanted them to have, even if in so doing it should prove necessary to translate his assertions into another 'language'" (NII 163–64; Niv 115). Descartes's language is essentially that of scholasticism, but Heidegger decided to give credit to Descartes's intentions. It is what Descartes wants to say—although he lacks the resources to say it—which exceeds the previous epoch.

Of course, readiness to translate a philosopher into a subsequent terminology is not normally understood by Heidegger as a defensible procedure. The whole meditation on Descartes in these lectures had, after all, begun in an attempt to show that the language of subjectivity was not appropriate for the interpretation of Protagoras's saying, "Man is the measure of all things." But, as already noted, the language of subjectivity that is said to identify Descartes's position rarely, if at all, dominates his texts and is more characteristic of subsequent writers like Leibniz.[16] Heidegger appears, therefore, to authorize the translation of Descartes's thinking into the language of Leibniz (among others) according to Descartes's intentions. What is supposed to give legitimacy to this procedure is the distinction between the historical and the historiological. The historiological sees only the continuity of previous metaphysical positions, as a consequence of the continued use of the language in which they are usually couched. Such language impedes a new beginning. It was a meditation of this kind which dominated in *Being and Time*. The distinction used here between the historiological (*historisch*) and the historical (*geschichtlich*) may not be the same as that found in *Being and Time*, but "the historiological destruction of the history of philosophy" (SZ 392; BT 444) to be found in *Being and Time* still stands. It was the historiological evidence of Descartes's continued use of scholastic terminology which put in question the neo-Kantian interpretation of Descartes as the founder of modern philosophy, just as it also concealed the ontological dogmatism which Descartes introduced into modern philosophy.

In contrast to the historiological approach, which affirms the power of the *logos* to control and contain whatever is said in it, according to the terms in which it is said, it is the task of historical meditation to translate what was said into another language. Heidegger even attempted a defense of this procedure on what would appear to be historiological grounds. "Through his many efforts to make what was new in his grounding of metaphysics intelligible to his contemporaries by responding to their doubts, Descartes was forced to discourse at the already prevailing level and so to explain his fundamental position superficially, that is, always inappropriately, a contingency that threatens *every essential thinking* [Heidegger's italics]..." (NII 167–68; Niv 118). What Heidegger describes as a contingency, or perhaps more neutrally as an event or occurrence (*Vorgang*), is a necessity, but it is not the necessity of the history of Being but of historiography. Descartes found himself obliged to use the inherited language, whereas those who came after him used a subsequent language more attuned to what was to be said. "The nature of such a transformation implies that the transformation often pursues its course within the very 'language' and representations of what is left behind by the transformation. On the other hand, an unequivocal characterization of the transformation cannot avoid speaking in the language of what is first attained in the transformation" (NII 143; Niv 97). The account of language presupposed here is not unimpeachable, but it should not be forgotten that Heidegger does not place a value on unequivocal language as such. It is ambiguity which is "the sign of a genuine transition" (NII 428; EP 25).

My investigation here into the transformation in Heidegger's reading of Descartes as a consequence of the discovery of the history of Being has come to focus on the difference between the historical and historiological. It should always be remembered that the two are initially to be conceived as in conflict with each other. In one place Heidegger warned that all historiology "systematically destroys the future and our historic relation to the advent of sending [*Geschick*]" (H 301; EGT 17). In another he observed that if one were "to construct the history of Being in accordance with the *historiological* representational thinking common today, the dominance of the oblivion of Being's destiny would be confirmed in the most blatant way" (VA 80; EP 93). But Heidegger was also well aware of the problems involved in maintaining the distinction. These are well exhibited by an examination of Heidegger's appeal to it at the culmination of the lecture course on European Nihilism. Heidegger there sought to establish a connection between Descartes and Nietzsche which would confirm the unity of the modern epoch as the epoch of the completion of Western metaphysics (NII 173; Niv 122). The attempt to enclose Nietzsche, along with Leibniz, Kant, and Hegel, in an epoch that found its beginning in Descartes was not meant to be a way of reducing them all to Descartes. Heidegger marked this by providing various lists of the words of Being in metaphysics. Each of the words says Being in a unique manner so that none of them can be reduced to any of the others. But together they are supposed to show the completeness of metaphysics and to confirm the unity of the modern epoch within it. Heidegger addressed this question by again appealing to the distinction between *Geschichte* as "the experience of the most concealed history of Being," on the one hand, and *Historie* as "a historiological report of various interpretations of the Being of beings," on the other, even though he was ready to concede that the two were "barely distinguishable" (NII 235; Niv 178).

The sketch of the history of Being which follows the introduction of this distinction provides a dramatic confirmation of how difficult it is to draw the distinction between *Geschichte* and *Historie*. First, Heidegger refers to Plato's interpretation of the beingness of beings as *idea*, its revision into the Latin *idea* as *perceptio* in Descartes, Kant's doctrine of the objectivity of objects, and Hegel's unconditioned subjectivity as absolute idea. This introduces the question of whether or not Nietzschean "will to power" descends on metaphysics without historical precedent as an arbitrary explanation of beings as a whole. It seems to Heidegger that he can satisfactorily solve this problem only by introducing the names of Aristotle and Leibniz. They provide the missing links of the chain, which enable Heidegger to announce triumphantly, "Thus it seems that we have found the historical thread along which we can pursue the historical provenance of the projection of beings as will to power." Or at least, the announcement would have had a triumphal tone had it not been somewhat muted by the interruption of the phrase *der geschichtliche Strang*, with the bracketed question *oder nur der historische?* (NII 237; Niv 180). There is no affirmation of the distinction between *Geschichte* and *Historie*, but only an extraordinary hesitation at the culmination of its application.

That Heidegger wavered at this point was no momentary lapse. In the following year, 1941, he addressed the same dilemma at the beginning of "Metaphysics as History of Being," which was an attempt to present, in continuous prose and in terms of the transformation of the essence of truth, what stands only as a list in, for example, the document simply labelled "Being" among the notes collected under the title "Sketches for a History of Being as Metaphysics." "Metaphysics of History of Being" begins by saying that "one could take what follows as an historiological [*historischen*] report on the history [*Geschichte*] of the concept of Being. Then what is essential would be missed. But perhaps what is essential can at times scarcely be said otherwise" (NII 399; EP 1). The distinction between history and historiology is not the solution to a problem, but rather a precarious way of recognizing an unavoidable dilemma.

The question may be posed as follows: Why is the sequence Plato, Descartes, Kant, Hegel, Nietzsche to be dismissed as arbitrary, while the sequence Plato, Aristotle, Descartes, Leibniz, Kant, Hegel, Nietzsche is supposed to have some persuasive force, an explanatory power, a certain necessity? Or better, why is the chain which runs *idea*, *perceptio*, objectivity, absolute idea, will to power presumed to lack conviction, whereas the chain which runs *idea*, *energia*, *perceptio*, *vis*, objectivity, absolute idea, will to power thought to show the guiding thread of metaphysics?

Heidegger attempted to make the list convincing by showing its explanatory force. But what carries conviction in explanatory terms is the guiding thread of a story. This only accentuates the difficulty, as Heidegger's remarks about the nature of explanation from "The Age of the World Picture" show. To take just one of them, "The unique, the rare, the simple—in short, the great—in history is never self-evident and hence remains inexplicable" (H 76; QT 123). Heidegger's dilemma was that to make his account seem less arbitrary, he needed to make it look more and more like a story or an explanation. And historiology, representation, and explanation all belong together, enclosed in the modern epoch as "The Age of the World Picture" and other texts indicate (e.g. VA 63; QT 175). And yet, of course, without this coherence borrowed from representation, all talk of necessity with reference to the history of Being appears shallow and arbitrary.

What status does any one of Heidegger's lists of the words of Being have? What are they lists of? Heidegger introduces such lists by saying that "there is only Being in this or that historic [*geschicklich*] character" (I 64; ID 66) or by referring to "the abundance of transformations of presencing" which we can historiologically (*historisch*) pin down (*feststellen*) (SD 7; TB 7). And he adds a warning that the historical is not lined up like apples, pears, or peaches on the counter of historiological representational thinking (I 64; ID 66). That, we are told, is not how it is given. But how else can it be said or thought?

What form does the saying of Being take in Descartes? The question is not the same as that which asks what Descartes may have said about what the tradition calls Being. The saying of Being is a very different matter from what a thinker says *about* Being or what a thinker says *with* the word Being. Descartes, on Heidegger's account, is such an extreme case of the oblivion of Being that, if it were a question of what he contributed to the explicit discussion of Being, his would not be an important place. Only in the 1925 lecture course does Heidegger seem to attempt to find in Descartes's texts—

and then perhaps in spite of Descartes himself—a saying of the Being of the world, albeit that in *Being and Time* the emphasis is placed rather on Descartes's evasion of the question of Being.

But it is a different question when attention is directed to the transformations of Being as presence. With Descartes the epoch of representation is introduced, so that it would seem that the word of Being in Descartes is representedness (*Vorgestelltheit*) or *repraesentatio* (NII 162–67; Niv 114– 18), although such words as *certitudo*, *percipere* as *cogitatio*, and *subjectum* are so closely related to it that they also serve in its place, bound (one feels tempted to say) as elements in the same story. All these words play a central role in the history of metaphysics to which they belong. "From Being as presence, Being comes to be as the representedness for a subject" (NII 474; EP 69). Furthermore, this sense of representation may be referred back to Plato's *eidos*, so that it could be said to have declared itself among the Greeks without yet having any determinate force over them, to have been inscribed by them without being prescribed for them.[17] Representation functions as a presupposition that, already well in advance of the modern age, has sent the world which would become an image (H 84; QT 131). But how could a charting of the sedimented layers of *Geschichte* along these lines avoid taking the form of an accumulation, a *Historie*, a coherent story, another bad novel?

It is certainly true that Heidegger did not confine himself to declaring the unity of metaphysics. Indeed, the very notion of the step back into the essence of metaphysics shows how alien that possibility would have been to him. Heidegger most often observed this with relation to the beginning of metaphysics. So, for example, he wrote with reference to the truth of beings as founded by Plato: "In the first beginning of naming Being as *phusis* and *aletheia*, this truth was prepared as that which exceeds metaphysics, too, so that the latter could never be able to know the first beginning essentially of itself, not even in terms of the whole of its history" (SA 227; ST 187). Hölderlin offered another example of that which exceeds metaphysics. To take a further example, more obviously from within metaphysics, *Der Satz vom Grund*, the principle of sufficient reason, came in the lecture course of that name to resound in a key quite alien to metaphysics. Heidegger, having provided a brief history of aesthetics at the beginning of the lecture course "The Will to Power as Art," toward the end announced as a "historical fact" that every true aesthetics explodes itself, and offered the Kantian as an example (NI 154; Ni 131). Other similar examples could be given. All of them warrant the most careful attention. All of them exemplify a saying which cannot be confined within the historical strand of the transformations of presencing, but exceed that dimension. What happens when, in the context of Heidegger's reading of Descartes, we raise the question of the saying of Being not as the saying of a transformation of presence, but as an excess which interrupts the unity of metaphysics? Does Heidegger's reading of Descartes find such an excess?

If one raises the question of the excess of Being in Descartes, one must beware the danger of demanding that such a word be found simply for the sake of completeness. A still greater danger would be to want to import such a word from outside Heidegger's own reading. This would be the case if one attempted to supplement Heidegger's reading with Levinas's reading of Descartes's infinite. The latter is an excess, but its introduction would run counter to Heidegger's account of the role of God in Descartes and his insistence on the onto-theological constitution of metaphysics. Furthermore, one must always be suspicious of acknowledging as excess simply that which exceeds a certain version of the story. The excess cannot simply be defined negatively by its opposition to the history of metaphysics or to the history of Being as story. For, if it is defined only as what a specific historiological account has not yet succeeded in explicating, then a subsequent story—another bad novel—might always succeed in integrating it.

Heidegger could be said to have already tamed *repraesentatio, certitudo,* and *subjectum* in Descartes by giving them a role in his story, by making them the plot of a novel. They do not form the saying of Being as an excess, having been overtaken or reabsorbed by the re-telling of the story. But there is more to Heidegger's account. What eventually struck Heidegger as excessive was something else which, particularly at first, he was at such pains to resist: *Descartes* as the name for a thinking that attempts to overthrow what has gone before and thereby to begin anew; in other words, Descartes as the name for the philosophical ambition to mark a new beginning. Descartes does not constantly talk about the new. Bacon, it seems, was more devoted to the rhetoric of novelty than Descartes. Indeed, in his correspondence Descartes actually criticized this rhetoric, for example, as it is found in Campanella's *De sensu rerum.*[18] Nevertheless, by his attempt to begin again and on a new and firmer foundation, Descartes came to be the image—perhaps one could even say the representative—of the modern age, of the *Neuzeit.*

The novelty of the new may be determined historiologically as that which breaks the continuity of the tradition as established by historicity. But the historiological is threatened by the new and so seeks to exclude or rather reduce it, as Heidegger himself suggested. "The unique, the rare, the simple—in short, the great—in history is never self-evident and hence remains inexplicable. It is not that historical research denies what is great in history; rather it explains it as the exception. In this explaining, the great is measured against the ordinary and the average" (H 76; QT 123). The new—in the sense that it concerned Heidegger—was not the new in the sense of the exceptional, but the new as the gift of a sending. Heidegger nowhere explored the problems of the new and of a new beginning more deeply than in his attempts to determine the place of Descartes. But the new was also a problem for his determination of his own place, or rather for the determination of the thinking which comes after the final possibilities of metaphysics have been exhausted and which thinks that exhaustion. The question of the new in this way came to be raised by Heidegger in dialogue with Descartes and particularly with regard to the questions of the advent of subjectivity and of Descartes's place in the history of philosophy. Heidegger will even use the observation that human beings have not always been determined as subjects, that this "has not always been the sole possibility belonging to the essence of historical man," to suggest that this determination will not always prevail (H 103; QT 153). But it is far from clear whether this remark—assuming it is neither a prophecy nor a false inference—is anything else but a historiological observation, inviting openness to the epochality of *Geschichte* (both the epochs within metaphysics and the epoch of metaphysics).

When in "The Age of the World Picture" Heidegger explored the novelty of the modern age, he proposed that it lay not so much in its specific difference from the medieval and Greek epochs with regard to representation, subject, or world-picture, but in novelty itself. Representation, world-picture and the determination of human being as subject were new in a sense, but they were not—as we have seen—entirely unprepared for. Hence, its determination as new is shifted elsewhere. "The age that is determined from out of this event is, when viewed in retrospect, not only a new one in contrast with the one that is past, but it settles itself firmly in place expressly as the new. To be new is peculiar to the world that has become picture" (H 85; QT 132). Here the new is not measured against the ordinary and the average, or even the earlier. It is acknowledged as a sending. But this is not how the new itself is thought in the modern age (NII 24–25; Niii 178) or even in its own determination of itself. Unlike Descartes—whose language is saved by his intentions—the relatively recent word *Neuzeit* "says more than it intends" (NII 424; EP 22). An indication of how, according to Heidegger, the modern age itself thought novelty may be found in the way Descartes is very often not only situated at the beginning of modern philosophy, but regarded as its founder. "What is decisive is that man himself expressly takes up this position as one constituted by himself, and that he intentionally maintains it as that taken up by himself, and that he makes it secure as the solid footing for a possible development of humanity" (H 84; QT 132). By contrast, even though Heidegger does not make the point specifically, it can be said that Being speaks in the language of Descartes in spite of the fact that Descartes wrote in what was essentially traditional language. It is as if

Descartes's place in the history of Being was secured in spite of Descartes.

Hence, not only representation and thus historiology, but also a certain decisive notion of the new belongs to the new time, the modern age. The new in this way finds its place historiologically defined. Heidegger says that the transformation of the question of the being into the question of method "*is* the beginning of a new thinking, whereby the old order passes into the new and the ensuing age becomes the modern age [*Neuzeit*]" (NII 142; Niv 97). But it is not the method which claimed Heidegger so much as the break with the past that the method was supposed to introduce. Heidegger took the word "new" from modernity's subsequent self-definition of itself as the new time, and both confirmed and denied its novelty. This he did by interweaving the history of the transformations of truth or presencing (reinforced by the notion of epochality), on the one hand, and the historiological perspective, on the other. The *Geschichte des Seins* which introduces itself by opposing itself to *Historie* comes to rely on *Historie* in order to show itself—and this notwithstanding the insistence on the part of the history of Being that it remain hidden from *Historie*. *Historie* is not simply one more stage in the *Geschichte des Seins*. Although *Historie* is itself both a sending and a holding back or forgetting of Being, it is a precondition for the *Geschichte des Seins* to show itself, and not merely as that which precedes the latter, but as that which accompanies it. *Historie* conceals the *Geschichte des Seins*, but it may also allow it to appear fleetingly. And something else takes place over and beyond this conflict that attempts to maintain the impossible distinction between the *Geschichte des Seins* and *Historie*.

Heidegger was not only concerned to place Descartes in a history or to expose his dogmatism. Even though it is tempting to suppose that Descartes alone, of all the great philosophers with whom Heidegger occupied himself, was the one from whom Heidegger took nothing, he was nevertheless claimed by Descartes. The claim concerned the destruction of the old foundation, a ridding oneself of prejudices, a breaking with the tradition, a beginning anew. In a sense this is the original Cartesian novel. It is a dream which had retained its power, as Heidegger could clearly see by observing his former teacher, Edmund Husserl. And, as section 6 of *Being and Time* shows, it is precisely in opposition to this conception that Heidegger developed his own rival account of the destruction of the history of ontology, which recognized in its positivity what the Cartesian dream refused: the sedimented layers of history. But what, then, was it that claimed Heidegger *in spite of* or perhaps even *on account of* this opposition? What claimed Heidegger was less an actual thought of Descartes than Descartes's place at the beginning of modern philosophy, the history of Descartes's text now rethought through an interweaving of *Geschichte* and *Historie*. Heidegger thought this place epochally in the special sense he gave to that word by returning to its Greek meaning: "To withhold itself is, in Greek, *epoche*" (SD 9; TB 9). Chronological distance from the Greeks is a question of *Historie*; the manner in which one is governed by the withholding of Being through one's relation to Greek antiquity is a matter of *Geschichte* (H 311; EGT 26–27). The epochs of the destiny of Being are to be understood in this way as both a sending and a withholding (SD 23; TB 22). By situating the passage from the Greek epoch to the medieval epoch in the translation of the Greek language into Latin, with a consequent loss in the saying power of language, Heidegger gave an essentially negative characterization to the Middle Ages. But having initially presented the passage from the Middle Ages to the modern epoch as a further decline, marked by a growth of dogmatism, Heidegger came to recognize in it the sending of that which brings the completion of Western metaphysics: representation, subjectivity, certainty, and *Historie* itself.

To summarize, Descartes stands at the beginning of the modern age (*Neuzeit*), which is a new era of philosophy (*eine neue Zeit der Philosophie*) (WDP 40; WP 85). It is a new beginning within the epoch of metaphysics and it takes place not only without compromising the unity of metaphysics, but in such a way as to begin to bring the various possibilities of the history of Being to unity and completion (NII 435; EP 31).[19] This is where the emphasis of Heidegger's account lies and not in the conviction that Descartes's philosophy was without precedent. If I emphasize this point it is as a corrective to Hans Blumenberg's caricature of the treatment accorded to Descartes by Heidegger's *Seinsgeschichte*. Blumenberg wrote that "The negative idealization of the modern age in the 'history of Being'—which perhaps has only one thing in common with the self-consciousness of the Enlightenment, namely, the capacity to designate Descartes's *cogito* as the epochal beginning that lacks any intelligible antecedents—has the methodical advantage of being in possession of an *a priori* typification of the epoch."[20] But it is unjust to suppose that the history of Being is uninterested in the "genetic presuppositions" underlying Descartes's *cogito*. This interest had played its part in Heidegger's objections against the neo-Kantians in the Marburg years, and Heidegger clearly retained an interest in such questions. He made clear that the history of Being does not propose a model according to which an epoch makes a sudden appearance at a single place and without preparation. So, for example, he wrote that "The epochs overlap each other in their sequence so that the original sending of Being as presence is more and more obscured in different ways" (SD 9; TB 9). And in another place Heidegger actually offers his own account of the prelude to Descartes (VS 30). But such considerations belong to historiology rather than to the history of Being, and therefore must be referred to the question of the sense in which historiology itself belongs to the history of Being.

Heidegger learned in his study of Descartes that the sending of Being was not inhibited by the lack of a new language. A wholly new language, a language without heritage, is no language. The language of rupture is inevitably also the language of that which is to be broken with. What matters is not only the individual words as seen from the perspective of historiology (although that cannot be ignored, since that heritage belongs to language and is a part of it), but the transformation language undergoes. Heidegger observed the translation of Descartes's sentences into "another" language. Having emphasized that the *cogito* was sketched into "the old framework" of the *ens creatum*, he quickly stressed that "in the realm of the dominion of the subject" *ens* is no longer *ens creatum* but *ens certum* (NII 166; Niv 117). Similarly, he reads *sum res cogitans* as "I am being whose mode *to be* consists in representing in such a way that the representing copresents the one who is representing into representedness" (NII 164; Niv 115). Is the translation of Descartes confined to a translation into the language of Leibniz? Does Heidegger confine Descartes to a specific interpretation of him? To hand Descartes over to Leibniz would be to imprison him within a single historically determined reading and to confine him to a reading which would assure him a place in the historiological series which "shows" the unity of metaphysics.

But there is a further sense which can be attributed to Heidegger's statement that Descartes's intentions are to be translated into "another language." The other language in this case would not be another metaphysical language, in the sense that the language of Leibniz is a language within metaphysics. The suggestion that Heidegger echoes Descartes whenever he writes of a new beginning—or, as he prefers, another beginning—does not reduce Heidegger to the order of metaphysics any more than it makes Descartes a postmodernist. Rather, this encounter with the excess over historiography is an indication that there never has been metaphysical language pure and simple, that it is only defined as such at the culmination of metaphysics, and that the culmination is recognized less by its ability to order and place metaphysics than by its capacity to hear non-metaphysical language always already interrupting what we might otherwise have properly called metaphysics. From the historiological point of view Descartes's language is the language of metaphysics, and wherever it is echoed metaphysics continues to prevail. Even if it remains impossible today to dismiss such considerations, they do not exhaust the possibilities of language. And this is what is acknowledged by the project of translating Descartes into "another language," not another metaphysical language, but another language of another beginning.

It has, of course, not proved possible to give this presentation without making a story of Heidegger's developing position. That Heidegger placed

Descartes at the beginning of the modern age is a story about a story. That he was claimed by Descartes is a story about a sending. The two stories are barely distinguishable. More important, the two are inseparable. They belong to the same story, a story which is itself a sending. The distinction between *Geschichte* and *Historie* is here, as always, impossible to maintain, and each term remains dependent on the other. There is no need or way to choose between historiology as representation and history as sending. Historiology remains inevitable, indeed, indispensable. Heidegger made the point in these terms: "Can we nevertheless make a representation and presentation [*Vorstellung* and *Darstellung*] of the dawn of an age in ways different from those of historiology? Perhaps the discipline of history is still for us an indispensable tool for making the historical contemporary. That does not in any way mean however that historiology, taken by itself, enables us to form within our history a truly adequate, far-reaching relation to history" (H 301; EGT 17–18). The claim that Descartes stands at the beginning of modern philosophy must in this way be understood in terms of both *Historie* and *Geschichte*, the latter interrupting but also sending the former, the former a precondition dominating—dissembling—the latter.

10

Bridging the Abyss: Heidegger and Gadamer

I

It is surprising that the question of Gadamer's relation to Heidegger has not provoked more study. It is well enough known that Gadamer was a student of Heidegger's at Marburg in the 1920s and that he has always littered his writings—whether they are on hermeneutics, time, or the interpretation of Plato—with references, both explicit and implicit, to his former teacher. Indeed, Gadamer has written a number of largely expository essays on Heidegger, 15 of which are collected in *Heideggers Wege*.[1] One of these, the introduction to the Reclam edition of "The Origin of the Work of Art," was written at Heidegger's express invitation and was subsequently recommended by him as "containing a decisive hint for the reader of my later writings" (UK 5; PLT xxiv). The collection as a whole not only shows the relaxed mastery which is characteristic of Gadamer's essay style, but it is also richly instructive, not least because of Gadamer's fund of personal anecdotes, which he frequently calls upon to illuminate a point. *Heideggers Wege* shows how Gadamer continued to devote himself to the self-effacing work of explicating the thinking of his former teacher, even after he himself had come to occupy the center of philosophical attention in Germany, a place which had once been Heidegger's own. Not that, as the years went by, certain reservations about Heidegger's work did not emerge, tempering the atmosphere of homage. Specifically, Gadamer came to regard Heidegger's language as artificial, and this provided a justification for Gadamer's attempts to translate Heidegger into a more accessible language.

When in 1979 Jürgen Habermas delivered a *laudatio* for Gadamer, his old sparring partner, who had been awarded the Hegel Prize, he offered two models or images for thinking Gadamer's relation to Heidegger. Habermas may have emphasized Gadamer's distance from Heidegger, but in so doing he was simply evoking the familiar motif of Gadamer's hermeneutics that distantiation as much as familiarity is a precondition of understanding.

Habermas did not attempt to establish Gadamer's independence from Heidegger; he did not attempt to set Gadamer against Heidegger. He was rather suggesting that the violence performed by a thinking as radical as Heidegger's sets a distance, like that between different languages or different times, which needs to be recouped. Gadamer, according to Habermas, had "*urbanised the Heideggerian province*": he had "bridged the gorge" which Heidegger had dug about himself. That was where "the greatness of Gadamer's achievement lay."[2]

Habermas, of course, did not use this occasion to revitalize the famous Gadamer-Habermas debate which had dominated the philosophical scene in Germany for a decade and which has since been exported to America. But he did quote one long passage from the introduction to *Truth and Method* which reminds us of what Habermas found questionable in Gadamer, as well as instructing us on why we should not expect Gadamer to approach Heidegger in a fundamentally critical frame of mind. Gadamer there dwells on the way that "the classics of philosophical thought" posit "a claim to truth that the contemporary consciousness can neither reject nor transcend." He says that in understanding the texts of great thinkers a truth may be recognized "that could not be attained in any other way."[3] Gadamer's examples are Plato, Aristotle, Leibniz, Kant, and Hegel, but there is no doubt that for him Heidegger also had this classic status, even if he has not yet had to stand the test of time. Gadamer is clear on this point: it may offend "the naive self-esteem of the present moment," but it is a weakness of philosophical thinking not to acknowledge this claim to truth and to apply instead the contemporary standards of scientific research and progress. Gadamer in this way seems to rule out any possibility of a Heidegger-Gadamer debate, if that would imply that they would both stand as equals before the neutral authority of reason. Indeed, in *Truth and Method* Gadamer presents Heidegger as the fulfillment of previous thinking and as providing the standard according to which he wants his own work to be measured.[4] Habermas, who does not share these qualms about philosophical debate, had little interest in exploring the substantial differences between Gadamer and Heidegger: so long as Gadamer can serve as a surrogate Heidegger, as he had already done in the famous Gadamer-Habermas debate of the late 1960s, Gadamer's deficiencies come to reflect on Heidegger himself. Gadamer's displacement of Heidegger at the center of German philosophy in the 1960s was in some ways more a form of representation. Gadamer, with his greater accessibility, was often called upon to serve as a substitute for Heidegger, the reading of whom required a greater exertion of effort.

Habermas is not alone in thinking that one of Gadamer's major contributions has been to present the work of the later Heidegger in a more accessible language than Heidegger was either prepared or able to do himself. It is an interpretation which is not without its merits, if one is ready to reserve one's doubts about the conception of language which it appears to imply. There is no doubt, for example, that Gadamer's many essays on art and poetry take up aspects of Heidegger's essay "The Origin of the Work of Art" and provide it with a range of reference which it did not have in the original. Indeed, one might suspect that by attempting to apply Heidegger's ideas to the generality of art, Gadamer had essentially transformed an account which was, so far as Heidegger himself was concerned, confined to the discussion of great art (H 29; PLT 40). But whether Gadamer's extension of the range of Heidegger's concepts is in this instance justified or not, this development of Heidegger's essay surely cannot be confused—and this will be important for what follows—with an attempt to provide it with a firmer foundation. In general our experience of reading Gadamer is the reverse; we constantly find ourselves forced to turn back to Heidegger to fill certain lacunae in his presentation, particularly in respect of the explication of concepts. The most notable example, and the one which has done most to establish the view that Gadamer's position is essentially Heidegger's, arises because of the striking omission of an identifiable theory of truth in the book called *Truth and Method*. Its readers were forced by default to assume that Gadamer was relying on Heidegger's conception of truth.[5] But can Heidegger's references to "truth," which are part of an investigation of the history of *aletheia* as "unconcealment," be isolated from that context to be reinstated as a theory of truth?

Even before I begin my examination of the issues which arise from Gadamer's indebtedness to Heidegger, I raise two caveats to qualify Habermas's image of Gadamer as having "urbanised" Heidegger-Gadamer the bridge-builder. First, it must be remembered that in 1960, when *Truth and Method* was published, many of the essays and lectures in which Heidegger shows with most penetration his relation to previous thinking had either not yet appeared or had only just appeared. For example, *On the Way to Language* was published only one year earlier, the two-volume *Nietzsche* one year later, and the essays comprising *Time and Being*, from which we derive so much of our understanding of Heidegger's notion of the end of philosophy, were in 1960 not yet written. Whether we are identifying Gadamer as a spokesman of the later Heidegger or drawing attention to the limitations of Gadamer's understanding of the later Heidegger at this time, we should not forget how many of the sources which today determine our reading of Heidegger were not available to him. Secondly, a reading of Gadamer's presentation of Heidegger would have to examine Gadamer's practice of returning to the familiar philosophical vocabulary of the tradition. It is his customary procedure to take whatever word of Heidegger's is under review and to remark on its strangeness at first encounter (something Gadamer often accomplishes with an anecdote recalling Heidegger's first presentation of it); then he attempts to persuade us that Heidegger is directing us to something which we can recognize as very familiar. But does not Gadamer thereby reduce what is radical in Heidegger to what is already familiar to us? We must ask whether, in building a bridge for ordinary understanding, Gadamer has not fallen into the trap of assimilating Heidegger's thinking to ordinary understanding, so depriving it of much of its challenge.

Habermas raises this question only to dismiss it in explaining why he prefers the image of urbanization to that of bridge-building. "The image of the bridge . . . awakens the impression that here someone is furnished with a pedagogical crutch for the purpose of getting closer to an unreachable place. I do not intend it in this way"[6] (EH 13; PP 190). Gadamer's contribution is that he fulfills the need for someone who "forges paths over which Heidegger can return from his self-chosen isolation." It is, of course, not we who are isolated from Heidegger, so much as Heidegger who, in his "thick-skinned uniqueness and originality" has opted for isolation. So far as Habermas is concerned, in marked contrast with Gadamer's quest to renew the humanistic tradition and his emphasis on the openness of dialogue, Heidegger has turned away from every articulate figure of the tradition in the interests of a mysticism of Being."[7] (EH 23; PP 194 and EH 31; PP 197). Later in his *laudatio*, Habermas has Gadamer building bridges again—three of them this time—reestablishing the continuity of the tradition over "chasms that have opened up between ourselves and the philosophy of the Greeks":

the breaks brought about in the nineteenth century by historicism, in the seventeenth century by physics, and at the start of modernity by the transition to the modern apprehension of the world.[8]

Habermas does not attempt to characterize explicitly how Heidegger stands in relation to these chasms. But one could restate Habermas's essay in terms of the contrast between Heidegger, as one who brings discontinuity and rupture, and Gadamer, as one who restores continuity. This emerges most clearly when Habermas seeks to understand the conditions which have allowed Gadamer to follow Heidegger "farther than most" and to recognize him as a thinker and not simply a pseudo-poet.

Gadamer can so emphatically defend as thinking the meditation that characterizes the speechlessness of the mystic only because he renders an account of Being as tradition, because he does not deliver himself up to the shapeless undertow of an ethereal Being, but, casting his gaze back to Hegel, takes into account the massive stream of the tradition of words that have become objective and concrete, actually spoken in their place at their time.[9]

Habermas is presumably not offering a portrait of Heidegger as a speechless mystic, which would be hard to take seriously under the weight of the ever-growing *Gesamtausgabe*. Habermas must be saying that it is Heidegger's unacknowledged reliance on the tradition which gives him his voice. Gadamer makes explicit Heidegger's debt to those thinkers whom he is supposed to have devalued and from whom he turned away. His bridge-building, his urbanization of the Heideggerian province, draws Heidegger back into the tradition which he seeks to overcome. This would be not so much an attack on Heidegger as—and here I am going beyond anything Habermas says in order to prepare for a claim Gadamer makes on his own behalf—an uncovering of the conditions governing Heidegger's thinking. The implication is that Gadamer learned enough from Hegel to reverse Heidegger's turn away from previous thinking in order to reestablish Heidegger within the continuity of the philosophical tradition. This is the model which is to be investigated in what follows.

II

Gadamer's statement, to which I have already referred, that "When we try to understand the classics of philosophical thought, they posit, of themselves, a claim to truth that the contemporary consciousness can neither reject nor transcend," may be illustrated by one of Gadamer's personal reminiscences. He tells how the students at Marburg went to hear Heidegger's lectures on Aristotle and found themselves so captivated by his presentation of that philosopher that Heidegger appeared to them as a latter day Aristotelian.[10] This sense of being claimed by the classics of philosophy is one Gadamer never forgot and it became a central example for his presentation of the hermeneutical experience. Whereas for some a reading of a text is not to be counted as philosophical unless it issues in specific criticisms directed against identifiable arguments, for Gadamer there is simply no encounter with the text unless we find ourselves claimed by what is said there. Nevertheless, to return to the anecdote, Gadamer is confident in retrospect that Heidegger's fundamental intention was the destruction of the history of ontology: Heidegger's lectures may have had a cutting edge, but they do not serve as an illustration of the diminishing kind of criticism common in Germany at that time.

For Gadamer, understanding occurs as an encounter with something that addresses us. "Understanding does not consist in a technical virtuosity of 'understanding' everything written. Rather, it is a genuine experience, i.e., an encounter with something that asserts itself as truth."[11] The question is not whether we should or should not set ourselves the impossible task of understanding everything. Gadamer discounts that question as irrelevant to "understanding." He is not seeking to give an account of what we ought to do. The point is rather that the encounter with truth is in an important sense beyond our control and thus beyond method. And when we read a text from the history of philosophy it can happen that we are not simply confronted by unfamiliar ideas which strike us as strange; we may find that it has something to say to us, so that in our encounter with it we come to experience its claim to truth. Familiarity with the tradition and being claimed by a truth which speaks from the tradition exemplifies what Gadamer means when he writes of our belonging to the tradition. And yet, Gadamer also insists that a text only addresses us once it has struck us by its strangeness. The greatest obstacle to a thoughtful reading of a text is not that complexity which cannot be penetrated without a great deal of effort; it is the apparent self-evidence of what is over-familiar to the point of seeming obvious. Hence, the exemplary status of the work of art for Gadamer, as well as for Heidegger, is not unconnected with the fact that it takes place as a demolition of the familiar.[12] Although temporal distance is sometimes regarded as an obstacle to understanding, we find that, once we have freed ourselves from the supposition that the meaning of a text resides in reconstructing the sense it had for its authors or their contemporaries, we are in a position to experience historical distance as something positive. It is when we no longer treat Plato or Aristotle as our contemporaries that we are in a position to be struck by what they have to say and have our horizons opened by them. Rather than dismiss straightaway an argument or line of thought in which there is an apparent jump, hermeneutical inquiry seeks to unearth the unstated presupposition as the mark of our historical distance. But what thus comes to light as—in Heidegger's phrase—"the unsaid in what is said" (W 109; P 251) does not simply emerge as something foreign to us. Insofar as it is part of the tradition to which we belong, we find ourselves addressed by it. Indeed, it is because we belong to the tradition, rather than it belonging to us, that we can never disown it and should rather approach it, expecting to recognize ourselves in it.

In this way we can readily understand how Gadamer comes to see the advent of historical consciousness as amounting to a continuation rather than a break with the tradition. Historical distance is not an obstacle to be overcome. "Distance in time," Gadamer says, is "a positive and productive possibility of understanding," and he appeals to the example of contemporary art to remind us that if what is at issue is contemporaneous with us, contemporaneity seems to be an obstacle to forming a reliable judgment.[13] The hermeneutical experience is situated within a polarity between familiarity and strangeness and is not to be directed toward one of the terms at the expense of the other.[14] But there is a degree of uncertainty about Gadamer's position here. That distance is positive, that it is an essential moment of understanding, is clear. But is the sense of distance always to be retained, so that we remain estranged from what is understood in this way? Or is this distance always recouped in a familiarity without remainder? Gadamer seems to answer both questions affirmatively at one time or another, but I would suggest that we would do better not to regard this as a contradiction so much as a reflection of his essential ambiguity toward the tradition, which—as we shall see—he also acknowledges on occasion. For the moment it may be sufficient to see it as a result of the multiplicity of influences to which Gadamer holds that we must be open. If we are latterday Aristotelians, we are equally latterday Platonists, latterday Leibnizians, latterday Kantians, and latterday Hegelians. This is enough to show that whatever it is he has in mind, it is not equivalent to being at home in Aristotelianism as traditionally conceived.

In order to indicate the difficulties which face the attempt to pose the question simply in terms of *distance*, I shall examine Gadamer's attempt to consider the issue of his own lack of a critical principle. In the foreword to the second edition of *Truth and Method*, he raises the following possible objections to his own enterprise:

> Does not the universality of understanding involve a one-sidedness in its contents, inasmuch as it lacks a critical principle in relation to tradition and, as it were, espouses a universal optimism? However much it is the nature of tradition to exist only through being appropriated, it still is part of the nature of man to be able to break with tradition, to criticize and dissolve it, and is not what takes place in the work of remaking the real into an instrument of human purpose something far more basic in our relationship to being? To this extent, does not the ontological universality of understanding result in a certain one-sidedness?[15]

Reading these possible objections today, one is liable to suppose that Gadamer has taken them from the mouth of Habermas, that is, until one remembers that Habermas did not present his critical account of *Truth and Method* until 1967, two years after Gadamer presented these questions.[16] Remarkably, Gadamer—prior to the debate with Habermas—imagines Heidegger as a spokesman for these views. He suggests that Heidegger would bemoan the emphasis placed on assimilation (*Aneignung*) at the expense of the projective character of understanding. "Like many of my critics, Heidegger too would probably feel a lack of an ultimate radicality in the conclusions I draw." Gadamer then poses certain questions about the meaning of the end of metaphysics as a science and of the "forgetfulness of Being." But it seems that the questions are only rhetorical, indicating how the alleged one-sidedness of hermeneutic universalism may possess the truth of a corrective. "What man needs is not just the persistent posing of ultimate questions, but the sense of what is feasible, what is possible, what is correct, here and now."[17]

So Gadamer, contrary to his usual reserve, on this occasion allows himself at least an imaginary debate with Heidegger. He portrays the latter as insisting upon a task which Gadamer neglects. This is the task, as Heidegger called it in *Being and Time*, "of destroying the history of ontology" (SZ 19; BT 41). But if Gadamer is indeed suggesting this, is he right to understand the destruction in terms of critique? How could the oblivion of Being serve as a critical tool when that would require that we were somehow in possession of it so that we could use it as a standard? If that question is not without consequence for some of Heidegger's harsh words about Descartes in *Being and Time*, one can at least say in respect of the later Heidegger that criticism no longer retains its previous function when it is a question of destiny—specifically, the destiny of Being.

But the most important thing here—because it addresses the issue of distantiation itself—is that it is not legitimate to regard Heidegger's relation to the tradition as a one-sided rejection of it, in contrast to Gadamer's insistence on belongingness. When announcing the task of the destruction of the history of ontology in *Being and Time*, Heidegger was clear that it implied the appropriation (*Aneignung*) of what has been thought (SZ 21 and 220; BT 42 and 262). Later writings confirm—against popular misunderstandings of Heidegger's thought—that "the tradition remains rich in truth" (US 202; WL 96). This insistence never wavered. For Heidegger, "the end of philosophy" means not that the tradition no longer has anything to say to us, but that there is a transformation in the way in which it speaks to us. With the end of metaphysics there is a transformation of the way in which we belong to language, so that we come to hear certain words of the tradition as words of Being; the tradition passes into the truth of Being. This notion of the truth of Being is the stumbling block for Gadamer, who would probably dismiss it as a kind of metaphysical speculation, if to do so were not, as we shall see, in contradiction to the sense he also wants to give to the claim that metaphysics has already been overcome.

It is therefore not quite right to say that Heidegger opts for distantiation and against belongingness, for discontinuity and against continuity. To understand the matter this way, to express it in a Gadamerian phrase, has "the truth of a corrective"; but it accomplishes no more than a reversal of traditional terms and so renders the issues in only the most fragile manner.

III

Truth and Method attempts to show that the human sciences, whatever their own account of their goals, are really concerned with the illumination of "self-understanding." When Gadamer uses "self-understanding," it does not bear the sense of self-transparency. "Self-understanding" is always bound to a certain concealment which renders self-transparency impossible.[18] One can recognize here Heidegger's account of the play between the concealment and unconcealment of *aletheia*. Furthermore, Gadamer also turns to Heidegger, and specifically to Heidegger's account of metaphysics, to justify going against what the human sciences say of themselves. Gadamer reads Heidegger's lecture "What Is Metaphysics?" as an attempt to ask what metaphysics really is in contrast with what it thinks itself to be.[19] The formulation is unfortunate; Gadamer, no more than Heidegger, is attached to the idea of a definitive reading of a text as it is "in itself," whether a single text or the "text" of metaphysics is meant. Anyway, what Gadamer is attempting with this characterization of Heidegger's 1929 inaugural lecture is to show it as an application of the idea, central to his hermeneutics, that the meaning of a text cannot be equated with what its author intended. Whereas Heidegger applies this principle to metaphysics, Gadamer in *Truth and Method* applies it to the human sciences. Gadamer believes that the human sciences have tended to be governed by certain "scientific" ideals which are not appropriate to that sphere. He is attempting to correct the description, which is implicit in those ideals, of what happens when we attain understanding in that realm. His concern in respect of the procedures of the human sciences is "not what we do or what we ought to do, but what happens to us over and above our wanting and doing"[20] (WM xvi; TM xvi). He is attempting to characterize not what the human sciences think themselves to be, but what they are.

It seems on the surface that this is a further instance of Gadamer drawing on a lesson learned from Heidegger. Gadamer himself sees it differently. In an important essay published 12 years after *Truth and Method*, "Hermeneutics as Practical Philosophy," Gadamer repeats his claim that Heidegger's question, "What is metaphysics?" is concerned with what metaphysics really is, in contrast to what it understands itself to be. But Gadamer insists that the question can only be understood in the light of the new concept of interpretation that he, and not Heidegger, has elucidated.[21] Nor is this claim an afterthought. A letter written to Leo Strauss at the time of the publication of *Truth and Method* confirms that even then Gadamer understood his task to be that of providing a basis for Heidegger's thinking, though one which would go against Heidegger's own self-understanding:

> Perhaps the tendency of my book will become clearer to you if I add: I have advocated against Heidegger for decades, that also his "bound" or "leap" back *behind* metaphysics is alone made possible through this itself (=historically operative consciousness!). What I believe to have understood through Heidegger ... is, above all, that philosophy must learn to do without the idea of an infinite intellect. I have attempted to draw up a

corresponding hermeneutics. But I can only do that, in that I—much against Heidegger's intentions—make visible in such a hermeneutic *consciousness* in the end everything that I see.[22]

What exactly is it that Gadamer opposes to Heidegger here? And how can he claim to provide the basis for Heidegger's thinking, when the reverse appears to be so manifestly the case? Gadamer, who unceasingly affirms his debt to Heidegger and his dependence upon him, seems to harbor the ambition to supplement the work of his teacher in the one way that would supplant the priority he accords to the latter, that is, by establishing the conditions which make his work possible.

It is noteworthy in this regard that, in the last sentence of the passage from the letter to Strauss just quoted, Gadamer appears to reassert the notion of consciousness. And yet, there is no doubt that Gadamer was well aware that what had led Heidegger to insist on the term *Dasein* was precisely his effort to evade what he took to be the irretrievably metaphysical notion of consciousness. If Gadamer generally refuses to introduce Heidegger's word *Dasein* into his own thinking, it is not from ignorance of what Heidegger was striving to say with the word, so much as in revolt against what he took to be Heidegger's attempt to transform—simply by decree—the word's meaning, from "existence" in the sense of "thatness" to the sense of standing out in the clearing (*Lichtung*). Gadamer is trying to draw Heidegger's insight back into the sphere of the tradition, and this is at the heart of the bridge-building identified by Habermas. The conditions for the possibility of Heidegger's thinking are found within the tradition itself. To translate Heidegger into the language of the tradition in this way may already be to replace Heidegger's own self-understanding of his place in relation to it with another. But to say that such a translation of Heidegger is impossible would be to concede that Heidegger makes no sense by withdrawing in advance the conditions for the possibility of construing him. So the argument might run. And it is on this basis that it is sometimes claimed that Gadamer's codicil to Heidegger is a "substantial" improvement on the original—both modifying and revolting against the original—and not simply a more *urbane* (in the sense of "elegant") version of the same.

Gadamer does not attempt to establish an independent position that would explain how Heidegger came to think as he did. Gadamer maintains rather that Heidegger misunderstood himself, just as Heidegger maintained that the tradition misunderstood itself. The terms of the debate could be restated as a question about what it means to pass "beyond" metaphysics. Gadamer does not use the word "metaphysics" in the sense it has for Heidegger, where it is equivalent to philosophy itself. "Metaphysics" for Gadamer is used in the more familiar sense of speculative inquiry, so that when Gadamer talks of "overcoming metaphysics" there is something of

Carnap's usage of that phrase, as well as Heidegger's. Indeed, for Gadamer "the overcoming of metaphysics" had already taken place in Dilthey,[23] which is something Heidegger would never have said, given his assessment of Dilthey as someone who remained within the metaphysical sphere of subjectivity (US 129–30; WL 35–36). The point is that, although Gadamer was prepared to concede that dogmatic metaphysics had come to an end, he did not acknowledge that a decisive rupture had thereby taken place with what had gone before. The division of *Truth and Method* into three parts corresponds to a threefold overcoming—of aesthetics, epistemology, and philosophy of language. But when Gadamer writes of "overcoming," he tends to think of it in such a way that it allows for a simple reinstatement of the tradition. For Gadamer, "overcoming" tended to be directed against the modern period, particularly the Enlightenment; what Gadamer sought to reinstate as often as not were Greek insights—and this is the other sense of bridge-building referred to by Habermas. In Heidegger, by contrast, "overcoming" is not a restoration. It introduces an ambiguous relation to what has gone before. Because of this ambiguity we have to be cautious about understanding Heidegger's conception of the end of philosophy as a decisive rupture. But Gadamer refuses to concede any sense to the end of "philosophy" except as the end of dogmatic speculation, because for him philosophy has the status of a natural inclination.[24]

When Gadamer attempts to explicate the conditions of Heidegger's questioning of Being and of the tradition, he is not doing something for which there is no parallel in Heidegger himself. In fact, Heidegger gives at least two different accounts of the relation of the question of Being to the philosophical tradition, one in *Being and Time* and another with the history of Being. Gadamer—in spite of a reputation which associates him with the later Heidegger—largely remains within the parameters of the earlier version. Gadamer places Heidegger firmly within the context of "the rise of historical consciousness,"[25] just as in section 6 of *Being and Time* the destruction of the history of ontology is introduced by reference to "the discovery of tradition" (SZ 20; BT 41). Similarly, when Gadamer insists on the natural inclination toward philosophy which survives the end of metaphysics, he would not find himself opposed by the early Heidegger, for whom the question of Being was a radicalization of an essential tendency of *Dasein* itself (SZ 15; BT 35). The sense in which Being comes to be identified with metaphysics and hence superseded by what Heidegger later calls *Ereignis* is absent at this "early" stage of Heidegger's thinking (SD 44; TB 41). The later emphasis on discontinuity had not yet been developed in 1927. The concept of interpretation that Gadamer offers, far from providing the basis for Heidegger's thinking, is not so very different from that given by Heidegger in *Being and Time*.

At various points Gadamer insists that Heidegger's decisive discovery lies in his exhibition of the continuity of the tradition. In other words, he does not find it in Heidegger's account of the "history of Being" as essentially discontinuous. So, for example, in an essay entitled "To What Extent Does Language Preform Thought?" Gadamer draws attention to Heidegger's claim that Greek metaphysics is the beginning of modern technology: "I am convinced that Heidegger's discovery will later become part of the common knowledge of humanity, for we see with increasing clarity today—as he has taught us to see—that Greek metaphysics is the beginning of modern technology."[26] Gadamer is referring to a point that Heidegger makes in "The Letter on Humanism": "Technology is in its essence a destiny within the history of Being and of the truth of Being, a truth that lies in oblivion. For technology does not go back to the *techne* of the Greeks in name only but derives historically and essentially from *techne* as a mode of *aletheuein*, a mode, that is, of rendering beings manifest" (W 171; BW 220). But, in the subsequent essay, "The Question concerning Technology," Heidegger attempts to do much more than show that modern technology is a revealing which as such has an affinity with the Greek thinking of *techne*. The crucial point of that essay lies in the recognition that the mode of revealing of *techne* is obstructed within modern technology (VA 38; QT 30). So, when Heidegger says that the essence of technology can only be seen on the basis of permanent enduring (VA 39; QT 30), it is not continuity between Greek metaphysics and modern technology that he is emphasizing. Rather, he is quite explicit that modern technology demands us to transform our thinking and, specifically, to think "essence" not as "permanent enduring," but in another way. And this demand arises because of a discontinuity evidenced in the obstruction of revealing.

This is not the place to enter into the complexities of Heidegger's account of technology, but Heidegger does there bring to light a certain continuity and also a discontinuity which interrupts the tradition.[27] The important point is that the rupturing of the tradition constitutes what has gone before as a unity. Heidegger sometimes makes claims about metaphysics as a whole, and these claims find their basis, one might say, in the distance which now separates us from the tradition of metaphysics. But this does not mean that Heidegger understands the rupture as an absolute break with what has gone before. Heidegger's careful formulations—as, for example, when he talks of "another beginning" rather than a "new beginning"—rule out any such thought, which would, of course, be vulnerable to the strategy of referring every attempt to pass outside metaphysics to the impossibility of escaping metaphysical language. It is Heidegger's sensitivity to that issue which Gadamer plays on: If there is no decisive break, does this not mean that the principle of continuity has been reestablished? We reach here the source of a certain unease in the face of Gadamer's reconstruction. For Heidegger, to think of the history of Being as epochal means to recognize the giving and withholding of Being as always taking place as an excess; any attempt to understand that history as continuous expels the excess of Being. When Gadamer accepts the point about the roots of technology in Greek metaphysics, without granting to Heidegger the legitimacy of the history of Being, we find ourselves wondering whether Gadamer has not opted for a one-sided interpretation of Heidegger's analysis, one which refuses its central insight.

We find something very similar in respect of metaphysics itself. Heidegger's own attempt to explicate what gave rise to the questioning of metaphysics in "What Is Metaphysics?" can be found in the Postscript and Introduction that Heidegger subsequently added to the lecture in 1943 and 1949 respectively. For Heidegger, it was only possible to raise the question of metaphysics, in the far-reaching way that he did, because metaphysics had already come to an end. At the time of the lecture itself there was no hint of that; the lecture ends with a clear affirmation of the metaphysical and its essential relation to human being, one which Gadamer would readily endorse: "So long as man exists, philosophizing of some sort occurs" (W 19; BW 112). It was only subsequently, with the recognition of the history of Being, that it seemed to Heidegger that metaphysics came into question in the experience of the Nothing, because the task of the thinker in the time of metaphysics is to say Being, and the Nothing arose in the lack of a word for Being in our epoch.

For Heidegger, the questioning of metaphysics—"the overcoming of metaphysics"—is something that happens to us over and above our wanting and doing. It is the destiny of the thinker of our epoch and should not be confused with an attack on metaphysics or an attempt to discover its transcendental condition. One must be cautious about presenting Heidegger's relation to metaphysics as an attempt to pass beyond metaphysics by going "behind" it in a return to the earliest Greek thinkers, an interpretation which Gadamer adopts in the letter to Strauss quoted earlier. Remembrance of *a-letheia* plays the central role it does in Heidegger's thinking, not simply because *aletheia* stands prior to metaphysics, but because at the end of metaphysics we come to hear in this word the play of concealment and unconcealment *within* metaphysics.

This is what Heidegger tells Gadamer in a letter written in response to the latter's two essays "The Idea of Hegel's Logic" and "Hegel and Heidegger." This letter, written at the end of 1971, together with another written early in 1972, constitutes the only documented evidence currently available of Heidegger's response to Gadamer, and it is to Gadamer's credit that he has made them available.[28] Heidegger wrote to Gadamer, "This experiencing of *aletheia* is the step back to the 'oldest of the old,' the turning to the 'other beginning,' i.e., the one and the same single beginning of Western European thought, but this beginning thought in another manner."[29] The phrase "the step back" recalls Heidegger's 1949 discussion of "The Way Back into the Ground of Metaphysics" (W 195–97; WB 207–09). The thinker leaves metaphysics not by putting it to one side, but by going back into the ground of metaphysics. It is therefore a question not only of returning to the origins of metaphysics, but also of turning to its essence. "The essence of metaphysics" does not mean what metaphysics is "in itself," but its manner of granting. Far from being an attempt to accomplish a complete break, a total emancipation from the tradition, the "overcoming of metaphysics" takes place as an insight into metaphysics, a reappropriation of it.

This insight is, of course, what Gadamer has in mind when he appeals in *Truth and Method* to the model of Heidegger's account of metaphysics. In the essay "Heidegger and the Language of Metaphysics" Gadamer records that "the break with tradition that took place in Heidegger's thought represented just as much an incomparable renewal of the tradition."[30] Gadamer has rightly insisted that the phrase "the overcoming [*Überwindung*] of metaphysics" is to be understood in the sense of *Verwindung*: we remain with metaphysics, which is not simply eliminated.[31] But if we were to allow that Heidegger was concerned simply with a renewal of the tradition, it would be difficult to know where we might find the words to express the difference between Heidegger and Gadamer. This is reflected in Gadamer's own attempts to distance himself from Heidegger, attempts which have not always exhibited the same careful appreciation of Heidegger's relation to the tradition of metaphysics. Gadamer can be found saying, for example, that he has "sought to reacknowledge, against Heidegger, that beginning in Plato and Platonism and also in Hegel (and not only in Schelling), which Heidegger's destruction of metaphysics was calling into question."[32] To suppose that Heidegger is somehow rejecting the tradition of philosophy begun by Plato is to make the very mistake against which the term *Verwindung* is supposed to guard. Gadamer presents Heidegger's frequent returns to Anaximander, Parmenides, and Heraclitus as "attempts to explicate the aboriginal situation of these thinkers as an antitype to the actual course taken by Western thought, the course represented by the history of metaphysics."[33] This interpretation probably has its source in the 1935 lecture course that we know under the title *Introduction to Metaphysics*. But even there Heidegger writes of "another beginning," a phrase which, as I have suggested, carries the full force of the ambiguity of Heidegger's relation to the tradition; "another beginning" is not a new beginning, but a beginning which remembers the first beginning of the Greeks and at the same time illuminates it (EM 29; IM 29).

IV

So, Gadamer is ready to acknowledge the end of metaphysics without conceding that in that end there takes place "another beginning." He says in the essay "Hegel and Heidegger" that "It seems difficult to me to avoid the thought which forces itself upon us regarding Heidegger's historical justification of himself and his return to the question of Being, specifically, that such a return is not itself a beginning, but rather, that it is made possible by an end."[34] But for Heidegger it is precisely the inseparability of the end and "another beginning" which is his way of insisting on the fact that through discontinuity we are still bound to what has gone before. This inseparability is attested to in the lines from Hölderlin's "Patmos" frequently quoted by Heidegger:

> Wo aber Gefahr ist, wächst
> Das Rettende auch.
>
> Where danger is, that which rescues
> burgeons too.

That Gadamer admits the notions of "the overcoming" and "the end" of metaphysics, as I have said, is not what is important, for those phrases have a more limited sense for Gadamer than for Heidegger. Gadamer insists on the continuity of philosophy over and above any overcoming or completion. The task that he gives to philosophy today, that of "achieving a new self-understanding of humanity," is no more than a renewal of a task that philosophy has served "for ages."[35]

Nevertheless, in insisting on continuity, Gadamer is not saying that we are bound by the metaphysical *logos*. The grammar of our languages does not bind our thoughts to metaphysics. When Gadamer refuses to characterize a family of languages as the language of metaphysics,[36] he intends this point to score against Heidegger. And yet it does not run counter either to Heidegger's remarks about using metaphysical language non-metaphysically (VS 88) or to his discussion of the possibility of a transformation of language (US 267; WL 136). It is clear that both thinkers allow that language carries within itself the inner resources to overcome itself. But it is clearly remarkable to find Gadamer appealing to the possibility of a language other than that of metaphysics. For here he clearly means "metaphysics," not in the sense he normally uses it, but in Heidegger's sense. Is Gadamer not reversing roles by allowing that metaphysical language might be left behind? Gadamer's point is not clearly made, and the fact that it is directed against Heidegger can only be established because elsewhere he says that it was.[37] What Gadamer seems to be denying, on the basis of the infinite resources of language, is the breakdown of language before its limits.³⁸ Of course, the breakdown of metaphysical language is a crucial component of everything that Heidegger said after the mid-1930s. But by that he meant both the experience of the lack of the word to say Being and the transformation of our relation to language, which accompanies that experience, whereby it becomes more appropriate to say—as with our relation to the tradition— that we belong to language, rather than that language belongs to us. Now, it is striking that this discussion of language is echoed in the third part of *Truth and Method*, where Gadamer adopts Heidegger's phrase, "language speaks."³⁹ It is in order to deny the implications of Heidegger's testimony about the transformation of language that Gadamer is obliged to posit an infinite capacity of language to transcend itself.

There is in the essay "Plato and Heidegger" a fine illustration of the difficulties this poses for Gadamer. Gadamer says that through Heidegger's step back it became possible to experience the limits of Greek thought and *aletheia*. The German version concludes with the words *Denken darf dieser Grenze nicht ausweichbar*, "Thinking may not evade these limits."⁴⁰ But, when Gadamer gave the lecture in English, because it was in the context of a symposium on "East-West Perspectives," he altered the last sentence to read, "It may be that by virtue of this a dialogue has become possible with philosophical traditions which have developed outside these limits, if they learn to free themselves from any tendency to parallel Western thought."⁴¹ Gadamer is committed to the idea that Western predicative judgment and Eastern figurative expression are "only different modes of utterance within one and the same universal, namely within the essence of language and reason"⁴² (KS III 219–20; PH 239). It emerges that what lies behind Gadamer's account of the infinite resources of language is not an appeal to explore these resources, but a conviction that we must leave it to language to undertake that exploration for us. Gadamer learned from Heidegger, as he acknowledged in his letter to Strauss, that philosophy must renounce appeals to an infinite intellect. And yet, it sometimes seems that he has retreated into maintaining a "bad infinity" of language.

For Heidegger the words of Being still address us and make a claim on us. We cannot simply brush off, for example, what Aristotle says with the word *logos*, for we are his heirs and can recognize his legacy to us in our own conceptions. Gadamer also emphasizes the possibility of a recovery of the past in this way (e.g. KS I 119; PH 26), and he is well aware that what it says to us will be in some way determined by our own situation.⁴³ But Heidegger's concern is the ambiguous status of the words of Being once they are recognized as such. They give thinking its essential character, determining thinking to this day without, because of their archaic status, being able simply to take up a place in the language and thinking of today (WD 102 and

98–99; WT 163 and 153). They belong to what Heidegger elsewhere calls "a saying not-saying" (I 72; ID 73). This is most clearly the case with the word *aletheia*, which does not provide the basis for a theory of truth, but rather has for Heidegger come to speak of the hidden concealment which accompanied all such theorizing throughout the tradition.

For Heidegger the discontinuity of the history of Being arises from the excess of each word of Being, an excess both over what has gone before, in terms of which it can never be explained, and over what comes after, so that it can never be given a definitive reading. For Gadamer the tension between familiarity and distance always seems to be resolved in favor of the former. In the essay "Hermeneutics and Historicism," for example, even though he concedes that the task of hermeneutics is complicated by the advent of historical consciousness, when the historical distance between the text and its interpreter becomes visible, he nevertheless describes the task of hermeneutics as "overcoming and removing the strangeness and making its assimilation [*Aneignung*] possible."[44] As he puts it in the essay "Hegel and Heidegger," "Does not history always present a continuity?"[45] It is no doubt according to this maxim, which we readily think of as "Hegelian," that Gadamer is suspicious of anything but continuity.

How does Gadamer conceive the relation between Heidegger and Hegel? There is no doubt that he attempts to assimilate Heidegger's relation to the history of philosophy to the Hegelian model. It is sometimes said that Heidegger's history of Being is basically only a reversal of Hegel's ladder of ascent to absolute Spirit. Heidegger, of course, denied it. But Gadamer claimed to have reversed the path of the *Phenomenology of Spirit*. He said that *Truth and Method* is supposed to show not how spirit comes to be freed, but the sense in which subjectivity is bound by substantiality.[46] If we rely on Gadamer as a spokesman for Heidegger, we are also liable to read Heidegger as a reversal of Hegel.[47]

Gadamer's adoption of the notions of experience (*Erfahrung*) and remembrance (*Erinnerung*) from both Hegel and Heidegger seems to overlook the very significant differences in the way these two concepts are determined for each of them. Is Gadamer attempting to forge a philosophical position of his own from what is common to Hegel and Heidegger? How could the two positions be reconciled? Certainly at times it seems that Gadamer is trying to purify the concepts—to discharge himself from any obligation to what he leaves behind—by playing one thinker off against the other. Gadamer appeals, on the one hand, to Heidegger's account of finitude in order to dismiss absolute knowing and, on the other, to Hegel's account of substance becoming subject in order to show how every apparent break is taken up in a new synthesis is which restores the continuity of history and renders impossible Heidegger's sense of discontinuity. Hence, Gadamer presents

Heidegger's account of modern technology in relation to the tradition; Gadamer must ignore the sense in which, according to Heidegger, insight into the essence of technology is only possible because of the completion of philosophy in the disruption of *poiesis*. Gadamer insists only on the continuity between our epoch and the beginnings of Greek thought.

However, what makes remembrance possible for Hegel is the standpoint of absolute knowing, as for Heidegger it is the experience of the oblivion of Being. Without reference to either of these it is entirely obscure what might allow Gadamer to integrate Hegelian and Heideggerian concepts into his thinking. Gadamer would no doubt say that his refusal to adopt a "standpoint" from which history is to be viewed is what provides the basis for that openness which is the condition for hearing the claim of previous thinking, including the thinking of Hegel and Heidegger. Gadamer borrows from Hegel both the philosophical means for maintaining the continuity of the tradition and also the notion of "self-recognition in otherness," to which he appeals in order to explicate the relation of familiarity and distance thereby established in respect of the tradition. But not only does the appeal to Hegel on these points run counter to the tendency of Heidegger's thinking. There is also much in Hegel to suggest that only the standpoint of absolute knowing provides the perspective from which what would otherwise be a discontinuous history displays retrospectively its continuity. And yet, it is precisely that standpoint which Gadamer abandons. It becomes a matter of serious concern whether Gadamer's eclectic attempt to fuse the response of these two thinkers to philosophy's historicality is ultimately defensible. The fashionable picture of Gadamer as a more acceptable version of Heidegger must confront the fact that Gadamer's apparent plausibility is compromised by his refusal to acknowledge the presuppositions in Hegel and Heidegger on which his own account depends. His reliance on them for his fundamental concepts is ambiguous, in much the same sense as Heidegger's relation to previous thinkers is ambiguous. Indeed, in "Heidegger and the History of Philosophy" Gadamer takes note of the ambiguity of Heidegger's relation to those metaphysical thinkers with which he occupied himself throughout his life and never put behind him—thinkers like Heraclitus, Parmenides, Aristotle, Hegel, and Nietzsche.[48] But Gadamer refuses to acknowledge that the ambiguity of Heidegger's relation to individual thinkers within the tradition has its source in our ambiguous relation to the language of Being and thus in our ambiguous relation to previous thinking.

Gadamer refuses to acknowledge the sense of assertions about "the night" of the foregetfulness of Being.[49] Although he intends this refusal as a corrective to Heidegger, Gadamer succeeds only in rendering his own thinking incoherent. The silence of the extreme oblivion of Being is nothing else than the Nothing of the lack of a word of Being, that silence which opens us to the grant of language, the experience of the truth of Being. And yet, there is another side to Gadamer. In the Introduction to *Truth and Method*, for example, he acknowledges a characteristic of language which cannot but suggest a parallel with what Heidegger calls "a saying not-saying," when, referring to the emergence of historical consciousness, Gadamer writes that "we have lost the naive innocence with which traditional concepts were made to support one's own thinking."[50] In the same place he actually says that "the continuity of the Western philosophical tradition has been effective only in a fragmentary way." If we were to recognize this emphasis on the *brokenness* of continuity as Gadamer's fundamental experience, an experience quite different from anything Hegel had in mind, it opens the way to another reading of his hermeneutics.

That Gadamer seems to meet the demand for a philosophy which recognizes historicity without succumbing to an apparently arbitrary philosophy of history is no doubt what endears him to those philosophers who refuse to engage in anything but second-order reflection. But the self-denying ordinance of hermeneutics, its confinement to the level of response, has its source in a refusal to take up issues except where the reader has the experience of the text making a claim on him or her. In consequence, hermeneutics offers less a continuous history than a philosophy of fragments. This framentation, coupled with a denial of critical reason, is a powerful testimony to the description given by Heidegger of the transformation of our relation both to the tradition and to language. Gadamer's is not a second-order enterprise, but a supplementary endeavor, a way of trying to keep faith with Heidegger.

Is Gadamer a bridge-builder, as Habermas says? What is a bridge? Does a bridge connect two banks separated from each other by an abyss? This is the image to which Habermas appeals. But Heidegger in "Building, Dwelling, Thinking" invites us to think of bridges in terms of "gathering." "The bridge does not first come to a location to stand in it; rather a location arises only by virtue of the bridge," that is to say, only through gathering (VA 154; PLT 154). Such a place of gathering is the end of philosophy (SD 63; TB 57). Is there gathering in Gadamer? Or only the accumulation of disparate sources? In that case Heidegger, not Gadamer, would be the bridge-builder.

It might seem on first reading that Gadamer's modifications of Heidegger's position, in particular his refusal to adopt the history of Being and his insistence on belongingness and continuity, constitute improvements which bring Heidegger into line with what is generally acceptable, urbanizing him. From this perspective, Gadamer might be thought to have ironed out the excesses of Heidegger's thinking—and precisely by turning his back on the crucial notion of excess. I have attempted to show that, judged as a revision of Heidegger, this is unacceptable. But it can be regarded in another way. Gadamer's refusal to choose between Hegel and Heidegger might indicate not indecision, but the genuineness of his own thinking. Even if it renders his own position incoherent when taken in isolation, it also makes his work a powerful testimony to the situation in which we find ourselves. It is a situation attested to by Heidegger in one of his letters to Gadamer.

> I myself do not know clearly enough how my "position" vis-à-vis Hegel is to be determined—it would not be enough to put it down as a "counterposition" . . . I have repeatedly opposed talk about the "breakdown" of the Hegelian system. What has broken down, that means to have sunk away, is what came after Hegel—Nietzsche included.[51]

The ambiguity of Gadamer's relation to Hegel and Heidegger must be seen in the light of the ambiguity of Heidegger's own appreciation of Hegel. We do not have to choose between Hegel and Heidegger as between two rival positions; that is not how the options present themselves. If Gadamer refuses to construct a third position which would borrow from Hegel and Heidegger and yet would attempt to challenge both, this is not a failing so much as a recognition that to attempt to do so would be to resort to metaphysical speculation of a kind no longer regarded by him as legitimate. In this readiness to depend on Heidegger without attempting to compete with him, Gadamer at times finds the one way open to him to supplement Heidegger. Gadamer is no substitute for Heidegger, and still less can he provide Heidegger with a firm foundation. But if Gadamer refuses to engage in metaphysical speculation out of a recognition of the fragmentation of language and of the tradition, then he has found a way of being faithful to Heidegger without either mimicking him or translating him back into the language of metaphysics. It is to acknowledge that after Heidegger's introduction to the end of philosophy and to the unity of metaphysics, as it arises out of this end, we shall be led—as we are already discovering—to forsake talk of both in favor of the plurality of dispersed forms by which we are claimed in their wake. This plurality is not defensible from within the confines of philosophical reason traditionally conceived; its incoherence corresponds to the situation where the *logos* no longer retains its mastery while recouping what precedes it. In Gadamer's openness to this plurality we may on occasion find a certain displacement of Heidegger the bridge-builder, the gatherer, who finds the unity of metaphysics, but who must withdraw from it at the very same time: for this unity is not established by opposition to what is not metaphysical (as what stands on one bank might be defined by the fact that it stands opposed to what lies on the other side of the river), but is simply another name for the *resources* of dispersion.

11

The Transformation of Language at Another Beginning

I

Derrida's starting point is the end of philosophy, or, as he would prefer to say, "the closure of metaphysics." The terms "philosophy" and "metaphysics" are for Derrida, as they became for Heidegger, equivalent ways of referring to the tradition. "End" is not equivalent to "closure."[1] Derrida uses "closure" because he refuses to speak of the "end" of philosophy in the sense of a termination. That philosophy is if not finished, at least *at an end*, is something Derrida does not see any need to establish; he points to Hegel, Marx, Nietzsche, and Heidegger.[2] It is for him quite simply the context in which "those who are still called philosophers . . . in remembrance at least" ask the one question left to them—the question of the closure, that is, the question of the relation between belonging to philosophy and achieving an opening beyond philosophical discourse.[3] Derrida's word "closure" states his fundamental insight that it is impossible for us simply to transgress metaphysics, to leave it unambiguously behind us and stand unequivocally outside it. But it does not bear only this negative sense.

Derrida's name has come to be associated with a number of strategies which govern his approach to a text and whose function is to impose closure on it. His procedure is most apparent in those places where he goes into greatest detail, as, for example, in his reading of Plato's *Phaedrus* in *Dissemination* and of Rousseau's *Essay on the Origin of Languages* in *Of Grammatology*. Metaphysics, according to Derrida, is marked by a certain series of oppositions, the most fundamental being presence versus absence. In each of the metaphysical oppositions (inside/outside; speaking/writing; remedy/poison) one of the terms is privileged over the other, and the privileging of presence governs all these others. Derrida's first task is to render the metaphysical reading of the text in hand, and he tends to accomplish this by drawing attention to the oppositions and priorities whereby what was primary becomes secondary and vice versa. Finally, this gives way to a reading in which neither term is privileged and we are introduced to a sense in which the terms (which at first—and second—reading were opposed) are "at play" one with the other; the play takes place according to a logic which we do not associate with metaphysics. This play, which exceeds metaphysics, is thus found inscribed in texts which we provisionally took to be metaphysical. The inscription of this excess is in Rousseau borne by the word *supplement* and in Plato by the word *pharmakon*.

These various stages (which I have described rather more schematically than they are practiced by Derrida) take the form of a series of readings of a specific text. We pass from a reading which is referred to the author's intentions or an influential interpretation or even a standard translation and arrive at a reading which displays a logic which is not that of traditional metaphysics working through the text. And yet, this passage is not arbitrarily enforced on the text, but is attained, by and large, through fairly conventional hermeneutical techniques. The difference between Derrida and, for example, Gadamerian hermeneutics lies more than is generally realized in the greater resolution with which Derrida applies these techniques. The sense in which Derrida's readings are immanent is indicated by his claim that every metaphysical text carries within itself the resources that will be borrowed from the metaphysical system to criticize it.[4] The justification for reversing the hierarchy of terms is found inscribed within the text itself; the means for surpassing metaphysics are to be found within metaphysics itself. But this surpassing is not to be understood as a Hegelian *Aufhebung*.

Derrida clarifies his approach somewhat in a discussion at the close of the 1968 essay "The Ends of Man."[5] The context of the discussion is the apparent dilemma of our relation to metaphysics: we find ourselves on the inside yet recognize that "a radical trembling can only come from the outside." Two strategies present themselves. The first is "to attempt an exit and a deconstruction without changing terrain," where the risk is that we would simply be confirming, consolidating, or subsuming (*relever*, the French equivalent of *aufheben*) what we claim to be deconstructing. The second is "to decide to change terrain, in a discontinuous and irruptive manner, by brutally placing oneself outside, and by affirming an absolute break and difference." The second can never be successful on its own because "the simple practice of language ceaselessly reinstates the 'new' terrain on the oldest ground." Thus the call is for "a new writing" to "weave and interlace these two motifs of deconstruction." The first strategy is said by Derrida to be the one which predominates in Heidegger, whereas the second was the dominant one in France at the time of the essay. But Derrida is quite clear that both strategies can be found in Heidegger.

Derrida's debt to Heidegger is obvious. The identification of metaphysics with the privileging of presence is found already in Heidegger's *Being and Time*—*Sein* as *Anwesenheit*. The very term "deconstruction," which Derrida sometimes uses to describe his procedure, clearly echoes Heidegger's notion of a "Destruction of the History of Ontology."[6] Nevertheless, some of Derrida's followers, by emphasizing those passages in which Derrida draws attention to the metaphysical within Heidegger's texts, have tried to find a straightforward answer to the complex question of whether Derrida represents in any way an advance on Heidegger. Of course, Derrida also finds the rupture within Heidegger's texts, but those same Derridians give the credit for this to Derrida himself as if it could be isolated as "his" contribution. And yet, this is to forget the sense in which Derrida's reading, like any other good reading, disappears into the text and becomes interwoven with it. The ambiguity of the Heideggerian situation is well described by Derrida himself when in *Of Grammatology* he writes that it is contained within the metaphysics of presence and logocentrism and yet it transgresses that metaphysics.[7] For Derrida, to impose closure on a text does not only mean to draw back within metaphysics what has pretensions to transgress it; it is at least just as much to force outside of metaphysics whatever seems to stand within it. Of course, and this is crucial, the inside-outside opposition used here to situate the closure is itself metaphysical. The two strategies of drawing within and forcing outside are inseparable. They belong together in an ambiguity for which Derrida prefers the title "play."[8]

The temptation to see Derrida as simply representing the impossibility of any transgression of metaphysics, and thus only the first of the two strategies described in "The Ends of Man," is easy to appreciate. It arises because the case against the possibility of transgressing the history of metaphysics can be so clearly stated: "We have no language—no syntax and no lexicon—which is foreign to this history."[9] On the other hand, Derrida is adamant that this is not the last word: "No concept is by itself, and consequently in and of itself, metaphysical, outside all the textual work in which it is inscribed."[10] In the present essay, by means of a reading of Heidegger's lecture "The Way to Language," I shall attempt to investigate this language which is not simply metaphysical and which lies at the heart of the play of the closure interweaving the twin strategies. In Heidegger's own terms, it is the question of how the overcoming of metaphysics can take place when it is "within certain limits, compelled to speak the language of that which it helps to overcome" (W 99; EB 380–81). This last quotation shows clearly enough that Derrida's question about "the conditions for a discourse exceeding metaphysics" is also one of Heidegger's questions, and is not brought to him from "outside."[11]

II

It is not difficult to imagine Derrida himself setting about a reading of Heidegger's essay "The Way to Language" by first emphasizing the tendency of its translators or its commentators to reinscribe Heidegger's text within metaphysics. The standard English translation in particular could readily be singled out for this purpose. By itself this could not constitute a reading Derrida himself might give: it would be but the first step on the way to such a reading. What I am concerned with is what happens when this "part of a reading" is taken as a result. The partial reading, which could never be Derrida's reading, can nevertheless be called "Derridian" in a sense often heard today: Derridian as opposed to Heideggerian. What characterizes a Derridian reading in this sense is the almost ritualistic attention to certain metaphysical prejudices, to which Derrida himself has in his writings frequently called our attention. But in this case the reader fixes the prejudices in the text so that they cannot be undone from within the text, save only by a virtuoso performance which remains outside the text.

In order to sketch such a "Derridian" reading of Heidegger's essay I shall consider six of these metaphysical gestures, all of which seem to be operative there:

(i) Reliance on experience
(ii) The priority accorded to speech over writing
(iii) The quest for origins
(iv) Logocentrism
(v) The privilege accorded to possession
(vi) The tendency to unite or unify

The list is not exhaustive. Taken singly or together, the items are directed to the question of the inside/outside of metaphysics. I shall consider them in turn always with two points in mind: first, to indicate how on a first reading Heidegger's essay "The Way to Language" might appear to be under the sway of these metaphysical motifs and, second, to show that to read Heidegger as falling prey to them seems to be in conformity with certain remarks of Derrida himself. Because my concern here is not a reconstruction of Derrida's own reading of Heidegger, I shall not restore those remarks to their proper context and to the strategy from which they can be detached only at the risk of distortion.

First, there is Heidegger's reliance on experience. Derrida has always insisted that the notion of experience is "fundamentally inscribed within onto-theology . . . by the value of presence."[12] And yet, Heidegger in "The Way to Language" clearly defines his task as that of "experiencing the unbinding bond within the web of language" (US 243; WL 113). Companion essays to that one, "The Word" and "The Essence of Language," similarly insist on undergoing an experience with language.

Secondly, we find the charge of phonocentrism, which means to uphold the priority accorded to speech over writing, the voice over the line. Again, what is at issue is the privilege of presence over absence, this time as it concerns the presence of the speaker. In the essay "The Ends of Man" Derrida charges Heidegger with privileging spoken language.[13] When we turn to "The Way to Language" it seems that writing is scarcely referred to, that the discussion is about speaking, and that there is even a sentence, seemingly Heidegger's description of his own position, which says that "here too language shows itself first as our way of speaking" (US 250; WL 120).

Thirdly, the notion of origin is also inscribed with the metaphysics of presence. The major part of Derrida's *Of Grammatology* is occupied with a deconstruction of Rousseau's texts on the origin of languages by means of a reading which gives rise to the notion of a "nonorigin" of language, an "incessant supplementarity."[14] And yet, in "The Way to Language" Heidegger can be found ascribing the origin of the word to Appropriation (US 265; WL 133).

Fourthly, Derrida charges Heidegger with logocentrism (G 33/20). Insofar as the issue of the closure is that of metaphysical language, it amounts to the question of how one stands in relation to the *logos*. Heidegger's essay "The Word" culminates in the word *logos* (US 237; WL 155). It also seems to figure in "The Way to Language" in Heidegger's adoption of the word "monologue" from Novalis and the discussion of "gathering," a notion Heidegger frequently appeals to when explicating *logos*.

Fifthly, Derrida draws attention to what he regards as the ethico-ontological ground of Heidegger's notion of *Verfallenheit*, or fallenness, in spite of Heidegger's denials that they are relevant. Derrida's justification is that it is the language and not the intention which is decisive.[15] The objection extends also to cover the notions of authenticity and inauthenticity, and then to the whole family of words in Heidegger that bear the same root and allude to the idea of owning. In this way Derrida in *Spurs* seeks to draw the fundamental word of Heidegger's later-thinking *Ereignis* back into the orbit of onto-theology. The translation of *Ereignis* as "appropriation" would, if correct, support Derrida's claim.

Finally, Heidegger's emphasis on the unifying unity of the essence of language seems to reflect the totalizing tendency of metaphysics and offers itself as a suitable target for dissemination.

Is one not forced to acknowledge, in the light of this catalogue—which could readily be extended—that Heidegger remains tied to the language of metaphysics? It would seem unnecessary to pursue the matter further, particularly as Heidegger himself seems to concede as much in the final

The Transformation of Language at Another Beginning / 195

pages of the essay where he describes the present era as one in which the old is completed and nothing new begins (US 265; WL 133).

But, as I have explained, it would be entirely uncharacteristic of Derrida himself to decide the question of the inside/outside simply by drawing Heidegger's text back within metaphysics. He would only want to show the possibility of a metaphysical reading of Heidegger to place alongside it another reading, one which would show Heidegger transgressing metaphysics.[16] Derrida gives such a reading of Heidegger's text "The Way to Language" in an important article published in 1978, "Le Retrait de la metaphore." It is accomplished by concentrating on the families of two words, *Ziehen* and *Reissen*. I shall not give an account of Derrida's essay here, both because I have had to leave to one side the question of metaphor with which it is concerned (highly relevant though it is to the topic of metaphysics) and because I am for the moment more concerned with Derridian readings than reconstructing Derrida's own reading.

For my purpose the question which needs to be clarified is whether this second reading, which shows the transgressive gesture at work in the text, would simply replace the first and metaphysical reading, or whether the point is to leave us undecided between the two readings so that the ambiguity of the text becomes a means of reflecting the sense in which at the closure we find ourselves unable to say what lies inside and what outside. The answer no doubt lies in the notion of a history of textuality, indicated but not developed in *Of Grammatology*. In our own epoch, this history recognizes that a logic other than the traditional structures the texts that hitherto have served to define "the tradition." Texts like Plato's *Phaedrus* or Rousseau's *Essay* belonged unambiguously to the tradition before their deconstruction; and yet the deconstructed reading did not simply replace previous readings. It only existed in relation to those readings which constituted the text in its historicality. Derrida, having dismissed the idea of the original meaning of a text, whether it was to be identified with the author's intentions or not, found that when he came to identify the text of a contemporary such as Heidegger or Levinas, the issue became more acute. Could we not have a text which is written and read only in accordance with this "other" logic?

Sometimes Derrida addresses this question by suggesting that he is concerned with the contemporary reader of Heidegger and not Heidegger himself. The contemporary reader draws the text back within metaphysics. But over and beyond that is the fact that we have at our disposal only the traditional language. And yet, how can that point be made without rendering any transgression of metaphysics impossible, whereas Derrida never left any doubt that he recognizes the possibility of such transgressions or ruptures? The questions remain: How can there be any transgression at all?

And if metaphysical language can be transgressed, why is Derrida so insistent as part of his strategy in showing the metaphysical language operating where he will find the transgression? Or to put it another way, why does Derrida insist on both the strategies outlined at the end of "The Ends of Man," and how are they to be united? I shall look for answers to these questions in the reading of Heidegger's "The Way to Language," which shall occupy the next three sections of my essay (corresponding to the three sections of Heidegger's own essay).

III

After an important introductory section to which I shall return later, "The Way to Language" begins with a discussion of the way language has been thought in the tradition, concentrating on two of the most influential accounts—Aristotle's in *Peri Hermeneias* and Wilhelm von Humboldt's in *Uber die Verschiedenheit des menschlichen Sprachbaues*. Heidegger ended his 1957 lecture, "The Principle of Identity," by saying that "only when we turn thoughtfully toward what has already been thought, will we be turned for what is yet to be thought" (I 106; ID 41). This is more than the customary warning that to remain ignorant of the tradition is to be in danger of repeating it. Heidegger is suggesting that there is a close relation between the dialogue with previous thinking and freeing oneself for what he elsewhere describes as "the no-longer metaphysical." The thinker attains the "no-longer metaphysical" by the step back into the essence or ground of metaphysics (W 100; EB 382).

Heidegger has always insisted on a close link between what is transmitted by the tradition and what we regard as self-evident, what we take for granted (SZ 21; BT 43). In outlining the traditional conception of language he also has in mind the "ordinary" conception of language (US 255; WL 125). Three common prejudices are highlighted in Heidegger's account. The first is that we tend to understand language in terms of speaking and not the other way round. The second is that we tend to conceive of speaking as an activity. The third is that we tend to take the activity of speaking for granted. At this juncture Heidegger reminds us that language is not a fixed possession and that sometimes we cannot speak through fear or because of some accident. But he is not thereby attempting to issue a direct challenge to the conception that man is the animal who "has" the *logos*. The tradition was well aware that the capacity to speak is sometimes disrupted. The point would seem to be rather—and it has to be conceded that Heidegger in no way spells it out—that such cases of disruption came to provide the basis for the analysis of language, just as cases of hallucination or illusion tended to serve as the starting point for the analysis of perception. The essential character of speaking came to be determined on the basis of those cases where speech fails us. One may have the intention to speak, but whoever does not make sounds does not speak; whoever has lost the capacity to activate the organs of speech has lost speech. Thus one of the primary ways in which speaking came to be regarded was in terms of the making of sounds.

To take the very clear, though relatively late, example of the Stoics, their treatment of language operates within the distinction between the word and what it signifies. This distinction is not given to the speaker or hearer deep in conversation, but arises only in the face of the barbarian. When the outsider addresses us, we fail to understand anything of what he or she says; we hear only noises. In this way the word is reduced to a word-thing or sign, and the analysis of language concentrates on what the barbarian lacked, which the Stoics called *to lekton*—the sense of significant discourse.[17] Essentially the same procedure can still be found to provide the basis of Husserl's analysis in the *Logical Investigations*. In such analyses the Being of language always goes missing, not so much because the investigation takes as its basis the case where language fails, but because the Being of language is not one constituent among others.

This response to the analysis of language is at best only hinted at by Heidegger. He is more directly concerned to provide the broad outlines of a history of the philosophy of language. He concentrates on three stages. First, using the example of Aristotle, he suggests that the Greeks of the classical age understood the relation between the various analytic constituents of language—letters, sounds, passions in the soul, that which strikes the passions—in terms of showing, letting appear, letting shine. Secondly, following the time of the Stoa, the relation of showing gives way to that of the sign understood as an instrument. The subsequent history of language is treated simply by reference to Humboldt, although later in the essay Heidegger gives some indication of how the conception of language as an instrument reaches its peak in the modern view of language in terms of information. Heidegger refers this history of language to the account of the change in the essence of truth which he had developed in the essay "Plato's Doctrine of Truth."

Heidegger makes the point that Aristotle's discussion of language is not to be read in terms of truth as correctness, but in terms of *aletheia* as unconcealment. Heidegger provides a somewhat unconventional translation of the well-known passage at the beginning of *Peri Hermeneias*, which explicates both the relation between the making of vocal sounds and the soul's passions and the relation between what is written and vocal sounds in terms of *sumbola*. William of Moerbeke in his translation had understood *sumbola* to mean *notae* (tokens). Heidegger understands it in terms of showing. The interpretation on which this translation is based goes back at least 30 years to the 1925/26 Marburg course, where the focus of his reading is the interpretation of *logos* as synthesis (GA 21, 166–68). In "The Way to Language" Heidegger does not refer to earlier translations and more familiar interpretations of the passage. Nevertheless the companion essay, "The Essence of Language" (contrary to the impression given by the standard English translation), gives the more conventional translation in terms of "signs" (US 203–04; WL 97). There is concealed in the translation Heidegger offers in "The Way to Language" what at an earlier time he might have called a "destruction" of the tendency "of all later considerations of language" to take the sign as their standard (US 204; WL 97). These later considerations Heidegger regards as derivative of the more fundamental conception of language, which recognizes it as a showing. Heidegger says nothing at this point in the essay to suggest that he recognizes this passage from Aristotle as an example of phonocentrism, which is how Derrida refers to it in *Of Grammatology*.[18] Indeed, in general there is no indication at this stage that any attempt will be made to go beyond Aristotle, let alone a clue as to how this might be done.

By contrast, Heidegger's discussion of von Humboldt follows the assessment of him already to be found in *Being and Time*, where "the philosophical horizon" within which he made language a problem was put in question (SZ 166; BT 209). A similar point is made here. Humboldt speaks the language of metaphysics, specifically that governed by Leibniz, as when he writes of language as an activity, *energeia*. Furthermore, Humboldt's account is inadequate because it grasps language in terms of a higher universal. Language is not experienced in its own terms, but is explicated with reference to the notion of a "world view." Nevertheless there are hints of a more sympathetic treatment of Humboldt. His treatise is described as "astounding, obscure and yet continuously stimulating." Indeed, at the end of the essay Humboldt receives that rare honor, usually only accorded to Hölderlin, of having the last word.

In general this first section of Heidegger's essay is a very broad survey of the approach to language taken by two of the most eminent representatives of the philosophical consideration of language, with only brief indications of what passed between. For the most part the survey is not very different from one Heidegger might have given 30 years earlier. Even the discussion of the transformation of the sign in terms of "the change in the essence of truth" is striking for being out of line with other discussions at about this time. Both in "Hegel and the Greeks" six months earlier and "The End of Philosophy and the Task of Thinking" five years later, and in spite of what seem to be striking differences between those two accounts, Heidegger was especially cautious that the passage away from *aletheia* not be referred to "truth," as if that notion encompassed both terms of the transformation. And yet, one has to say that because Heidegger does not give the conventional reading of Aristotle, but only his own rereading of Aristotle, this first part of the essay does not seem to be setting up a straightforward metaphysical account simply in order for it to be "overcome" subsequently.

IV

The philosophical consideration of language has tended to take the form of an analysis that breaks language into its components. In the face of this diversity it has tended to let one aspect of language predominate (US 251; WL 121) or else it has grasped language in terms of something other than language, such as activity, spirit, or worldview (US 250; WL 119). But this means that the attempt to find the unifying unity of language, that which we might call the "essence of language," fails because the universal only succeeds in coordinating or synthesizing relative to the analysis (US 250; WL 120). For Heidegger the failure to attain language as language defines the traditional approach; the "ownmost" character of language has always eluded it. Indeed, so long as we think *das Eigentumliche* not as the "ownmost" character of language, but—and this is how the standard English translation renders it—as what is "peculiar" to it in distinction from other things, language is still being referred to what is not language and, in Heidegger's terms, is being thought metaphysically.

In consequence, Heidegger in the second part of the essay sketches an alternative account of language to that of the tradition of Aristotle and Humboldt (US 250–01; WL 120). He does not indicate a source for this view of language. Nevertheless, in certain important respects it resembles the account of discourse given in section 34 of *Being and Time*. Heidegger had already there dismissed previous attempts to grasp the essence of language as not only one-sided and partial, but as also inadequate in terms of their starting point (SZ 163; BT 206). Furthermore, *Being and Time* rejected one of the pillars of the analytic approach when it insisted that "word-things do not get supplied with significations" (SZ 161; BT 204). Language was not to be understood in terms of constituents revealed by analysis. Heidegger was careful not to individuate constitutive items, but emphasized instead what he called "the structure of discourse." The essence of language as the unifying unity of language is anticipated in this notion, but it is not experienced and is not named. Both the metaphysical attempt and that of *Being and Time*— whose relation to metaphysics is still an open question—fail in this. The account of language offered in *Being and Time* may claim superiority over previous accounts on the basis that it alone attempts the task of working out the structure of discourse on the basis of the analytic of *Dasein*. A close reading of section 34 suggests that there we are already invited to understand the relation between *Dasein* and language in such a way that this task is nevertheless to think language in terms of itself, and not in terms of something other than language. But there is no indication—the discussion of "keeping silent" notwithstanding—that to bring language as language to language means anything other than finding a name for it.

Indeed, in "The Way to Language" Heidegger evokes this earlier discussion of keeping silent, where hearing and keeping silent were presented as "possibilities belonging to discursive speech [*Sprechen*]" (SZ 161; BT 204). In *Being and Time* Heidegger, with the introduction of a distinction between discourse and speech, had addressed the question of the privilege accorded to speech in the traditional accounts of language. No doubt a certain kind of reading would latch onto the phrase used to describe keeping silent—"discursive speech"—in order to suggest that the privilege is not addressed there resolutely enough. Certainly the relation in which silence stands to speech needs further clarification, leaving the possibility that the conventional subordination of silence to speech has simply been reversed. In "The Way to Language" Heidegger introduces a distinction between "saying" and "speech" (US 252; WL 122) which runs parallel to that between "discourse" and "speech" in *Being and Time*. This distinction is no more successful in displacing the traditional hierarchical ordering in favor of speech, as is conceded when, in the second part of "The Way to Language," we read, "here, too, language shows itself first as our way of speaking" (US 250; WL 120). It is only later in the essay, when the task of naming the essence of language comes to be associated with silence, that the traditional priority accorded to speaking is addressed radically.

At this point in "The Way to Language" the issue of the essence of language remains, as in *Being and Time*, that of the failure to grasp it, to bring it to language. "That which must remain wholly unspoken is held back in the unsaid, abides in concealment as unshowable, is mystery" (US 253; WL 122). And this is the fate of the essence of language which remains hidden in mystery for us. Heidegger in "The Way to Language" makes one more attempt and immediately concedes that it has failed according to the standard he has already recognized: "With regard to the manifold ties of saying [*Sagen*] we shall call the essence of language in its totality *die Sage*—and admit that even now we have not caught sight of what unifies those ties" (US 253; WL 122–23). I shall leave aside for the moment the question of what conception of language might make possible such an arbitrary act of naming, if that is indeed what it is. For the moment it is enough to notice that this is not the first occurrence of the word *Sage* in Heidegger's writings: it arises both in the discussion of the projective saying of poetry (H 61; PLT 74) and in another place in reference to the thinking of Being (W 188; BW 236). *Sage* is Heidegger's word for that originary language through which the destiny of Being happens, and, to that extent it goes beyond what in *Being and Time* was named as *Rede*.

In "The Way to Language" the essential being of language as *Sage* is referred to showing (US 254; WL 123). "Showing" is not to be understood in the sense that is given to it in Part One of *Being and Time*, where its understanding, as so often in that book, should be approached in terms of the repetition of Aristotle referred to above. Here showing is that "realm" which already in *Being and Time* had been called "Lichtung" (SZ 133; BT 171). In the 1964 essay "The End of Philosophy and the Task of Thinking" Heidegger insists that *Lichtung* should be thought neither as a transcendental condition nor as a spatial metaphor. Indeed, it has remained unthought by metaphysics and presumably cannot be thought from within it (SD 74; TB 67).

In this way Heidegger attempts in "The Way to Language" to guard us against thinking of showing, and thus saying, primarily as a human activity (US 254; WL 123). Self-showing marks (*Kennzeichen* is Heidegger's warning to his reader that the matter is still not thought deeply enough) the presence and absence of what-comes-to-presence. It is not human saying which lets things appear. Rather, human saying is preceded by a *Sichzeigenlassen* which takes place as the speaking of language itself. It is language itself which reaches into the regions of presencing and lets what-comes-to presence appear and disappear. The notorious phrase "language speaks" was first introduced nine years before this essay in 1950. The showing of saying takes place when language itself speaks. Human saying is only a *Nachsprechen*, literally, a "saying after," a reiteration (US 255; WL 124–25).

At the end of the second part of the essay Heidegger makes this speaking of language the context for an attempt to displace the metaphysical account of speech as a human activity. In a conversation it is not the case that one person speaks while another listens. Still less, we can add, is it the case that a person speaks and listens to himself. When Heidegger refers to a simultaneity of speaking and listening he is referring to something very different from the pure auto-affection of the voice as heard by its speaker. The listening is a listening neither to oneself nor to another, but to language before we speak. The recognition that we belong to language was not absent from *Being and Time*; and reticence was there already referred to a potentiality for hearing. One may even wish to attribute to the Heidegger of *Being and Time* the view, more openly stated in lectures given in the mid-1930s, that language had its origin in keeping silent (GA 39, 218). But Heidegger addresses that view in the third part of the essay, where it is exposed as an inadequate basis for entering into the essence of language, or, as one might rather say, it is brought to the closure and deconstructed.

V

In his introductory remarks to the essay, Heidegger described "The Way to Language" as an attempt to bring "language as language to language." The stages of the path which constitutes "The Way to Language" may be measured by the transformations that phrase undergoes. What at first seems nothing more than a vague directive takes on a greater determinacy as the essay proceeds, so that along the way it comes to be understood to mean bringing the essence of language (in the sense of the unifying unity) into the sounded word (*Sage* as a name for the essence of language) (US 261; WL 130). In the third part of Heidegger's essay, of which I shall give only a highly selective account, the phrase comes to mean letting the essence of language resound in all human saying. There is no word for the essence of language according to the metaphysical way of naming; indeed, the attempt to name this essence is itself only a metaphysical ambition if it means to crack open and divulge the mystery of the unsaid. What is at issue is not "the procurement of newly formed words" (US 266–67; WL 134), but the transformation of our relation to language. To bring the essence of language to language now comes to mean to hear the essence of language in every word or, one might say, to enter into the essence of language to which in a sense we already belong. We can only take the step back into the essence of language insofar as we have stepped outside all attempts to grasp language. What thereby enters the sounded word is the silent speaking of language itself. Heidegger is at great pains to point out that this does not mean that the accounts of language discussed in the first and second parts of the essay are now to be dismissed as invalid (US 261; WL 130). And he adds that the way to language taken in the second part of the essay becomes "possible and necessary" only through the way taken in the third part, just as Heidegger would later say in response to Father Richardson that although Heidegger I is the only access to Heidegger II, Heidegger I becomes possible only if it is contained in Heidegger II (BR xxiii). On the present reading, the second part of "The Way to Language" corresponds to Heidegger I, in the same way as the third part corresponds to Heidegger II, and the manner of their presence together in this essay should serve as a confirmation that Heidegger II cannot be separated from, nor understood in simple opposition to, Heidegger I.

Although there is a sense in which the essence of language is always brought to language whenever there is speaking, we are appropriated to it in our ownmost essence only when we hear the stillness speaking in language or correspond to it in our saying—as when we remain silent and renounce the attempt to name the essence of language metaphysically. The renunciation arises as a matter of destiny, specifically that of our time as the time of *der Fehl des Gemeinsamen*, the lack of something common—a universal—

which binds together and to which we may refer language. Through this lack we enter into dwelling in *Ereignis*. What looked lie a task we set ourselves—to bring language to language as language—becomes the way-making (*Be-wegung*) which is *Ereignis* itself (US 261; WL 130). The transformation of the formula about bringing language as language to language is the passage from Being to *Ereignis*.

The essay "The Way to Language" directs us to the special conditions which prevail in our epoch. "That we cannot know the essence of language—know it according to the traditional concept of knowledge defined in terms of cognition as representation, is not a defect, but rather an advantage by which we are favoured with a special realm" (US 266; WL 134). Previous thinkers both did and yet did not know the essence of language in terms of the presencing of representation. They approached language in terms of *Vorstellung*, but for that very reason did not enter into the essence of language, which only becomes accessible once all attempts to "know" it have failed and are renounced. The mystery of language only gives itself over to those who accept it as mystery; the essence of language is unconcealed only as concealed within the sounded word. The entry into *Ereignis*—whereby each is brought into his own—means that each is no longer mediated by the universal, by the governing representation. The universal acts as a binding relation between language, as *Sage*, and man. The lack of this universal turns us toward the insight which takes place as *Ereignis*—"the unbinding bond" (US 243 and 262; WL 113 and 131)—whereby man does not seek to bind language but is himself bound over to *Ereignis*, into his own, as he who belongs to language. And yet, because Heidegger is describing the destiny of our epoch he can also call this lack "the most binding relation" (US 265; WL 134).

Heidegger indicates the nature of the transformation of language by the phrase, already introduced in 1950, *des Geläut der Stille*, "the ringing of stillness" (US 215; WL 108; US 30; PLT 207). The phrase says that through the lack of a name for the essence of language, all language comes to be infused with silence. To bring the essence of language as *Sage* to the sounded word means to bring silence to the sounded word, to bring the unspeakable to the spoken. Indeed, the directive "to bring language as language to language" itself becomes "a soundless echo" (US 243; WL 113). That does not mean it comes to be negated, but that to experience language is to enter into the grant whereby the silence transforms speaking. Heidegger's word for language—*die Sage*—says but does not say "the essence of language" as the unnameable, the unsayable.

But what then is the place of *logos* in Heidegger's thinking on language? Does not *logos* enter into Heidegger's thinking as a word of Being? Both the companion essays to "The Way to Language"—"The Essence of Language" and "The Word"—point to the word *logos*, "the oldest word for the rule of the word" (US 237; WL 155). And they both recognize it as a name for Being and for saying (US 185; WL 80). Does that not mean that *logos* is the word for the Being of saying? In which case how can we talk of the continuing failure to find a name for the Being of language? Of course, the Greeks did not hear the word *logos* as a word for Being, but if we accept Heidegger's reading of *logos* as a word of Being, does it not follow that it now stands for us as the word for the Being of language—*logos* as gathering?

Heidegger's answer would be that such questions ignore the very transformation of language which is at issue. The transformation does not mean that the word *logos* no longer imposes a claim on us; the recognition of a word as a word of Being takes place in its addressing us through the tradition which thereby shows how it still has a hold on us today. The word *logos* still determines thinking to this day (WD 102; WCT 163), but like other archaic words it is no longer able to take up a place in the language and thinking of today (WD 98–99; WCT 153). For the thinkers at the end of philosophy, at the closure, *logos* no longer speaks directly as it once did. It no longer asserts itself, but slips away into the abyss, *Abgrund*. Slipping into the abyss, the word returns to where it came from—the silence of speaking language. *Logos* and the other words of Being still claim us, but we can no longer assert them nor read them without their undergoing this transformation. For metaphysics the no longer metaphysical is unsayable. For us the metaphysical is no longer sayable. We read Plato and are introduced to a non-metaphysical Plato; we read Hegel and find a non-metaphysical Hegel, and so on. Or rather, the metaphysical disappears as metaphysical for recollective thinking. For the rest, Heidegger leaves us in no doubt that where we do not in our questioning listen to language and entertain what it grants, the metaphysical is simply perpetuated.

For a word to be heard as a word of Being and for that word to transgress metaphysics are the same, for thereby it is no longer held back in the oblivion which marks the limits of metaphysics. And yet, the word, heard or read, does not pass from oblivion into unconcealment in the sense of being brought to presence. Heidegger's essay "The End of Philosophy and the Task of Thinking" is particularly valuable for showing this transformation of language. *Lichtung* is *der Ort der Stille*—the place of stillness. *Lichtung* is named by Parmenides, but not thought by him as such, through the word *aletheia* (SD 76–77; TB 69). What *aletheia* as *Lichtung* grants *is* experienced and thought within metaphysics; what it is as such remains concealed (SD 78; TB 71). Read by Heidegger as *a-letheia*, it announces in advance its own concealment within metaphysics. When we read *aletheia* as *a-letheia* we pass into the "speaking of language." When Aristotle's discussion of language is read in terms not only of *aletheia* but of *a-letheia* his text is brought to the closure. When Heidegger in "The Way to Language" introduces his word *Ereignis*, calling it the earliest and oldest, he is also referring to *a-letheia* (US 258; WL 127; cf. SD 25; TB 24). It cannot be discussed or placed. There can be no *Erörterung* of it, for it is the *Ortschaft* or region of all places. The experience to which "The Way to Language" is directed and from which it speaks is "the plain, sudden, unforgettable and hence forever new look" not into a new dawn, but into that dawn from which the changing cycle of day and night begins. The transformation of language was prepared for at the very beginning of philosophy—as a "trace."

What takes place with the transformation of language is that the old region of metaphysics is fitted with new ways by what Heidegger calls "recollection" and "way-making" (*Be-wegung*) and Derrida calls "displacement" and "transgression." For Heidegger the preferred phrase is not "a new beginning," but "another beginning," an expression which occurs at least eight times in his published writings. In this notion of "another" the reference to what went before is maintained in its discontinuity with it. A similar language is found in Derrida, though perhaps not always with the same consistency. In "The Ends of Man" Derrida uses the phrase "a new writing." The more careful formulation which corresponds to Heideggerian usage—"another writing"—can also be found.[19]

The question is whether there is available for us a language other than the language of metaphysics. The two quotations from Humboldt which end Heidegger's essay must be read in the light of it. The first passage includes the sentence: "A people could by inner illumination and favourable external circumstances, impact so different a form to the language handed down to them that it would thereby turn into a wholly other, wholly new language." Strictly speaking, a wholly new language is impossible. It could arise only through the "application of an already available phonetic form." This is confirmed by the second quotation, where Humboldt writes of filling an old shell with new meaning. This is what happens when the transformation of language becomes operative in our reading of the history of philosophy, transforming it into the history of Being: metaphysical language comes to echo with the *Geläut der Stille*.

The end of philosophy, or rather its closure (*Verendung*), takes place in both Heidegger and Derrida, therefore, only as a transformation of our relation to previous thinking. It is not a termination of the tradition, a "dead end," nor does it take place in turning one's back on what has gone before. And yet, even though there is no clean break with metaphysics there is a rupture, a discontinuity which cannot be understood simply as a dialectical reversal.

VI

How does it stand with the Derridian strategies listed in part two, above, after this rereading of Heidegger's essay?

First is the inscription of presence in the notion of experience. Just as Derrida has provided a "deconstructed" reading of certain metaphysical texts and their concepts, Heidegger, in *Hegel's Concept of Experience*, in his reading of Hegel's word "experience" as a word of Being, has heard its claim from beyond metaphysics. There Heidegger establishes the relationship in Hegel between experience and presence as *parousia*, precisely to call it into question. In seeking an experience with language, what is experienced is not a presence but a lack, the lack of a word of Being in our epoch. And yet, Heidegger is careful to insist that this lack is not a simple defect or something merely negative (US 266; WL 134). This experience is for thinking the passage from the realm of the opposition of presence and absence into "the special realm" within which that opposition arises and which as such is not governed by it.

Secondly, Heidegger mentions the priority accorded to speaking only to displace it. Speaking is secondary, not to the originary nature of silence, but to that relation of silence which Heidegger describes as an *Entsprechen* or "corresponding" (US 262; WL 131). Given that for Derrida the reversal of the priority of speaking and writing is for the sake of disturbing the privilege accorded to speech within the tradition, and not in order to privilege writing (for that would be to maintain the metaphysical system of opposition), Heidegger subverts the metaphysical schema. The privilege is disturbed, but not in favor of another oppositional system.

Thirdly, there is the question of origins. We have seen how Heidegger turned away from regarding silence as an origin in the sense of *Ursprung*, but there remains the discussion of the origin of the word in the sense of *Herkunft* (US 265; WL 133). This origin is not thought of as a first word, but in terms of *Ereignis* as the oldest of the old. In this way the quest for origins as a quest for a ground is abandoned (US 256; WL 125). So far as the spoken word is concerned, it is rethought as "an answer, a countersaying" (US 260; WL 129). But there are of course not two separate events—the speaking of language and the human speaking which answers to it. That the origin of human speaking takes place as an answer must be understood as obeying that same "logic" that Derrida describes with Rousseau's word "supplement."

Fourthly, Heidegger's recollection of *logos* takes place from the experience of the end of philosophy. The recollection of *logos* does not remain within the logocentrism of metaphysics. The word *logos* like the word "experience," as we saw, is no longer determinative for us nor available to us for our use as it was within metaphysics.

Fifthly, how can *Ereignis* overcome the connotations of ownership and property? What we witness here is the deconstruction of man as appropriating, man as the measure. Rather, he is appropriated. Nor does Heidegger seek to appropriate the *lethe* but lets it be as *lethe*.

Finally, with the lack of a universal, the essence of language in the sense of the unifying unity passes into the unbinding bond (US 262; WL 131). In being bound over to *Ereignis* the search for the unifying unity of language gives way to *Gelassenheit*. Or to put it another way, there takes place a transformation in the notion of "essence." This transformation is parallel to that we find in the essays "The Essence of Truth," "The Question concerning Technology," and "The Essence of Language," and which we here recognize as a transformation of language.

How does it stand, then, between Heidegger and Derrida? In the 1968 essay "Ousia and Gramme" Derrida sets himself against a complicity between devoted Heideggerians and anti-Heideggerians in their refusal to *read* the texts of the history of metaphysics. Derrida describes the opening of the Heideggerian breakthrough as the only place where the excess of metaphysics is thought, recalling to us the sense in which *a-letheia* has hitherto remained unthought. But at the same time, Derrida insists that the texts of metaphysics be read "beyond certain propositions or conclusions within which the Heideggerian breakthrough has had to constrain itself, propositions or conclusions which it has had to call upon or take its support from."[20] Derrida refers explicitly to the place of Aristotle and Hegel during the epoch of *Being and Time*. It is striking how modest is the position Derrida allots himself here vis-à-vis Heidegger. Nevertheless, the question remains how and how far Derrida succeeds in going "beyond" the propositions or conclusions that Heidegger, in his reading of the history of metaphysics, drew on from that history for his support. The question is concerned with the sense of this "beyond."

What Derrida was indicating at this point of the 1968 paper as the great danger was the "closing off of questions" brought about by the complicity of Heideggerians and anti-Heideggerians. The danger lay in the difficulties which would ensue were Heidegger's readings of the history of philosophy to fall into self-evidence, to be presented not as a dialogue between thinkers, but as a standard interpretation. It would reduce to assertion what lives only in the transformation of language away from assertion. By the same token, the ambiguity of Derrida's own relation to Heidegger, the way in which he seeks to sustain a metaphysical reading of Heidegger and yet find a transgression within the Heideggerian text, must be maintained.

The complicity of "Heideggerians" and "Derridians" is that their very stance toward each other closes off that non-oppositional relation to texts which is the hallmark of both Heidegger and Derrida. If the essay "The Way to Language" appears now as Heidegger's own attempt to "deconstruct" *Being and Time*, there can be little doubt that we are conceding that, when we read Heidegger today, we find Derrida's Heidegger. We are no longer in a position to say how much of our current reading of Heidegger is indebted to Derrida. We can always point to those moments when we can distinguish the two, when (as Derrida himself would say) "the seam does not hold," but that does not make it possible for us to use the distinction more universally. One consequence is that it ill behooves Derridians to try and contrast Heidegger with Derrida to the latter's advantage. If Derrida has helped us to a reading of Heidegger which gives the destruction of metaphysics the central place already allotted to it in *Being and Time*, we cannot subsequently identify Heidegger exclusively with, for example, the ahistorical readings of Heidegger which were at one time fashionable. Derrida's reading of the text belongs to the text just as much as those other readings.

But do Derrida's readings nevertheless attain a certain priority over other readings? If they do, would not the only way of justifying it be by referring those readings to the epoch, the time which we share with them? But would not that be just another way of maintaining the privilege of the present? The notion of "trace" or, as in the explication of Heidegger's essay above, the notion of *a-letheia* or of *Ereignis* as the oldest of the old, must be understood as addressing precisely that issue. The closure is not brought to a text from outside; one should not really speak of "imposing the closure on a text." So Derrida writes:

> Henceforth the closure of metaphysics ... would not occur *around* a homogeneous and continuous field of metaphysics. Rather, it would fissure the structure and history of metaphysics, *organically* inscribing and systematically *articulating* the traces of the *before* and the *after* both from within and without metaphysics. Thereby proposing an infinite, and infinitely surprising, reading. An irreducible rupture, an excess, can always be produced within an era, at a certain point of its text (for example, in the "Platonic" fabric of "Plotinism"). Already in Plato's text no doubt.[21]

And in "The Way to Language" Heidegger also makes an attempt to save us from the idea that the transformation of language is something that simply happens in our time and thus is our contribution. "But it is only to us and only with regard to ourselves that the change of the way to language appears as a shift which has taken place only now" (US 261; WL 130). The shift from understanding language in terms of human activity to the entry of the essence of language into *Ereignis* implies the shift away from thinking the closure as situated at an end-point.

A further consequence is the disappearance of the idea that texts like those of Heidegger or Levinas should, because of their contemporaneity, not be given a "double reading" on the grounds that they stand unambiguously outside metaphysics. If the notion of "outside" has any meaning in this context it would have to be thought in terms of the entry into the "ambiguity" of the *Geläut der Stille*, which ambiguity precisely disturbs the definition of the outside. It is in this light that we must reexamine Derrida's practice of "prefacing" his readings of the "philosophical" classics with a presentation of translations of them or the standard interpretations which at one time seemed quite adequate to that for which they served proxies. Derrida's use of these surrogates is the conventionalizing of a common Heideggerian practice, especially visible in his essays on Greek thinkers, where he would remind us either of the conventional translation or of Hegel's interpretation before providing his own. But this is no idle preparation for the "real" reading of the text. The space of the Heideggerian reading is the between-space, which relates the multiplicity of different translations, the previous ones and his own. By conventionalizing this relation and turning it into a strategy Derrida misleads the Derridian. The language of strategy as a human activity is applied to the reading, but that reading takes place only as a necessity. This "necessity," to which Derrida often refers, is the necessity of responding to what has already happened, specifically that the words no longer say the same to us, we can no longer follow the old ways.

The reference to inadequate translations and blatantly metaphysical interpretations belongs to the ambiguity of the text, its play, and is supported by the memory of what has gone before. This memory is kept alive in a history of textuality, a history of reading, a notion which in the absence of any detailed explication by Derrida should presumably be understood as similar to Heidegger's history of Being. So Derrida keeps open the space of Heidegger's thinking, which is in danger of collapsing as Heidegger's readings fall into self-evidence. If the translations and previous interpretations were forgotten or ignored, the so-called ambiguity would be lost, the ringing of stillness would fade into silence, the discontinuity of rupture would dissolve into continuity. The maintenance of the rift is essential. (This would be the point to introduce Derrida's reading of the rift in "The *Retrait* of Metaphor.") It is not that the metaphysical is needed as one term in an oppositional structure. The advantage of the account of the "ringing of stillness" over an account presented in terms of inside and outside lies precisely in avoiding that impression.

The fact that Derrida is parasitic on Heidegger is not a weakness from a Derridian point of view.[22] Heidegger *experiences* the end of philosophy; but even if it is conceded that this is no longer a metaphysical concept of experience, it would still be the case that according to the logic of supplementarity the parasite is more original than the original. The difficulty in assessing the relation between Derrida and Heidegger is a much more complex issue when we look to see what Derrida has done to keep open the ambiguity—the play—of the Heideggerian space. This is most apparent when we return to the question of the two strategies that Derrida outlines at the end of "The Ends of Man." It is Derrida who here (and elsewhere) accentuates the inside-outside opposition, which may be present in Heidegger but certainly does not dominate his texts as they have dominated so many of Derrida's. By identifying Heidegger's strategy predominantly with that of attempting an exit without changing ground, while conceding that the other strategy of deciding to change ground was also operative in his works, Derrida both imposes a distinction born of a metaphysical opposition where it did not belong and at the same time denies its appropriateness. The opposition Heideggerian-Derridian as a cultural event has come to serve as a reinscription of the metaphysical dualism of inside and outside. But the discussions of *Ereignis* and *a-letheia* which arise out of the transformation of the language of the history of philosophy into the language of the history of Being have precisely the effect of rendering otiose the application of the two strategies to a discussion of what Heidegger understands by "another beginning." With the notions of "another beginning" and "another writing" Heidegger and Derrida have attempted to think the sense in which there is today both a changing of ground and a dissolution of the notion of ground.[23]

12

Deconstruction and the Possibility of Ethics: Reiterating the "Letter on Humanism"

It seems that everyone is demanding that Derrida give us an ethics, or at least make manifest an ethical significance to deconstruction. And yet, in the face of this situation we might be forgiven for suffering from a sense of déjà vu. Heidegger had similarly faced the demand for an ethics. In the "Letter of Humanism," he remembers how, soon after the publication of *Being and Time*, a young friend asked him when he was going to write an ethics (W 183; BW 231). Is the response rehearsed by Heidegger in 1946 equally appropriate to Derrida now? Will what was said then of the relation of ethics to the destruction or overcoming of philosophy serve now, when we prefer to talk of its deconstruction?

Whatever Heidegger's reply may have been to his young friend, in the "Letter on Humanism" he repeats the story within a philosophical context. The "Letter on Humanism," as is well known, is a revised version of a letter written in response to certain questions put to Heidegger by Jean Beaufret. Heidegger quotes Beaufret as saying that he had for a long time been trying "to determine precisely the relation of ontology to a possible ethics." Beaufret's sentence has an almost studied cautiousness about it which Heidegger instantly penetrates (perhaps on the basis of other comments in Beaufret's still unpublished letter). Heidegger assimilates Beaufret's position to that which insists that "'ontology' be supplemented [*ergänzt*] by 'ethics.'" It is at that point that Heidegger remembers the incident almost 20 years earlier of the young friend demanding an ethics. Heidegger's reply to Beaufret focuses on the relation of ethics and ontology, but no longer as two philosophical disciplines. "Ethics" is referred to the basic meaning of the

Greek word *ēthos*: "'Ethics' ponders the abode of man." In consequence "original ethics" is a "thinking which thinks the truth of Being as the primordial element of man, as one who eksists" (W 187; BW 235). "Ontology," as "fundamental ontology," is likewise referred to the "truth of Being." Ethics and ontology are in this way brought together, but so withdrawn from our conventional understanding of them that it is not easy to tell what their conjunction amounts to. So long as we take this to be the thrust of Heidegger's reply, the story of the young friend is a digression, like the anecdote about Heraclitus's encounter with some strangers over the kitchen stove, which Heidegger retells a page or two later. These apparent digressions lend credence to the common view that since the letter had its source in a private correspondence, it is less rigorous than other of Heidegger's essays.

But to return to the two questioners, the unnamed young friend and Jean Beaufret, the former was disappointed. Heidegger did not write an ethics, but wrote the "Letter on Humanism" instead. It might seem that Beaufret, the original recipient of the letter, was also refused by Heidegger. Heidegger wrote that the very question of supplementing ontology with an ethics "no longer has any basis in this sphere" of the truth of Being (W 188; BW 236). And yet, Beaufret's question, understood not as a question about ethics as the production of rules, but "thought in a more original way, retains a meaning and an essential importance" (W 188; BW 236). What is most important for human beings, according to Heidegger, is coming to abide in the truth of Being (W 191; BW 239). Understood in its traditional sense, ontology thinks the truth of Being no more than ethics does. But it seems to Heidegger that we could as readily call the thinking which attempts to think the truth of Being "original ethics" as call it "fundamental ontology," which is the title given to the thinking to be found in *Being and Time* (W 187; BW 235). Whatever we call it, the task is not to dismiss ethics and ontology as human invention, but to attain to the realm from which they arise. Insofar as *Being and Time* was indeed "fundamental ontology"—in the sense Heidegger gives to the phrase in the "Letter on Humanism"—*Being and Time* was already original ethics.[1]

That does not mean that we should be trying somehow to reread *Being and Time* in the expectation of finding that it prescribes laws and ethical directives of its own. Laws and ethical directives are assigned according to the dispensation or sending of Being, which conditions, determines, and makes ethics possible. There is an original sense of law, as there is of ethics and ontology.

> Nomos is not only law but more originally the assignment contained in the dispensation of Being. Only the assignment is capable of dispatching man into Being. Only such dispatching is capable of supporting and obligating. Otherwise all law remains merely something fabricated by human reason. (W 191; BW 238–39)

Heidegger thus refers ethical rules back to the destiny of Being as that which rules them; and it is more essential to belong to that destiny than it is to follow these rules or to devote oneself to questions about ethics and ontology.

It might, therefore, seem to be appropriate for a thinking informed by Heidegger to respond to the demand for an ethics by subjecting the notion of "ethics" to examination, indicating its different senses as both a specific set of directives and a specific philosophical discipline. It would trace them back to a more "original" sense, governed by the notion of "sending" or destiny. In this way the demand for an ethics undergoes instruction. It is informed that the demand betrays traditional presuppositions about ethical systems. Ethics is not impossible. It is a possibility which can be realized in principle. Yet an ethics cannot simply be produced to order. Nor is it what is most pressing or most essential. It is as if the thinker *qua* thinker must remain deaf to demands which come from elsewhere in order to concentrate on coming to abide in the destiny of Being. The thinker cannot do more than this without coming up against the boundaries set by the truth of Being (W 182; BW 230).

In "Violence and Metaphysics," Derrida's first essay on Levinas, Heideggerian considerations of this kind are prominent. To ask this essay, which predates Derrida's adoption of the word *deconstruction*, to bear the weight of determining the relation of deconstruction to the possibility of ethics is no doubt to ask too much. But "Violence and Metaphysics" warrants most careful consideration, not least because it is a key document both in Derrida's development of deconstruction and in the reception of Levinas's own ethical thinking. Indeed, in "Violence and Metaphysics" Derrida has given a reading of Levinas which in large measure has determined the reception of Levinas ever since—notwithstanding the fact that the essay has not been read carefully, as is clear from the fact that it is almost invariably referred to as Derrida's *critique* of Levinas. I shall suggest that the essay would better merit its influence if it were better understood.[2]

Derrida draws heavily on the "Letter on Humanism" in "Violence and Metaphysics." He does so not simply to question Levinas's interpretation of Heidegger, though this proves a major preoccupation of the second half of the essay. In its opening pages Derrida uses the "Letter on Humanism" in order to situate his own inquiry within "the impossible." And "the impossible has *already* occurred."[3] In raising the impossible question of the death of philosophy, the question of the relation of philosophy and non-philosophy, Derrida announces an injunction: "The question must be maintained." Or one might say (in recollection of the word which is associated with the English translation of Heidegger) "preserved." And, asking about the meaning of this injunction, Derrida writes that "if this commandment has an ethical meaning, it is not in that it belongs to the *domain* of the ethical, but in that it ultimately authorizes every ethical law in general."[4] The implicit reference to the distinction introduced in the "Letter on Humanism" is clear. The domain of the ethical corresponds to ethics as a discipline; the authorization of every ethical law is equivalent to what Heidegger calls law as the assignment of the dispensation of Being. This question, which Derrida redefines in the second version of the essay as "the question of the relations between belonging and opening, the question of closure," is imposed on us by an injunction, an imposition perhaps similar to that which Heidegger refers to as the dispensation of Being.[5]

Thus Derrida in "Violence and Metaphysics" follows Heidegger's treatment of ethics in the "Letter on Humanism." In particular, Derrida at one point offers a sustained attempt to measure how Levinas fares according to the standard Heidegger established.

> It is true that Ethics, in Levinas's sense, is an Ethics without law and without concept, which maintains its non-violent purity only before being determined as concepts and laws. This is not an objection: let us not forget that Levinas does not seek to propose laws or moral rules, does not seek to determine *a* morality, but rather the essence of the ethical relation in general. But as this determination does not offer itself as a *theory* of Ethics, in question, then, is an Ethics of Ethics. In this case, it is perhaps serious that this Ethics of Ethics can occasion neither a determined ethics nor determined laws without negating and forgetting itself. Moreover, is this Ethics of Ethics beyond all laws? Is it not the Law of laws? A coherence which breaks down the coherence of the discourse against coherence—the infinite concept, hidden within the protest against the concept.[6]

Leaving aside for the moment the question of how we should read these remarks about coherence, Derrida seems to bring Levinas into correspondence with the Heidegger of the "Letter on Humanism."[7] What is the "Law of laws" except "the assignment contained in the dispensation of Being"? That is why Derrida is at such pains to show that what Levinas says of ontology does not hold for Heidegger's thinking of Being, and that Heidegger's attempt to separate them in the "Letter on Humanism" is to be accepted. On this interpretation, what Levinas has to say can be reconciled with Heidegger. Of course, this will run quite contrary to the whole rhetoric of Levinas's discussion of Heidegger, from the moment in *Existence and Existents* when Levinas, declaring his debt to Heidegger's thinking, also announces his "profound need to leave the climate of that philosophy."[8] Such a reassimilation of Levinas to Heidegger would no doubt be attractive to all those who have already pledged their allegiance to Heidegger but who cannot overlook his relative silence, after the discussion of *Mitsein* in *Being and Time*, about our fellow human beings. What matter that Levinas on every page protests his distance from Heidegger, when we now know better than to be bound by authorial intentions?

Certain remarks in Derrida's more recent essay on Levinas, "At This Very Moment in This Work Here I Am," are germane to this reassimilation. In one of the strands of his many-sided essay, Derrida investigates the curious structure of the ethical relation as explicated by Levinas.[9] He recalls that for Levinas gratitude can serve to compromise the generosity of the Self which in work goes toward the Other. To give thanks in return is to destroy transcendence and return an apparently gratuitous act to the order of the same. Levinas puts it this way: "Work fundamentally considered . . . demands an ingratitude from the Other. Gratitude would be precisely the return of the movement to its origin."[10] It would seem to follow that to preserve the ethical relation of the giver I am obliged to show no gratitude. That is a strange ethical requirement whereby, in order to let the Other be as Other, to preserve the alterity of the Other, to *be* grateful, I must be ungrateful. Derrida explores a certain kind of "radical ingratitude" beyond all restitution. This idea has a hermeneutical application. As the gift is preserved as gift only in a radical ingratitude, so the text is only preserved as text when one is in a certain way unfaithful to it. The text is not to be returned to its author.

As I have attempted to show, Derrida already in "Violence and Metaphysics" does not return Levinas's text to its author, but to another—namely, Heidegger. It is not a question of insisting upon Heidegger's influence on Levinas, which Levinas has never sought to deny. Derrida is concerned both with the extraordinary violence that Levinas seems to do to Heidegger's texts in order to arrive at his interpretations and with the tone of his remarks about Heidegger.[11] One is even tempted to speak here of an attempt at *parricide*, just as Derrida refers to parricide when recalling Levinas's attempt to break with Parmenides.[12] Derrida's references to the "Letter on Humanism" show how little Levinas succeeds in distancing himself from Heidegger. How could Levinas attack Heidegger for having subordinated ethics to ontology when Heidegger goes to such pains to displace that question? Indeed, Derrida's question of parricide could be juxtaposed with Levinas's own discussion of the impossibility of murder. Levinas interprets the command "Thou shalt not commit murder" not as a law to obey or disobey, but as the essence of the ethical relation, a necessity which we cannot evade. At one point in *Existence and Existents* Levinas refers to Macbeth's inability to rid himself of Banquo.[13] On Derrida's reading, Levinas cannot rid himself of Heidegger's ghost. And so Derrida finds himself in a position to situate Levinas and the ethics he proposes with reference to the thought of Being: "Not only is the thought of Being not ethical violence, but it seems that no ethics—in Levinas's sense—can be opened without it."[14] And again, "Levinas must ceaselessly suppose and practice the thought or precomprehension of Being in his discourse, even when he directs it against 'ontology' . . . Ethico-metaphysical transcendence therefore presupposes ontological transcendence."[15] So, according to Derrida, who sees at work here an instructive necessity, Levinas's metaphysics presupposes what it seeks to put in question in such a way that it remains haunted by it. And parricide proves just as difficult in the case of Parmenides. Derrida again and again draws attention to "some indestructible and unforeseeable resource of the Greek logos . . . by which he who attempts to repel it would always already be *overtaken*."[16]

Nevertheless, we would fail completely to recognize how far this early reading of Levinas accomplished the double movement of a deconstruction if we see in "Violence and Metaphysics" only an attempt to reassimilate Levinas to the tradition. The necessity which imposes itself on Levinas is that of "lodging oneself within traditional conceptuality in order to destroy it."[17] That is to say, if Levinas at times succumbs to philosophical discourse, this is not a failing but, according to Derrida, the only way he can renounce it. The question which Derrida does not clearly pose, but which his essay seems to provoke, is whether Levinas knew that that was what he was doing. And because Derrida seems sometimes to indicate that he did not, the reader of Levinas who disagrees is likely to ask whether Derrida's reading of Levinas must not be corrected, just as Derrida himself corrected Levinas's reading of Heidegger.

So, for example, Derrida seems to have thought that Levinas opposed infinity to totality and ethical metaphysics to the Western philosophical tradition of ontology. If this were the case, it could be shown, by what Derrida elsewhere calls "a Hegelian law," to be self-defeating: "The revolution against reason can be made only within it."[18] The attempt to overcome philosophy by situating oneself outside it remains within the order of the same. This is what underlies Derrida's attempt to show how the negative prefix of the very word *infinity* renders "unthinkable, impossible, unutterable" Levinas's attempt to construe a positive infinity.[19] But then the question arises as to whether certain remarks that Derrida makes later in the essay are to be understood as developments of this objection or as a renewed exposition of Levinas. For example, Derrida writes: "How could there be a 'play of the Same' if alterity itself was not already *in* the Same, with a meaning of inclusion doubtless betrayed by the word *in*? Without alterity *in* the same, how could the 'play of the Same' occur, in the sense of playful activity, or of dislocation, in a machine or organic totality which *plays* or *works*?"[20] Is Derrida here explicating Levinas or correcting him? The "in" of *in*finity can be understood not simply negatively, but also as conveying the sense of "inclusion" that Derrida seems to think he is bringing to Levinas. Levinas not only explicitly evokes this sense of inclusion in the 1975 essay "God and Philosophy"; the sense in which infinity is already *in* the finite provides *Totality and Infinity* with its structure, guiding the descriptions of, for example, both desire and labor.[21] Similarly, because of his charge of an ahistoricism against Levinas, Derrida might be thought not to have recognized the extent to which another conception of history—other than Hegel's totalizing history—already pervaded *Totality and Infinity*, not least in the use made there of Plato and Descartes to say the beyond Being from within Western ontology. In *Otherwise than Being or Beyond Essence* Levinas refers explicitly to this other history of the West, which announces the beyond of Being within Western ontology.[22] But since Levinas's *explicit* recognition of this "history of the departures from totality" comes only after Derrida misses it, it could be suggested that Derrida has again anticipated Levinas as much as he has overlooked what was always to be found there.[23] It would be curious indeed simply to dismiss these moments in Derrida's essay as instances of criticism which failed, when their failure is only that they fail as criticisms, that is, fail to redirect Levinas's thinking elsewhere. It is not only in his discussion of history that Derrida seems to confirm what—at least retrospectively—appears to have been always at the core of Levinas's thinking. There is no need to insist that Levinas's subsequent development shows the marks of his having read carefully and learned from Derrida's "Violence and Metaphysics"—although there is evidence for such an assertion. A seemingly grand claim like that in fact reduces the question to one of influence, a notion whose philosophical value is questionable, as Derrida himself observed.[24] The affinity between the course Levinas follows and that which Derrida lays out for him raises the question of the character of the dialogue between thinkers after Heidegger. And incidentally, it also serves to establish the rigor of Derrida's reading and to contradict the accusation of arbitrariness which is commonly brought against him.

That said, it does seem that Derrida's gesture of distinguishing Levinas's intentions from his text, the classic early deconstruction mechanism for the production of a doubled text, appears somewhat forced in this case: "Levinas is resigned to betraying his own intentions in his philosophical discourse."[25] Certainly Derrida could not have replaced this distinction with the distinction between a text and its standard interpretation, which is what he tends to use to "double" Heidegger without having recourse to indiscreet conjectures about intentions. It was Derrida who in some ways set the standard reading of Levinas by offering the first extended reading of him; and no doubt against Derrida's intentions what was adopted from "Violence and Metaphysics" was the idea that certain of Levinas's central terms were incoherent. This understanding of Derrida's essay disregards the strategy guiding it, as I have tried to show elsewhere.[26] Yet, even though Levinas's announcement in *Time and the Other* that he intended to break with the tradition of Parmenides was not without a certain naive innocence—as indeed he showed an extraordinary presumption 14 years later, when he claimed to have successfully made the break[27]—on what basis could Derrida insist that Levinas was naive in his use of philosophical language? No doubt Derrida maintains that there is a certain necessity whereby Levinas could not avoid the use of such language. But when Derrida writes that "Levinas is resigned to betraying his own intentions in his philosophical discourse," he seems to have had no warrant for attributing to Levinas the naive idea that one can break with a discourse simply by an edict, an edict which he is supposed to have betrayed. Already in *Totality and Infinity* Levinas shows himself to be fully aware of the difficulty of rupturing a tradition.

And yet, to throw doubt on Derrida's use of the distinction between text and intention is not to correct Derrida. Derrida had already acknowledged that in Levinas's writing more than anywhere the distinction between intentions and stylistic gestures is a "violence of commentary."[28] The whole question of intention, of how much Levinas or Derrida knew what they were doing, is not only unimportant and often unanswerable; the interest in posing it arises from the false assumption that the relation between Levinas and Derrida is to be viewed as if they were taking part in some sort of competition. When Levinas introduced the *trace* as "the presence of that which properly speaking has never been there, of what is always past,"[29] it was already with reference to the "unthinkable."[30] So when Derrida called the trace "impossible-unthinkable-unstatable" he was not correcting Levinas, but instructing us on how to maintain or preserve it in its denial of the (onto)logical tradition on which it depends. Those commentators who have been puzzled by the thought that Derrida could whole-heartedly reject Levinas's concept of the trace one day and embrace it with equal enthusiasm the next read "Violence and Metaphysics" as a *critique*. Rather, it is by saying the unsayable, in resigning himself to "incoherent incoherence," that Levinas satisfies his "intentions."[31] That is the only way, in Derrida's phrase, that "the question of the relations between belonging and the opening, the question of closure," can be posed within language.[32] But it is important to recognize that at the very beginning of the essay Derrida resigns himself to this same "incoherent incoherence": "Therefore we will be incoherent, but without systematically resigning ourselves to incoherence."[33] A *systematic* incoherence is not a systematic *incoherence*, because it would in the end amount to a *coherent* incoherence.[34] Derrida warns against such a coherent incoherence whenever it threatens to deprive Levinas of absolute incoherent incoherency. That is what Derrida means when at one point in "Violence and Metaphysics" he refers to "a demonstration which contradicts what is demonstrated by the very rigor and truth of its development."[35] And it explains the passage quoted earlier, where Derrida describes the "Law of laws" as a "coherence which breaks down the coherence of the discourse against coherence"; this is not a refutation of Levinas, but an illustration of the only way his text can work. Only thereby can the infinite concept be "hidden within the protest against the concept."[36]

So Derrida by no means simply returns Levinas to Heidegger. He shows how Levinas maintains the impossible discourse of the ethical and infinite relation to the Other. Over and beyond that, Derrida "returns" Heidegger to Levinas. That is to say, he allows a Levinasian interpretation of Heidegger. It is not the one which bears Levinas's own name. Derrida neither confirms nor denies Levinas's central charge against Heidegger, that he shares the tradition's refusal of transcendence. It is at all events a charge which can be brought against Derrida at least as readily as against Heidegger. But the remarkable pages at the end of "Violence and Metaphysics" which attempt to establish a proximity between Levinas and Heidegger have not, so far as I am aware, been taken up by any commentator. Derrida there writes of "the proximity of two 'eschatolgies' which by opposed routes repeat and put into question the entire 'philosophical' adventure issued from Platonism."[37] He suggests that God as positive infinity might be "the other name of Being." It would not be one word of Being among others (which Heidegger might accept, according to my interpretation of him); nor would it be one eventual determination of the simplicity of Being (which is what Derrida imagines Heidegger might have accepted).[38] But Being and God, twin non-concepts, proving to be the same name! As if this were not remarkable enough, Derrida adds that "the question about the Being of the existent would not only introduce—among others—the question about the existent-God; it already *would suppose* God as the very possibility of its question."[39] No wonder there has been a conspiracy of silence! Derrida here is not simply gathering Levinas and Heidegger together. He is suggesting that the thought of infinity opens the question of the ontico-ontological difference, thereby raising the issue of the relative priority of Being and God, and thus in a certain sense the relative priority of Heidegger's thinking as compared with that of Levinas. In the light of Heidegger's discussion of the onto-theo-logical constitution of metaphysics, Derrida's claim is extraordinary, and all the more so for appearing in the context of an essay in which he has been severe with Levinas for failing to attend sufficiently closely to the letter of the "Letter on Humanism." But just as Derrida returns Levinas to Heidegger by showing that ethico-metaphysical transcendence presupposes ontological transcendence, so Heidegger is "returned" to Levinas by the suggestion that the question of Being presupposes God. I am not commenting here on Derrida's reading of Heidegger but, as Derrida himself might say, on the *necessity* which forbids Derrida from according to the subject-matter of either thinker an absolute priority over that of the other.

The response of deconstruction to the demand for an ethics was not, need not, and indeed should not be the one I suggested earlier. Ethics is not simply to be put in its place—even if that place is the exalted one of an "original ethics" which already contests the name and place traditionally given to ethics. Heidegger's original ethics can in no way be equated with Levinasian ethics. Indeed, more telling than the very little that Heidegger has to say about original ethics is the fact that Heidegger constantly writes of the destiny of Being in ethical terms. For example, the very word *Schicklichkeit*, which in Heidegger's text evokes the destiny or sending of Being, also marks the fittingness of Being to which we should submit ourselves: "Rigor in meditation, carefulness in saying, frugality in words" (W 194; BW 241). Have we not seen how Heidegger constantly enjoins us to come to abide in the truth of Being (W 191; BW 239)? It is a tone which Derrida himself adopts at the beginning of "Violence and Metaphysics": "The injunction must be maintained." Perhaps on the basis of this ethical language one might attempt to reread Heidegger's answer to Beaufret as saying that ethics does indeed supplement ontology, not as a mere addition, but in *accordance with the logic of the supplement*, and that this is the meaning of original ethics. Perhaps one could rejoin such an effort to that by which Derrida showed that the question of Being presupposes God. Or one could even apply Derrida's own caricature of the deconstructive strategy, whereby overturning the hierarchy precedes its neutralization. One could thereby come to suggest that Levinas's attempts to subordinate ontology to ethics serve only as the reversal of the traditional privilege accorded to ontology, whereas it is Heidegger, with his notion of "original ethics," who neutralizes the privilege and renders the conceptual pair "undecidable."

But suppose one grants that it is in some sense an *ethical* demand that imposes itself on the thinker, a demand which says that he or she should abide in the truth of Being, "maintain the injunction," rather than, for example, write an ethics. How would this stand as a reply to the demand for an ethics? However rigorous, careful, and frugal that thinking might be, would we not also have to call it patronizing for addressing the demand for an ethics in this way? Do we not need to attend more humbly to the demand for an ethics?

What is the relation of thinking to the demands made on it from "elsewhere"? In the context of this question another meaning can be given to Aristotle's story of Heraclitus found at his stove by strangers come to visit him.[40] I have always felt uneasy about Heidegger's retelling of the story, not least because I cannot help wondering whether Heidegger could read the story without thinking of the numerous sightseers who came to catch a glimpse of him. Heidegger introduces the story about Heraclitus into the "Letter on Humanism" in order to deepen our appreciation of the Greek understanding of *ethos* as abode or dwelling place, even though the word appears nowhere in Aristotle's discussion of it. Fragment 119, *ethos anthropo daimon*, is not to be read as "A man's character is his *daimon*," but as follows: "The abode is for man the open region for the present of god." The "here" of Heraclitus's invitation to the strangers—"even here the gods are present"—is read by Heidegger as a reference to the stove, "the ordinary place where every thing and every condition, every deed and thought is intimate and commonplace" (W 186–87; BW 234). Both sayings of Heraclitus are thus to be understood as referring the familiar to the unfamiliar, the abode to the gods.

Heidegger refuses to speculate on whether or not these strangers might have understood Heraclitus's phrase. Having heard it, did they or did they not come to see everything otherwise? Certainly Heidegger seems to have a low opinion of them. Aristotle tells us nothing about their motives for wanting to visit Heraclitus; but Heidegger assumes that they merely wanted "the material for entertaining conversation." Heidegger describes them three times as "curious," and curiosity in *Being and Time* has the "everyday" characteristic of lacking an abode. It is because Heraclitus is, from the look of it, engaged in the everyday, like themselves, that they turn away disappointed. Furthermore, Heidegger's translation of Aristotle's story is already an expansion of it. It is Heidegger who provides the detail that the consternation of the strangers grew all the greater when Heraclitus issued his saying. And one effect of this addition is to complete the reader's perplexity both whether the statement was eventually understood by the strangers and how it came to be handed down, assuming for the sake of argument that the story is genuine. Who retold the story generation after generation? Did these curious strangers tell it as an amusing anecdote, not knowing what philosophers might subsequently make of it? Or did it enter at once into the philosophical repertoire, enthusiastically recalled because of the rigor, carefulness, and frugality of the response and the way it put the common people to shame? Or were there philosophers who were haunted by the fact that before the face of the stranger the thinker had so little to offer? Heidegger imagines "the frustrated curiosity of these faces" (W 186; BW 234). Could philosophers be haunted by the memory of these disappointed faces as Macbeth was haunted by Banquo?

What could Heraclitus have offered to the strangers? Bread and wine after their journey? This would have been all the more disappointing, at least as Heidegger presents the story. The strangers came to see a thinker at work. They saw him in the mode of everyday existence and they turned away disappointed. But Heraclitus uttered a word which perhaps might have enabled him to see what they would already have seen, had they eyes to see at all. He gave them what they wanted, but perhaps they never penetrated the surface, which was all that concerned them. What more could Heraclitus have said and done for the strangers?

Heraclitus's saying went unrecognized, which is to say, that it went unreturned. Perhaps Heraclitus learned in the process that the crucial question is not what one must do to fulfill one's obligations. Perhaps he learned more from the encounter than the strangers appear to have done. Perhaps their response taught him that whatever we say as teachers or authors, it is never enough.[41] We always approach the Other with empty hands. And yet, would this not make Heraclitus all the more correct when he said, "Even here there are gods present"? Even here: *kai entautha*: even now: at this very moment: *en ce moment même*. Not in the sense Heidegger gives it: in every thing, condition, deed, and thought. Not there only. But because the gods are present, the infinite in the finite, in the encounter itself between thinker and strangers.[42]

And is it not in some sense the same story when the young friend comes to Heidegger and asks about ethics? Heidegger does not record exactly what he said on that occasion. Recalling the event in the "Letter on Humanism," he says of *Being and Time* that "Where the essence of man is thought so essentially, i.e. solely from the question concerning the truth of Being, but still without elevating man to the center of beings, a longing necessarily [*muss*] awakens for a peremptory directive and for rules that say how man, experienced from eksistence towards Being, ought to live in a fitting [*geschichlich*] manner" (W 183; BW 231). A hasty reading might suppose that Heidegger is doing no more in this sentence than insisting—in his own inimitable language—on the impact made by his first great work: What can you expect after a book like *Being and Time* than that young people, strangers even, would want to live according to it? But it invites another reading. To demand an ethics which will provide rules and directives no doubt misunderstands what it means to live in a fitting manner, that is to say, according to the destiny (*Geschick*) of Being. But that the demand is made in such a way, that it arises out of a necessity—a necessity in the destiny of Being—shows that the person who makes it abides in the destiny of Being and responds to it in his or her own way. Heidegger in this passage effectively refers the demand for ethics to the truth of Being which conditions or dispatches ethics. That means that the *demand* for ethics itself arises from "original ethics." It is by refusing the demand for *an* ethics that Heidegger ensures that he does not deny the person who demanded it. To follow rules is to uproot oneself from dwelling. To provide ethical directives is to condemn to the everyday the person who adopts them.

Just as Heidegger sees the demand for an ethics as a destiny of Being, so for Levinas the demand would already be a manifestation of "the ethical relation." As Derrida himself presents Levinas: "Not a theoretical interrogation, however, but a total question, a distress and denuding, a supplication, a demanding prayer addressed to a freedom, that is, to a commandment; [this is] the only possible ethical imperative, the only incarnated violence in that it is respect for the other."[43] The demand for an ethics already enacts the ethical relation, is already "original ethics" as Levinas understands it, ethics in its primacy. But it seems that the demand for *an* ethics can only be satisfied by denying the ethical relation. It is as though the thinker were to respond by offering tablets of stone. It is, of course, no better a response to issue the instruction which refers ethics to the truth of Being. And yet, it is at least the case that to refuse the demand is not necessarily to deny the relation.

The demand that deconstruction provide *an* ethics betrays not only traditional presuppositions about the possibility of generating ethical systems, but also a miscomprehension about the nature of deconstruction, confusing it for one philosophy among others. Hence, in the face of the demand for an ethics deconstruction can reply, in the course of its reading of Levinas, that *the ethical relation is impossible and "the impossible has already occurred" at this very moment*. In other words, the ethical relation occurs in the face-to-face relation, as witnessed in the demand for an ethics itself, a demand which it is as impossible to satisfy as it is to refuse. To acknowledge this is to submit the demand for an ethics not to instruction, but to deconstruction. And the *possibility* of ethics is referred not to its actuality, but to its *impossibility*. This does not mean that writing ethical systems is impossible; only that the attempt to do so is a denial of the ethical relation, though this denial happily can never be complete. When ontology presents its ethical system, ontology both denies the ethical relation and at the same time gives birth to the ethical relation afresh in the saying of its said. The impossibility of murder.

Though the ethical relation as described by Levinas is thought both by logic and by deconstruction to be impossible, logic dismisses this "original ethics," while deconstruction maintains it by insisting on its impossibility. Deconstruction can—and to a certain extent does in "Violence and Metaphysics"—give a rigorous reading of Levinas which preserves the ethical relation without reducing it to the order of ontology. But the insistence that the logos of the ethical relation is impossible-unthinkable-unsayable might be said to preserve the *thought* of the ethical relation (a thought which is not yet also practice) rather than the ethical relation itself. The issue, then, is whether deconstruction enacts the ethical relation, as I have attempted to show Heidegger in the "Letter on Humanism" enacting it in his response to the young friend, or as Heraclitus perhaps enacted it in his dealings with the strangers, at least on a certain reading of Aristotle's story as retold by Heidegger. We might look at the way deconstruction seems rigorously to hold to the limits of thinking, not without a certain resignation, or at the way it responds with matchless energy to the apparently limitless appetite for more of its efforts. Of course, the *saying* of the said, its writerly saying, is also to be found in deconstruction—whenever it finds a "voice" of its own. But we find the ethical enactment above all in the way deconstruction ultimately refuses to adopt the standpoint of critique, renouncing the passing of judgments on its own behalf in its own voice.

Notes

PREFACE

1. By consulting the *Philosopher's Index*, David Kolb found that 27% of the 1,924 indexed items mentioning Heidegger in their title, abstract, or descriptor have appeared in the last five years. He found a similar percentage when he consulted the database for both Social Science Research and Religion, whereas a massive 36% of all references to Heidegger in the *MLA Bibliography* belong to the last five years. See David Kolb, "Heidegger at 100, in America," *Journal of the History of Ideas* 52, 1991, p. 140. For the sake of Kolb's reputation, it should be noted that he does not confine himself to statistics, but proceeds to offer a balanced view of recent Heidegger research in the United States, focusing in particular on the difference between what might be called the analytic and the continental readings of Heidegger.
2. O. Pöggeler, *Der Denkweg Martin Heideggers* (Pfullingen: Neske, 1963, second expanded edition, 1983); trans. D. Magurshak and S. Barber, *Martin Heidegger's Path of Thinking* (Atlantic Highlands: Humanities Press International, 1987).
3. They will be volumes 19 and 17 respectively of the *Gesamtausgabe*.
4. The quotation and a discussion of precisely what is scandalous about it can be found in Philippe Lacoue-Labarthe, *La fiction du politique* (Paris: Christian Bourgois, 1990), pp. 58–59; trans. Chris Turner, *Heidegger, Art and Politics* (Oxford: Basil Blackwell, 1990), pp. 34–35. What is scandalous is both that Heidegger neglected to mention that the death camps had as their aim the extermination of the Jews and that he failed to think the spiritual logic of the West that revealed itself in that phenomenon. It might be mentioned that Lacoue-Labarthe repeats the claim that of the four lectures only one has not been published, the one in which this extract is to be found. However, whenever this is said, it is forgotten that the second lecture has been published only in an expanded version as "The Question concerning Technology," and so may read very differently in its original form.
5. See my "Seeing Double: *Destruktion* and Deconstruction," in *Dialogue and Deconstruction*, ed. Diane Michelfelder and Richard Palmer (Albany: State University of New York Press, 1989), pp. 233–50.
6. This was already the focus of my previous book, *The Question of Language in Heidegger's History of Being* (Atlantic Highlands: Humanities Press, 1985). Here, as in the earlier book, I often use the phrase "history [*Geschichte*] of Being" to cover what Heidegger subsequently refines and presents as the "destiny [*Geschick*] of Being."

7. See Bernasconi, "Seeing Double," pp. 239–47.
8. See for an initial step in this direction "'We Philosophers': Barbaros medeis eisito," in *Endings. The Question of Memory in Hegel and Heidegger*, ed. Rebecca Comay and John McCumber, forthcoming.
9. See Graham Parkes, ed., *Heidegger and Asian Thought* (Honolulu: University of Hawaii Press, 1987), and Parkes's essay "Heidegger and Japanese Thought" in Christopher McCann, ed., *Heidegger: Critical Assessments* (London: Routledge, forthcoming).

INTRODUCTION

1. Many important texts, and not just the early lecture courses, circulate among a few scholars, often in imperfect copies, but it seems that the current generation of scholars is doomed never to have all the materials at its disposal, especially Heidegger's correspondence.
2. For further discussion of the Appendix see chapter 2 below.
3. Heidegger says the same in *Being and Time*: "Our way of exhibiting the constitution of Dasein's Being remains only *one way* which we may take it" (SZ 436; BT 487). Cf. KPM 213; KPM 161.
4. Reiner Schürmann developed the notion of a "practical a priori," without which thinking is impossible, in order to clarify this idea. Praxis determines thinking, so that existing authentically must be understood as a condition for understanding authentic temporality in *Being and Time*, just as "letting be" was a condition for Heidegger's working through the domination characteristic of technology. "On Self-regulation and Transgression," *Social Research* 49, 4, 1982, p. 1039. However, it should be recognized that in same year Schürmann was giving a more nuanced formulation of the practical a priori, perhaps in an effort to meet some of the difficulties here indicated, in a major work, *Le principe d' anarchie* (Paris: Seuil, 1982), pp. 282–91; *Heidegger on Being and Acting: From Principles to Anarchy* (Bloomington: Indiana University Press, 1987), pp. 236–45.
5. On the distinction between *ethos* and *nomoi*, see Charles Scott, *The Question of Ethics* (Bloomington: Indiana University Press, 1990), pp. 142–47.
6. Much is heard of the Hegelian structures of Heidegger's history of Being. It is certainly true that Heidegger draws heavily on the story that Hegel tells about the history of philosophy, not least his insistence on its Greek origins and its division into three epochs, but the history of Being is much more than a story. I have questioned the claim about the Hegelian structures of the Heideggerian history in *The Question of Language and Heidegger's History of Being*, chapter 1.
7. See Rebecca Comay's "Questioning the Question: A response to Charles Scott," *Research in Phenomenology* 21, 1991, pp. 149–50.

CHAPTER 1. THE FATE OF DISTINCTION BETWEEN *PRAXIS* AND *POIESIS*

1. *Nicomachean Ethics*, VI.iv.2. 1140a 2–3. At one time it was assumed that these "exoteric discourses" referred to Aristotle's own more popular writings, but for some time it has been generally accepted that the phrase is more usually meant to

suggest that some idea or distinction was widespread. See, for example, *The Ethics of Aristotle*, with essays and notes, by Sir Alexander Grant (London: Longmans, Green & Co., 1874), Vol. 1, pp. 397–408, and *Notes on the Nicomachean Ethics* by J. A. Stewart (Oxford: Oxford University Press, 1892), Vol. 1, p. 162. For a recent discussion which reverts to the older view, see R. A. Gauthier and J. Y. Jolif, *L'éthique à Nicomaque, tome II* (Paris: Béatrice-Nauwelaerts, 1970), deuxième partie, pp. 456–58.

2. For a recent example of this tendency, which also challenges the standard interpretation of the distinction, see Theodor Ebert, "Praxis und Poiesis. Zu einer handlungstheoretischen Unterscheidung der Aristoteles," *Zeitschrift für philosophische Forschung* 30, 1976, pp. 12–30.

3. Gauthier and Jolif are surely correct that the distinction between *praxis* and *poiesis* in Plato's *Charmides* (163 b-e) is not the same as that in Aristotle. See also J. Hintikka, "Some Remarks on Praxis, Poiesis and Ergon in Plato and in Aristotle," *Studia Philosophica in honorem Svena Krohn*, Annales Universitatis Turkensis, ser. B. 126 (1973), pp. 53–62, who goes much farther than I would in claiming (p. 60) that the tendency to understand the distinction as one between action and fabrication or production was due to Aristotle's conceptual framework.

4. The following books and essays offer general overviews of Heidegger's debt to Aristotle in the Marburg period, with only limited attention to Heidegger's reading of the *Ethics*: F. Volpi, *Heidegger e Aristotle* (Padova: Daphne Editrice, 1984), and "Heidegger in Marburg. Die Auseinandersetzung mit Aristotles," *Philosophischer Literaturanzeiger* 37, 2, 1984, pp. 172–88. T. Sheehan, "Heidegger, Aristotle, Phenomenology," *Philosophy Today* 19, 2, 1975, pp. 87–94, and "Heidegger's Philosophy of Mind," *Contemporary Philosophy. A New Survey*, Vol. 4, ed. G. Floistad (The Hague: Martinus Nijhoff, 1983), pp. 287–318. Helene Weiss's book on Aristotle still serves as an important source for Heidegger's reading of Aristotle at this period: *Kausalität und Zufall in der Philosophie des Aristoteles* (Basel: Haus zum Falken, 1942). She acknowledges her debt to Heidegger's unpublished interpretations of Greek philosophy in the introduction and repeats it specially with reference to her account of the *Nicomachean Ethics* in a chapter entitled "Praxis," p. 100n.

5. On the importance of Aristotle's *Ethics* for Heidegger see, for example, "Brief an P. William J. Richardson," *Heidegger through Phenomenology to Thought* (The Hague: Martinus Nijhoff, 1963), pp. x–xiii. Among the first to draw the *Ethics* into their interpretation of Heidegger was Reiner Schürmann in his innovative study, *La principe d'anarchie* (Paris: Seuil, 1982), pp. 116–25, trans. C.-M. Gros, *Heidegger on Being and Acting* (Bloomington: Indiana University Press, 1987), pp. 98–105. Since the original publication of the present chapter a flood of essays has tried to locate Heidegger's reading of Aristotle in *Being and Time*, with very little agreement among scholars as to how that might best be done. Among them are: J. Taminiaux, "Phenomenology and the Problem of Action." *Philosophy and Social Criticism* 11, 1986, pp. 207–19; "*Poiesis* and *Praxis* in Fundamental Ontology," *Research in Phenomenology* 17, 1987, pp. 137–69; "*Poiesis* et *Praxis* dans l'articulation de l'ontologie fondamentale," *Heidegger et l'idée de la phénoménologie* (Dordrecht: Kluwer, 1988), pp. 107–25. F. Volpi, *Heidegger e Aristotele* (Padua: Daphne Editrice, 1984), pp. 90–116; "Dasein comme praxis": L'assimilation et la radicalisation heideggerienne de la philosophie pratique d' Aristote," in *Heidegger et l'idée de la phénoménologie*, pp. 1–41. W. Brogan,

"Heidegger and Aristotle: Dasein and the Question of Practical Life," and D. Schmidt, "Economies of Production: Heidegger and Aristotle on *Poiesis*," in *Crises in Continental Philosophy*, ed. A. Dallery and C. Scott (Albany: SUNY Press, 1990), pp. 137–46 and 147–59 respectively. John van Buren, "The Young Heidegger, Aristotle, Ethics," *Ethics and Danger*, ed. A. Dallery and C. Scott (Albany: SUNY Press, 1991). See also the papers cited in note 6 below.

6. This volume, which was one of the first to be announced at the time of writing, is not yet published, and will be volume 19. At least two different transcripts of the Sophist lectures are in limited circulation. I had access to an incomplete and sometimes illegible typescript of Helene Weiss's notes when writing "Heidegger's Destruction of Phronesis," *Southern Journal of Philosophy* 27, Supplement, 1989, pp. 127–47. I would certainly be very hesitant about any conclusions drawn on the basis of the copy at my disposal. For another account of the Sophist lectures, based apparently on Simon Moser's transcript, see Jacques Taminiaux, "On Heidegger's Interpretation of *The Nicomachean Ethics*," in *Heidegger: A Centenary Appraisal* (Pittsburgh: The Simon Silverman Phenomenology Center, Duquesne University, 1990), pp. 1–12, and the appendix to the republication of "*Poiesis et Praxis* dans l'articulation de l'ontologie fondamentale," in *Lectures de l'ontologie fondamentale* (Grenoble: Jérôme Millon, 1989), pp. 183–89.

7. Published as "Phänomenologische Interpretationen zu Aristoteles," *Dilthey Jahrbuch* 6, 1989, pp. 237–69. For initial interpretations, see H.-G. Gadamer, "Heideggers 'theologische' Jugendschrift," *Dilthey Jahrbuch* 6, 1989, pp. 228–34; Rudolf Makkreel, "The Genesis of Heidegger's Phenomenological Hermeneutics and the Rediscovered 'Aristotle Introduction' of 1922," *Man and World* 23, 1990, pp. 305–20; R. Bernasconi, "Heidegger's Destruction of Phronesis," cited above. The prospectus for the *Gesamtausgabe* also refers to a lecture to the Kant-Gesellschaft of Cologne a year earlier under the title "Wahrsein und Dasein. Aristotles, Ethica Nicomachea Z." J. Caputo makes the case for *Verstehen* in *Radical Hermeneutics* (Bloomington: Indiana University Press, 1987), p. 109. The case for *Gewissen* is supported by the anecdotal evidence of Gadamer and Oskar Becker. See Gadamer, "Die Marburger Theologie," p. 200; trans. "Heidegger and Marburg Theology," p. 201, and O. Pöggeler, "Nachwort zur zweiten Auflage," *Der Denkweg Martin Heideggers* (Pfullingen: Neske, 1983), p. 352; trans. D. Magurshak and S. Barber, *Martin Heidegger's Path of Thinking* (Atlantic Highlands: Humanities Press International, 1987), p. 285. For *phronesis* as *Entschlossenheit*, see, for example, Taminiaux, *Praxis* and *Poiesis* in 'Fundamental Ontology,'" pp. 147, 152, and 166–67. All these texts will be considered by Ted Kisiel in his forthcoming study of the young Heidegger, which promises to be required reading for anyone seeking an understanding of Heidegger.

8. H. Arendt, *The Human Condition* (New York: Doubleday Anchor, 1959); *Vita Activa oder Vom tätigen Leben* (Munich: R. Piper, 1981). As I am unable here to give my own account of *praxis*, Arendt's discussion in chapter 5 must serve provisionally in its place. However, it is clear that as an account of the Greek sources her account of the distinction between *praxis* and *poiesis* needs some revision. Furthermore, her general overview needs to be supplemented by a fuller discussion of the oblivion of *praxis* in Western metaphysics and an appreciation of how to construe the occasional witnessing to *praxis* which interrupts this oblivion. Finally, there is a further and less accidental sense in which I

cannot here give an account of *praxis*, which should become clearer by the end of this essay. According to this understanding my appeal to Arendt will turn out to be all the more provisional and, by the same token, less easy for me to replace.
9. H.-G. Gadamer, *Wahrheit und Methode* (Tübingen: J. C. B. Mohr, 1975), pp. 295–307; trans. Joel Weinsheimer and Donald G. Marshall, *Truth and Method*, second revised edition (New York: Crossroad, 1988), pp. 278–89. Gadamer is quite explicit about his debt to Heidegger's seminars and lectures on the *Nicomachean Ethics* in a number of essays. See chapter 10 below; Paul Schuchmann, "Aristotle's *Phronesis* and Gadamer's Hermeneutics," *Philosophy Today* 23, 1979, pp. 41–50; and Joseph Dunne, "Aristotle after Gadamer: An Analysis of the Distinction between the Concepts of Phronesis and Techne," *Irish Philosophical Journal* 2, 2, 1985, pp. 105–23.
10. See chapter 11 below.
11. For example, GA 26, 197; MFL 155. But as an indication of how insecure the distinction between the notion of "repetition" and that of "another beginning" is, see EM 29; IM 39.
12. See further, Jacques Taminiaux, "Heidegger et les Grecs à l'époque de l'ontologie fondamentale," *Etudes Phénoménologiques* 1, 1985, pp. 95–112.
13. GA 24, 153; BP 108–09. See also GA 20, 258; HCT 190. There are differences in emphasis between the various formulations of this distinction in the Marburg lectures, and one should not insist that they be brought into absolute consistency.
14. Arendt draws on section 18 of *Being and Time* when she explores the difficulties confronting utilitarianism and all philosophies which draw on the experience of instrumentality. Her main references to the "for the sake of" are, however, neither to Aristotle nor Heidegger, but to Kant. That she does not adopt the Aristotelian "solution" and refer the "for the sake of" to action indicates her alertness to the dangers of substituting making for doing. *Human Condition*, sec. 21, pp. 134–37; *Vita Activa*, pp. 140–43.
15. *Praxis* is also understood in this broad sense, which includes *poiesis*, in a discussion of Plato in GA 40, 62 and EM 44; IM 58.
16. When Aristotle introduced the distinction earlier, he described it, in the same phrase he used for the distinction between *praxis* and *poiesis*, as current "in exoteric discourses." *Nicomachean Ethics* I. xiii. 9, 1102a28.
17. Heidegger in a discussion of this passage understands *logismos* as circumspective calculation, consideration, and so relates it to choice and decision. GA 33, 125–28.
18. *Nicomachean Ethics* VI. vi. 2, 1141a6–9.
19. *Nicomachean Ethics* VI. ii. 5, 1139a35–1139b4, my translation. For further discussion of the interpretation underlying this translation see R. Bernasconi, "Technology and the Ethics of Praxis," *Acta Institutionis Philosophiae et Aestheticae* (Tokyo) 5, 1987, pp. 93–108. A complementary discussion of this passage can be found in Troels Engberg-Pedersen, *Aristotle's Theory of Moral Insight* (Oxford: Oxford University Press, 1983), pp. 29 and 166.
20. Andronicus Rhodius, *Ethicorum Nicomacheorum Paraphrasis* (Cambridge: Johannes Hayes, 1679), pp. 254–55. By contrast, Thomas Aquinas in his Commentary understands this whole chapter of the *Ethics* in terms of chapters 10 and 11 of Book III of the *De Anima*. Hence, he does not see any ordering of *praxis* and *poiesis* implied in this passage, but rather understands it in terms of the distinction between speculative and practical reason. *In dicem libros ethicorum*

Aristotelis ad Nicomachum (Torino: Marietti, 1964), paras. 1135–36, p. 311; trans. C. I. Litzinger, *Commentary of the Nicomachean Ethics* (Chicago: Henry Regnery, 1964), pp. 547–48. Aquinas thereby finds a way of avoiding any suggestion of the superiority of *praxis* over *poiesis*.

21. That there is in Aristotle an "assimilation of moral reasoning to technical deliberation" is now a common observation in the contemporary interpretation of his *Ethics*, but it is provided with a very different significance than that which I am attempting to give it here. See, for example, John M. Cooper, *Reason and Human Good in Aristotle* (Cambridge: Harvard University Press, 1975), p. 2.

22. In "The Question concerning Technology" Heidegger challenges the conventional interpretation of the four causes as offering a further illustration of the transformation which Greek philosophy underwent with its translation into Latin. Insofar as I have myself in this paragraph relied on such conventional terms as final and efficient cause, the later Heidegger might have judged my reading of Aristotle anachronistic. Whether and in what way a reading of these passages from the *Ethics* in terms of *veranlassen* or occasioning would make a difference cannot be answered here, but I shall say more later on what lies behind Heidegger's attempt to reconstrue the Greek notion of *poiesis*. VA 15–18; QT 6–11.

23. Arendt, *Human Condition*, sec. 26, p. 171; *Vita Activa*, pp. 184–85.

24. For further evidence to this effect, see my "Heidegger's Destruction of *Phronesis*" and the important qualifications I introduce there about too close an identification of *Umsicht* with *phronesis*. Other candidates have been proposed. Although I have read nothing in these essays that lead me to revise the general approach offered in this chapter, the measure of disagreement provides a salutary warning about the complexities that arise when one tries to do justice to the deconstructive aspect of *Being and Time*, which was—and still is being—overlooked by the interpretations of Heidegger as either an existentialist or a pragmatist. For a record of some of these complexities, see Walter Brogan, "A Response to Robert Bernasconi's 'Heidegger's Destruction of Phronesis,'" *Southern Journal of Philosophy* 28, Supplement, 1989, pp. 149–53.

25. One might refer in this context to the 1939 lectures on *The Will to Power as Knowledge and as Metaphysics*, where *praxis* is described as "the securing of stability, a need for schemata" (NI 572, Niii 86). However, as the lecture course develops, it becomes clear that the outlook here being opened up is to be referred to "the poetizing [*dichtende*] nature of positing a horizon within a perspective," which is itself understood as a kind of constructing or building (*Bauen*) (NI 640–41; Niii 143–44). This suggests that *praxis* in this text is being understood as equivalent to *poiesis* in the broadest sense.

26. The problems of the rival claims are discussed—and at various points exaggerated—by Gerold Prauss in *Erkennen und Handeln in Heideggers 'Sein und Zeit'* (Freiburg: Alber, 1977). Unfortunately, Prauss does not recognize the underlying questions which are being entertained by Heidegger, because like so many readers before him he does not read *Being and Time* in terms of its stated task of destroying the history of ontology.

27. I discuss Heidegger's essay in chapter 5 of *The Question of Language in Heidegger's History of Being*. See also Michael Haar, "The End of Distress: The End of Technology?" *Research in Phenomenology* 13, 1983, pp. 43–63.

28. See also "Vom Wesen und Begriff der *phusis*." "Making, *poiesis*, is *one* kind of production, whereas 'growing' (the going back into itself and emerging out of

itself), *physis*, is another" (CW 359); trans. T. Sheehan, "On the Being and Conception of *phusis*," *Man and World* 9, 3, 1976, p. 20. Also VS 130 and GA 24, 151; BP 107. Notice further that Heidegger also hears the word *Tun*, in the sense of *Wirken*, as related through the same Indo-Germanic word stem to the Greek *thesis*. This latter is not only understood so that it refers to *phusis* as well as human activity. It also serves as another route by which Heidegger thinks the unity of metaphysics in relation to doing in a broad sense, this time through the various words related to *Stellen* (VA 49; QT 159).

29. Although Aristotle is clear that the *eidos* of every part of the intellect is to attain truth, he is more explicit about truth in respect of *praxis* (VI.ii.3) and *phronesis* (VI.vi.5) than about *techne*. Indeed, he omits any reference to *techne* in one of two lists which record the excellences whereby the mind achieves the truth (VI.vi.2, 1141a2–8). The omission could be explained as an error in transcription or as an acknowledgment of the dependence of *techne* on *phronesis*.

30. M. Heidegger, *Die Künste im technischen Zeitalter* (Munich: R. Oldenberg, 1954), pp. 59–62.

31. The lecture was part of a series on "The Arts in the Age of Technology." I discuss this passage in the context of the discussion of art in chapter 6.

32. *Nicomachean Ethics* II.i.1, 1103a17.

33. *Metaphysics* V.i.5, 1025b25. Also *Nicomachean Ethics* I.i.1. 1139a27 and *Eudemian Ethics* I.i.2, 1214a8–12.

34. On the "Letter on Humanism" see chapter 12 below and the following discussions: John Sallis, "Reason and Ek-sistence" in *Delimitations. Phenomenology and the End of Metaphysics* (Bloomington: Indiana University Press, 1986), pp. 152–59; Charles Scott, *The Question of Ethics* (Bloomington: Indiana University Press, 1990), pp. 178–90; Murray Miles, "Heidegger and the Question of Humanism," *Man and World* 22, 1989, pp. 427–51.

35. This is of course an un-Aristotelian conception. In the *Ethics* Aristotle offers Anaxagoras and Thales as evidence for the separation of *sophia* and *phronesis*. *Nicomachean Ethics* VI.vii.3, 1141b4.

36. I discuss this story at greater length in chapter 12 below.

37. "The element of the truth of being," according to the text to be found in the *Gesamtausgabe: Wegmarken, Gesamtausgabe Band 9* (Frankfurt: Klostermann, 1976), p. 315.

38. The difference disappears in the typography of the English translation.

39. Even if the word "deconstruction" might seem to evoke the name of Derrida, it should be recognized that I am not by any means referring to Derrida, but rather to the misuse to which his thinking has sometimes been put.

40. H. Arendt, *The Human Condition*, sec. 11, pp. 72–81; *Vita Activa*, pp. 76–85. See also Aristotle, *De partibus animalium* 4. 10, and Klaus Bartels, "Der Begriff Techne bei Aristotles," *Synusia*. Festgabe für Wolfgang Schadewaldt, ed. H. Flashar and K. Gaiser (Pfullingen: Neske, 1965), pp. 275–87.

41. I explore the conception of ethics further in chapters 2 and 12 below.

42. *Die lateinischen Werke*, edited by J. Quint (Stuttgart and Berlin: W. Kohlhammer, 1962), V, pp. 197–98; translated by E. Colledge and B. McGinn, *Meister Eckhart* (New York: Paulist Press, 1981), pp. 250–51. See also R. Schürmann, *Meister Eckhart: Mystic and Philosopher* (Bloomington: Indiana University Press, 1978), p. 256n. 103, and J. D. Caputo, *The Mystical Elements in Heidegger's Thought* (Athens: Ohio University Press, 1978), p. 156.

CHAPTER 2. "THE DOUBLE CONCEPT OF PHILOSOPHY"

1. See, in particular, "Die Idee der Philosophie und das Weltanschauungs problem," *Zur Bestimmung der Philosophie, Gesamtausgabe Band 56/57* (Frankfurt: Klostermann, 1987), pp. 7ff.
2. For a history of these distinctions, see Ernst Vollrath, "Die Gliederung der Metaphysik in eine Metaphysics generalis und eine Metaphysics specialis," *Zeitschrift für Philosophische Forschung*, 16, 2, 1962, pp. 258–84; Gerd Buchdahl, "Kant's 'Special Metaphysics' and *The Metaphysical Foundations of Natural Science*," in *Kant's Philosophy of Physical Science*, edited by Robert Butts (Dordrecht: D. Reidel, 1986), pp. 127–61; Michael Frede, "The Unity of General and Special Metaphysics: Aristotle's Conception of Metaphysics," *Essays in Ancient Philosophy* (Oxford: Oxford University Press, 1987), pp. 81–95.
3. Heidegger had already referred to the discordance (*Zwiespalt*) of Aristotelian metaphysics as pure formal ontology and as the theology of the *nous* in the 1925/26 lecture course (GA 21, 410n). In 1927 he took up this division in the context of the ontical foundation of ontology, which he saw already expressed in "Aristotle's dictum that the first science, the science of being, is theology" (GA 24, 26; MFL 20). See also GA 24, 38, and 111; BP 29 and 79, where the focus is essentially on the role of theology in subsequent metaphysics.
4. Klaus Held, the editor of volume 26 of the *Gesamtausgabe*, does not explain in his Editor's Epilogue the status of this Appendix. He does not say whether this material was delivered as part of the lecture course, nor whether Heidegger himself designated it an Appendix. The fact that the word *Anhang* is used in the previous paragraph is not decisive (GA 26, 195; MFL 154).
5. The first reference outside the Appendix to metontology is to a "metontology of spatiality," a phrase which in context has all the appearances of a marginal note incorporated into the text by the editor (GA 26, 174; MFL 138). The other reference throws very little light on Heidegger's understanding of the word (GA 26, 185; MFL 146).
6. The problematic of metontology has been tracked to *Introduction to Metaphysics* in three studies. See John Sallis, *Echoes* (Bloomington: Indiana University Press, 1990), pp. 139–68; Kelly Mink, *Heidegger: Ontology, Metontology, and the Turn*, doctoral dissertation, Loyola University of Chicago, 1987; and Will McNeill, "Metaphysics, Fundamental Ontology, Metontology 1925–1935," *Heidegger Studies* 8, forthcoming. Note also David Krell's "Fundamental Ontology, Meta-Ontology, Frontal Ontology," in *Intimations of Mortality* (University Park: Pennsylvania State University Press, 1986), pp. 27–46. Krell was among the first to insist on the importance of metontology.
7. In a supplement (*Beilage*) entitled "Distance and Nearness," at the end of the published version of *The Metaphysical Foundations of Logic*, Heidegger returns to the problem: "Philosophy . . . is more primordial than every science and, at the same time, more primordial than every world-view" (GA 26, 285; MFL 221). At this point he appears to turn against a version of the double concept of philosophy: "As long as we waver back and forth on the surface by doubling (*Doppelung*) theoretical and practical maxims, we are not yet in philosophy." However, the intervening sentence explains that what is at issue in philosophizing is "to transform each and everything in ourselves and to ourselves." What differentiates the relation between scientific philosophy and worldview philosophy from the "double concept of philosophy" (both in its traditional forms and in the forms given it by Heidegger) is that the former is a wavering while the

latter is an interweaving, an integration without unity, a discordance.
8. This is not to say, however, that the much discussed *Kehre* in Heidegger's thinking can be situated at this point. What is later called the *Kehre* is a turn from metaphysics to *Ereignis*, Heidegger's response to an event in the history of Being. This perspective was missing from Heidegger's thinking at the time of *Being and Time*. In the "Letter on Humanism" it becomes clear that it is in terms of the truth or history of Being that Heidegger will later attempt to rethink the question of the "foundation" of ontology (W 187; BW 235).
9. Heidegger also refers to this passage in the "Letter on Humanism," so underlining its importance (W 173; BW 222). It is ultimately his explanation of why fundamental ontology must from the outset be an existential analysis (GA 26, 196; MFL 154).
10. The translation of *Metontologie* as meta-ontology would therefore be misleading if it suggested that the prefix was to be understood in any of the ways usually applied to the word "meta-physics" ("beyond" or "after"). The first occurrence of the word *Metontologie* in the Appendix comes immediately after Heidegger has indicated that *Umschlag* is his translation of the Greek word *metabole* (GA 26, 199; MFL 157). See also *The Basic Problems of Phenomenology*, where *metabole* is introduced as the most general concept of motion or *kinesis* in Aristotle, and where it is again translated by Heidegger into German as *Umschlag*.
11. E. Husserl, *Die Krisis der Europäischen Wissenschaften und die Transzendentale Phänomenologie* (The Hague: Martinus Nijhoff, 1962), p. 508; translated by David Carr, *The Crisis of European Sciences and Transcendental Phenomenology* (Evanston: Northwestern University Press, 1970), p. 389.
12. See chapter 5, where I attempt to show this in more detail.
13. I hesitate to apply the phrase "original ethics" to *Being and Time* because it is used in the "Letter on Humanism" specifically with reference to the truth of Being. It thus presupposes an insight into the history of Being that was lacking to Heidegger at that time. The "original ethics" already in place in *Being and Time* is rather an ethics relevant to the philosopher at the *existentiell* level.
14. It is necessary to remember that "theology" in this context has the same meaning in *The Metaphysical Foundations of Logic*, where it is referred to "the overwhelming" (*das Übermächtige*). In *Being and Time* the same word refers to the power of *Dasein*'s "finite freedom" (SZ 384; BT 436).
15. Another example might be found in the way that in the beginning of section 25 of *Being and Time* Heidegger refers back to the sentence from the beginning of section 9 that "Dasein is an entity which is in each case I myself; its Being is in each case mine." In returning to it Heidegger refers both to its ontological meaning, as a definition indicating an ontologically constitutive state, and to its ontical meaning: "At the same time it tells us *ontically* (though in a rough-and-ready fashion) that in each case an 'I'—not Others—is this entity." There is no suggestion here that because the sentence has an ontological meaning it must at all costs be denied an ontical reading. The two are seen to accompany each other. The danger lies rather in excluding the one or the other. Here the threat of an exclusively ontical reading receives the most attention: "Indeed it remains questionable whether even the mere ontical content of the above assertion does proper justice to the stock of phenomena belonging to everyday Dasein. It could be that the 'who' of everyday Dasein just is *not* the 'I myself'" (SZ 115; BT 150). But similar difficulties would arise for an exclusively ontological reading were that possibility ever to be realized.

CHAPTER 3. JUSTICE AND THE TWILIGHT ZONE OF MORALITY

1. For further discussion of the distinction between *Geschichte* and *Historie* and the difficulty of maintaining it, see chapter 9.
2. Because Heidegger's essay is so familiar and is not the real subject of this paper, my reading shall be brief and will not reflect all the nuances of Heidegger's text. See Robert Bernasconi, *The Question of Language in Heidegger's History of Being* (Atlantic Highlands: Humanities Press, 1985), pp. 15–27; John Sallis, "At the Threshold of Metaphysics," in *Delimitations* (Bloomington: Indiana University Press, 1986), pp. 170–85; and Adriaan Peperzak, "Heidegger and Plato's Idea of the Good," *Commemorations: Reading Heidegger*, ed. John Sallis (Bloomington: Indiana University Press, 1992).
3. The discussion in the lecture course, particularly of the textual problems associated with the fragment, are not sufficiently extensive to satisfy the reference to such discussions in "The Anaximander Fragment" (H 314; EGT 30). This suggests more extensive discussions in other, yet-to-be-published lecture courses.
4. John Burnet, *Early Greek Philosophy* (London: A. and C. Black, third edition, 1920), p. 52. Heidegger read Burnet in German translation.
5. Other commentators who begin the quotation from *kata to chreon* include Heidel, "On Anaximander," *Classical Philology* 7, 1912, p. 233; and J. B. McDiarmid, "Theophrastus on the Presocratic Causes," in *Studies in Presocratic Philosophy*, Vol. 1, ed. D. J. Furley and R. E. Allen (London, Routledge & Kegan Paul, 1970), pp. 190–93. Attribution of the whole passage to Anaximander is defended by Paul Seligman, *The "Apeiron" of Anaximander* (London: Athlone Press, 1962), pp. 66–83.
6. Heidegger explicitly notes his agreement with Franz Dirlmeier's delimitation of the text, while at the same time distancing himself from the reasons he gives (H 344; EGT 1): "Der Satz des Anaximandros von Milet," *Rheinisches Museum für Philologie* 87, 1938, pp. 376–82. The phrase expelled by Heidegger is defended by, for example, G. S. Kirk, "Some Problems in Anaximander," in *Studies in Presocratic Philosophy*, Vol. 1, pp. 345–46, and Charles H. Kahn, *Anaximander and the Origins of Greek Cosmology* (New York: Columbia University Press, 1960), pp. 170–71.
7. Even if recent commentators have tended to dismiss the interpretation which has Anaximander saying that existence is an injustice, the interpretation has maintained a certain resilience, as Gregory Vlastos has shown in "Equality and Justice in Early Greek Cosmologies," in *Studies in Presocratic Philosophy*, Vol. 1, pp. 76–80.
8. See further Marlène Zarader, *Heidegger et les paroles de l'origine* (Paris: Vrin, 1986), pp. 91–95.
9. The argument that there is an abrupt transition when, at *Republic* 331C, Socrates describes Cephalus's speech about *dike* as a speech about *dikaiosune*, is made by Eric Havelock in *The Greek Concept of Justice* (Cambridge: Harvard University Press, 1978), pp. 308–23. For the context, see also Havelock, "Dikaiosune: An Essay in Greek Intellectual History," *Phoenix* 22, 1969, pp. 49–70.
10. Reiner Schürmann in a brief but helpful discussion of justice in Heidegger reads this passage as a denial of "any kinship" between Nietzschean "justice" and Heraclitean *dike*. He appears to believe that this is a necessary consequence of the fact that "the concept of justice translates 'truth as *homoiosis*' for the age of

closure" (NI 632f). *Heidegger on Being and Acting: From Principles to Anarchy* (Bloomington: Indiana University Press, 1987), p. 364n 62. However, as I try to show, this would eradicate the ambiguity of the history of Being in respect of Western metaphysics. As with the thought of chaos, Nietzsche's word "justice" is both metaphysical and yet not entirely confined to metaphysics, but heard from beyond it. This parallels the way the Anaximander fragment is said to lay a claim on subsequent thinking while at the same time being reducible to it.

11. Heidegger had already in 1937 observed "a dual significance" (*eine zweifache Bedeutung*) in Nietzsche's concept of chaos, but it does not appear to be conceived in the same way as the double meaning (*Doppelbedeutung*) identified two years later (NI 569; Niii 82). Only in the first of the two cases does Heidegger explicitly observe that Nietzsche "fails to liberate himself from the traditional sense of chaos as something that lacks order and lawfulness" (NI 349–50; Nii 91).

12. F. Nietzsche, *Sämtliche Werke. Kritische Studienausgabe, Band II* (Berlin: de Gruyter, 1980), p. 506, 34 [253]; trans. Walter Kaufmann, *The Will to Power* (London: Weidenfeld and Nicholson, 1967), p. 272, no. 493.

13. Levinas, who clearly differentiates what he calls "ethics" from Heidegger's retrieval of the Greek *ēthos*, suggested in a recent essay that in spite of himself Heidegger could not succeed in eradicating the ethical from Anaximander. "It [love] puts into question the ego's natural position as subject, its perseverance—the perseverance of its good conscience—in its being. It puts into question its *conatus essendi*, the stubbornness of its being [*étant*]. Here is an indiscreet—or 'unjust'—presence, which is perhaps already an issue in "The Anaximander Fragment," such as Heidegger interprets it in *Holzwege*. It puts into question the 'positivity' of the *esse* in its *presence*, signifying, bluntly, encroachment and usurpation! Did not Heidegger—despite all he intends to teach about the priority of the 'thought of being'—here run up against the original significance of ethics?" "Diachronie et representation," *Revue de l'Université d'Ottawa* 55, 4, 1985, p. 92; trans. R. Cohen, "Diachrony and Representation," in *Time and the Other* (Pittsburgh: Duquesne University Press, 1987), pp. 108–09.

14. The echo of *dike* in *Gerechtigkeit* thus belongs among those moments in Heidegger where the ethical exceeds the "twilight zone of morality." I have explored other cases in chapters 1, 2, and 12.

15. On the relation of Nietzsche's *Gerechtigkeit* and technology, see Schürmann, *Heidegger on Being and Acting*, pp. 192–93.

16. David Krell has shown that the importance Heidegger gives to *Gerechtigkeit* in Nietzsche is not quite as idiosyncratic as it might at first appear. He does this by showing that previous writers on Nietzsche had already come to focus on the term. See the Analysis to Niii, pp. 272–74. Nevertheless, Heidegger gives Nietzsche's thought of justice an entirely different role from either Ernst Bertram or Alfred Baeumler. The task that Heidegger assigns to *Gerechtigkeit* is one that he and he alone could have identified, relying as it does on his unique conception of *Geschichte*. Nothing that can be found in Bertram and Baeumler prepares one for the role Heidegger gives to Nietzsche's *Gerechtigkeit*. They had cited the relevant Nietzsche texts but their discussion is at another level. It is almost certainly they, for example, whom Heidegger has in mind when he dismisses the observation about Nietzsche's debt to Heraclitus as *historisch*. See Bertram, *Nietzsche. Versuch einer Mythologie* (Berlin: Georg Bondi, 1929), pp. 114–16, and Baeumler, *Nietzsche der Philosoph und Politiker* (Leipzig: Phillipp Reclam,

1931), pp. 65–70. Heidegger explicitly criticizes Baeumler for not seeing "the metaphysical essence of *Gerechtigkeit*," in the reworked version of the final lecture of the 1939 course on Nietzsche recently published in the *Gesamtausgabe* (GA 47, 297).

CHAPTER 4. HABERMAS, ARENDT, AND LEVINAS ON THE PHILOSOPHER'S "ERROR"

1. Aristotle, *Protrepticus*, fragment 106, ed. Anton-Hermann Chroust (Notre Dame: University of Notre Dame Press, 1964), p. 44.
2. Plato, *Protagoras*, 352 c-d.
3. By now, of course, there have been numerous attempts to connect Heidegger's politics to his philosophy. For a recent study which stands out from the crowd, see Dominique Janicaud, *L'ombre de cette pensée* (Grenoble: Jerome Millon, 1990).
4. *The Times Higher Educational Supplement*, no. 850, 17 February 1989, p. 12.
5. Jean-Francois Lyotard, *Heidegger et "les juifs"* (Paris: Galileé, 1988), p. 90; trans. Andreas Michel and Mark S. Roberts, *Heidegger and "the Jews"* (Minneapolis: University of Minnesota Press, 1990), p. 52.
6. Michael Dummett, *Frege. Philosophy of Language* (London: Duckworth, 1973), p. xii.
7. David Krell has attempted to identify some specific places in Heidegger's texts where this failure of thinking can be marked. See *Daimon Life: Heidegger and Life-Philosophy* (Bloomington: Indiana University Press, 1992), chapter 4.
8. See chapter 5 below.
9. See Cicero, *De finibus*, III.2.5.
10. See Plato, *Republic*, Book V, 473.
11. Martin Heidegger, "Nationalsozialistische Wissenschulung," *Nachlese zu Heidegger*, ed. G. Schneeberger (Bern: Suhr, 1962), pp. 192–202; trans. William S. Lewis, "National Socialist Education," *New German Critique* 45, Fall 1988, pp. 110–14.
12. See chapters 6 and 8 below.
13. See, for example, Martin Heidegger, "Brief über den 'Humanismus,'" *Wegmarken* (Frankfurt: Klostermann, 1967), pp. 183–94; trans. Frank A. Capuzzi and J. Glenn Gray, "Letter on Humanism," *Basic Writings*, ed. D. F. Krell (New York: Harper and Row, 1977), 213–42.
14. Victor Farias, *Heidegger et le nazisme* (Lagrasse: Verdier, 1987), p. 7. I have not discussed Farias's book in detail here, nor Hugo Ott's *Martin Heidegger. Unterwegs zu seiner Biographie* (Frankfurt: Campus Verlag, 1988). For my comments on these texts, see "The Heidegger Controversy," *German Historical Institute London. Bulletin* XII, 1, 1990, pp. 3–9.
15. Richard Rorty, "Taking Philosophy Seriously," *The New Republic*, 11 April 1988, p. 32.
16. Rorty, "Taking Philosophy Seriously," p. 34.
17. Jürgen Habermas, "Heidegger—Werk und Weltanschauung," in Victor Farias, *Heidegger und der Nationalsozialismus* (Frankfurt: S. Fischer, 1989), p. 14 n15; trans. John McCumber, "Work and Weltanschauung: The Heidegger Controversy from a German Perspective," *Critical Inquiry* 13, 1989, p. 436 n15.
18. Habermas, "Werk und Weltanschauung," p. 12; "Work and Weltanschauung" p. 433.

19. ibid.
20. ibid.
21. Habermas, "Werk und Weltanschauung," p. 32; trans. p. 453.
22. ibid., p. 14; p. 435–36.
23. ibid., p. 33; p. 454.
24. ibid., p. 12; p. 433.
25. The last four paragraphs of the German text of Habermas's essay are not in the English version. They relate more specifically to Farias's book, but do not seem adequate to the often justified criticisms the book had already elicited following its publication in France.
26. Habermas, "Werk und Weltanschauung" pp. 14–15; "Work and Weltanschauung," p. 436.
27. Habermas, "Werk und Weltanschauung," p. 28; trans. p. 449.
28. Now that two draft versions of "The Origin of the Work of Art" have been made available, it is possible to see Heidegger already engaged in the process of ontologizing, and even in a sense denazifying, his texts in 1935 and 1936. It is not that the final version lacked political content. Rather, Heidegger had already begun to withdraw from the historical context as a result of disillusionment about his own role vis-à-vis the regime. This disappointment is reflected in the greater distance he takes from the disputes of the day and the omission of certain contemporary references. See chapter 6 below.
29. Habermas, "Werk und Weltanschauung," p. 18; trans. p. 440.
30. ibid., p. 16; p. 438.
31. ibid., p. 19; p. 440.
32. ibid., p. 19; p. 441.
33. See, for example, Martin Heidegger, *Ontologie. Hermeneutik der Faktizität, Gesamtausgabe 63* (Frankfurt: Klostermann, 1988), pp. 58–66.
34. Habermas, "Werk und Weltanschauung," p. 33; trans. p. 454.
35. ibid.
36. Martin Heidegger, "Die Idee der Philosophie und das Weltanschauungsproblem," *Zur Bestimmung der Philosophie, Gesamtausgabe 56/57* (Frankfurt: Klostermann, 1987).
37. Habermas, "Werk und Weltanschauung," pp. 34–35; "Work and Weltanschauung," p. 455.
38. For a more precise account of their relation, see chapter 2 above.
39. Hannah Arendt, *The Life of the Mind*, Vol. I (New York: Harcourt Brace Jovanovich, 1978), p. 3.
40. Emmanuel Levinas, "Liberté et Commandement," *Revue de Métaphysique et de Morale* 58, 1953, p. 265; trans. A. Lingis, "Freedom and Command," *Collected Philosophical Papers* (The Hague: Martinus Nijhoff, 1987), p. 16.
41. Hannah Arendt, *The Origins of Totalitarianism* (London: George Allen and Unwin, revised edition, 1967).
42. Arendt, "Martin Heidegger at Eighty," in *Heidegger and Modern Philosophy*, ed. Michael Murray (New Haven: Yale University Press, 1978), p. 303.
43. Hannah Arendt, *The Human Condition* (Chicago: University of Chicago Press, 1958), p. 5.
44. Hannah Arendt, *Eichmann in Jerusalem* (Harmondsworth: Penguin, revised and enlarged edition, 1979), p. 252.
45. ibid., p. 287.
46. ibid., pp. 287–88.

47. This essay was originally entitled "Thought and Moral Propositions," when it was delivered as a lecture at Loyola University of Chicago on 5 January 1970. It was subsequently published as "Thinking and Moral Considerations," *Social Research* 38, 1971, p. 418. "Thinking and Moral Considerations" was subsequently incorporated into the first volume of *The Life of the Mind*, with some modifications.
48. Arendt, "Thinking and Moral Considerations," p. 442.
49. ibid., p. 418.
50. ibid., p. 425.
51. ibid., p. 445.
52. ibid.
53. Arendt, *Eichmann in Jerusalem*, p. 295.
54. Arendt, "Thinking and Moral Considerations," p. 445.
55. ibid., p. 295.
56. Hannah Arendt, "What Is Existenz Philosophy?" *Partisan Review* 13, 1, 1946, p. 52.
57. Cited by Elisabeth Young-Bruehl, *Hannah Arendt. For Love of the World* (New Haven: Yale University Press, 1982), p. 303.
58. "Hannah Arendt an Karl Jaspers, 29 September 1949," *Briefwechsel 1926–1969* (München: Piper, 1985), p. 178. In the same letter she again revealed her ambiguous relation to Heidegger by describing him as lacking character, even bad character, but possessing a depth and passion that was unforgettable.
59. Arendt, "Heidegger at Eighty," p. 303.
60. Aristotle, *Nicomachean Ethics*, VI, vii, 1141b 2–5.
61. Arendt, "Heidegger at Eighty," p. 302n.
62. Arendt, *Life of the Mind*, I, p. 179. Cf. "Thinking and Moral Considerations," p. 438.
63. Arendt, "Thinking and Moral Considerations," p. 444.
64. Arendt, *Life of the Mind*, I, p. 192.
65. George Kateb, *Hannah Arendt. Politics, Conscience, Evil* (Totowa, NJ: Rowman and Allanheld, 1983), pp. 189, 195.
66. Arendt, "Thinking and Moral Considerations," p. 425. *Life of the Mind*, I, p. 191.
67. Arendt, "Thinking and Moral Considerations," p. 445. *Life of the Mind*, I, p. 191.
68. Arendt, *Life of the Mind*, I, p. 212.
69. Arendt, "Heidegger at Eighty," p. 297.
70. Arendt, "Thinking and Moral Considerations," p. 446.
71. Arendt, *Life of the Mind*, I, p. 177. Commentators have noticed that Arendt tends to focus on the judgment of spectators after the event, rather than on the judgment of actors beforehand; even to the point of confusing the two. The conscience which precedes action and which is presumably what is required in cases of political emergency, where, as she liked to say, "the chips were down" or "the stakes are on the table" (*Life of the Mind*, I, 192–93), is only a modification of the first kind: it is "the anticipated fear of such afterthoughts" ("Thinking and Moral Considerations," 444). See, for example, Richard Bernstein, "Judging—the Actor and the Spectator," *Philosophical Profiles* (Oxford: Polity Press, 1986), pp. 221–37. It should not be forgotten, however, that every judgment of the past intervenes with the future, as indeed current judgments on

the Heidegger affair clearly indicate by being as much concerned with the future of philosophy as with its past.
72. Hannah Arendt, *Men in Dark Times* (New York: Harcourt, Brace and World, 1968), p. 71.
73. Young-Bruehl, *Hannah Arendt For Love of the World*, p. 301.
74. Arendt, "What Is Existenz Philosophy?" pp. 50 and 55.
75. Arendt, *Men in Dark Times*, p. 72.
76. ibid., p. 74.
77. Arendt, "Heidegger at Eighty," p. 303.
78. Arendt, *Origins of Totalitarianism*, p. 459.
79. Hannah Arendt, *The Jew as Pariah* (New York: Grove Press, 1978), p. 251. In *Visible Spaces* (Baltimore: Johns Hopkins University Press, 1990), Dagmar Barnouw recognizes that there is nevertheless a certain continuity between the two treatments of evil (pp. 250–51).
80. Arendt, *Eichmann in Jerusalem*, p. 150, and *Life of the Mind*, I, p. 177.
81. Emmanuel Levinas, "Comme un consentement à l'horrible," *Le nouvel observateur* 22–28 January 1988, p. 48; trans. Paula Wissing, "As If Consenting to Horror," *Critical Inquiry* 15, 1989, p. 486.
82. Levinas, "Comme un consentement," p. 48; trans. p. 485.
83. ibid., pp. 48–49; p. 487.
84. ibid., p. 48; p. 487.
85. ibid., p. 49; p. 488.
86. Emmanuel Levinas, *De l'existence à l'existant* (Paris: Fontaine, 1947), p. 19; trans. A. Lingis, *Existence and Existents* (The Hague: Martinus Nijhoff, 1978), p. 19.
87. Levinas, "Comme un consentement," p. 48; "As If Consenting to Horror," p. 486.
88. Emmanuel Levinas, *Totalité et Infini* (The Hague: Martinus Nijhoff, 1961), p. 173; trans. A. Lingis, *Totality and Infinity* (Pittsburgh: Duquesne University Press, 1969), pp. 198–99. Cf. p. 205; trans. 229. I shall not attempt here to justify the somewhat unusual reading of Levinas indicated by this last remark. See, for example, my essay "The Ethics of Suspicion," *Research in Phenomenology* 20, 1990, pp. 3–18.
89. Levinas was present in Chicago when Arendt delivered the lecture "Thinking and Moral Propositions," but I am not aware of his having made any response to it.

CHAPTER 5. LITERARY ATTESTATION IN PHILOSOPHY

1. L. Tolstoy, *The Death of Ivan Ilyich*, translated by Rosemary Edmonds (Harmondsworth: Penguin, 1983), p. 102.
2. ibid., p. 104.
3. ibid.
4. ibid., p. 149.
5. ibid., p. 130.
6. ibid., p. 134.
7. ibid., p. 134. See also p. 151.
8. John Macquarrie, *Existentialism* (Harmondsworth: Penguin, 1973), p. 153.

9. Tolstoy, *The Death of Ivan Ilyich*, p. 137.
10. ibid., p. 138.
11. ibid., p. 142.
12. ibid., p. 159.
13. ibid.
14. Walter Kaufmann, "Existentialism and Death," in *Existentialism, Religion and Death* (New York: New American Library, 1976), p. 198. The first version of this essay was published in the *Chicago Review* in 1959.
15. Walter Kaufmann, *Discovering the Mind*, Vol. 2 (New York: McGraw-Hill, 1980), p. 214.
16. Kaufmann, *Existentialism, Religion and Death*, p. 199. Also *Discovering the Mind*, Vol. 2, p. 213.
17. Tolstoy, *The Death of Ivan Ilyich*, p. 161.
18. William Spanos, "Leo Tolstoy's 'The Death of Ivan Ilych': A Temporal Interpretation," *De-Structing the Novel: Essays in Applied Postmodern Hermeneutics*, edited by Leo Orr (Troy, N.Y.: The Whitson Publishing Company, 1982), pp. 1–64.
19. Tolstoy, *The Death of Ivan Ilyich*, p. 159.
20. ibid., p. 160.
21. Spanos, "Leo Tolstoy's 'The Death of Ivan Ilych,'" p. 34.
22. ibid., p. 17.
23. ibid., p. 19.
24. ibid., p. 17.
25. ibid., p. 32.
26. ibid., p. 33.
27. Quoted by Temira Pachmuss in "The Theme of Love and Death in Tolstoy's 'The Death of Ivan Ilyich,'" *The American Slavic and East European Review* 20, 1, 1961, pp. 76–77.
28. Spanos, "Leo Tolstoy's 'The Death of Ivan Ilych,'" p. 3.
29. Levinas does not, to the best of my knowledge, discuss Tolstoy's "The Death of Ivan Ilyich," but in *Otherwise than Being or Beyond Essence* he does take up another of Tolstoy's stories about death. There he refers to "Tolstoy's tale where an order for enough boots for 25 years is sent by one that will die that very evening he gives the order." *Autrement qu'être ou au delà de l' essence* (The Hague: Martinus Nijhoff, 1974), p. 165; *Otherwise than Being or Beyond Essence*, translated by Alphonso Lingis (The Hague: Martinus Nijhoff, 1981), p. 129. This seems to be a reference to Tolstoy's "What Men Live By," although in that story the man makes provision for only one year, not 25. Tolstoy, *Twenty-Three Tales*, translated by Louise and Aylmer Maude (London: Oxford University Press, 1919), p. 72. For a juxtaposition of Heidegger and Levinas on death, see Tina Chanter, "The Question of Death: The Time of the I and the Time of the Other," *Irish Philosophical Journal* 4, 1 and 2, 1987, pp. 94–119, and "The Alterity and Immodesty of Time: Death as Future and Eros as Feminine in Levinas," *Writing the Future*, ed. David Wood (London: Routledge, 1990), pp. 137–54.
30. Levinas, *Totalité et Infini*, pp. 212–13; *Totality and Infinity*, pp. 235–36.
31. Tolstoy, *The Death of Ivan Ilyich*, p. 160. E. Levinas, *Le temps et l'autre* (Montpellier:Fata Morgana, 1979), p. 61; translated by Richard Cohen, *Time and the Other* (Pittsburgh: Duquesne University Press, 1987), p. 73.
32. Tolstoy, *The Death of Ivan Ilyich*, p. 157.

33. Levinas, *Totalité et Infini*, pp. 153–54; *Totality and Infinity*, p. 178.
34. ibid., p. 210; p. 234.
35. ibid., p. 213; p. 236.
36. It would not be accurate to suggest that Heidegger forgoes the distinction altogether in his later writings. See, for example, NII 477–80; EP 71-74. The difficulty of maintaining the distinction is apparent from chapter 2 above.
37. For a discussion of these issues, see among others: Klaus Hartmann, "The Logic of Deficient and Eminent Modes in Heidegger," *Journal of the British Society for Phenomenology* 5, 2, 1974, pp. 118–34; Joan Stambaugh, "An Inquiry into Authenticity and Inauthenticity in *Being and Time*," in *Radical Phenomenology*, edited by John Sallis (Atlantic Highlands: Humanities Press, 1978), pp. 153–61; Robert J. Dostal, "The Problem of 'Indifferenz' in *Sein und Zeit*," *Philosophy and Phenomenological Research* 43, 1, 1982, pp. 43–58; Charles B. Guignon, "Heidegger's 'Authenticity' Revisited," *Review of Metaphysics*, 38, 1984, pp. 321–39; Jay A. Ciaffa, "Toward an Understanding of Heidegger's Conception of Inter-relation between Authentic and Inauthentic Existence," *Journal of the British Society for Phenomenology* 18, 1, 1987, pp. 49–59; and William McNeill, "Heidegger and the Modification of *Being and Time*," Ph.D. dissertation, Essex University, 1986.
38. Tolstoy, *The Death of Ivan Ilyich*, p. 109.
39. ibid., p. 109.
40. I have provided in an appendix a list of works consulted and it will be seen that for the most part I have confined myself to secondary literature in English. Two essays stand out as being particularly relevant for the reading I have given. John Wiltshire claims that Tolstoy "seems to work with two different and logically contradictory accounts of Ivan Ilyich's life and death, and to work with them simultaneously." Nevertheless, he denies that there are two accounts in the last chapter, which he seems to regard as a failure. This is because he regards the contradictory strands of the story to be, first, that current which leads to conversation and, secondly, a sub-current which gives a sense of the arbitrary and senseless aspect of Ivan's life history. Wiltshire is dissatisfied with the last chapter because Tolstoy immediately converts the relinquishing of the ego or dissolution of the will into a "conduct-morality," which requires Ivan to act "when his power for 'acting' could never have been less." John Wiltshire, "The Argument of Ivan Ilyich's Death," *The Critical Review* 24, 1982, pp. 53–54. Jan Van der Eng finds "three contrastive descriptions of Ivan Il'ic's dying." "There is a description that registers his physical reactions. It is preceded by two accounts of the exact moment of death, one rendered by Ivan Il'ich himself, the other by someone who witnesses his dying." "The Death of Ivan Il'ic," *Russian Literature* 7, 1979, pp. 181–82. I am grateful to Tina Chanter for helping me establish this bibliography.
41. Tolstoy, *The Death of Ivan Ilyich*, p. 153.
42. Often interpreted as the womb, Boris Sorokin understands the black bag to refer to the blind gut which Ivan suspects as a cause of his illness. "Ivan Il'ich as Jonah: A Cruel Joke," *Canadian Slavic Studies* 5, 4, pp. 487–507.
43. Tolstoy, *The Death of Ivan Ilyich*, p. 159.
44. Tolstoy draws an analogy at this point between being drawn into the black sack and the experience of motion in a railway carriage, where one thinks one is going forwards but suddenly becomes aware of the fact that one is going backwards. Tolstoy is perhaps mistakenly recalling the experience of thinking one is in a

moving train when, in fact, one's own is stationary and it is another train which is moving. If Tolstoy has indeed misdescribed the experience, then it is probably in his eagerness to draw a parallel between this image and another, to be found earlier in the story, where Ivan imagined he was climbing, although he was in fact going steadily downhill (*The Death of Ivan Ilyich*, p. 153).

45. Tolstoy, *The Death of Ivan Ilyich*, p. 159.
46. ibid., p. 160.
47. ibid.
48. ibid., p. 161. The translation by Louise and Aylmer Maude decides in favor of concealing the inconsistency by reading at this point "two hours before his death": *Ivan Ilych and Hadju Murad* (Oxford: Oxford University Press, 1934), p. 72. I am grateful to Angela Livingstone of the Department of Literature at the University of Essex for confirming that the Penguin translation provides the correct translation of the Russian text.
49. If Tolstoy gives the impression of being confused about the objective time of the last events of Ivan's life, he nevertheless makes sure that the reader is well aware that Ivan experiences the temporality of his death differently from his wife, and that neither of them follow clock time: "To him all this happened in a single instant, and the meaning of that instant suffered no change thereafter" (*The Death of Ivan Ilyich*, p. 161).
50. Tolstoy, *The Death of Ivan Ilyich*, p. 143.
51. ibid., p. 160.
52. Robert Russell, "From Individual to Universal: Tolstoy's 'Smert' Ivana Il'icha," *Modern Language Review* 76, 1981, p. 631. Perhaps the most illuminating contrast is how Ivan Ilyich had, at a time when he was looking for pity, found his son's frightened look of pity dreadful to see (*The Death of Ivan Ilyich*, p. 150).
53. Tolstoy, *The Death of Ivan Ilyich*, p. 101.
54. ibid., pp. 111 and 116.
55. ibid., p. 160.
56. ibid., pp. 159–60.
57. ibid., p. 160.
58. For a reading which gives special significance to this confusion, see Gary R. Jahn, "The Role of the Ending in Leo Tolstoi's 'The Death of Ivan Il'ich,'" *Revue Canadienne des Slavistes* 24, 3, 1982, p. 235n. However, his focus is on the way the two words unify the two themes and principles of organization of the story. Angela Livingstone suggested to me that *prosti* could in Tolstoy's time also mean "goodbye." In that case a further possibility is introduced arising from the fact that in the first chapter Ivan's wife tells Piotr Ivanovicsh that Ivan had "said good-bye to us a quarter of an hour before he died, and even asked us to take Volodya away" (*The Death of Ivan Ilyich*, p. 107). In spite of the inconsistency about the time, the fact that she mentions Volodya suggests that she had this incident in mind. It would mean that a further ambiguity had been introduced. If he meant "forgive" when he meant to say *prosti* but said *propusti*, he was not understood by his wife. But if he meant "goodbye," then he was understood. Tolstoy leaves no indication of which is the correct interpretation. Angela Livingstone has also emphasized to me the problems posed by the phrase "whoever was concerned would understand," and suggested the more literal translation "he to whom it was necessary [to understand] would understand."
59. *The Death of Ivan Ilyich*, p. 161.

60. John 19:30. See also Jahn, "The Role of the Ending in Leo Tolstoi's 'The Death of Ivan Il'ich,'" p. 237.
61. Edward Wasiolek, *Tolstoy's Major Fiction* (Chicago: University of Chicago Press, 1978), p. 167.
62. I am again indebted to Angela Livingstone, this time for pointing out to me that there is no pluperfect tense in Russian so that flashbacks are not distinguished by a change in tense.

CHAPTER 6. THE GREATNESS OF THE WORK OF ART

1. If we follow not the published text of 1953, but Pöggeler's reconstruction it would seem that the manuscript referred to "the inner truth and greatness of N.S." and that in the lecture he actually said "the inner truth and greatness of the movement." There is also reason to believe that the explanatory phrase "namely, the encounter between global technology and modern man" was not in the manuscript, as he claimed later, although it is clear that the confrontation with technology was a, perhaps *the*, crucial political question at this time (EM 28–29; IM 37–38). On the difference between Heidegger's account of these events and the historian's reconstruction of them, see, for example, Otto Pöggeler, "Nachwort zur zweiten Auflage," *Der Denkweg Martin Heideggers* (Pfullingen: Neske, 1983), pp. 340–42; trans. D. Magurshak and S. Barner, *Martin Heidegger's Path of Thinking* (Atlantic Highlands: Humanities Press, 1987), pp. 275–77. Also Pöggeler "Heideggers politisches Selbstverständnis," in *Heidegger und die praktische Philosophie*, ed. Annemarie Gethmann-Siefert and Otto Pöggeler (Frankfurt: Suhrkamp, 1988), p. 59 n11.
2. As an example of Heidegger's fascination for this theme, see his inscription in the copy of Burckhardt's *Grösse, Glück and Unglück in der Weltgeschichte* that he gave to the art historian Kurt Bauch at Christmas in 1937. Karin Schoeller-von Haslingen, "'Was ist Grösse?,'" *Heidegger Studies* 3/4, 1987/88, pp. 15–23. In particular Burckhardt's comments on great poets in the essay "Das Individuum und das Allgemeine (Die historische Grösse)" should be compared with certain aspects of Heidegger's discussion.
3. Heidegger's claim that parts of the epilogue were written at the same time as the lecture has been confirmed by the publication of earlier versions of the lecture. The 1950 text was revised—although most of the modifications were relatively minor—when it was published separately in 1960 in the Reclam series. At the same time Heidegger included an Addendum which was written in 1956. The addendum tries in a certain way to rewrite the essay from the standpoint that Heidegger had attained in the 1950s. It was this text which formed the basis for the Hofstadter translation in *Poetry, Language, Thought*. The Reclam text, and not the 1950 version, served as the basis for the edition of Heidegger's *Holzwege* which appeared as volume 5 of Heidegger's *Gesamtausgabe*. Some notes were added drawn from Heidegger's copies of the third edition of *Holzwege* (1957) and the Reclam edition. The most recent version of *Holzwege* published independently of the *Gesamtausgabe* follows this text.
4. Hans-Georg Gadamer, *Kleine Schriften* I (Tübingen: J. C. B. Mohr, 1967), pp. 102–03; trans. David E. Linge, *Philosophical Hermeneutics* (Berkeley: University of California Press, 1976), p. 5.

5. H.-G. Gadamer, "Zur Einführung," in M. Heidegger, *Der Ursprung des Kunstwerkes* (Stuttgart: Reclam, 1967), pp. 102–25.
6. Philippe Lacoue-Labarthe recently reminded his readers that in 1933 Heidegger never said that "the beginnings of 'a *Verwindung*' of nihilism are to be found in poetic thinking." *La fiction du politique* (Paris: Christian Bourgois, 1987), p. 86; trans. Chris Turner, *Heidegger, Art and Politics* (Oxford: Basil Blackwell, 1990), p. 55. Whereas the turn to Hölderlin is dramatic in 1934 with the lecture course on the poems *Germanien* and *Der Rhein*, Heidegger's ambiguity toward National Socialism continues for some time through the turn to art and poetry. The details of that ambiguity are chartered by recent biographical studies of Heidegger.
7. For another discussion of the relation of Heidegger's "The Origin of the Work of Art" to Hegel based on Heidegger's brief sketch of the history of aesthetics and of art, see J. Taminiaux, "Le dépassement Heideggérien de l'esthétique et l'héritage de Hegel," *Recoupements* (Brussels: Ousia, 1982), pp. 175–208. Andreas Grossmann insists that Heidegger's approach is opposed to that of Hegel, but he does not take into account Heidegger's sketch of the history of aesthetics that helps establish the complexity of the relation as detailed in the present chapter. See "Hegel, Heidegger, and the Question of Art Today," *Research in Phenomenology* 20, 1990, pp. 112–35.
8. G. W. F. Hegel, *Vorlesungen über die Ästhetik* I, Werke in zwanzig Bänden 13 (Frankfurt: Suhrkamp, 1970), 25; trans. T. M. Knox, *Aesthetics* Vol. 1 (Oxford: Oxford University Press, 1975), p. 11.
9. At one point it looks as if Heidegger might have attempted to displace the concept of art by narrowing his focus and adopting the concept of poetry (H 59; PLT 72), but there is no evidence of him sustaining the attempt beyond *The Origin of the Work of Art*.
10. See W. Tatarkiewicz, "Classification of Arts in Antiquity," *Journal of the History of Ideas* 24, 1963, pp. 231–40, and P. O. Kristeller, "The Modern System of the Arts," *Renaissance Thought and the Arts* (Princeton: Princeton University Press, 1980), pp. 163–227.
11. The question of the status of the example of the Van Gogh painting has also been raised, though with a somewhat different resolution, by Jay Bernstein. See "Aesthetic Alienation: Heidegger, Adorno and Truth at the End of Art," *Life After Postmodernism*, ed. John Fekete (New York: St. Martin's Press, 1987), pp. 86–119.
12. The triumvirate of the poet, the thinker, and the founder of the state can already be found in the Hölderlin lectures at the end of 1934, and so presumably predates all three versions of "The Origin of the Work of Art," thereby raising the question as to why art was singled out in the draft. As a provisional response it can be noted that the conflict may be more apparent than real. In the relevant passage in the Hölderlin lectures Heidegger was addressing not truth specifically, but the people, and already in this respect the poet was given a certain priority (GA 39, 51).
13. At one point in the *Beiträge zur Philosophie*, written in the years immediately following "The Origin of the Work of Art," Heidegger introduces the notion of artlessness (*Kunstlosigkeit*) to address precisely this issue (GA 65, 506). Artlessness has nothing to do with art as understood by the culture industry: "An *art-less* moment of history can be more historical and creative than times with an extensive art industry." It is only by traversing artlessness that art happens, when it does, which is seldom enough.

14. We have the lecture in the version delivered in Munich in November 1953. An earlier version was given as the second of a series of four lectures delivered in Bremen in December 1949 under the title "Einblick in das was ist." Every indication is that the publication of this earlier version will be as instructive as the publication of the earlier versions of "The Origin of the Work of Art." The sense in which the essay on technology is a continuation of "The Origin of the Work of Art" is confirmed by a fragment in which, again drawing on Hegel, Heidegger situates his thought in the space between the "no longer of an essential relation to art" and the "not yet of an essential relation to technology." "Technik und Kunst—Ge-stell," in *Kunst und Technik*, ed. Walter Bienel and Friedrich-Wilhelm von Herrmann (Frankfurt: Klostermann, 1989), pp. xiii–xiv.
15. In the margin of his copy of the Reclam edition of the essay Heidegger did include a reference to *poiesis*. See *Holzwege, Gesamtausgabe 5* (Frankfurt: Klostermann, 1977), p. 70n. Contrast Heidegger's attempt to rule out the reference from *Dichtung* to *poiesis* in 1934 (GA 39, 29).
16. I shall not discuss the role of the quotation in any more detail here. Meanwhile see my discussion in *The Question of Language in Heidegger's History of Being* (Atlantic Highlands: Humanities Press, 1985), pp. 69–75.
17. Compare Habermas's description of Heidegger's tendency in the 1940s and 1950s to efface the traces of nationalism from his philosophy of the 1930s by a process of "abstraction via essentialization." Jürgen Habermas, "Heidegger—Werk und Weltanschauung," in Victor Farias, *Heidegger und der Nationalsozialismus* (Lagrane: Verdier, 1987), p. 28; trans. John McCumber, "Work and Weltanschauung: The Heidegger Controversy from a German Perspective," *Critical Inquiry*, 15, 1989, p. 449.
18. The question of whether in the contemporary world dominated by industrial society the work can still remain a work was posed in a 1967 lecture, but not with the same urgency as earlier. "Die Herkunft der Kunst und die Bestimmung des Denkens," *Distanz und Nähe*, ed. Petra Jaeger and Rudolf Lüthe (Würzburg: Königshausen and Neumann, 1983), p. 19.

CHAPTER 7. *NE SUTOR ULTRA CREPIDAM*

1. Pliny, *Natural History* IX, trans. W. Jones, Loeb Classical Library (Cambridge: Harvard University Press, 1956), XXXV, 84–85, pp. 323–25. A last is the wooden model of the foot on which shoemakers shape boots and shoes.
2. M 22–26; PLT 33–37. Meyer Shapiro, "The Still Life as a Personal Object—A Note on Heidegger and Van Gogh," in *The Reach of the Mind. Essays in Memory of Kurt Goldstein*, ed. Marianne L. Simmel (New York: Springer, 1968), pp. 203–09.
3. J. Derrida, *La verité en peinture* (Paris: Flammarion, 1978), p. 321; trans. Geoff Bennington and Ian McLeod, *The Truth in Painting* (Chicago: University of Chicago Press, 1987), p. 281.
4. Shapiro, "The Still Life as a Personal Object," p. 206.
5. In this context I am unable to give a thematic discussion of Derrida's essay. See Dorothea Olkowski, "If the Shoe Fits—Derrida and the Orientation of Thought," *Hermeneutics and Deconstruction*, ed. H. J. Silverman and D. Ihde (Albany: State University of New York Press, 1985), pp. 262–69; and Tina Chanter, "Derrida and Heidegger: The Interlacing of Texts," *The Textual Sublime: Deconstruction and Its Differences*, ed. H. J. Silverman and G. Aylesworth

(Albany: State University of New York Press, 1990), pp. 61–68.
6. Shapiro, "The Still Life as a Personal Object," p. 205.
7. Heidegger first published the lectures *Nietzsche. The Will to Power as Art* in 1961 (NI) in an edition reworked and supervised by him. Recently they have been republished as part of the *Gesamtausgabe* by going back to the text of his lecture notes. Because there are minor but not insignificant differences between the two versions of the passage I discuss here, I shall cite both editions. Where only one edition is documented, this is an indication that the phrase in question is missing from the other edition.
8. Erasmus, *De recta Latini Graecique sermonis pronunciatione*, Opera Omnia I–4 (Amsterdam: North Holland Publishing Company, 1973), p. 40. Notice that there is an error in the transcription in NI and Ni which has been corrected in GA 43. For a translation of Erasmus's discussion see Erasmus, *Literary and Educational Writings*, 4, Collected Works Vol. 26, ed. J. K. Sowards (Toronto: University of Toronto Press, 1985), p. 399.
9. Albrecht Dürer, *Diary of His Journey to the Netherlands 1520–21* (Greenwich, Ct.: New York Graphic Society, 1971). The diary tells us that in August 1520 in Antwerp Erasmus gave Dürer a small Spanish "mantilla" and three men's portraits (p. 59), and that Dürer reciprocated with one of his favorite presents, an engraved Passion (p. 65). We know that Erasmus sat for Dürer on two occasions and that they dined together at least once, but what they spoke about is not clear, except that Erasmus, wrongly as it turns out, confided that he had only two years of work left in him. For some reason, I imagine Dürer wanting to discuss the religious disputes of the day with Erasmus, and Erasmus wanting to discuss art instead.
10. Erwin Panofsky, "Erasmus and the Visual Arts," *Journal of the Warburg and Courtauld Institutes* 32, 1969, pp. 205 and 223.
11. Erasmus, "Letter to Stanislaus Turzo, 8 February 1525," *Opus Epistolarum Des. Erasmi Roterodami* VI, ed. P. S. and H. M. Allen (Oxford: Oxford University Press, 1926), p. 19.
12. Matthias Mende, "Dürer—der zweite Apelles," *Dürer heute*, ed. Willi Bongard and Matthias Mende (Munich: Heinz Moos, 1971), pp. 23–41.
13. Erasmus, "Letter to Willibald Pirckheimer, 28 August 1525," *Opus Epistolarum des Erasmi Roterodami* V, p. 351.
14. E. Panofsky, "Nebulae in Pariete: Notes on Erasmus' Eulogy on Dürer," *Journal of the Warburg and Courtauld Institutes* 14, 1951, p. 37.
15. Pliny, *Natural History* XXXV, 88, p. 326.
16. ibid., xxxv, 95, p. 330.
17. ibid., xxxv, 88, p. 326.
18. E. Panofsky, *The Life and Art of Albrecht Dürer* (Princeton: Princeton University Press, 1971), p. 58.
19. Panofsky drew attention to the phrases not drawn from Pliny in "Nebulae in Pariete," pp. 37–40. He noted the misquotation in "Erasmus and the Visual Arts," pp. 124–27. Erasmus claimed that Apelles was supposed to be irreproachable "except that he did not know when to take his hand off the panel." However, Erasmus knew very well—he discussed the phrase in the *Adages*—that Pliny actually said Apelles knew when to take his hand off the panel and this alone made him superior to Protogenes. Panofsky speculated that the misquotation was inspired by the fact that even if the criticism did not apply to Apelles, it did apply to Dürer.

20. H. Wölfflin, *Die Kunst Albrecht Dürers* (Munich: F. Bruckmann, 1926), p. 356.
21. ibid., pp. 400 and 357.
22. Panofsky, "Nebulae in Pariete," p. 38.
23. ibid.
24. Pliny, *Natural History* xxxv, 67, p. 310.
25. Panofsky, *The Life and Art of Albrecht Dürer*, p. 260.
26. ibid., p. 261.
27. In a note added to the *Gesamtausgabe* edition of the lecture course Heidegger explains that *species* is the Latin translation of the *phantasma* of the one, of the *tauton* (GA 43, 230 n2).
28. William M. Ivins, Jr., *On the Rationalization of Sight* (New York: Da Capo Press, 1973), pp. 34–43.
29. Fritz Koreny, *Albrecht Dürer and the Animal and Plant Studies of the Renaissance* (Boston: Little, Brown and Company, 1988), p. 132.
30. ibid., p. 134.
31. Erasmus, *De recta Latini Graecique sermonis pronunciatione*, p. 40; *The Right Way of Speaking Latin and Greek*, p. 399.
32. Koreny, *Albrecht Dürer and the Animal and Plant Studies of the Renaissance*, pp. 134, 154, and 156.
33. Notice how the criterion seems to have diminished, particularly by the omission of the phrase "definitively and commandingly" (*massgebend und führend*), from the 1961 edition. Cf. GA 43, 98. On Van Gogh's painting as great art, see chapter 6 above.
34. E. Panofsky, "Der Begriff des Kunstwollens," *Aufsätze zu Grundfragen der Kunstwissenschaft* (Berlin: Bruno Hessling, 1964), p. 40; trans. K. J. Northcolt and Joel Snyder, "The Concept of Artistic Volition," *Critical Inquiry* 8, 1981, p. 28.
35. Panofsky, "Der Begriff," p. 44; trans. p. 32.
36. ibid.
37. See Michael Podro, *The Critical Historians of Art* (New Haven: Yale University Press, 1982), p. 191.
38. ibid. pp. 186–89.
39. E. Panofsky, "Die Perspektive als 'symbolische Form,'" *Aufsätze zu Grundfragen der Kunstwissenschaft*, pp. 103–04; trans. Christopher S. Wood, *Perspective as Symbolic Form* (New York: Zone Books, 1991), pp. 32–34. See also the extended discussion of this essay in Michael Ann Holly, *Panofsky and the Foundations of Art History* (Ithaca: Cornell University Press, 1984), pp. 130–57.
40. E. Panofsky, "Zum Problem der Beschreibung und Inhaltsdeutung von Werken der bildenden Kunst," *Aufsätze zu Grundfragen der Kunstwissenschaft*, p. 92. See further the discussion by Silvia Ferretti, *Cassirer, Panofsky and Warburg*, trans. R. Pierce (New Haven: Yale University Press, 1989), pp. 222–25.
41. "Dann wahrhaftig steckt die Kunst in der Natur, wer sie heraus kann reissen, der hat sie." *Dürers Schriftlicher Nachlass*, ed. K. Lange and F. Fuhse (Wiesbaden: Martin Sandig, 1970), p. 226. A somewhat dated translation can be found in Alfred Werner, ed., *The Writings of Albrecht Dürer*, trans. W. M. Conway (London: Peter Owen, 1958), p. 247. Although for convenience I have cited Conway's translation, I have not followed it.
42. Panofsky, *The Life and Art of Albrecht Dürer*, p. 273.
43. ibid. See also *Dürers Kunsttheorie* (Berlin: Georg Reimer, 1915), pp. 178–80, where Panofsky links this sense to the Greek *techne* in a way which evokes Heidegger's discussion at H 47–78; PLT 58–59.

44. *Dürers Schriflicher Nachlass*, p. 222; *The Writings of Albrecht Dürer*, p. 245.
45. In the first book of his treatise on art Dürer lists five different kinds of figure, but proceeds to grade them in a way that would no longer be found acceptable. So Dürer compares "the two races (*Geschlecht*) of mankind, white and black," admiring the arms and limbs of the latter, but judging that their faces are seldom beautiful. *Dürers Schriftlicher Nachlass*, p. 226; *The Writings of Albrecht Dürer*, p. 247. The issue was of practical significance to artists because paintings of the adoration of the Magi tended to include an African figure.
46. For another discussion of the key sentence quoted by Heidegger and one which places it in the context of Dürer's thought, see Hermann Beenken, "Dürers Kunsturteil und die Struktur des Renaissance—Individualismus," *Festschrift Heinrich Wölfflin* (Munich: Hugo Schmidt, 1924), pp. 186–87.
47. Panofsky, *The Life and Art of Albrecht Dürer*, pp. 275–79.
48. *Dürers Schriftlicher Nachlass*, p. 351; *The Writings of Albrecht Dürer*, p. 250.
49. Panofsky, *Dürers Kunsttheorie*, p. 351; *The Life and Art of Albrecht Dürer*, p. 288.
50. See E. Panofsky, *Idea. A Concept in Art Theory* (Columbia: University of South Carolina Press, 1968), pp. 186–87.
51. Panofsky, *Idea*, pp. 124–25.
52. *Dürers Schriftlicher Nachlass*, p. 295.
53. *Dürers Schriftlicher Nachlass*, p. 316; *The Writings of Albrecht Dürer*, p. 178n.
54. Panofsky, "Erasmus and the Visual Arts," p. 213.
55. *Dialogus Ciceronianus*, *Opera Omnia*, I-2 (Amsterdam: North Holland Publishing Company, 1971), p. 635.
56. As an extreme example there is Dürer's engraving *The Knight, Death and Devil*, which seems to portray Erasmus's writings, in particular the *Enchiridion militis Christiani*. See Panofsky, "Erasmus and the Visual Arts," p. 221. Not that Dürer was entirely capable of disassociating the author from his works. When Dürer suspected that Luther had been killed, he addressed Erasmus in his diary as a soldier of Christ and called on him to take Luther's place: "Hear, thou knight of Christ! Ride on by the side of the Lord Jesus. Guard the truth. Attain the martyr's crown" (Dürer, *Diary of His Journey*, p. 92). As historians point out, Dürer mistook Erasmus for someone he was not. But are errors of that kind, where Dürer presents his idea of what Erasmus could have been, simply to be dismissed as departures from verisimilitude?
57. Erasmus, "Letter to Henri Botteus, 29 March 1528," *Opus Epistolarum Des. Erasmi Roterodami* VII, p. 376.
58. Dürer, *Diary of His Journey*, p. 92.
59. Wilhelm Waetzoldt, *Dürer and His Times* (London: Phaidon, 1950), p. 119.
60. W. N. Howe, "The Eye of Erasmus," in *Charlton Lectures on Art*, by Lord Northbourne et al. (Oxford: Oxford University Press, 1923), pp. 111–12.
61. Erasmus, "Letter to Willibald Pirckheimer, 8 January 1524," *Opus Epistolarum Des. Erasmi Roterodami* V, p. 382. Panofsky gives a reconstruction of the allusion in "Nebulae in Pariete," p. 34n.
62. *Dürers Schriftlicher Nachlass*, p. 297.
63. Derrida, *La verité en peinture*, p. 291; *The Truth in Painting*, p. 255.

CHAPTER 8. "POET OF POETS. POET OF THE GERMANS."

1. Heidegger confirmed the point in his 1942 lectures: "The poetic never lets itself be construed in terms of the poet, but only from the essence of poetry" (GA 53, 149). See also GA 52, 6.
2. Even Karsten Harries can be found attempting to maintain the myth in the face of the evidence when he wrote recently that it was "only in the Winter semester 1934/1935, following the disappointment of his hope to help bring about a spiritual revolution of the German people, that Heidegger, having resigned his political ambitions and with it political responsibility, offered for the first time a lecture course on Hölderlin" (HNS xxxvi).
3. For examples of the new scholarship which uses the recently published lecture courses to develop an appreciation of the role of politics in Heidegger's lectures on Hölderlin's poetry, see Fred Dallmayr, "Heidegger, Hölderlin and Politics," *Heidegger Studies* 2, 1986, pp. 81–96; Véronique Fóti, "Textuality, Totalization and the Question of Origin in Heidegger's Elucidation of *Andenken*," *Research in Phenomenology* 19, 1989, pp. 43–58; and Annemarie Gethmann-Siefert, "Heidegger and Hölderlin: The Over-usage of Poets in an Impoverished Time," *Research in Phenomenology* 19, 1989, pp. 59–88.
4. Max Kommerell, *Briefe und Aufzeichnungen 1919–1944*, ed. Inge Jens (Freiburg in Breisgau: Walter, 1967), pp. 396–405.
5. ibid., p. 405.
6. Elsewhere I have developed this account of how it was largely as a consequence of the dialogue of thinking with poetizing that Heidegger came to tell the story of how the words of Being were interruptions of philosophy. See *The Question of Language and Heidegger's History of Being* (Atlantic Highlands: Humanities Press, 1985), chapter 2.
7. See chapter 6 above.
8. For Heidegger's understanding of the *polis* see especially GA 53, 97–107.
9. Even in the never completed lecture course from the winter semester 1944/45, "Introduction to Philosophy, Thinking and Poetizing," Heidegger seemed to be suggesting that the special sense in which the Germans were recognized as "the people of poets and thinkers" provided them with a basis on which foreigners might be made questionable in their essence (GA 50, 102–03).
10. Heidegger similarly poses the question "Who are these 'others'?" in 1974, when commenting on the lines from Hölderlin's "Dichterberuf": "And a poet gladly joins with others/so that they may help him understand." This shows the continuity of Heidegger's concerns. "Der Fehl Heiliger Namen," GA 13, 231; trans. Bernhard Radloff, "The Want of Holy Names," *Man and World* 18, 1985, p. 263.
11. See Andrzej Warminski, who, in *Readings in Interpretation* (Minneapolis: University of Minnesota Press, 1987), chapters 1–3, has established the distortive effects of this omission from Heidegger's reading of Hölderlin. See also Christopher Fynsk's review article of Warminski's book in the *Bulletin of the Hegel Society of Great Britain* 18, Autumn/Winter 1988, pp. 43–57.
12. Heidegger developed this question in the context of a discussion of Valéry's essay "La Crise de l'esprit." Valéry's essay has recently been the subject of Derrida's scrutiny in *L'autre cap* (Paris: Minuit, 1991).
13. Warminski offers a brief analysis of this portion of the interview in "Monstrous History: Heidegger Reading Hölderlin," *Yale French Studies* 77, 1990, pp. 194–95.

"Monstrous History" continues the approach of *Readings in Interpretation* and extends it to Heidegger's reading of "Der Ister" in GA 53. Warminski in his essay and book gives extensive consideration to Heidegger's readings of Hölderlin's letters to Böhlendorff. I would maintain that a comparison of Heidegger's readings of these letters in his lecture courses and essays throw an important light not only on the role he assigns to the Germans, but also on the way he comes to think of the task of overcoming metaphysics. I intend to take up this aspect of the topic in a future essay, the outline of which was set out in a lecture delivered at the Collegium Phaenomenologicum in Perugia, August 1991.

14. Some commentators have argued for a change in Heidegger's relation to poetry after the war, with the publication of essays on George and Trakl. See, for example, Gerald Bruns' illuminating book *Heidegger's Estrangements* (New Haven: Yale University Press, 1989). Without wanting at this point to address in detail the question of a reversal or reversals in Heidegger's thinking, I am sympathetic to the idea of a general shift in Heidegger's thought which can most conveniently be dated around the time of *Einblick in das was ist* (1949). However, some of the differences noted by Bruns are better understood as differences between Hölderlin, on the one hand, and George or Trakl, on the other, rather than as differences in Heidegger's relation to poetry, which remains relatively constant. Indeed, the 1968 essay on Hölderlin, "Das Gedicht," shows a striking continuity with the earlier essays, contrary to Bruns' specific characterization of the change (EHD 191. Cf. Bruns 80).
15. Wilhelm von Humboldt, "Uber die Verschiedenheit des menschlichen Sprachbaues und ihren Einfluss auf die geistige Entwicklung des Menschengeschlechts," *Werke* 3, ed. Andreas Flitner and Klaus Giel (Stuttgart: J. G. Cottsche, 1963), p. 457; trans. Peter Heath, *On Language* (Cambridge: Cambridge University Press, 1988), p. 76.
16. von Humboldt, "Über die Verschiedenheit," p. 472; trans. pp. 86–87.

CHAPTER 9. DESCARTES IN THE HISTORY OF BEING

1. Some further qualifications will appear in the course of my paper, but it should be noted that Heidegger himself sometimes complicated the question by referring to Eckhart as the beginning of German philosophy (GA 39, 133–34). But a year later, in 1935–36, Heidegger explicitly rejected Eckhart's claims in order to place Descartes at the beginning of modern philosophy: FD 76; WT 98. That rather more is at issue than a hesitation on Heidegger's part is suggested by the references to Descartes and Eckhart in the lecture course of summer 1936: SA 36–38; ST 30–31.
2. Jean-Luc Marion has provided a helpful survey of Heidegger's various discussions of Descartes in "Bulletin Cartésien IV," *Archives de Philosophie* 38, 1975, pp. 253–309. See also, R. von Gumppenberg, "Über die Seinslehre bei Descartes," *Salzburger Jahrbuch für Philosophie* 12–13, 1968, pp. 131–39. F.-W. von Herrmann, "Sein und Cogitationes," *Durchblicke. Martin Heidegger zum 80. Geburtstag* (Frankfurt: Klostermann, 1970), pp. 235–54. B. C. Flynn, "Descartes and the Ontology of Subjectivity," *Man and World* 16, 1983, pp. 3–23. Paul Ricoeur, *Le conflit des interprétations* (Paris: Seuil, 1969), pp. 222–32; trans. *The Conflict of Interpretations*, ed. D. Ihde (Evanston: Northwestern, 1974), pp. 223–35.

3. I am grateful to Geoff Bennington of Sussex University for informing me that Heidegger was by no means the first to refer to Descartes in this way. He refers me in particular to Voltaire, who in "Letter XIV" of the *Letters Philosophiques* said of Descartes that "sa philosophie ne fut plus qu'un roman ingénieux." *Mélanges*, ed. Jacques van den Heuvel (Paris: Gallimard, 1961), p. 57; trans. *Letters concerning the English Nation* (London: Peter Davies, 1926), p. 91.
4. Descartes, *Discours de la Méthode*, ed. Etienne Gilson (Paris: Vrin, 1976), p. 4; trans. John Cottingham, Robert Stroothoff, and Dugald Murdoch, *The Philosophical Writings of Descartes* (Cambridge: Cambridge University Press, 1985), Vol. 1, p. 112. Dalia Judovitz explores the distinction between fable and narrative in her "Autobiographical Discourse and Critical Praxis in Descartes," *Philosophy and Literature* 5, 1981, pp. 91–107.
5. Descartes, *Discours de la Méthode*, pp. 7 and 15; *Philosophical Writings of Descartes*, Vol. 1, pp. 114 and 118. Descartes' designation of the *Discourse* as a *fable* is, of course, more significant than I have acknowledged here. See Jean-Luc Nancy, "Mundus est fabula," *Ego sum* (Paris: Flammarion, 1979), pp. 95–127; trans. Daniel Brewer, "Mundus est fabula," *MLN* 93, 4, 1978, pp. 635–53.
6. Hegel, *Vorlesungen über die Geschichte der Philosophie*, Teil 4, ed. P. Garniron and W. Jaeschke (Hamburg: Felix Meiner, 1986), p. 88; trans. Robert F. Brown and J. M. Stewart, *Lectures on the History of Philosophy (1825–1826)*. Vol. III. *Medieval and Modern Philosophy* (Berkeley: University of California Press, 1990), p. 131. The passage is quoted by Heidegger from earlier editions of Hegel's lectures at H 118; HCE 27. See also W 257 and SD 68; TB 61.
7. Schelling, "Zur Geschichte der neueren Philosophie," *Schriften von 1813–1830* (Darmstadt: Wissenschaftliche Buchgesellschaft, 1976), p. 286.
8. Jean Beaufret, *Dialogue avec Heidegger. 11. Philosophie Moderne* (Paris: Minuit, 1973), pp. 52–53.
9. Jean-Luc Marion has situated his own indispensable work on Descartes "in one sense, on the margin" of Heidegger's comment that Descartes was far behind the scholastics and had evaded the question of Being. On this account, Heidegger's reading serves as an answer to Hegel's and Schelling's praise of Descartes: see *Sur la théologie blanche de Descartes* (Paris: Presses Universitaires de France, 1981), p. 453n. See also *Sur l'ontologie grise de Descartes* (Paris: Vrin, 1981) and, for a later discussion of Heidegger's claim that Descartes left undetermined and undiscussed the meaning of Being enclosed within the idea of substantiality, *Sur le prisme métaphysique de Descartes* (Paris: Presses Universitaires de France, 1986), pp. 177–80.
10. Heidegger recognized that "everyone who is acquainted with the Middle Ages sees that Descartes is 'dependent' upon medieval scholasticism and employs its terminology" (SZ 25; BT 46). In 1913 Etienne Gilson had published alongside his major doctoral thesis, *La liberté chez Descartes et la théologie*, his "pètite these," *Index scholastico-cartésien*.
11. This shift toward modern mathematical physics in the modern period remains a constant focus of Heidegger's Descartes interpretation. For the Marburg period, see GA 20, 245; HCT 181–82. For the later period, see N II 161–62; Niv 114.
12. For example, GA 24, 175; BP 125 and GA 20, 139; HCT 101. A marginal note to Heidegger's own copy of *Being and Time* confirms that the discussion of Descartes there was also directed against Husserl: "Kritik an Husserls Aufbau der 'Ontologien!' wie überhaupt die ganze Descartes-Kritik in dieser Absicht

mit hierher gesetzt!" *Sein und Zeit, Gesamtausgabe* Band 2 (Frankfurt: Klostermann, 1977), p. 132n.
13. *Oeuvres de Descartes* VIII–I, ed. Charles Adam and Paul Tannery (Paris: Vrin, 1973), p. 25; trans. *The Philosophical Writings of Descartes* Vol. 1, p. 210.
14. Michel Henry has recently questioned Heidegger's tendency to refer to the Cartesian *subjectum* as a determination of "man," whereas Descartes himself is more careful, for example in the Second Meditation. See *Généalogie de la psychanalyse* (Paris: Presses Universitaires de France, 1985), pp. 87–123. The change in Heidegger's attitude toward the determination of man as a subject reflects in no small measure Heidegger's growing appreciation of the difficulty of twisting free from subjectivity. The destruction of subjectivity calls for a history of Being that marks the event of subjectivity precisely because the former must confront the danger of becoming merely another entrenchment of subjectivity. In 1940 Heidegger apparently offered this as part of an account of the difficulties in attempting to complete *Being and Time* (NII 194; Niv 141). On the degree to which Heidegger later found it necessary to revise his reading of Descartes in *Being and Time* because *Being and Time* was more Cartesian or bound to subjectivity than he had realized, see J. Taminiaux, "Heidegger lecteur de Descartes," *Kunst und Technik*, ed. W. Biemel and F.-W. Herrmann (Frankfurt: Klostermann, 1989), pp. 109–23, and Jean-Luc Marion, "L'ego et le Dasein. Heidegger et la 'destruction' de Descartes dans *Sein und Zeit*," *Revue de Métaphysique et de Morale* 92, 1987, pp. 25–53.
15. "Metaphysik ist eine Epoche der Geschichte des Seins selbst" (H 245; QT 110). As the *Gesamtausgabe* edition shows, Heidegger's marginal note to his own copy asks if metaphysics is not *the* epoch of the history of Being itself. *Holzwege Gesamtausgabe* Band 5 (Frankfurt: Klostermann, 1977), p. 265.
16. Heidegger had always been clear that it was not Descartes so much as his successors that developed the metaphysics of subjectivity (GA 24, 178, and 217; BP 127 and 152). This is said particularly clearly in the lectures on European Nihilism. "The metaphysics of subjectivity completes its decisive beginning in the metaphysics of Descartes" (NII 237; Niv 179). For a brief but careful comparison of the contribution of both Descartes and Leibniz to the metaphysics of subjectivity, see SA 221; ST 182.
17. See J. Derrida, "Envoi," *Psyché Inventions de l'autre* (Paris: Galilée, 1987), pp. 123–24; trans. Peter and Mary Ann Craws, "Sending: On Representation," *Social Research* 49, 2, 1982, pp. 312–13.
18. Descartes, "Letter to Huygens, March 1638." *Oeuvres de Descartes. Correspondance II*, ed. C. Adam and P. Tannery, p. 48. Heidegger himself rejected the rhetoric of novelty in a very similar tone in notes written in connection with his 1921/22 lecture course at Freiburg (GA 61, 193–94).
19. I thus agree with Dalia Judovitz's characterization: "The question of the 'end' of philosophy was implicit in its Cartesian 'origin,' in its fictitious illusion of a new beginning. The sense of crisis that defines modernity, its obsession with newness, with the 'avant-garde,' emerges as the legacy of the Cartesian belief that philosophy begins with him anew, in discontinuity with all previous traditions. The crisis of modern metaphysics, its 'end,' thus emerges as a metaphysical experience." *Subjectivity and Representation in Descartes* (Cambridge: Cambridge University Press, 1988), p. 197.
20. Hans Blumenberg, *Säkularisierung und Selbstbehauptung* (Frankfurt: Suhr-

kamp, 1983), pp. 226–27; trans. Robert M. Wallace, *The Legitimacy of the Modern Age* (Cambridge: MIT Press, 1983), pp. 192–93.

CHAPTER 10. BRIDGING THE ABYSS

1. H.-G. Gadamer, *Heideggers Wege* (Tübingen: J. C. B. Mohr, 1983).
2. H.-G. Gadamer, *Das Erbe Hegels* (Frankfurt: Suhrkamp, 1979), p. 13; trans. Frederick G. Lawrence, *Philosophical-Political Profiles* (London: Heinemann and Massachusetts: MIT, 1983), p. 190.
3. H.-G. Gadamer, *Wahrheit und Methode* (Tübingen: J. C. B. Mohr, 1972), p. xxviii; trans. Joel Weinsheimer and Donald G. Marshall, *Truth and Method* (New York: Crossroad, 1989), p. xxii.
4. Gadamer, *Wahrheit und Methode*, p. xxxi; *Truth and Method*, xxv.
5. Wolfhart Pannenberg has also pointed to the theological origins of Gadamer's notion of claim (*Anspruch*), specifically its indebtedness to Bultmann. *Theology and the Philosophy of Science* (Philadelphia: Westminster, 1976), p. 169n.
6. Gadamer, *Das Erbe Hegels* p. 13; *Philosophical-Political Profiles* p. 190.
7. Gadamer, *Das Erbe Hegels*, pp. 23 and 31; trans. pp. 194 and 197.
8. ibid., p. 19; pp. 192–93.
9. ibid., p. 24; pp. 194–95.
10. H.-G. Gadamer, *Kleine Schriften I* (Tübingen: J. C. B. Mohr, 1967), p. 84; trans. D. E. Linge *Philosophical Hermeneutics* (Berkeley, University of California Press, 1976), p. 201. Also *Philosophische Lehrjahre* (Frankfurt: Klostermann, 1977), pp. 36 and 216; trans. R. Sullivan, *Philosophical Apprenticeships* (Cambridge: MIT Press, 1985), pp. 38 and 49.
11. Gadamer, *Wahrheit und Methode*, p. 463; *Truth and Method*, p. 489.
12. H.-G. Gadamer, *Kleine Schriften II* (Tübingen: J. C. B. Mohr, 1967), p. 8; *Philosophical Hermeneutics* p. 104.
13. Gadamer, *Wahrheit und Methode*, p. 281; *Truth and Method*, p. 296.
14. Gadamer, *Wahrheit und Methode*, p. 279; trans. p. 295.
15. ibid. p. xxv; p. xxxvii.
16. J. Habermas, *Zur Logik der Sozialwissenschaften, Philosophische Rundschau 14*, Beiheft 5, 1966–67. The section on Gadamer is translated as "A Review of Gadamer's 'Truth and Method,'" *Understanding and Social Inquiry*, eds. F. Dallmayr and T. McCarthy (Notre Dame: University of Notre Dame Press, 1977), pp. 335–63.
17. Gadamer, *Wahrheit und Methode*, p. xxv; *Truth and Method*, pp. xxxvii–xxxviii.
18. Gadamer, *Kleine Schriften I*, p. 88; *Philosophical Hermeneutics*, p. 206.
19. Gadamer, *Wahrheit und Methode*, p. 95; *Truth and Method*, p. 100.
20. Gadamer, *Wahrheit und Methode*, p. xvi; trans. p. xxviii.
21. H.-G. Gadamer, *Vernunft im Zeitalter der Wissenschaft* (Frankfurt: Suhrkamp, 1976), p. 95; trans. F. G. Lawrence, *Reason in the Age of Science* (Cambridge: MIT Press, 1981), p. 101.
22. H.-G. Gadamer (with Leo Strauss), "Correspondence Concerning *Wahrheit und Methode*," *Independent Journal of Philosophy* 2, 1978, p. 11.
23. Gadamer, *Wahrheit und Methode*, p. 216; *Truth and Method*, p. 230.
24. Gadamer, *Vernunft im Zeitalter der Wissenschaft*, p. 110; *Reason in the Age of Science*, p. 139.

25. H.-G. Gadamer, "Heidegger und die Geschichte der Philosophie," *The Monist* 64, 4, 1981, p. 423; trans. Karen Campbell, "Heidegger and the History of Philosophy," *The Monist* 64, 4, 1981, p. 434.
26. H.-G. Gadamer, *Kleine Schriften IV* (Tübingen: J. C. B. Mohr, 1977), p. 89; *Truth and Method* p. 545.
27. For a fuller treatment, see my *The Question of Language in Heidegger's History of Being* (Atlantic Highlands: Humanities Press, 1985), esp. chapter 5.
28. The fullest published text of the letters is to be found in an Italian translation by Ricardo Dottori as an appendix to *La dialettica di Hegel* (Torino: Marietti, 1973), pp. 148–51. Gadamer quotes extensive extracts from them in the notes to *Das Erbe Hegels*, pp. 89–94; *Reason in the Age of Science*, pp. 65–67.
29. Gadamer, *Das Erbe Hegels*, p. 93; *Reason in the Age of Science*, p. 67.
30. Gadamer, *Kleine Schriften III* (Tübingen: J. C. B. Mohr, 1972), p. 212; *Philosophical Hermeneutics*, p. 230.
31. H.-G. Gadamer, *Hegels Dialektik* (Tübingen: J. C. B. Mohr, 1971), p. 83; trans. P. Christopher Smith, *Hegel's Dialectic* (New Haven: Yale University Press, 1976), p. 101. See also *Das Erbe Hegels*, p. 94; *Reason in the Age of Science*, p. 68.
32. Gadamer, *Das Erbe Hegels*, p. 80; *Reason in the Age of Science*, p. 61.
33. Gadamer, "Heidegger und die Geschichte der Philosophie," p. 427; "Heidegger and the History of Philosophy," pp. 437–38.
34. Gadamer, *Hegels Dialektik*, p. 90; *Hegel's Dialectic*, pp. 108–09.
35. Gadamer, *Vernunft im Zeitalter der Wissenschaft*, p. 123; *Reason in the Age of Science*, p. 149.
36. Gadamer, *Kleine Schriften III*, p. 219; *Philosophical Hermeneutics*, p. 239.
37. Gadamer, *Das Erbe Hegels*, p. 71; *Reason in the Age of Science*, p. 57.
38. Gadamer, *Kleine Schriften III*, p. 219; *Philosophical Hermeneutics*, p. 239.
39. Gadamer, *Wahrheit und Methode*, p. 439; *Truth and Method*, p. 463.
40. Gadamer, *Heideggers Wege*, p. 80.
41. H.-G. Gadamer, "Plato and Heidegger," trans. I. Sprung, *The Question of Being*, ed. M. Sprung (University Park: Pennsylvania State University, 1978), p. 53.
42. Gadamer, *Kleine Schriften III*, pp. 219–20; *Philosophical Hermeneutics*, p. 239.
43. For example, Gadamer, *Kleine Schriften I*, p. 119; *Philosophical Hermeneutics*, p. 26.
44. Gadamer, *Wahrheit und Methode*, p. 508; *Truth and Method*, p. 487.
45. Gadamer, *Hegels Dialektik*, p. 90; *Hegel's Dialectic*, p. 109.
46. Gadamer, *Wahrheit und Methode*, p. 286; *Truth and Method*, p. 269.
47. R. Bubner, *Modern German Philosophy* (Cambridge: Cambridge University Press, 1981), pp. 60–66. For further references and a more detailed discussion of the issues involved see the first chapter of *The Question of Language in Heidegger's History of Being*.
48. Gadamer, "Heidegger und die Geschichte der Philosophie," p. 433; "Heidegger and the History of Philosophy," p. 443.
49. Gadamer, *Wahrheit und Methode*, p. xxv; *Truth and Method*, p. xxxvii.
50. Gadamer, *Wahrheit und Methode*, p. xxx; trans. xiv–xv.
51. Gadamer, *Das Erbe Hegels*, p. 89; *Reason in the Age of Science*, p. 65.

CHAPTER 11. THE TRANSFORMATION OF LANGUAGE AT ANOTHER BEGINNING

1. J. Derrida, *De la grammatologie* (Paris: Minuit, 1969), p. 14; trans. G. Spivak, *Of Grammatology* (Baltimore: Johns Hopkins University Press, 1976), p. 4.
2. J. Derrida, *L'écriture et la différence* (Paris: Seuil, 1967), p. 117; trans. Alan Bass, *Writing and Difference* (Chicago: University of Chicago Press, 1978), p. 79.
3. Derrida, *L'ecriture*, p. 163; trans. p. 110.
4. J. Derrida, *Marges de la philosophie* (Paris: Minuit, 1972), p. 70; trans. Alan Bass, *Margins of Philosophy* (Chicago: University of Chicago Press, 1982), p. 60.
5. Derrida, *Marges*, pp. 162–64; trans. pp. 134–36. I discuss the strategies of this essay in more detail in "Politics beyond Humanism: Mandela and the Struggle against Apartheid," forthcoming.
6. For further reflections on the relation of Heidegger's *Destruktion* to Derrida's *déconstruction*, see my essay "Seeing Double: *Destruktion* and Deconstruction," *Dialogue and Deconstruction*, ed. Diane Michelfelder and R. E. Palmer (Albany: State University of New York Press, 1989), pp. 233–50. The essay also includes a reading of "Envoi," *Psyché. Inventions de l'autre* (Paris: Galilée, 1987); partially translated by Peter and Mary Ann Caws, "Sending: On Representation," *Social Research* 49, 2, 1982. "Seeing Double" can thus be understood as a necessary supplement to the present chapter, providing as it does a consideration of Derrida's relation to Heidegger's history of Being.
7. Derrida, *De la grammatologie*, p. 36; *Of Grammatology*, p. 22.
8. Derrida, *De la grammatologie*, p. 104; trans. p. 71.
9. Derrida, *L'écriture et la différence*, p. 412; *Writing and Difference*, p. 280.
10. Derrida, *Positions* (Paris: Minuit, 1972), p. 78; trans. Alan Bass, *Positions* (Chicago: University of Chicago Press, 1981), p. 57.
11. Derrida, *Marges*, p. 70; *Margins*, p. 61.
12. Derrida, *De la grammatologie*, pp. 400–01; *Of Grammatology*, p. 283.
13. Derrida, *Marges*, p. 159; *Margins*, p. 132.
14. Derrida, *De la grammatologie*, pp. 343 and 334; *Of Grammatology*, pp. 241 and 235.
15. Derrida, *Marges*, p. 50; *Margins*, p. 45.
16. Derrida, *De la grammatologie*, p. 36; *Of Grammatology*, p. 22.
17. Sextus Empiricus, *Adversus Math.* VIII, 11–12.
18. Derrida, *De la grammatologie*, pp. 21–22; *Of Grammatology*, p. 11.
19. Derrida, *Positions*, p. 72; trans. p. 53. *La Dissemination* (Paris: Seuil, 1972), p. 172; trans. Barbara Johnson, *Dissemination* (Chicago: University of Chicago, 1981), p. 149.
20. Derrida, *Marges*, p. 72; *Margins*, p. 62.
21. Derrida, *Marges*, p. 206; *Margins*, p. 172.
22. In fact the reading of Derrida suggested here can be characterized as a "parasitic reading," as opposed to the "systematic reading" offered by Rodolphe Gasché in *The Tain of the Mirror* (Cambridge: Harvard University Press, 1986). See my review, "Deconstruction and Scholarship," *Man and World* 21, 1988, pp. 223–30.
23. Since I wrote this essay Derrida has not only continued to provide some of the most illuminating readings of Heidegger (as noted from time to time elsewhere in this volume), the literature on Derrida's relation to Heidegger has grown massively. In addition to John Llewelyn's *Derrida on the Threshold of Sense*

(London: Macmillan, 1986) and David Wood's *The Deconstruction of Time* (Atlantic Highlands: Humanities Press, 1989), pp. 251–64 and 293–309, I would particularly draw attention to the following: John Caputo, *Radical Hermeneutics* (Bloomington: Indiana University Press, 1987), pp. 153–206, and the debate it spawned between John Sallis and John Caputo, interesting above all for showing the impact of Derrida on what now concerns Heidegger's readers: *Man and World* 22, 2, 1989, pp. 251–61.

CHAPTER 12. DECONSTRUCTION AND THE POSSIBILITY OF ETHICS

1. For the sense in which *Being and Time* is and is not fundamental ontology and for the sense in which ethics is and is not postponed to the role of a supplement, see chapter 2 above. On the issue of ethics as a supplement, see, already, SZ 316; BT 364. On fundamental ontology, see GA 26, 196–202; MFL 154–59.
2. "First, let it be said, for our own reassurance: the route followed by Levinas's thought is such that all our questions already belong to his own interior dialogue, are displaced into his discourse and only listen to it, from many vantage points and in many ways." Jacques Derrida, "Violence et métaphysique," *L'écriture et la différence* (Paris: Seuil, 1967), p. 161; trans. Alan Bass, *Writing and Difference* (Chicago: University of Chicago Press, 1978), p. 109. The essay was first published in two parts in the *Revue de métaphysique et de morale* in 1964. A number of changes were made to the essay for its republication in 1967; most of them were minor, but a few of them show Derrida engaged in the process of "Derridianising" his own text. I shall usually quote the second version, noting the changes where appropriate. I give more details in *Between Levinas and Derrida* (Bloomington: Indiana University Press, forthcoming).
3. Derrida, *L'écriture et la différence*, p. 118; *Writing and Difference*, p. 80.
4. Derrida, *L'écriture*, p. 119; trans. p. 80.
5. ibid., p. 163; p. 110.
6. ibid., p. 164; p. 111. Levinas himself wrote, "My task does not consist in constructing ethics; I only try to find its meaning. . . . One can without doubt construct an ethics in function of what I have just said, but this is not my own theme." *Éthique et infini* (Paris: Fayard, 1982), pp. 95–96; trans. Richard Cohen, *Ethics and Infinity* (Pittsburgh: Duquesne University Press, 1985), p. 90. But to agree that Levinas does not provide *an* ethics is not a straightforward issue. I shall make the point later in the essay that to write an ethics in the sense of a set of directives (and incidentally, Aristotle's *Ethics* need not be read as being of that kind) is only possible while denying the ethical relation. The question, then, is whether maintenance of the ethical relation is not thereby accorded the status of a directive or a rule. My answer would be that Levinas understands it to be not so much an obligation, which we must choose to follow, as an irremissible necessity. The sense in which this necessity cannot be evaded is precisely the same as that by which it is impossible to commit murder. Indeed, "Thou shalt not commit murder" would mean to Levinas "It is impossible to annihilate the Other." Levinas refers to this as a "moral impossibility" and distinguishes it from "pure and simple impossibility." The interdiction dwells in this possibility "which precisely it forbids." *Totalité et Infini* (The Hague: Martinus Nijhoff, 1961), p. 209; trans. Alphonso Lingis, *Totality and Infinity* (Pittsburgh: Du-

quesne University Press, 1969), pp. 232–33. I would claim that Levinas's "moral impossibility" comes much closer to the sense of necessity governing Heidegger's history of Being than it does to logical impossibility. We can see yet again how Levinas's ethics of ethics is brought close to fundamental ontology, understood as a coming to abide in the sending of Being. See "Fundamental Ontology, Metontology, and Ethics," *Irish Philosophical Journal* 4, 1 and 2, 1987, pp. 76–93, and Jean Greisch "Ethics and Ontology: Some Hypocritical Reflections," *Irish Philosophical Journal* 4, 1 and 2, 1987, pp. 64–75.

7. A further example of the convergence of Heidegger's "Letter on Humanism" and Derrida's "Violence and Metaphysics" occurs when Derrida says of Levinas that he has to "define metaphysical transcendence . . . as a not (yet) practical ethics." *L'écriture et la différence*, p. 199; *Writing and Difference*, p. 135. Derrida quotes the passage where Heidegger announces a thinking which is "neither theoretical nor practical" (W 192; BW 240) and juxtaposes it to the remark in the preface to *Totality and Infinity* where Levinas says that he will refer both theory and practice to metaphysical transcendence. *Totalité et Infini*, p. xvii; *Totality and Infinity*, p. 29.

8. Emmanuel Levinas, *De l'existence à l'existant* (Paris: Fontaine, 1947), p. 19; trans. Alphonso Lingis, *Existence and Existents* (The Hague: Nijhoff, 1978), p. 19.

9. Jacques Derrida, "En ce moment même dans cet ouvrage me voici," *Textes pour Emmanuel Levinas*, ed. F. Laruelle (Paris: Jean-Michel Place, 1980), p. 24; trans. Ruben Berezdivin, "At This Very Moment in This Work Here I Am," *Re-Reading Levinas*, ed. R. Bernasconi and S. Critchley (Bloomington: Indiana University Press, 1991), p. 13.

10. Emmanuel Levinas, "La signification et le sens," *Humanisme de l'autre homme* (Montpellier: Fata Morgana, 1972), pp. 41–42; trans. Alphonso Lingis, "Meaning and Sense," *Collected Philosophical Papers* (The Hague: Martinus Nijhoff, 1987), pp. 91–92. Also "La trace de l'autre," *En découvrant l'existence avec Husserl et Heidegger* (Paris: Vrin, 1974), p. 191; trans. Alphonso Lingis, "The Trace of the Other," *Deconstruction in Context*, ed. Mark Taylor (Chicago: University of Chicago Press, 1986), pp. 348–49.

11. Derrida, *L'écriture et la différence*, p. 131; *Writing and Difference*, p. 88.

12. Derrida, *L'écriture*, pp. 132–33; trans. 89.

13. Levinas, *De l'existence à l'existant*, p. 101; *Existence and Existents*, p. 62.

14. Derrida, *L'écriture et la différence*, p. 202; *Writing and Difference*, p. 137.

15. Derrida, *L'écriture*, p. 208; trans. 141.

16. ibid., p. 165; pp. 111–12.

17. ibid., p. 165; p. 111. In "Tout Autrement," an essay written in 1973 for an edition of *L'Arc* devoted to Derrida, Levinas was tempted by the thought of applying against Derrida the argument which Derrida had used against him in "Violence and Metaphysics"—specifically the argument which challenges the recourse to logocentric language in the fight against logocentric language. *Noms Propres* (Montpellier: Fata Morgana, 1976), p. 85; trans. Simon Critchley, "Wholly Otherwise," *Re-Reading Levinas*, p. 5. But Levinas turns his back on this argument on the grounds that it would bypass the "non-simultaneity" between *le dire* and *le dit*, the saying and the said. This shows very clearly the extent to which Levinas believes that that distinction addresses Derrida. See, further, Levinas's *Autrement qu'être ou au-delà de l'essence* (The Hague: Martinus Nijhoff, 1974), pp. 56–61; trans. Alphonso Lingis, *Otherwise Than Being or*

Beyond Essence (The Hague: Martinus Nijhoff, 1981), pp. 43–48.
18. Levinas, *Autrement*, p. 59; trans. p. 36.
19. ibid., p. 168; p. 114.
20. ibid., p. 186; pp. 126–27.
21. Levinas, "Dieu et la philosophie," *De Dieu qui vient à l'idée* (Paris: Vrin, 1980), pp. 105–06; trans. Alphonso Lingis, *Collected Philosophical Papers*, p. 160. *Totalité et Infini*, p. xi; *Totality and Infinity*, p. 23. See further my essay "Levinas: Philosophy and Beyond," *Philosophy and Non-Philosophy Since Merleau-Ponty* (London: Routledge, 1988), pp. 244–45.
22. Levinas, *Autrement qu'être*, pp. 224–25; *Otherwise than Being*, p. 178. See further my essay "Levinas and Derrida: The Question of the Closure of Metaphysics," *Face to Face with Levinas*, ed. Richard Cohen (Albany: State University of New York Press, 1986), pp. 181–202. Among the changes introduced by Derrida in 1967 to the 1964 version of "Violence and Metaphysics" a number are concerned with the concept of history. See, for example, *L'écriture et la différence*, pp. 220 and 222; *Writing and Difference*, pp. 148 and 149.
23. Derrida, *L'écriture et la différence*, p. 173; *Writing and Difference*, p. 117.
24. Derrida, *L'écriture* p. 164; trans. p. 110.
25. ibid., p. 224; p. 151.
26. See my essay "The Trace of Levinas in Derrida," *Derrida and Différance*, ed. D. Wood and R. Bernasconi (Chicago: Northwestern University Press, 1988), pp. 17–44. To insist on the proximity of Derrida and Levinas is not to deny numerous differences between them, many of which are, of course, set out in "Violence and Metaphysics." The point is to develop an appreciation of Derrida's *strategy*. Compare, for example, Joseph Libertson, *Proximity. Levinas, Blanchot, Bataille and Communication* (The Hague: Martinus Nijhoff, 1982), p. 286n: "Derrida's essay ... is a virulent attempt to reduce the pertinence and originality of all the Levinasian concepts, from a philosophical perspective which is surprisingly traditional ... Derrida's astonishing incomprehension of Levinas is noteworthy less for the ambiguity of its intention, which is a virtual constant in his theoretical practice, than for the extreme intimacy of the Levinasian text to those concepts (trace, *espacement*, supplementarity, temporal alteration in *différence*, etc.) which were to structure Derrida's own text."
27. Levinas, *Totalité et Infini*, p. 247; *Totality and Infinity*, p. 269.
28. Derrida, *L'écriture et la différence*, p. 124n; *Writing and Difference*, p. 312 n7.
29. Levinas, "La trace de l'autre," p. 201; "The Trace of the Other," p. 358.
30. Levinas, "La trace," p. 190; trans. 347.
31. Derrida, *L'écriture et la différence*, p. 224; *Writing and Difference*, p. 151.
32. Derrida, *L'écriture*, p. 163; trans. p. 110.
33. ibid., p. 125; p. 84.
34. By echoing the penultimate paragraph of Leszek Kolakowski's essay "In Praise of Inconsistency" in *Marxism and Beyond* (London: Pall Mall, 1969), p. 240, I do not mean to imply that the logic of inconsistency is "identical" with that of incoherency.
35. Derrida, *L'écriture*, p. 224; trans. p. 151.
36. ibid., p. 164; p. 111.
37. ibid., p. 221; p. 149.
38. ibid., p. 222; p. 150.
39. ibid., p. 223; p. 150.
40. The source of the story is Aristotle's *De partibus animalium* 645a, 15–23. It is

not usually included in collections of Heraclitus's sayings. Heidegger's retelling of the story can now be seen to have been extracted from his lecture course on Heraclitus held in the summer semester of 1943, so making all the more pressing the question of its place in the "Letter on Humanism." See GA 55, 6–10 and 22–23. For further details of Heidegger's retelling of the story, see David Krell, "Daimon Life, Nearness and Abyss: An Introduction to Za-ology," *Research in Phenomenology* xvii, 1987, pp. 23–25.

41. This is true even if the "more" that is required of us as teachers is that of holding back and refusing the demands of our students for more. Heidegger's discussion of the teacher-student relation recognizes this very clearly and can serve as another example in his work of the ethical relation. See WD 50; WCT 15.

42. The attempt to refer Heidegger's discussion of the familiar and the unfamiliar (the gods) to Levinas's discussion of the finite and the infinite is not supposed to indicate that these two conceptual pairs are equivalent across the two thinkers. There is a pressing need for a discussion of Heidegger's notion of finitude (and also of the notion of infinity that he adopts from Hölderlin in later essays) in relation both to Levinas's and Derrida's discussion of these terms. I have not undertaken that task here; it cannot effectively be done without consideration of Hegel, particularly his *Glauben und Wissen*. See Rodolphe Gasché, "Nontotalization without Spuriousness: Hegel and Derrida on the Infinite," *Journal of the British Society for Phenomenology* 17, 3, 1986, pp. 289–307.

43. Derrida, *L'écriture et la différence*, p. 142; *Writing and Difference*, p. 96.

Index

Aesthetics, xxi–xxii, 99, 102–6, 108, 116, 125–27, 133, 136, 147, 163, 180
Akrasia, 57
Aletheia, 11, 13–14, 40–49, 54, 163, 172, 178, 182, 185, 186, 197–98, 204–5, 207–8, 210
Anaximander, xxi, 42–47, 54, 138, 183, 234–35
Andronicus of Rhodes, 8, 229
Aneignung, 52, 176–77, 186
Another beginning, ix, xxiii, xxiv, 3, 14, 16, 23, 53, 168, 181, 183, 184, 195, 205, 210, 229
Anxiety, 79, 82–83, 89, 95
Apelles, 117, 120–21, 130, 133
Appropriation. *See Ereignis*
Aquinas, Thomas, 41, 155, 229–30
Arche, 8
Arendt, Hannah, xx, 3, 9, 64–71, 73, 228–31, 237–39
Aristotle, 27–33, 41, 56–57, 67, 155, 161–62, 220–21, 224, 232–33, 236, 258–59; *Ethics*, xx, 2–3, 5–18, 23, 226–31, 238, 256; *Peri Hermeneias*, 196–99; Heidegger's lectures on, 3, 174
Art, xxi–xxiv, 101–16, 117–34, 244; death of, 103–4, 106, 108, 111, 115, 136
Art history, xxii, 117–21, 126, 133–34
Art of existing. *See Existierkunst*
Asian thought, x, 226
Assimilation. *See Aneignung*

Bacon, Francis, 164
Basic Problems of Phenomenology, 9, 27–28, 35, 152–53, 233

Beaufret, Jean 19–20, 211–12, 251
Beauty, xxii, 127, 130, 136
Becker, Oskar, 228
Beginning, xxiii–xxiv, 153–59, 163. *See also* Another beginning
Being: truth of, 45, 179, 212; history of, ix, xxi, 49, 62, 126, 139, 150–69, 181–82, 205, 225, 226
Being and Time, xviii, 4–14, 62, 66, 71–72, 106–7, 119, 142, 144, 192, 221–22, 229, 233; and ethics, 25–28, 33–40, 58, 212, 256; on death, 76–97; on Descartes, 153–59, 163; on language, 199–201. *See also* Destruction
Bennington, Geoff, 251
Bernstein, Jay, 244
Blumenberg, Hans, 167, 252–53
Brogan, Walter, 227–28, 230
Bruns, Gerald, 250
Buber, Martin, 84
Bubner, Rüdiger, 254
Bultmann, Rudolf, 253
Burckhardt, Jacob, 243
Burnet, John, 42, 234

Cajetan, Cardinal (Thomas de Vio), 155
Caputo, John, 228, 231, 256
Care, 26, 76, 87
Cassirer, Ernst, 127
Chanter, Tina, 240–41, 245
Cicero, Marcus Tullius, 58, 236
Clearing, 9, 53, 151, 179, 201, 204
Closure, 190, 192, 194, 205, 208, 214
Cogito, 153, 159
Comay, Rebecca, 226
Completion, 54, 104, 115, 158

261

Dallmayr, Fred, 249
Death, xxi, 76–97
Deconstruction, viii, ix, xvii, 4, 21, 22, 190–210, 211, 213–20, 231, 255
Derrida, Jacques, viii–ix, xvii, xxi, xxiii, xxiv, 190–96, 205–10, 211, 213–20, 223–24, 249, 252, 255–59; *La verité en peinture*, 117–18, 123, 133, 245, 248
Descartes, René, xxiii, 41, 49, 150–69, 177, 217, 250–52
Destiny, ix, 22, 40, 225
Destruction, viii, xvii, 3, 10, 12, 60–61, 153–54, 157, 159, 183, 198, 230, 255; in *Being and Time*, 100, 166, 177, 192, 208
Dike. See Justice
Dilthey, Wilhelm, 180
Dostal, Robert, 241
Dummett, Michael, 58, 236
Dunne, Joseph, 229
Dürer, Albrecht, xxii, 119–34, 246–48
Dwelling, 15–17, 19, 21, 23, 222

Eckhart, 23–24, 125, 231, 250
Egoism, 25–26, 28, 33, 38, 70, 86
Egypt, 144
Eichmann, Adolf, 64–65, 68, 71
Eidos. See Ideas
End of Philosophy. See Closure *and* Completion
Epoch, 165, 167, 252
Equipment, 5–7, 12, 14, 100–101, 105–6. See also Readiness to hand
Erasmus, Desiderius, 119–25, 129–33, 246–48
Ereignis, 180, 194, 203, 206–7, 208, 210, 232
Erinnerung. See Remembrance
Essence, 181, 207
Ethics, xx, xxi, 15, 17, 23, 25–39, 43, 47, 64–73, 95, 211–24, 233, 235, 256. See also Justice
Ethos, xx, 15, 17, 23
Everydayness, xix, xx, 9, 37, 76–78, 80, 85–92, 221
Evil, xx, 64ff, 71
Excess, 164, 182
Existentiell, xviii, xix, xxi, xxiv, 26, 28, 36, 38, 58, 77–79, 81–83, 85–91, 96–97, 232

Existierkunst, xvii–xxii, xxiv, 58, 63
Experience, 175, 193–94, 206–7, 209–10

Farias, Victor, 60, 61, 62, 236–37
Finitude, x, xviii, xix, xxiv, 30, 34, 259
Flynn, Bernard, 250
Fóti, Véronique, 249
Frege, Gottlob, 58
Fundamental Ontology, xviii, 29–39, 88, 90, 212, 256
Fynsk, Christopher, 249

Gadamer, Hans-Georg, xxiii, 3, 102, 116, 170–89, 191, 228, 229, 243–44, 253–54
Gasché, Rodolphe, 255, 259
Gelassenheit, 24, 83, 85, 207
George, Stefan, 250
German language, x, xxiv, 17, 22, 48, 116, 144–47, 154
Germans, x, 107, 109–13, 142–45, 249. See also People
Gethmann-Siefert, Annemarie, 249
Gilson, Etienne, 251
Greatness, rhetoric of, 99, 103–4, 110, 116, 118–19, 132–33, 137, 164, 243
Greek language, x, xxiv, 17, 104
Greek philosophy, x, 147, 173
Greisch, Jean, 257
Grossmann, Andreas, 244
Guignon, Charles, 241

Haar, Michael, 230
Habermas, Jürgen, xx, 61–64, 71, 170–74, 176, 179–80, 188, 236–37, 245, 253–54
Harries, Karsten, 249
Hegel, Georg Wilhelm Friedrich, x, xv, xxii, xxiii, 152, 155, 161, 173, 182, 186–89, 191, 204, 216–17, 226, 251, 259; *Aesthetics*, 103–4, 108, 111, 115, 125–26, 136, 244
Heisenberg, Werner, 13, 14
Held, Klaus, 232
Henry, Michel, 252
Heraclitus, 11, 19, 44–46, 50, 54, 105, 138–39, 183, 220–23, 258–59
Hermeneutics, 170–89, 191
Herrmann, Friedrich-Wilhelm von, 250
Hesiod, 50
History, xx–xxiii, 109, 112, 175, 217;

and historiology (*Historie*), ix, 33, 40, 49, 50, 150–53, 159–69, 234; of philosophy, x, 40–43, 184–89. See also Being, history of
Hölderlin, Friedrich, xxii, 109–13, 116, 135–48, 163, 198, 244, 249–50, 259; *Patmos*, 14, 115, 135, 184; *Die Wanderung*, 110, 112, 143
Holocaust, viii, xix, 56, 65, 67, 71–72
Humboldt, Wilhelm von, 154–55, 196–99, 205, 250
Husserl, Edmund, 35, 36, 72, 90, 155, 166, 197, 233, 251–52

Ideas, 10–11, 41, 42, 49, 104, 121, 129, 133, 161–62, 163
Introduction to Metaphysics, 45–46, 53, 69, 99, 102–3, 114, 138, 144, 183, 229
Intuition, priority of, 4, 10, 11–12

Jambet, Christian, 60
Janicaud, Dominique, 236
Jaspers, Karl, 61, 66–67, 69–70
Judovitz, Dalia, 251, 252
Justice, xxi, xxiii, 42–55, 234–36

Kant, Immanuel, 4, 6, 10, 11, 27, 30, 49, 64–65, 68, 71, 152, 155–56, 161, 163, 229
Kant and the Problem of Metaphysics, 4, 5, 25, 29, 30, 127, 137
Kateb, George, 68
Kaufmann, Walter, 82–83, 85, 240
Kehre. See Turning
Kierkegaard, Sören, 48
Kisiel, Ted, 228
Kolakowski, Leszek, 258
Kolb, David, 225
Kolbenheyer, Erwin, 109
Kommerell, Max, 137, 249
Krell, David, 232, 235, 259

Lacoue-Labarthe, Philippe, 71, 225, 244
Law. See Nomos
Leibniz, Gottfried, 159, 161, 168, 252
Letter on Humanism, 12, 18–22, 32–33, 38, 43, 47, 53, 145, 181, 211–14, 219–24, 233, 257
Levinas, Emmanuel, xx, 64, 71–73, 85–86, 94, 164, 213–20, 223–35, 237, 239ff, 256–59

Libertson, Joseph, 258
Lichtung. See Clearing
Llewelyn, John, 255–56
Logos, 160, 184, 189, 194, 196, 198, 203–4, 206–7
Luther, Martin, 49, 125, 248
Lyotard, Jean-François, 57–58, 236

Macquarrie, John, 76, 80, 88, 239
Makkreel, Rudolf, 228
Marion, Jean-Luc, 250–52
Marx, Karl, 190
McNeill, Will, 232, 241
Metaphysical Foundations of Logic, xvii, xix, 8, 10–11, 20, 25–39, 58–59, 63
Metaphysics, 179–80, 184, 189, 190–91; unity of, 42, 189, 196
Metontology, xix, 29–34, 77, 233
Miles, Murray, 231
Mink, Kelly, 232
Mitsein, 25, 38, 214–15
Morality. See Ethics
Mörike, Eduard, 138

Nancy, Jean-Luc, 251
National Socialism, xix, 46–47, 56, 58–73, 99, 101, 102, 113, 114, 116, 243–44
Nazism. See National Socialism
Neo-Kantianism, 127, 152, 154, 157
Nietzsche, Friedrich, 41, 42, 47, 50–55, 103–4, 158, 161, 189, 190, 234–35
Nomos, 43, 212, 226
Nothing, 182, 187

Olkowski, Dorthea, 245
Ontic, xviii, 26, 29–30, 33–34, 36–37, 52, 77–79, 83, 85, 95, 144, 233
Ontology. See Fundamental Ontology
Origin, 109, 196, 206
Origin of the Work of Art, 12, 15, 59, 99–116, 117–19, 123–29, 133–34, 135–36, 140, 170, 172
Overcoming, 5, 45, 53, 179–80, 182–83

Paestum, 107, 119
Pannenberg, Wolfhart, 253
Panofsky, Erwin, xxii, 120–22, 126–28, 130–33, 246–48
Parkes, Graham, 226

Parmenides, 4, 10, 44–46, 47, 56, 138–39, 156, 183, 215–16
People, xxi–xxiv, 42, 59, 102, 108–9, 112, 114, 116, 140–48
Peperzak, Adriaan, 234
Permanence, 44, 53
Phenomenology, 35, 71, 77, 90
Philosopher, ideal of, xviii–xix, xxi, 29, 36–39, 56–73
Phronesis, 2–3, 7–9, 13, 15–16, 19, 58, 69, 228–31
Phusis, 13, 15, 21, 44, 46, 163, 231
Plato, 13, 18, 64, 68–69, 136, 152, 155, 163, 204, 208, 217, 229, 236; *Charmides*, 227; *Phaedrus*, 190–91; *Republic*, 6, 41, 46–48, 59, 122, 133: See also Ideas
Platonism, 122–23, 129–30
Pliny, 117, 120ff, 245
Podro, Michael, 127, 247
Poets, 113, 135–48, 249
Pöggeler, Otto, viii, 225, 228, 243
Poiesis, xvii, 2–24, 115, 226–30, 245
Polis, 66, 141, 249
Prauss, Gerold, 230
Praxis, xviii, 2–26, 227–30
Preontological, 87
Presence, 163, 190, 192, 206
Presence at hand, 4–5, 22
Production. See Poiesis
Protagoras, 14, 15, 159

Question Concerning Technology, 13–15, 53, 103, 114–16, 181, 225, 230

Race, 248
Readiness to hand, 4, 11, 22, 106. See also Equipment
Recollection. See Remembrance
Rectoral Address, viii, 59, 67, 99, 109, 136, 142
Releasement. See *Gelassenheit*
Remembrance, 16, 19, 23, 107, 182, 190, 205
Renunciation, 202–3
Retrieval (*Wiederholung*), 4, 6, 9, 11–12, 17, 46, 229
Richardson, William, 202, 227
Ricoeur, Paul, 250
Rorty, Richard, 60–61, 64, 69, 72, 236

Rosenberg, Alfred, 109
Rousseau, Jean-Jacques, 190–91, 194, 206
Ryle, Gilbert, 57–58, 60

Sallis, John, 231, 232, 234, 256
Sartre, Jean-Paul, 85
Scheler, Max, 30–31
Schelling, Friedrich, 152, 183, 251
Schmidt, Dennis, 228
Scholem, Gershom, 71
Schuchmann, Paul, 229
Schürmann, Reiner, 226, 227, 231, 234–35
Scott, Charles, 226, 231
Sextus Empiricus, 255
Shapiro, Meyer, 117–19, 121, 245–46
Sheehan, Thomas, 227
Socrates, 65, 67
Sophocles, 45–46
Spanos, Walter, 83–85, 240
Spatiality, 31–32, 154
Spengler, Oswald, 109
Staiger, Emil, 138
Stambaugh, Joan, 241
Step back, 17, 83
Strauss, Leo, 178–79, 182, 185
Suarez, Francisco, 155
Substance, 156, 159

Taminiaux, Jacques, 227, 228, 229, 244, 252
Techne, 2–3, 5, 7–8, 13–16, 19, 21, 53, 104, 129, 181, 231, 247
Technology, xxiii, 13–14, 17, 114, 181, 245
Temporality, 34, 84; of Being, xviii
Theophrastus, 42–44, 54
Theory, 7, 10, 11–12, 16, 19, 20
Thinkers, 108, 111, 112–13, 135–48, 221–22
Thinking, 16–21, 43, 65–73
Time and Being, 12, 35
Tolstoy, Leo, xxi, 76–97, 239–43
Trace, 205, 208, 218
Tradition, 24, 154, 173–77, 179–89
Trakl, Georg, 137, 250
Truth, 40–42, 48, 50, 54–55, 103, 107, 108, 110–11, 116, 122–23, 125. See also Aletheia
Turning, 34, 233

Unconcealment. *See* Aletheia

Valéry, Paul, 249
Van Buren, John, 228
Van Gogh, Vincent, 101, 107–8, 113–14, 117–18, 123, 125–26, 133
Verisimilitude, xxii, 120–22, 126–33
Vlastos, Gregory, 234
Volk. See People
Vollendung. See Completion
Volpi, Franco, 227
Voltaire, François-Marie Arouet de, 251

Warminski, Andrzej, 249–50
Weiss, Helene, 227, 228

What is Metaphysics?, 47, 137, 178, 182, 183
Wiederholung. See Retrieval
Wiltshire, John, 241
Wolfflin, Heinrich, 121, 247
Wood, David, 256
Words of Being, 19, 44, 54, 161–62, 177, 185, 204, 249; lack of, 182, 187. *See also* Being, history of
World, 4, 9, 14, 28, 107, 119, 156, 165
Worldview, 26–31, 37–39, 62–63, 73, 199, 232
Writing, 19–20, 106, 193, 206, 210

Zarader, Marlene, 234

www.ingramcontent.com/pod-product-compliance
Lightning Source LLC
Chambersburg PA
CBHW030131240426
43672CB00005B/101